ESSENTIALS

for
Child Development Associates
Working with Young Children
2nd Edition

Carol Brunson Day, *Editor*

Council for Professional Recognition
2460 16th Street NW
Washington, DC 20009-3575

Acknowledgments

This edition acknowledges the enormous writing and editorial contribution of Sue Bredekamp who, building on the underpinning of developmentally appropriate practice, moved the text forward a decade into the era of school readiness— capturing all the subtle shifts in emphasis, yet remaining true to the integrity of the developing child.

This edition also acknowledges from the first edition, Teresa Rosegrant and Sue Bredekamp for immeasurable assistance in conceptualization; Barbara T. Bowman, Januce E. Hale and Jan McCarthy for review and conceptual direction; and Jan Brown McCracken and Sharon Cronin for writing.

Finally for both editions, we acknowledge J.D. Andrews for oversight and general counsel.

Visit the Council's Website at http://www.cdacouncil.org

This text was prepared under the editorial direction of Carol Brunson Day, Ph.D., President/CEO, Council for Professional Recognition.

Contributing writer: Sue Bredekamp

Design/production: Elizabeth Pascucci and Cynthia DiBlasi

Photographs courtesy of: World Bank Children's Center, Jean-Claude Lejeune, Janet Brown McCracken, Cleo Photography, Nancy P. Alexander, and CentroNía Center

Library of Congress Catalog Card Number: 91-71482

ISBN 0-9759140-0-6

Printed in the United States of America.

Contents

Unit 6. Keys to establish productive relationships with families 363

Unit 7. Putting it all together as an early childhood professional working with preschoolers or infants and toddlers, or providing family childcare — 397

Unit 8. Preparing for final assessment as a Child Development Associate

How to use this book

Most likely you are eager to become a Child Development Associate. It represents a big step in your early childhood education career. You even may be tempted to skip this section so you can get started on your CDA. Go ahead and leaf through each unit to get an idea of what you will be doing with these materials during your CDA work. Then come back here to get the overall view of how this book fits into the next year of your life and beyond.

You probably read most books once and then put them on your shelf. On rare occasions you go back to look up something. This book is different. It contains **essential** information about what competent teachers of young children *do*. Some of the information and ideas probably will be familiar to you. Other ideas may be new or different—even contrary to what you always believed about teaching.

Before you complete your Child Development Associate professional preparation program, you will use this early childhood studies curriculum in three different ways:

1. On your own

CDA Candidates begin their work in real-life settings—work in family child care homes and other group programs for young children.

Whether you are already working with children or have selected a site to work in just to prepare for your CDA, you begin this first phase of your professional preparation by working on your own to learn more about yourself, your program, and the children you teach.

During the next six months, you will study at your own pace, and must set aside a regular time to do so. You will need at least two to four hours each week to think about ideas, to try out new techniques, to watch the videotape for each of the six units, and to find information that applies to your program and the children you teach. You will also talk with your *Field Advisor* at least once a week to discuss ideas, ask questions, and review your progress.

You are required to complete the six units in this book, which review what we know about young children and how we can help them learn, develop, and make the most of the many learning experiences that they will encounter in the early years. Begin with Unit 1 and continue to work in order through Unit 6, because each section builds upon the last one.

Contained in the first six units are *self-study activities* for you. They are practical, hands-on experiences. As you do them, you will be looking for answers to questions YOU have, and you will learn more about your profession, the children with whom you work, and about the best ways to teach.

Essentials is designed to become the backbone of your professional resources. Write in it. Check the checklists. Make notes in the margins. Tear out pages to add to a specific folder.

As you work during the self-study phase, you will begin to build your *CDA Professional Resource File*. You will write about the things you do with children and families and why you do them. You will also gather many things to help you in your teaching: curriculum ideas and resources, phone numbers, regulations, teaching strategies, and observations of children's progress. Make this book—and your growing CDA Professional Resource File—work for you. You will use this book all year and beyond: during your self-study work, again when you meet in the CDA Seminar, and while you put everything you are learning into practice. Much of it will be used again and again all during your teaching career—it contains the basics for good professional practice.

A videotape is also recommended for each unit of study to help you see many of these ideas in action. A Viewer's Guide is enclosed with the tapes. Think about the questions in the guide as you watch each unit of the tape. You can view these videos with your Field Advisor if you would like, and discuss together what you have seen.

Your CDA Field Advisor will keep in touch with you once a week to guide and verify your progress during this first phase of study. Now is the time to ask questions ... to search for information you can use ... to collect ideas. Get yourself off to a good start!

2.   With a small group

When the second phase of your study begins, you will join other CDA Candidates who have also completed their self-study materials. In these *CDA Seminars* you, your *Seminar Instructor*, and other CDA Candidates will discuss your experiences as you work in a real-life early childhood education setting. You will continue to use *Essentials* along with other reading assignments and exercises.

Expect lots of lively discussions to bring to life the ideas you have read about here. Your Seminar Instructor will also help you broaden your horizons and give you opportunities to learn even more about young children.

Attend regularly and get involved in each session! Follow through with your assignments. Your participation will enable you to make satisfactory progress toward earning your CDA. Your expanding Professional Resource File will be another indication of how much you are learning.

At the end of this phase, you and all other CDA Candidates will be prepared to take the CDA *Early Childhood Studies Review*, a written examination to verify your knowledge about the basics needed to teach young children. You will also be prepared to complete the final requirements to be assessed as a CDA.

3. As you work with children

After you complete your Seminar, you will continue to apply what you have learned, and prepare to demonstrate your skills with children. During this last phase, your Field Advisor will work with you to complete the last units in this book. You will continue to build your CDA Professional Resource File and you will be formally observed as you demonstrate your competency as a teacher of young children.

Your *Field Advisor* will distribute a Parent Opinion Questionnaire to each parent in your group to determine their opinion of your work.

A CDA *Council Representative*—the person who will verify that you can put what you have learned into practice—and your CDA Field Advisor will support you throughout this period.

The entire CDA Professional Preparation Program is designed to help you see what you are doing well, to identify where changes are needed, and to know how to make changes that are best for children and their families. You will demonstrate your competency to meet children's needs in two ways.

During this year, you will put what you know into **writing**. You will make notes in this book, build your Professional Resource File, and complete your CDA Early Childhood Studies Review.

You will put what you know into **practice**, too. You will share ideas with your CDA Seminar group, demonstrate appropriate strategies as you work with children, respond to parents' needs, join a professional organization, read to keep current with the field, attend conferences, and stand up for the needs of children.

To help you keep track of your efforts, a CDA progress record is provided in the back of this book. Each time you complete a unit of this book, or other major milestones in each of these three phases, you can check it off. You are to be congratulated on a job well done!

What if you have a question about the CDA professional preparation and Credentialing process? You have several places to turn. You can call the *CDA Candidate Connection*, CDA's toll-free number, 1-800-424-4310 from 8:30 a.m. to 6:00 p.m. (Eastern Time) weekdays to get a quick answer to your question. Your CDA Field Advisor or Seminar Instructor may also have the information you need.

How do you make changes in your work with children? If you are a family child care provider, you probably can make improvements in your program as you see fit. If you work in Head Start, preschool, or other center-based program, it may not be possible for you to make changes without first discussing them with your supervisor. You may work in a shared space, so someone else must be included in your decisions. Talk about your new learning opportunity with everyone involved. When your supervisors and co-workers share your commitment to making your program the best it can be, you can work together to make improvements.

Explain to the parents what you are doing. They will be proud to have you caring for and educating their child! Parents are thrilled that their children are cared for by people who take their work so seriously. Be sure to explain to them what you are doing and how it will affect their children.

By the time you are awarded your CDA Credential, your CDA Professional Resource File should be brimming over with materials. Each day with young children and their families is filled with challenges. Begin now to prepare yourself to meet them!

Carol Brunson Day, Ph.D.
President/CEO
Council for Professional Recognition

Introduction to the early childhood profession

WELCOME! You have made an important decision about your career with young children. You want to become a Child Development Associate, a CDA. As you follow the steps required to earn your CDA Credential—studying on your own, joining Seminar discussions, and applying what you know with young children—you will see how exciting and challenging it is to be a teacher.

When you have successfully completed your 120 clock hours of CDA training, your field experience, and your final assessment, you will be awarded your CDA Credential. Your skills as a primary caregiver and teacher of young children will be confirmed by this nationally recognized professional credential.

For some of you, the CDA program materials may be a review of how young children develop and learn. Many of the teaching strategies and guidance techniques will be familiar. For others, this is your introduction to the early childhood education profession.

Regardless of your experience or formal training in the field, we hope you discover some fresh, interesting ideas and information you can use in your work.

Parents, teachers, and other professionals have spent many years gathering information about how young children develop and learn. They have researched what teaching strategies are most effective. They have studied ways to encourage children to learn self-regulation.

Now, as a CDA Candidate, you are making a commitment to become a professional early childhood educator. Whether you call yourself a family child care provider, a teacher, a classroom assistant, a caregiver, or some other title, you are choosing a career of work with children from birth through age 5 and their families.

What you do with children during the day is somewhat like being a parent, but it is also very different. You are preparing to become a CDA because you want to be a good early childhood educator—a very special type of teacher of young children. Caring for one's own children is different from caring for and educating a group of other people's children.

Let's start your CDA professional preparation with a look at the real world: Why do you want to teach? What kind of person is a good teacher of young children? How is a teacher different from a parent? What kinds of work will you be prepared to do as a CDA?

PART 1

Why do you want to work with young children?

You are already working with young children, either in a center program or in your home. Before you started to work with children, you probably thought about what you wanted to do with your life. You may have tried other jobs first.

But something drew you to early childhood education. You surely have several reasons why you decided to work with young children. **You will be a better teacher if you know what motivates you—why you want to teach.** Write your reasons here. Be honest with yourself.

_____

_____

_____

_____

_____

_____

Many of you probably wrote at least one of these reasons:

- I love children.
- I always wanted to be a teacher.
- Many of my family members have been teachers
- Young children are ... so cute ... so energetic ... so curious ... so much fun.
- Children like me.

You will need about two weeks to complete your study of Unit 1. During this time you must:

1. Prepare for conferences with your Field Advisor to discuss three topics (*becoming a CDA, who early childhood educators are, and legal requirements*).
2. Complete two assignments (*an interview with an early childhood education professional, and learn about two national associations*) and two entries for the Professional Resource File.
3. Complete two assignments for Seminar (*visit an early childhood program, and locate state/local child care licensing requirements*).
4. View the accompanying videotape using the Viewer's Guide.

- I want to help young children ... who have different abilities *(such as deaf, emotionally challenged, chronically ill)*.
- I want to reach out to families who are ... struggling to get out of poverty ... trying to deal with difficult circumstances.
- There aren't enough good teachers ... for children who speak my first language ... who speak a language common in our community.
- This is my way to help make the world a better place to live.
- Teaching is the perfect part-time job for a busy mother.
- Child care was an easy course at my school.
- Children's early years are the most important time of their lives. I want to make those years as good as possible.
- I want to be in charge of children who will listen to me. *(Older children are hard to handle.)*
- I need to make some money.

Now it is time to take an honest look at your reasons for wanting to work with young children. As you consider them, remember, young children are very vulnerable. Their parents trust you to provide good care and education. Children thrive only in a stable, predictable, loving environment.

Educators can help children and families change and improve their lives and our society. You need to know a great deal about young children, families, and yourself. Becoming a teacher cannot be taken lightly.

Some of the reasons we listed here are not very good reasons for choosing teaching as a profession. These reasons may ignore the needs of children or families.

Some are misinformed ideas about what being a teacher of young children is really all about. Loving children is not sufficient reason to choose teaching as a career. Some children are not very lovable, and they are the ones who need you most. And teaching young children is hard work. The job should not be taken lightly.

Try to be objective when you think about your reasons for wanting to work with young children.

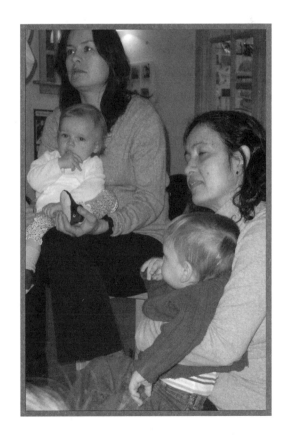

Your role as a caregiver is not the same as a parent, but children should feel loved and protected in your care.

If you want to become a teacher for sound reasons—if you really are committed to learning more about the best ways to work with children and families—you will surely make a positive difference in their lives. Becoming a CDA is an excellent step for you to take! Let your Advisor know why you are convinced this is the career for you.

What if you are not really sure whether your reasons are good enough? If most of your reasons seem questionable, now that you see them in writing, you may want to spend more time considering your future before you make a definite commitment to teaching.

Try something else, give yourself more experience with young children, or talk about your decision with your Advisor before you get further professional education.

Maybe your motives for being a teacher seem selfish or pretty weak, now that you see them on paper. Teaching is a difficult job. There is a lot to learn. You may want to reconsider your decision before you continue to work on a CDA Credential. **Discuss your reservations about becoming a teacher with your CDA Field Advisor.**

Rather than wasting your time preparing for a job that isn't suited to *you*, find a career counselor who can help you determine what kind of work fits you best. Children deserve only the best care and education. Being a CDA can help you become a *superior* teacher. When you are sure working with young children is for you, you are ready for Part 2 of your CDA studies.

PART 2

Will you be a good teacher?

You probably have a few doubts about whether you can be a **good** teacher. In fact, your desire to improve is probably what drew you to the CDA program—you want to become better! Let's think for a minute about how teachers are different from parents and who a good teacher *really* is.

Your image of a teacher probably comes from your memories of what school was like for you: You remember that teachers ... tell classes what to do ... make children sit quietly ... correct papers and give grades. But this is *not* what a good early childhood teacher does.

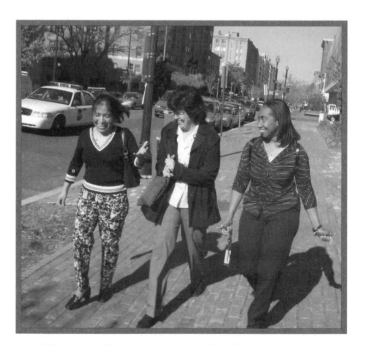

If you really are committed to learning more about the best ways to work with children and families, you will surely make a positive difference in their lives. Becoming a CDA is an excellent step for you to take!

Life is much more active in an appropriate program for young children! Early childhood educators plan and set up a rich, inviting environment filled with toys, equipment, and interesting, engaging learning experiences. Children learn best with hands-on, real-life experiences.

Children select many of their own activities and take as much responsibility as they can handle. They work alone or in small groups, talk with each other in their home languages, make choices, and pursue many of their ideas. The room hums with activity!

Early childhood teachers also change diapers, feed children, clean up messes, assist children with dressing, perform simple first aid, and administer medicine. Yes, teachers of young children do many of the same things parents usually do. But they also do much more.

Your image of parents also probably comes from your own experiences: Parents love their children ... raise their children based on the values of their own cultural group ... are disciplinarians ... have hopes and dreams for their children. Parents buy clothes, set bedtimes, and take care of you when you don't feel well! Parents think their child is the most important child of all.

As you have probably already found in your work with young children, whether it is in your own home or other group program, your role as a caregiver or teacher is different from that as a parent. You are not as emotionally invested in each child and don't show favorites—but children must feel loved and protected in your care. Like parents, you want children to be proud of who they are, the traditions they share, and the abilities they have. You want children to learn to be self-disciplined and to be self-motivated.

All through this book you will see how working with young children is *different:* Early childhood educators are different from

Well-qualified early educators

- plan interesting projects to engage children's thinking and learning,

- engage individual children in extended conversations about events that occurred in the past or will happen in the future,

- move about the room to assist individual children,

- help children expand upon an idea,

- take notes about children's individual development,

- help young children learn to solve their own real problems rather than solving problems for them,

- give children opportunities to succeed,

- strengthen children's appreciation for their own and others' languages and cultures,

- allow children to be as independent as possible, and

- help children learn to regulate their own behavior and make good decisions for themselves.

the teachers you had in elementary school. We are also different from children's parents.

Perhaps you remember the adults you looked up to as a child. You probably had a favorite teacher, a special grandparent or relative, or a neighbor who was dear to you. Why did you enjoy being with that person?

Jot down some of the qualities that made the person special to you.

_____

_____

_____

_____

Or perhaps you have always liked children—they just seem drawn to you and you to them. **Why do children find you appealing? Make a list of qualities that describe you.**

_____

_____

_____

_____

Compare your description of your favorite person—or of yourself—with this list of traits of good teachers of young children. You probably will find several matches. **You may have some other important ideas that are not included here. Add them to the list.**

As you work on your CDA during this next year, keep in mind that what you are learning is helping you to become the kind of teacher you want to be!

Good early childhood teachers

- **respect children, parents, and staff**—each person is valuable. We all are proud of our heritage and skills. Yet we all have biases about other people: Some of us are uncomfortable around children whose abilities are different and others harbor resentment about skin colors, languages, or cultures. We may hold stereotypes about rich or low-income families. Even a child's hairstyle or earrings may offend us. Unless you are willing to figure out what your biases are and to work to change them, you will not be a good teacher.

- **accept diverse ideas**—there are many ways to look at and do things. Good teachers prepare children to live and work in a pluralistic society. Each family has its own ways. Cultural groups have their own preferences and languages. Our lives are richer when we appreciate each other's diversity and get along together. You and the children stand up for what is fair for people.

- **develop warm, caring relationships with children**—children **know** you care about them by what you do and what you say. A beaming smile, a loving hand, and genuine affection bring out the best in young children. Good teachers demonstrate affection in ways that are consistent with children's culture.

- **are flexible**—you can change direction at a moment's notice. Many of children's best learning opportunities happen without advance planning.

- **really listen**—you pay attention to what children say with words and through their behavior. You talk *with,* not at, children.

- **show enthusiasm**—you laugh with the children, sharing life's big and little delights.

- **have lots of energy**—teaching is hard work. You carry heavy furniture, hold children, walk about the room and outdoor play area, deal with strong emotions.

- **teach children all about the world around them**—young children are constantly learning. They need adults to help them acquire skills to function independently as well as concepts that help them make sense of the world and their experiences in it.

- **are creative**—you love new ideas—yours and children's.

- **are patient**—children cannot be rushed. Growing up takes a long time. There is so much to enjoy and learn!

- **remain calm**—you don't get upset easily, even when everything seems to be going wrong!

- **are curious**—you are eager to learn more about children. You want to give children challenging but achievable learning opportunities.

- **have a great deal of inner strength**—children can rely on you to help them weather life's difficulties.

- **use knowledge, not opinion, when teaching**—you read professional journals and books, attend workshops, participate in groups that work on behalf of young children, and learn from your own experiences.

- **are constantly learning**—good teachers always want to improve.

- **know their strengths and weaknesses**—no teacher is perfect for all children, but good teachers know what they do well and work on the areas they need to improve.

What qualities do you think make a good early childhood teacher?

_____

_____

_____

_____

Do most of these traits describe you? Or do you really want to work on becoming this kind of person? Are you willing to try to figure out how your cultural perspective affects your teaching? Then you are probably in the right profession. Let's see what might happen once you become a CDA working with a group of young children.

> ### HOW we teach is just as important as WHAT we teach.
>
> ### Children copy what we do and say.

PART 3

What is a day in the life of a CDA like?

Perhaps you are a Head Start volunteer or assistant. You may be a family child care provider. Or maybe you work as an assistant in a pre-kindergarten in a public school or as a teacher in a child care program. Most likely you are a parent or plan to become one. No matter what your experience with young children, as you work toward becoming a CDA, you will change: **Teaching will look different to you.** You will have more questions. You will be a livelier person. You will see how much more you can learn about young children.

Following are some examples of what your day may be like depending on where you decide to work as a CDA.

A CDA as an Infant-Toddler Teacher

Imelda Gonzales co-teaches an infant class with her friend, Jane Bennet. Together, they are responsible for six babies who range in age from 3 to 14 months. Imelda recently completed her CDA Credential with an infant-toddler specialization. She and Jane will stay with the same group of children for 3 years. During that time, other children will join the group so there will eventually be 12 toddlers in their care.

As the babies arrive early in the morning, Imelda greets each one warmly and talks quietly with the parent or other family member who has brought the baby to the center. Imelda learns that Emilio is fussy because he's teething and that Brandon wouldn't eat breakfast before he left home. She comforts each child and helps the parents make the transition to leave for work.

After feeding, diapering, and hand washing routines are accomplished—activities that go on throughout the day—Imelda finds toys and books that interest each of her babies. She plays with, sings to, and talks to each baby. Each of the babies is developing different skills at different times and she is alert to how she can best support their developing abilities while keeping them safe. Sarah is beginning to cruise around, while holding on to furniture or someone's pant legs, so Imelda makes sure that Sarah has secure objects to grab onto as she takes each new step.

Each baby eats and rests as needed, without a rigid schedule. And, weather permitting, Imelda takes them out for outdoor play or a walk in the stroller every day.

As the children get older, Imelda adds challenges to the curriculum experiences she provides. Her emphasis for these young babies is on building a warm, positive relationship with each child and family, and promoting their development in all areas—physical, social, emotional, and intellectual. Whatever she does with them, she describes it in words and always responds to their attempts to talk. She gives them lots of first-hand, new experiences (like playing in water) and the words that go with them (*splash, slippery, pour, wet, cold*). She uses the routines of daily living—eating, diapering, dressing—to teach the children new concepts and skills. And she uses play as the primary context for their learning.

During the day, Imelda and Jane record important information about each baby—the food consumed, bowel movements, mood, any special events—to share with parents.

By staying with their group for three years, Imelda and Jane get to know the children very well and are able to use the children's personal interests and abilities to help each child make developmental and learning progress every day. These infant-toddler teachers also become very close to the families. Imelda is able to speak Spanish as well as English, so she can help Emilio and Maria, two of the children in her care, become bilingual.

A Family Child Care Provider CDA

Aleta Boykin chose to make Family Child Care her profession and obtained a CDA Credential, which demonstrates her competence to the families who use her services. Much of her work is similar to Imelda's because she cares for babies. But her work is especially interesting and complex because she has a multi-age group. She cares for 1-year-old Lauren, 18-month-old Erica, 4-year-old Joey, and 6-year-old Michael before and after school. Aleta's own son, Joshua, is also 6 and in the same class as Michael. Aleta views her family child care business as having the strengths of a true family because the children can model and learn from each other.

Aleta has toys and materials that are appropriate for each of the different age groups, and she is extra cautious about health and safety concerns. Some of the toys that Joey likes to play with such as Lego blocks and peg boards could be choking hazards for the toddlers. So Joey plays with those while the younger children are napping or after they go home. At other times during the day, he builds with blocks, reads books, paints, and writes. He, Joshua, and Michael play together too, and they especially enjoy dramatic play with blocks where they create elaborate scenarios like pirate ship, dress-up, and act-out stories.

Having the mixed age group is both a challenge and an opportunity for Aleta. Michael and Josh are learning to read at school so they practice their reading on the younger children. But at times, they want to do only "big boy" things so Aleta respects their choices, just as she does for Joey.

Mealtimes are also fun times, when children talk together and share experiences about what they did at home or will do in the future. The toddlers benefit greatly from having several people of different ages to talk with them.

Most of the families who use her family child care home stay with Aleta for years, so she becomes part of their family as well. She likes the intimate nature of this work—being a confidante and support for young parents—but she makes sure that she uses good business practices as well.

A Center-Based Preschool CDA

Sue Ridley has had a CDA Credential for three years and works as a preschool teacher in a Head Start program. She earned nine college credits while obtaining her formal training for her CDA and she has applied those credits toward an associate degree. She is now working on her associate degree and will be finished in another year, making her eligible for a salary increase.

Sue had never thought about going to college before entering her CDA program, but once she had the nine credits, she was motivated by knowing that she was one-third of the way toward finishing the professional portion of the associate program. She also found that she liked learning new things and that what she learned in school made her a better teacher. The children were happier and more engaged with the new teaching strategies she used. There were fewer discipline problems in her classroom and her director started sending other teachers to observe her work.

Sue was especially excited about what she learned in school about how to help children learn early literacy and math skills that prepare them for school. She had always thought it was developmentally inappropriate to teach the alphabet. But in her curriculum class, Sue learned that knowing the alphabet is an important predictor of children's success in kindergarten. More important, Sue learned lots of developmentally appropriate ways to teach the alphabet to young children. The children in Sue's Head Start class did not know their letters, so teaching the alphabet was an important goal for her.

She began by making sure the alphabet was displayed in places where children could see it, touch it, manipulate it, and use it in their work and play. She read alphabet books to small groups or individuals, and played alphabet games like lotto and puzzles. She setup a sign-in sheet and other ways for children to sign their names such as signaling their preferences for snack. Some children just made scribbles at first. But after lots of opportunities to see and work with the letters in their names, children gradually began to make letter-like symbols and some letters. By the end of the year, all the children were writing their first names and a few could write their last names as well.

Helping children learn the alphabet was only one of the ways Sue's teaching improved from her college work. She also included math and science experiences in her curriculum, which added lots of new words and concepts to children's vocabularies. The children began working on projects where they identified questions they wanted answered and problems they wanted to solve. Their interest and motivation to learn took off, and Sue's motivation as a teacher increased day-by-day.

CDAs in Every Early Childhood Setting

Imelda, Aleta, and Sue are just three examples of the type of work that CDAs do every day. We could describe many other career options for CDAs. Carlos has a CDA credential with a bilingual specialization. He works as a teacher assistant in a public school pre-kindergarten program, and is especially effective in supporting home language development for the seven children who speak Spanish at home. Dawn has a preschool CDA and is a teacher of 3-year-olds in a full-day, employer- sponsored child care center. Marilyn also has a center-based preschool CDA, but she teaches half-day in a church-sponsored preschool. There are many options for CDAs because early childhood education is such a diverse field.

But like Sue, every CDA should see her credential as the beginning of a professional journey. Professional knowledge is always growing and changing, and there is much more to be learned once your CDA credential is obtained. Qualification requirements for jobs in early childhood education are also increasing. In order to advance in your profession, you will want to think of CDA as the entry stage on a journey of lifelong professional preparation and development.

Now you have seen different kinds of situations where CDAs work and seen how much responsibility a CDA has in planning and supervising daily experiences. This is a good time for you to go see another program in action, and to watch the video for Unit 1.

Schedule a visit to another early childhood program. Try to visit one that you have never seen before, one that is as different as possible from the one in which you work—a family child care home, a public school pre-kindergarten, Head Start, or a full-day child care program.

Spend one or two hours watching what happens. Perhaps you can go on your lunch hour. If you just can't manage to take off more than an extra hour or two, at least visit a co-worker's classroom or a neighbor's family child care home.

After your visit, think about what it would be like to be a teacher or a child in that program.

Jot down some of your impressions here. How I would feel if I were a teacher in the program I visited:

_____

_____

_____

_____

_____

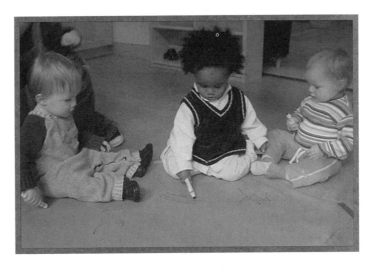

How do you observe children's behavior for clues about development and learning?

How I would feel if I were a child in the program I visited:

_____

_____

_____

_____

_____

What did you see that was similar to your program *(or similar between different programs)*?

_____

_____

_____

_____

_____

What was different from your program *(or different from the other programs you observed)*?

_____

_____

_____

_____

_____

You and your Field Advisor can discuss your observations and talk about any questions you may have about the variety of early childhood programs.

If you are not now working full-time with young children, you may have time to visit or even volunteer in several different types of programs. You need to have a really good feel for what happens with young children, and you just can't get it from reading. Use extra paper to write your responses to the same questions for each program.

If you can't schedule a visit, interview a family child care provider, group teacher, or program director. Ask her or him to describe a typical day. Perhaps a copy of the parent contract, statement of program goals and philosophy, curriculum plan, or other written materials will help you visualize what happens in the program. Then go back and see whether you can answer the questions about the program.

Each time you visit another program or talk with someone else in the field, you gain a new perspective on what teaching is all about. Most likely you either feel good about your own work or are eager to improve. You either gain new ideas or discover that what you do is so much more creative. **When your Seminar group of CDA Candidates meets, you will see how much you can learn from each other as professionals.**

Part 4 of this unit and the accompanying videotape will give you an even better picture of just what teachers of young children do and how CDAs fit into the broad picture of the entire field of early childhood education.

Who are early childhood educators?

Many teach young children

You probably remember busy days like those you read about in Part 3. Some are *more* hectic—there could have been an earthquake evacuation, a playground accident, a prospective parent visit, a substitute assistant teacher, or all of these!

Think back to the description of the CDA's days. Try to remember the day you visited another program. Review what you saw on the video. Did you see how some of the qualities of a good teacher were put to use? Now let's pull together all of the information you have gathered so far to see what good teachers do.

Teachers of young children ... prepare the environment to create learning opportunities—you set the stage for children to learn through play and teacher-planned experiences.

You prepare art supplies for children to use in their own creative ways.

You select toys and materials that present problems for children to solve.

You plan field trips to familiar as well as new and interesting places.

You read picture books and information books, and have paper and markers so children can write their own messages and stories.

You extend children's play by posing open-ended questions or introducing props used in many cultures and jobs.

What teachers of young children do

- prepare the environment to create learning opportunities
- have reasonable expectations
- know individual children
- know the social and cultural context of the children and families you serve
- offer appropriate learning experiences
- interact frequently with individuals and small groups
- provide time for children to be with each other and with loving adults
- are eager to learn more about children and teaching

You choose many types of music to listen and move to.

You give children quiet places to be alone, and other spaces to be together with their friends.

... have reasonable expectations—you know how children typically develop and learn, so you know what each child in your group is trying to understand and do. You know that children tend to work on different skills during each age range.

... know individual children—you know that each child is unique. You are aware of the strengths, needs, and interests of each child. You observe their learning and developmental progress so you can individualize your teaching.

... **know the social and cultural context of the children and families you work with**—you know the values of the culture(s) within the group and your community. You know how to support and respect children's home languages and cultures to strengthen their sense of their own identities.

... **offer appropriate learning experiences**—you select interesting topics of study and plan projects and other experiences that expand children's thinking and learning. Projects are challenging but not frustrating for children.

... **interact frequently with individuals and small groups**—children learn a great deal from adults and other children. To develop language and learn about the world, young children need many opportunities to

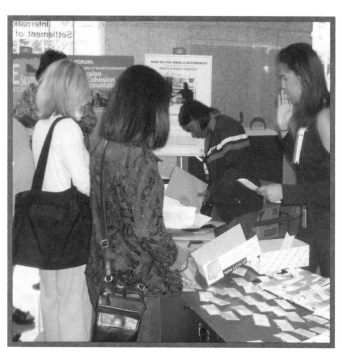

Each time you visit another program or talk with someone else in the field, you gain a new perspective on what teaching is all about.

engage in one-to-one conversations with adults. Children also need adults to give them information such as the names of objects or symbols such as letters or numbers.

... **provide lots of time for children to be with each other and with loving adults**—children learn how to get along well with people when they play with and solve problems with others. They also learn a great deal, especially language, from adults and other children. Children also need time alone.

... **are eager to learn more about children and teaching**—you are ready to adopt sound new ideas about teaching. You want those ideas to be based on research, theory, and practical experiences of others who keep children's long-range development in mind.

You learn at least some key words in each language spoken by the families in your program.

You become better at working with parents. You stand up for what you know is fair for children and families.

Early childhood education is more than teaching

Because you are on your way to becoming a CDA, this year of study concentrates on teaching young children. However, as you probably are aware, not everyone in our field teaches children. Regardless of what you do, there are many issues you need to know about that face our profession.

Let's take a brief look at the broader early childhood field.

Enjoy the variety of careers

Early childhood educators have lots of different jobs in various places.

Some teach young children or assist lead teachers. Others direct programs, plan curriculum for children, and supervise staff. Many others educate teachers in colleges, workshops, and through books, journals, and videotapes, for example.

Working with parents, as home visitors do, is another major area of our field.

Still others are researchers, finding new insights about how children develop and learn.

Some write children's books or produce children's television. Others may develop learning materials, design special clothing or equipment for differently abled children, or set up a variety of recreation programs for young children.

Many people are involved in government, perhaps in licensing child care or working on legislation to improve the lives of children and families. Some work in educational sales or as consumer advocates.

Others work "outside" the field but need knowledge of early childhood education or child development, such as medical staff, children's librarians, and social workers.

Where you work can also vary. Some early childhood educators work in offices, some in stores, some in churches, some in universities, some in their own homes. You have a lot of choices!

To be qualified for most of these positions, you must have a credential, such as the CDA, or a diploma such as an associate or bachelor's degree. Some positions require even more years of college education, such as advanced degrees. Many also require experience in teaching young children.

Although it is possible to be hired to work with young children while you are still in an educational program, one goal of our profession is to ensure that the care and education of young children is in the hands of people who are well educated.

The National Association for the Education of Young Children (NAEYC), which is the largest professional organization of early childhood educators in the United States, has identified four early childhood professional development levels (see page 16). Each level requires an increasing amount of education and/or experience. Each of these levels also varies greatly in salaries paid. You are probably aware that most paychecks in early childhood education are small compared to the amount of work and responsibility. Advocating for better salaries and working conditions is part of being a professional, too.

Get to know your colleagues better. **Interview someone who is in the field but works in a different type of job.** Perhaps you have met or heard about a person with an interesting career through your local early childhood association. You might choose a curriculum specialist, or a program director, or someone who writes books for children or parents. Consider someone from a cultural group different from yours, or who works with children speaking a home language other than English.

The following is designed to reflect a continuum of professional development. The levels identify levels of preparation programs for which standards have been established nationally.

Definitions of Early Childhood Professional Categories

Early Childhood Professional Level VI

Successful completion of a Ph.D. or Ed.D. in a program conforming to NAEYC guidelines; OR

Successful demonstration of the knowledge, performance, and dispositions expected as outcomes of a doctoral degree program conforming to NAEYC guidelines.

Early Childhood Professional Level V

Successful completion of a master's degree in a program that conforms to NAEYC guidelines; OR

Successful demonstration of the knowledge, performance, and dispositions expected as outcomes of a master's degree program conforming to NAEYC guidelines.

Early Childhood Professional Level IV

Successful completion of a baccalaureate degree from a program conforming to NAEYC guidelines; OR

State certificate meeting NAEYC certification guidelines; OR

Successful completion of a baccalaureate degree in another field with more than 30 professional units in early childhood development/education including 300 hours of supervised teaching experience, including 150 hours each for two of the following three age groups: infant and toddlers, 3- to 5-year-olds, or the primary grades; OR

Successful demonstration of the knowledge, performance, and dispositions expected as outcomes of a baccalaureate degree program conforming to NAEYC guidelines.

Early Childhood Professional Level III

Successful completion of an associate degree from a program conforming to NAEYC guidelines; OR

Successful completion of an associate degree in a related field, plus 30 units of professional studies in early childhood development/education, including 300 hours of supervised teaching experience in an early childhood program; OR

Successful demonstration of the knowledge, performance and dispositions expected as outcomes of an associate degree program conforming to NAEYC guidelines.

Early Childhood Professional Level II

II B. Successful completion of a one-year early childhood certificate program.

II A. Successful completion of the CDA Professional Preparation Program OR completion of a systematic, comprehensive training program that prepares an individual to successfully acquire the CDA Credential through Direct Assessment.

Early Childhood Professional Level I

Individuals who are employed in an early childhood professional role working under supervision or with support (*e.g., linkages with provider association or network or enrollment in supervised practicum*) and participating in training designed to lead to the assessment of individual competencies or acquisitions of a degree.

Your Field Advisor can help you locate people and figure out what to ask in your interview. Here are some questions you might talk about. Add your own questions to this list. Then write the person's responses here after your interview.

Interviewee _____

_____

Type of work _____

_____

_____

_____

What are some of the challenges of your work?

_____

_____

_____

_____

_____

What do you find most rewarding?

_____

_____

_____

_____

What *do* you find least rewarding?

_____

_____

_____

_____

_____

_____

_____

How can we work together to make lives better for young children?

_____

_____

_____

_____

_____

_____

_____

What education and experiences are needed to do your job?

_____

_____

_____

_____

_____

_____

There are so many different types of early childhood educators. Make a list here of other people that you would like to talk with in our field—either their name or job titles.

_____

_____

_____

_____

_____

Sometime, while you are working on your CDA, you may have a chance to get to know these people. One of them may be your Seminar Instructor. Another may be your CDA Field Advisor. Still others may be active in your local early childhood association. We all learn so much when we share ideas with other professionals.

Advocate for better wages and working conditions

Early childhood educators are proud professionals. However, as an occupational group, our wages and working conditions are less than ideal.

National studies of child care teaching staff show the following:

- Nearly all child care teachers are women.

- Many earn minimum wage or less.
- A large proportion receive no paid holidays or vacation.
- Few receive paid sick leave and even fewer have paid health insurance.
- Each year, as many as 40% of child care teachers leave their jobs for work in other occupations.

National early childhood organizations believe that if all child care teachers became advocates for improved wages and working conditions, this situation would change. NAEYC has also organized a campaign to help improve compensation and working conditions by advocating for financing of a system of early care and education. For more information, visit their Website: www.naeyc.org. As a start, you may want to ask questions to find out what salaries and benefits are provided in early childhood programs in your community.

What are average starting wages?

_____

_____

_____

_____

_____

_____

How do they compare with the wages received by other professionals in the community who have similar levels of educational preparation and responsibility?

_____

_____

_____

_____

Is there a career ladder that provides opportunities for career advancement and encourages individuals to continue to work with children?

_____

_____

_____

_____

Is there health insurance? Ample sick leave?

_____

_____

_____

_____

Are there retirement benefits?

_____

_____

_____

_____

Who/What organization keeps track of this information? Write down the Website or other contact information.

_____

_____

_____

_____

_____

_____

If you need help in getting this information, ask your Field Advisor. It is important to be active in helping improve the status of the profession, a topic explored again in Unit 7.

Meet legal requirements

Every state has its own laws about standards for early childhood programs and teacher qualifications.

For programs. In some states it may be mandatory for every group program and family child care home to be licensed.

In other states, family child care registration is optional, the number of children enrolled may make a difference, or some group programs may be exempt from licensing *(such as Head Start, church programs, or those sponsored by school districts).*

You need to know just how your program, or any other place you might want to work, fits into the whole picture of the regulation of programs for children from birth through age 5.

Talk with the program director where you work or volunteer, or use the Internet to find out about your local and state laws.

What state and/or local agencies regulate group programs in your state? Who regulates family child care programs? **Write the agency name(s) , address(es), Website, and/or phone number(s) here.**

Group programs

_____

_____

_____

_____

Family child care

_____

_____

_____

_____

_____

Which group child care programs in your state must be licensed?

_____

_____

_____

_____

Which programs are excluded?

_____

_____

_____

_____

Contact the agency that regulates group programs. Use the Internet to obtain a copy of your state's group program licensing requirements. (See Resources, p.24)

Look through every section and especially study the sections about the curriculum and teaching materials.

Do the requirements seem very strict? Or could almost any program meet the standards?

_____

_____

_____

_____

_____

What does the licensing law say about personnel qualifications for center directors? For teachers? For assistant teachers?

_____

_____

_____

_____

_____

Learn about the agency that governs family child care providers in your state or county. Save a copy of the section on personnel regulations for your Professional Resource File. (You will begin to build this me after you have met with your Field Advisor.)

Regardless of the type of program you work in, you need to know about family child care. Many families who use out-of-home care still prefer family child care, especially for very young children.

Does your state or county regulate family child care providers?

_____

_____

_____

_____

Do the standards seem easy to meet or fairly strict?

_____

_____

_____

If you work in Head Start, read through all the *Head Start Program Performance Standards*. List here some of the strengths and weaknesses your Head Start program has in meeting these standards.

_____

_____

_____

_____

Perhaps you work in a program that is supported at least in part by another agency that also has regulations to be met—maybe the program is housed in an elementary school or church, or you receive Children's Aid Society funds. Or perhaps your program is accredited and must meet those standards in addition to licensing requirements.

Find out from your program director what additional requirements your program must meet. Jot down some of them in this space.

_____

_____

_____

_____

_____

For teachers. Just as requirements for programs differ by state, so do regulations about teacher qualifications. For example, a lead teacher in some states might need a four-year college degree in early childhood education or a related field and even a year or two of experience, while in other states less training is required.

In the Seminar, you will discuss how your CDA Credential fits into your own state regulations, and the importance of continuing education.

In many states, people who are responsible for a group of children must be aged 18 or older. It is fairly common that people who work with young children cannot have a criminal record.

Observe professional ethics

Perhaps you feel that requirements for teachers and programs are unnecessary or that they just cause endless paperwork and red tape. Maybe you are uncertain about the value of child care regulation. You may find it hard to understand how anyone could want to take advantage of young children. Perhaps you feel that government should not interfere with child care.

It might help you to see the value of mandatory licensing if you think in these terms:

Laws governing teachers and programs for young children offer at least a minimum level of consumer protection.

Cats and dogs need rabies shots. Ice cream vendors must have a license. Even your car is registered. Surely children, who are so precious and vulnerable, deserve to be protected!

Parents, teachers, programs, and governments can work together to provide good care for our most vulnerable citizens. *Conscientious teachers and programs welcome regulation and want to help their states work toward laws that will help to ensure only the best care for young children.*

Legal requirements have been a controversial topic for many years and will be just one of the ethical issues you must face in our field. Some other typical problems, with no easy solutions, might be these:

- What do you do when parents ask you to spank their children?

- How do you handle suspected child abuse or neglect?

- How do you treat confidential information innocently passed on by a child that could be damaging to the parents?

- What should you do if your program has more children than its license allows?

You will have the opportunity to learn more about how to deal with issues such as these during your CDA Seminar.

As a CDA, you are expected to agree to the NAEYC Code of Ethical Conduct and Statement of Commitment printed at the end of Unit 1. This statement is just the beginning of your commitment to the well-being of young children. All during your career, you will struggle with ethical dilemmas similar to the ones you will touch on during your CDA professional preparation.

Fortunately, you are not alone in your struggle to do what is right for children. Professional organizations such as those listed on pages 26-27 are working to improve the quality of staff and programs for all young children.

The best way to keep up with professional issues is to be a member of an association. You may not be ready to join yet, but find out about one or two of the groups listed on pages 26-27 and obtain information. Locate one that has a state or local chapter in your area. The fastest and easiest way is to go the organization's website.

You will be off to a good start on finding the right association for you. **Name the two associations you have information about.**

_____

_____

_____

_____

Save the information you receive from them or print from the Internet in your Professional Resource File.

You have now completed Unit 1 of the self- study phase of your work toward your CDA. Turn to page 457 of these materials. There you will find your CDA progress record. Check off the box for the Unit 1 Self-Study.

You know that work with young children is not an easy job. Teaching—whether in a group program or as a family child care provider—is much more enjoyable and much more professional when you know a lot about children. You need to know about children in general and about those you work with in particular.

The next unit of *Essentials* will summarize for you what a large body of research and generations of people have found out about how children develop and learn. Children's development and learning become apparent every day when you know what to look for!

Resources for more information

Bellm, D. & Haack, P. *Working for quality child care: Good child care jobs = good care for children.* Washington, DC: Center for the Child Care Workforce, www.ccw.org. Also available from Redleaf Press at www. redleafpress.org.

Career Encounters: Early Childhood Education. (video 1994 and viewer's guide 2003). Produced by Gray-Davis Inc., with support of Rockefeller Brothers Foundation and Johnson and Johnson, 28 min. Washington, DC: National Association for the Education of Young Children.

Careers for men in early childhood education (brochure) (2001). Washington, DC: National Association for the Education of Young Children.

Careers in early childhood education (brochure). (2003). Washington, DC: National Association for the Education of Young Children.

Center for the Child Care Workforce. (2002). *Current data on child care salaries and benefits, 2002 edition.* Washington, DC: Available from www.ccw.org.

Feeney, S., Christensen, D.& Moravcik, E. (2000). *Who am I in the lives of children? An introduction to teaching young children.* Columbus, OH: Prentice Hall.

Feeney, S. & Freeman, N.K. (1999). *Ethics and the early childhood educator: Using the NAEYC Code.* Washington, DC: National Association for the Education of Young Children.

Head Start Program Performance Standards. (1998). Washington, DC: U.S. Department of Health and Human Services, Head Start Bureau. National Center for Early Childhood.

Hyson, M. (Ed.). (2003). *Preparing early childhood professionals: NAEYC's standards for programs.* Washington, DC: National Association for the Education of Young Children.

Johnson, J. & McCracken, J.B. (Eds.). (1994). *The early childhood career lattice: Perspectives on professional development.* Washington, DC: National Association for the Education of Young Children.

Modigliani, K., Rieff, M. & Jones, S. (1987). *Opening your door to children: How to start a family day care program.* Washington, DC: National Association for the Education of Young Children.

NAEYC Position Statement: A conceptual framework for early childhood professional development. (1994). *Young Children, 49(3),* 68–77.

NAEYC Position Statement on Licensing and public regulation of early childhood programs. (1997). Washington, DC: National Association for the Education of Young Children.

NAEYC Position Statement on Quality, compensation, and affordability in early childhood programs. (1995.) Washington, DC: National Association for the Education of Young Children.

National Resource Center for Health and Safety in Child Care, University of Colorado Health Science Center, provides access to licensing information for every state (http://nrc.uchsc.edu/STATES/states.htm).

Nurturing the promise: A set of multimedia training materials for the implementation of the Head Start Program Performance Standards (includes standards, videotape, user's guide, wall chart, brochure, transparencies). Available from: Head Start Publications Management Center, P.O. Box 26147, Alexandria, VA 22313-0417.

Whitebook, M.& Bellm, D. (1998). *Taking on turnover: An action guide for child care teachers and directors.* Washington, DC: Center for the Child Care Workforce. Available from www.ccw.org.

Membership and resource organizations

American Library Association
Association for Library Services
for Children
www.ala.org/ala/alsc/alsc.htm
50 E. Huron Street
Chicago, IL 60611
800-545-2433, ext. 2163

Association for Childhood Education
International
www.acei.org
headquarters@acei.org
17904 Georgia Avenue, Suite 215
Olney, MD 20832
301-570-2111
800-423-3563

Center for the Child Care Workforce
A project of the American
Federation of Teachers Educational
Foundation
www.ccw.org
555 New Jersey Avenue NW
Washington, DC 20001
202-662-8005

Child Care Information Exchange
www.childcareexchange.com
P.O. Box 3249
Redmond, WA 98073

Division for Early Childhood of the
Council for Exceptional Children
www.dec-sped.org
27 Fort Missoula Rd.
Missoula, MT 59804
406-543-0872

National Association for Bilingual
Education
www.nabe.org
1313 L Street NW, Suite 210
Washington, DC 20005
202-898-1829

National Association for the Education
of Young Children
www.naeyc.org
1313 L Street NW, Suite 500
Washington, DC 20005-4110
202-232-8777
800-424-2460

National Association for Family Child
Care
www.nafcc.org
1743 W. Alexander St.
Salt Lake City, UT 84119
801-886-2325

National Black Child Development
Institute
www.nbcdi.org
1313 L Street NW, Suite 110
Washington, DC 20005-4110
202-833-2220

National Child Care Association
www.nccanet.org
1325 G St. NW
Washington, DC 20005
800-543-7161

National Head Start Association
www.nhsa.org
1651 Prince Street
Alexandria, VA 22314
703-739-0875

National Latino Children's Institute
www.nlci.org
118 Broadway Street
San Antonio, TX 78205
210-228-9997

North American Reggio Emilia Alliance
www.reggioalliance.org
c/o Inspired Practices
2040 Wilson Ridge Court
Roswell, GA 30075
770-552-0179

T.E.A.C.H. Early Childhood Technical Assistance Center
www.childcareservices.org
Child Care Services Association
P.O. Box 901
Chapel Hill, NC 27514
919-967-3272

World Organization for Early Childhood Education
(OMEP) - U.S. National Committee
http://omep-usnc.org

Southern Early Childhood Association
www.southernearlychildhood.org
P.O. Box 55930
Little Rock, AR 72215-5930
800-305-7322

Zero to Three: National Center for Infants, Toddlers, and Families
www.zerotothree.org
2000 M Street NW, Suite 200
Washington, DC 20036
202-638-1144

National Association for the Education of Young Children

Statement of Commitment

AS AN INDIVIDUAL WHO WORKS WITH YOUNG CHILDREN,
I COMMIT MYSELF TO FURTHERING THE VALUES OF EARLY CHILDHOOD EDUCATION
AS THEY ARE REFLECTED IN THE NAEYC CODE OF ETHICAL CONDUCT.

TO THE BEST OF MY ABILITY I WILL:

- ENSURE THAT PROGRAMS FOR YOUNG CHILDREN ARE BASED ON CURRENT KNOWLEDGE OF CHILD DEVELOPMENT AND EARLY CHILDHOOD EDUCATION.

- RESPECT AND SUPPORT FAMILIES IN THEIR TASK OF NURTURING CHILDREN.

- RESPECT COLLEAGUES IN EARLY CHILDHOOD EDUCATION AND SUPPORT THEM IN MAINTAINING THE NAEYC CODE OF ETHICAL CONDUCT.

- SERVE AS AN ADVOCATE FOR CHILDREN, THEIR FAMILIES, AND THEIR TEACHERS IN COMMUNITY AND SOCIETY.

- MAINTAIN HIGH STANDARDS OF PROFESSIONAL CONDUCT.

- RECOGNIZE HOW PERSONAL VALUES, OPINIONS, AND BIASES CAN AFFECT PROFESSIONAL JUDGMENT.

- BE OPEN TO NEW IDEAS AND BE WILLING TO LEARN FROM THE SUGGESTIONS OF OTHERS.

- CONTINUE TO LEARN, GROW, AND CONTRIBUTE AS A PROFESSIONAL.

- HONOR THE IDEALS AND PRINCIPLES OF THE NAEYC CODE OF ETHICAL CONDUCT.

NAEYC POSITION STATEMENT ADOPTED 1989 AMENDED 1997

NAEYC Code of Ethical Conduct and Statement of Commitment

(Revised April 2005)

A position statement of the National Association for the Education of Young Children

Endorsed by the Association for Childhood Education International

Adopted by the National Association for Family Child Care

Preamble

NAEYC recognizes that those who work with young children face many daily decisions that have moral and ethical implications. The **NAEYC Code of Ethical Conduct** offers guidelines for responsible behavior and sets forth a common basis for resolving the principal ethical dilemmas encountered in early childhood care and education. The **Statement of Commitment** is not part of the Code but is a personal acknowledgement of an individual's willingness to embrace the distinctive values and moral obligations of the field of early childhood care and education. The primary focus of the Code is on daily practice with children and their families in programs for children from birth through 8 years of age, such as infant/toddler programs, preschool and pre-kindergarten programs, child care centers, hospital and child life settings, family child care homes, kindergartens, and primary classrooms. When the issues involve young children, then these provisions also apply to specialists who do not work directly with children, including program administrators, parent educators, early childhood adult educators, and officials with responsibility for program monitoring and licensing. (Note: See also the "Code of Ethical Conduct: Supplement for Early Childhood Adult Educators," online at http://www.naeyc.org/about/positions/ethics04.asp.)

Core values

Standards of ethical behavior in early childhood care and education are based on commitment to the following core values that are deeply rooted in the history of the field of early childhood care and education. We have made a commitment to

- Appreciate childhood as a unique and valuable stage of the human life cycle.
- Base our work on knowledge of how children develop and learn.
- Appreciate and support the bond between the child and family.
- Recognize that children are best understood and supported in the context of family, culture,[1] community, and society.
- Respect the dignity, worth, and uniqueness of each individual (child, family member, and colleague).
- Respect diversity in children, families, and colleagues.
- Recognize that children and adults achieve their full potential in the context of relationships that are based on trust and respect.

Conceptual framework

The Code sets forth a framework of professional responsibilities in four sections. Each section addresses an area of professional relationships: (1) with children, (2) with families, (3) among colleagues, and (4) with the community and society. Each section includes an introduction to the primary responsibilities of the early childhood practitioner in that context. The introduction is followed by a set of ideals (I) that reflect exemplary professional practice and a set of principles (P) describing practices that are required, prohibited, or permitted.

The ideals reflect the aspirations of practitioners. The principles guide conduct and assist practitioners in resolving ethical dilemmas.[2] Both ideals and principles are intended to direct practitioners to those questions which, when responsibly answered, can provide the basis for conscientious decision making. While the Code provides specific direction for addressing some ethical dilemmas, many others will require the practitioner to combine the guidance of the Code with professional judgment.

The **ideals** and **principles** in this Code present a shared framework of professional responsibility that affirms our commitment to the core values of our field. The Code publicly acknowledges the responsibilities that we in the field have assumed and in so doing supports ethical behavior in our work. Practitioners who face situations with ethical dimensions are urged to seek guidance in the applicable parts of this Code and in the spirit that informs the whole.

Often, "the right answer"—the best ethical course of action to take—is not obvious. There may be no readily apparent, positive way to handle a situation. When one important value contradicts another, we face an ethical dilemma. When we face a dilemma, it is our professional responsibility to consult the Code and all relevant parties to find the most ethical resolution.

Section I

Ethical responsibilities to children

Childhood is a unique and valuable stage in the human life cycle. Our paramount responsibility is to provide care and education in settings that are safe, healthy, nurturing, and responsive for each child. We are committed to supporting children's development and learning; respecting individual differences; and helping children learn to live, play, and work cooperatively. We are also committed to promoting children's self-awareness, competence, self-worth, resiliency, and physical well-being.

---

[1] Culture includes ethnicity, racial identity, economic level, family structure, language, and religious and political beliefs, which profoundly influence each child's development and relationship to the world.

[2] There is not necessarily a corresponding principle for each ideal.

Ideals

I-1.1—To be familiar with the knowledge base of early childhood care and education and to stay informed through continuing education and training.

I-1.2—To base program practices upon current knowledge and research in the field of early childhood education, child development, and related disciplines, as well as on particular knowledge of each child.

I-1.3—To recognize and respect the unique qualities, abilities, and potential of each child.

I-1.4—To appreciate the vulnerability of children and their dependence on adults.

I-1.5—To create and maintain safe and healthy settings that foster children's social, emotional, cognitive, and physical development and that respect their dignity and their contributions.

I-1.6—To use assessment instruments and strategies that are appropriate for the children to be assessed, that are used only for the purposes for which they were designed, and that have the potential to benefit children.

I-1.7—To use assessment information to understand and support children's development and learning, to support instruction, and to identify children who may need additional services.

I-1.8—To support the right of each child to play and learn in an inclusive environment that meets the needs of children with and without disabilities.

I-1.9—To advocate for and ensure that all children, including those with special needs, have access to the support services needed to be successful.

I-1.10—To ensure that each child's culture, language, ethnicity, and family structure are recognized and valued in the program.

I-1.11—To provide all children with experiences in a language that they know, as well as support children in maintaining the use of their home language and in learning English.

I-1.12—To work with families to provide a safe and smooth transition as children and families move from one program to the next.

Principles

P-1.1—Above all, we shall not harm children. We shall not participate in practices that are emotionally damaging, physically harmful, disrespectful, degrading, dangerous, exploitative, or intimidating to children. *This principle has precedence over all others in this Code.*

P-1.2—We shall care for and educate children in positive emotional and social environments that are cognitively stimulating and that support each child's culture, language, ethnicity, and family structure.

P-1.3—We shall not participate in practices that discriminate against children by denying benefits, giving special advantages, or excluding them from programs or activities on the basis of their sex, race, national origin, religious beliefs, medical condition, disability, or the marital status/family structure, sexual orientation, or religious beliefs or other affiliations of their families. (Aspects of this principle do not apply in programs that have a lawful mandate to provide services to a particular population of children.)

P-1.4—We shall involve all those with relevant knowledge (including families and staff) in decisions concerning a child, as appropriate, ensuring confidentiality of sensitive information.

P-1.5—We shall use appropriate assessment systems, which include multiple sources of information, to provide information on children's learning and development.

P-1.6—We shall strive to ensure that decisions such as those related to enrollment, retention, or assignment to special education services, will be based on multiple sources of information and will never be based on a single assessment, such as a test score or a single observation.

P-1.7—We shall strive to build individual relationships with each child; make individualized adaptations in teaching strategies, learning environments, and curricula; and consult with the family so that each child benefits from the program. If after such efforts have been exhausted, the current placement does not meet a child's needs, or the child is seriously jeopardizing the ability of other children to benefit from the program, we shall collaborate with the child's family and appropriate specialists to determine the additional services needed and/or the placement option(s) most likely to ensure the child's success. (Aspects of this principle may not apply in programs that have a lawful mandate to provide services to a particular population of children.)

P-1.8—We shall be familiar with the risk factors for and symptoms of child abuse and neglect, including physical, sexual, verbal, and emotional abuse and physical, emotional, educational, and medical neglect. We shall know and follow state laws and community procedures that protect children against abuse and neglect.

P-1.9—When we have reasonable cause to suspect child abuse or neglect, we shall report it to the appropriate community agency and follow up to ensure that appropriate action has been taken. When appropriate, parents or guardians will be informed that the referral will be or has been made.

P-1.10—When another person tells us of his or her suspicion that a child is being abused or neglected, we shall assist that person in taking appropriate action in order to protect the child.

P-1.11—When we become aware of a practice or situation that endangers the health, safety, or well-being of children, we have an ethical responsibility to protect children or inform parents and/or others who can.

Section II

Ethical responsibilities to families

Families[3] are of primary importance in children's development. Because the family and the early childhood practitioner have a common interest in the child's well-being, we acknowledge a primary responsibility to bring about communication, cooperation, and collaboration between the home and early childhood program in ways that enhance the child's development.

Ideals

I-2.1—To be familiar with the knowledge base related to working effectively with families and to stay informed through continuing education and training.

I-2.2—To develop relationships of mutual trust and create partnerships with the families we serve.

I-2.3. To welcome all family members and encourage them to participate in the program.

---

[3]The term *family* may include those adults, besides parents, with the responsibility of being involved in educating, nurturing, and advocating for the child.

I-2.4—To listen to families, acknowledge and build upon their strengths and competencies, and learn from families as we support them in their task of nurturing children.

I-2.5—To respect the dignity and preferences of each family and to make an effort to learn about its structure, culture, language, customs, and beliefs.

I-2.6. To acknowledge families' childrearing values and their right to make decisions for their children.

I-2.7. To share information about each child's education and development with families and to help them understand and appreciate the current knowledge base of the early childhood profession.

I-2.8—To help family members enhance their understanding of their children and support the continuing development of their skills as parents.

I-2.9—To participate in building support networks for families by providing them with opportunities to interact with program staff, other families, community resources, and professional services.

Principles

P-2.1—We shall not deny family members access to their child's classroom or program setting unless access is denied by court order or other legal restriction.

P-2.2—We shall inform families of program philosophy, policies, curriculum, assessment system, and personnel qualifications, and explain why we teach as we do—which should be in accordance with our ethical responsibilities to children (see Section I).

P-2.3—We shall inform families of and, when appropriate, involve them in policy decisions.

P-2.4—We shall involve the family in significant decisions affecting their child.

P-2.5—We shall make every effort to communicate effectively with all families in a language that they understand. We shall use community resources for translation and interpretation when we do not have sufficient resources in our own programs.

P-2.6—As families share information with us about their children and families, we shall consider this information to plan and implement the program.

P-2.7—We shall inform families about the nature and purpose of the program's child assessments and how data about their child will be used.

P-2.8—We shall treat child assessment information confidentially and share this information only when there is a legitimate need for it.

P-2.9—We shall inform the family of injuries and incidents involving their child, of risks such as exposures to communicable diseases that might result in infection, and of occurrences that might result in emotional stress.

P-2.10—Families shall be fully informed of any proposed research projects involving their children and shall have the opportunity to give or withhold consent without penalty. We shall not permit or participate in research that could in any way hinder the education, development, or well-being of children.

P-2.11—We shall not engage in or support exploitation of families. We shall not use our relationship with a family for private advantage or personal gain, or enter into relationships with family members that might impair our effectiveness working with their children.

P-2.12—We shall develop written policies for the protection of confidentiality and the disclosure of children's records. These policy documents shall be made available to all program personnel and families. Disclosure of children's records beyond family members, program personnel, and consultants having an obligation of confidentiality shall require familial consent (except in cases of abuse or neglect).

P-2.13—We shall maintain confidentiality and shall respect the family's right to privacy, refraining from disclosure of confidential information and intrusion into family life. However, when we have reason to believe that a child's welfare is at risk, it is permissible to share confidential information with agencies, as well as with individuals who have legal responsibility for intervening in the child's interest.

P-2.14—In cases where family members are in conflict with one another, we shall work openly, sharing our observations of the child, to help all parties involved make informed decisions. We shall refrain from becoming an advocate for one party.

P-2.15—We shall be familiar with and appropriately refer families to community resources and professional support services. After a referral has been made, we shall follow up to ensure that services have been appropriately provided.

Ethical responsibilities to colleagues

In a caring, cooperative workplace, human dignity is respected, professional satisfaction is promoted, and positive relationships are developed and sustained. Based upon our core values, our primary responsibility to colleagues is to establish and maintain settings and relationships that support productive work and meet professional needs. The same ideals that apply to children also apply as we interact with adults in the workplace.

A—Responsibilities to co-workers

Ideals

I-3A.1—To establish and maintain relationships of respect, trust, confidentiality, collaboration, and cooperation with co-workers.

I-3A.2—To share resources with co-workers, collaborating to ensure that the best possible early childhood care and education program is provided.

I-3A.3—To support co-workers in meeting their professional needs and in their professional development.

I-3A.4—To accord co-workers due recognition of professional achievement.

Principles

P-3A.1—We shall recognize the contributions of colleagues to our program and not participate in practices that diminish their reputations or impair their effectiveness in working with children and families.

P-3A.2—When we have concerns about the professional behavior of a co-worker, we shall first let that person know of our concern in a way that shows respect for personal dignity and for the diversity to be found among staff members, and then attempt to resolve the matter collegially and in a confidential manner.

P-3A.3—We shall exercise care in expressing views regarding the personal attributes or professional conduct of co-workers. Statements should be based on firsthand knowledge, not hearsay, and relevant to the interests of children and programs.

P-3A.4—We shall not participate in practices that discriminate against a co-worker because of sex, race, national origin, religious beliefs or other affiliations, age, marital status/family structure, disability, or sexual orientation.

B—Responsibilities to employers

Ideals

I-3B.1—To assist the program in providing the highest quality of service.

I-3B.2—To do nothing that diminishes the reputation of the program in which we work unless it is violating laws and regulations designed to protect children or is violating the provisions of this Code.

Principles

P-3B.1—We shall follow all program policies. When we do not agree with program policies, we shall attempt to effect change through constructive action within the organization.

P-3B.2—We shall speak or act on behalf of an organization only when authorized. We shall take care to acknowledge when we are speaking for the organization and when we are expressing a personal judgment.

P-3B.3—We shall not violate laws or regulations designed to protect children and shall take appropriate action consistent with this Code when aware of such violations.

P-3B.4—If we have concerns about a colleague's behavior, and children's well-being is not at risk, we may address the concern with that individual. If children are at risk or the situation does not improve after it has been brought to the colleague's attention, we shall report the colleague's unethical or incompetent behavior to an appropriate authority.

P-3B.5—When we have a concern about circumstances or conditions that impact the quality of care and education within the program, we shall inform the program's administration or, when necessary, other appropriate authorities.

C—Responsibilities to employees

Ideals

I-3C.1—To promote safe and healthy working conditions and policies that foster mutual respect, cooperation, collaboration, competence, well-being, confidentiality, and self-esteem in staff members.

I-3C.2—To create and maintain a climate of trust and candor that will enable staff to speak and act in the best interests of children, families, and the field of early childhood care and education.

I-3C.3—To strive to secure adequate and equitable compensation (salary and benefits) for those who work with or on behalf of young children.

I-3C.4—To encourage and support continual development of employees in becoming more skilled and knowledgeable practitioners.

Principles

P-3C.1—In decisions concerning children and programs, we shall draw upon the education, training, experience, and expertise of staff members.

P-3C.2—We shall provide staff members with safe and supportive working conditions that honor confidences and permit them to carry out their responsibilities through fair performance evaluation, written grievance procedures, constructive feedback, and opportunities for continuing professional development and advancement.

P-3C.3—We shall develop and maintain comprehensive written personnel policies that define program standards. These policies shall be given to new staff members and shall be available and easily accessible for review by all staff members.

P-3C.4—We shall inform employees whose performance does not meet program expectations of areas of concern and, when possible, assist in improving their performance.

P-3C.5—We shall conduct employee dismissals for just cause, in accordance with all applicable laws and regulations. We shall inform employees who are dismissed of the reasons for their termination. When a dismissal is for cause, justification must be based on evidence of inadequate or inappropriate behavior that is accurately documented, current, and available for the employee to review.

P-3C.6—In making evaluations and recommendations, we shall make judgments based on fact and relevant to the interests of children and programs.

P-3C.7—We shall make hiring, retention, termination, and promotion decisions based solely on a person's competence, record of accomplishment,

ability to carry out the responsibilities of the position, and professional preparation specific to the developmental levels of children in his/her care.

P-3C.8—We shall not make hiring, retention, termination, and promotion decisions based on an individual's sex, race, national origin, religious beliefs or other affiliations, age, marital status/family structure, disability, or sexual orientation. We shall be familiar with and observe laws and regulations that pertain to employment discrimination. (Aspects of this principle do not apply to programs that have a lawful mandate to determine eligibility based on one or more of the criteria identified above.)

P-3C.9—We shall maintain confidentiality in dealing with issues related to an employee's job performance and shall respect an employee's right to privacy regarding personal issues.

Section IV

Ethical responsibilities to community and society

Early childhood programs operate within the context of their immediate community made up of families and other institutions concerned with children's welfare. Our responsibilities to the community are to provide programs that meet the diverse needs of families, to cooperate with agencies and professions that share the responsibility for children, to assist families in gaining access to those agencies and allied professionals, and to assist in the development of community programs that are needed but not currently available.

As individuals, we acknowledge our responsibility to provide the best possible programs of care and education for children and to conduct ourselves with honesty and integrity. Because of our specialized expertise in early childhood development and education and because the larger society shares responsibility for the welfare and protection of young children, we acknowledge a collective obligation to advocate for the best interests of children within early childhood programs and in the larger community and to serve as a voice for young children everywhere.

The ideals and principles in this section are presented to distinguish between those that pertain to the work of the individual early childhood educator and those that more typically are engaged in collectively on behalf of the best interests of children—with the understanding that individual early childhood educators have a shared responsibility for addressing the ideals and principles that are identified as "collective."

Ideal (Individual)

I-4.1—To provide the community with high-quality early childhood care and education programs and services.

Ideals (Collective)

I-4.2—To promote cooperation among professionals and agencies and interdisciplinary collaboration among professions concerned with addressing issues in the health, education, and well-being of young children, their families, and their early childhood educators.

I-4.3—To work through education, research, and advocacy toward an environmentally safe world in which all children receive health care, food, and shelter; are nurtured; and live free from violence in their home and their communities.

I-4.4—To work through education, research, and advocacy toward a society in which all young children have access to high-quality early care and education programs.

I-4.5—To work to ensure that appropriate assessment systems, which include multiple sources of information, are used for purposes that benefit children.

I-4.6—To promote knowledge and understanding of young children and their needs. To work toward greater societal acknowledgment of children's rights and greater social acceptance of responsibility for the well-being of all children.

I-4.7—To support policies and laws that promote the well-being of children and families, and to work to change those that impair their well-being. To participate in developing policies and laws that are needed, and to cooperate with other individuals and groups in these efforts.

I-4.8—To further the professional development of the field of early childhood care and education and to strengthen its commitment to realizing its core values as reflected in this Code.

Principles (Individual)

P-4.1—We shall communicate openly and truthfully about the nature and extent of services that we provide.

P-4.2—We shall apply for, accept, and work in positions for which we are personally well-suited and professionally qualified. We shall not offer services that we do not have the competence, qualifications, or resources to provide.

P-4.3—We shall carefully check references and shall not hire or recommend for employment any person whose competence, qualifications, or character makes him or her unsuited for the position.

P-4.4—We shall be objective and accurate in reporting the knowledge upon which we base our program practices.

P-4.5—We shall be knowledgeable about the appropriate use of assessment strategies and instruments and interpret results accurately to families.

P-4.6—We shall be familiar with laws and regulations that serve to protect the children in our programs and be vigilant in ensuring that these laws and regulations are followed.

P-4.7—When we become aware of a practice or situation that endangers the health, safety, or well-being of children, we have an ethical responsibility to protect children or inform parents and/or others who can.

P-4.8—We shall not participate in practices that are in violation of laws and regulations that protect the children in our programs.

P-4.9—When we have evidence that an early childhood program is violating laws or regulations protecting children, we shall report the violation to appropriate authorities who can be expected to remedy the situation.

P-4.10—When a program violates or requires its employees to violate this Code, it is permissible, after fair assessment of the evidence, to disclose the identity of that program.

Principles (Collective)

P-4.11—When policies are enacted for purposes that do not benefit children, we have a collective responsibility to work to change these practices.

P-4-12—When we have evidence that an agency that provides services intended to ensure children's well-being is failing to meet its obligations, we acknowledge a collective ethical responsibility to report the problem to appropriate authorities or to the public. We shall be vigilant in our follow-up until the situation is resolved.

P-4.13—When a child protection agency fails to provide adequate protection for abused or neglected children, we acknowledge a collective ethical responsibility to work toward the improvement of these services.

The National Association for the Education of Young Children ("NAEYC") is a nonprofit corporation, tax exempt under Section 501(c)(3) of the Internal Revenue Code, dedicated to acting on behalf of the needs and interests of young children. The NAEYC Code of Ethical Conduct ("Code") has been developed in furtherance of NAEYC's nonprofit and tax exempt purposes. The information contained in the Code is intended to provide early childhood educators with guidelines for working with children from birth through age 8. Use, reference to, or review of the Code does not guarantee compliance with NAEYC Early Childhood Program Standards and Accreditation Performance Criteria and program accreditation procedures. It is recommended that the Code be used as guidance in connection with implementation of the NAEYC Program Standards, but such use is not a substitute for diligent review and application of the NAEYC Program Standards.

NAEYC has taken reasonable measures to develop the Code in a fair, reasonable, open, unbiased, and objective manner, based on currently available data. However, further research or developments may change the current state of knowledge. Neither NAEYC nor its officers, directors, members, employees, or agents will be liable for any loss, damage, or claim with respect to any liabilities, including direct, special, indirect, or consequential damages incurred in connection with the Code or reliance on the information presented.

NAEYC Code of Ethical Conduct Revisions Workgroup

Mary Ambery, Ruth Ann Ball, James Clay, Julie Olsen Edwards, Harriet Egertson, Anthony Fair, Stephanie Feeney, Jana Fleming, Nancy Freeman, Marla Israel, Allison McKinnon, Evelyn Wright Moore, Eva Moravcik, Christina Lopez Morgan, Sarah Mulligan, Nila Rinehart, Betty Holston Smith, and Peter Pizzolongo

NAEYC Staff

Glossary of Terms Related to Ethics

Code of Ethics. Defines the core values of the field and provides guidance for what professionals should do when they encounter conflicting obligations or responsibilities in their work.

Values. Qualities or principles that individuals believe to be desirable or worthwhile and that they prize for themselves, for others, and for the world in which they live.

Core Values. Commitments held by a profession that are consciously and knowingly embraced by its practitioners because they make a contribution to society. There is a difference between personal values and the core values of a profession.

Morality. Peoples' views of what is good, right, and proper; their beliefs about their obligations; and their ideas about how they should behave.

Ethics. The study of right and wrong, or duty and obligation, that involves critical reflection on morality and the ability to make choices between values and the examination of the moral dimensions of relationships.

Professional Ethics. The moral commitments of a profession that involve moral reflection that extends and enhances the personal morality practitioners bring to their work, that concern actions of right and wrong in the workplace, and that help individuals resolve moral dilemmas they encounter in their work.

Ethical Responsibilities. Behaviors that one must or must not engage in. Ethical responsibilities are clear-cut and are spelled out in the Code of Ethical Conduct (for example, early childhood educators should never share confidential information about a child or family with a person who has no legitimate need for knowing).

Ethical Dilemma. A moral conflict that involves determining appropriate conduct when an individual faces conflicting professional values and responsibilities.

Sources for Glossary Terms and Definitions
Feeney, S., & N. Freeman. 1999. *Ethics and the early childhood educator: Using the NAEYC code*. Washington, DC: NAEYC.
Kidder, R.M. 1995. *How good people make tough choices: Resolving the dilemmas of ethical living*. New York: Fireside.
Kipnis, K. 1987. How to discuss professional ethics. *Young Children* 42 (4): 26-30.

Statement of Commitment[4]

As an individual who works with young children, I commit myself to furthering the values of early childhood education as they are reflected in the ideals and principles of the NAEYC Code of Ethical Conduct. To the best of my ability I will

- Never harm children.

- Ensure that programs for young children are based on current knowledge and research of child development and early childhood education.

- Respect and support families in their task of nurturing children.

- Respect colleagues in early childhood care and education and support them in maintaining the NAEYC Code of Ethical Conduct.

- Serve as an advocate for children, their families, and their teachers in community and society.

- Stay informed of and maintain high standards of professional conduct.

- Engage in an ongoing process of self-reflection, realizing that personal characteristics, biases, and beliefs have an impact on children and families.

- Be open to new ideas and be willing to learn from the suggestions of others.

- Continue to learn, grow, and contribute as a professional.

- Honor the ideals and principles of the NAEYC Code of Ethical Conduct.

---

[4]This Statement of Commitment is not part of the Code but is a personal acknowledgement of the individual's willingness to embrace the distinctive values and moral obligations of the field of early childhood care and education. It is recognition of the moral obligations that lead to an individual becoming part of the profession.

Ways to study how children develop and learn

2

PART 1

Why do you need to know how children develop and learn?

Family picture albums. Baby books. Children's heights marked on the door each birthday. Nearly every family keeps a record of how its members grow and change. Have you looked at your family pictures lately? How did your family look five years ago? What a difference a short time makes!

You know young children grow and develop so fast! Babies seem to change overnight. Preschoolers acquire new skills almost everyday. As a parent, teacher, or family child care provider, you may watch whole families of children develop from infants into responsible young people.

You have been watching how children develop all your life. Now you want to become a

Child Development Associate. As you work toward your CDA, you will become even more curious about how children develop.

If you want to be a good teacher, you must know what you can reasonably expect of the children in your care. Otherwise, how will you know what learning experiences to plan ... what toys and materials to choose ... how to handle "difficult transitions" ... how to help children learn ... how to foster children's self-motivation ... how to nurture culturally important behaviors ... how to help children feel good about themselves ... how to help children develop self-regulation ... how to answer parents' questions ... and how to improve your work?

All around the world, people have been studying how children develop and learn. Some of these people are parents. Many are researchers at universities. Others are teachers. What they have learned will help you become a better teacher.

We have condensed some of the most important information about how children develop and learn in the chart in Part 2 of this unit. All of the ages given are approximate—some children will demonstrate these accomplishments earlier, some later—but most typically developing children will fall into the range listed.

Each part of the chart also has some extra space for you to fill in. There are probably other developmental accomplishments that are especially important to you or to the cultural groups with whom you work. Add them where they are appropriate.

This is your chart—make it work for you. Refer to these next few pages often. Use them as you watch the video for Unit 2. Keep the chart handy. Make a copy before it gets worn out. Most of what you do with young children is based on what you know about how children develop and learn.

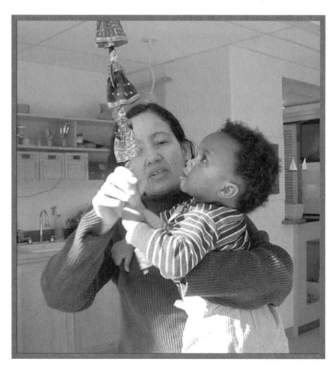

Children learn from their experiences with objects and people.

PART 2

What are the characteristics of children from birth through age 5?

You use developmental principles

Development is age-related change. We now know a great deal from research about child development. We know that development occurs as the result of interaction between children's maturation (their biological growth) and the experiences that they have—both experiences with the physical world and with other people. Because children are growing and changing so rapidly during the first years of life, the link between maturation and experience is fairly strong at this age. And therefore, it is possible to make some predictions about the kinds of abilities and interests young children will have at various ages.

But the role of experience is also important. Children learn from their experiences with objects and people. And experiences are culturally determined. So one important principle is that all development occurs in and is influenced by social and cultural contexts.

Another important principle of child development is individual differences. Every child is different. Some children are well coordinated, while others have less control of their changing bodies. Some children use lots of

Timelines

You will need about three weeks to complete your study of Unit 2.
During this time you must:

1. Prepare for conference with your Field Advisor to discuss three topics (what are the characteristics of children from birth through age 5, value of and methods for observing children's behavior, and how observations of children and adult-child interactions can be used to teach appropriately).

2. Complete two assignments (add developmental accomplishments to the chart and try four observation tools), and three entries for the Professional Resource File.

3. Complete three assignments for Seminar (choose an observation tool to demonstrate, collect samples of developmental checklists and screening instruments, and resource agencies for developmental disabilities).

words right away, but others' language is slower to develop. Some children are friendly, and others are shy. Some can figure out problems quickly, yet others give up easily. Children may spurt ahead for a while in one area, while they seem to be "on hold" in another.

Children grow at their own pace. What can make a difference in children's development?

- tendencies they inherit (some families have lots of tall people, for example),

- nutrition and good health (healthy foods encourage brains and bodies to grow),

- what families value (verbal and/or nonverbal expression), and

- experiences children have (for example, if a child's home is on one floor, the child will have little practice with steps).

Most of all, children need time, lots of experiences, and lots of skilled people like you to develop and learn to their fullest potential.

Your chart is divided into seven major areas in which young children change rapidly:

- children show interest in others

- children become more aware of themselves

- children's muscles grow stronger and coordination improves

- children learn to communicate and become literate

- children become aware of the world

- children solve problems and use tools

- children express feelings

You may have read other books that put these categories together into four areas of development: *physical, social, emotional,* and *cognitive or intellectual/language.* There are several ways to organize what we know about children's development and learning.

Whatever words you use to describe these areas, always remember that *all of the aspects of children's development and learning over-lap.* For example, there is no one part of a child's brain or body reserved just for feelings. When children run, they use more than just muscles.

You must also keep one other point in mind: *No child will ever develop exactly according to this chart.* The areas of development overlap, and so do the age groups. We have sorted out just a few of the most important developmental accomplishments that you can usually observe in young children.

Your chart is divided into two columns:

- what children are usually like at each age

- how you can help promote children's development and learning

Be sure to add other developmental accomplishments that seem especially appropriate for the children with whom you work. There are many, many more than we could fit into this book!

These are just a few accomplishments to watch for as children develop and learn. The ages tell you approximately when to expect typically developing children to begin to demonstrate these accomplishments.

 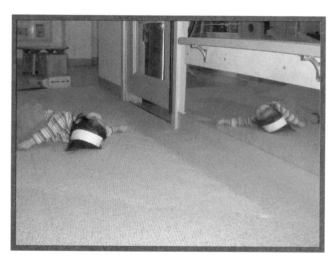

All aspects of a child's development overlap.

Developmental Accomplishments—Birth through age 5

The early months (birth to 8 months)

What children are usually like at this age

How adults can help promote children's learning and development

Children show interest in others

Newborns like to look at people's faces. They love to hear people talk and sing. Within the first few days they can recognize and prefer the sight, smell, and sound of the person who takes care of them.

Hold babies close. Look at babies in the eye. Talk. Sing.

• • • • • • •

Babies soon smile real smiles. They look you in the eye and then look away.

Smile back. Say, "What a wonderful smile you have!"

• • • • • • •

Older babies in this age range kick, smile, and/or hold out their arms when they know you are about to pick them up or to feed them.

Talk to babies as you approach. Tell babies what you are about to do. Tell babies what you are doing. " Here I come. It's time for a clean diaper now. Here's the fresh diaper, just for you. . . ." Pick babies up. Carry on a conversation with babies in their home language while you hold them to feed them.

• • • • • • •

Older babies love to play with people more than any toy.

PLAY with babies. Dance. Take walks with the stroller. Show them what you are doing. Sing. Make up poems. Read stories. Play games like "Peek-a-Boo" and "This Little Piggy."

What children are like	**How adults can help**
Babies may suck their fingers or hands. Soon they watch their hands in fascination.	Give babies time to play. Comment on what they are doing. "Look! You've found your hands. Dos manos! Your two hands can do so many things. They can . . ." Use the child's home language.

· · · · · · ·

Babies may move their hands in front of their faces as if to protect themselves when something comes close.	Be careful not to startle very young babies. Older babies may enjoy some surprises when they feel safe.

· · · · · · ·

When you touch them, babies look to the place where they were touched.	Touch babies gently to see how they respond.

· · · · · · ·

Older babies in this age range reach for toys. They begin to grasp them with their fingers.	Offer toys that are easy for tiny fingers to grasp: texture balls, rattles with narrow handles, spoons.

· · · · · · ·

Older babies can clasp their hands together and wiggle their fingers. They hold onto their toes. They watch themselves in a mirror.	Talk with babies as they explore their bodies. Place an unbreakable mirror at babies' eye level. Talk about what they see.

· · · · · · ·

Older babies try to make things happen: squeak a toy, push a ball.	Provide toys that babies can rattle, squeak, roll, or push. Firmly but safely attach large jingle bells to booties or wrists. Babies will be thrilled at the sound when they shake their arms or legs.

What children are like

Older babies in this age range usually begin to prefer being around people they know. Adult strangers may frighten them. This is called stranger anxiety. It is a great way to know that children are on target in their emotional and intellectual development.

How adults can help

Make sure babies get to know many friendly people. When you come up to strangers together, help babies feel secure. Talk with babies positively when they are afraid of strangers. Never be critical of such a natural event, such as saying, "Oh, come on, Grandma wants to hold you. What a bad boy to be so scared of Grandma."

Help parents understand that, although this is a difficult period, with experience and time children will again become friendly and will know that their parents will return after they leave.

It is probably not a good idea to put babies in new child care arrangements while they are afraid of strangers. It may be harder for them to adjust.

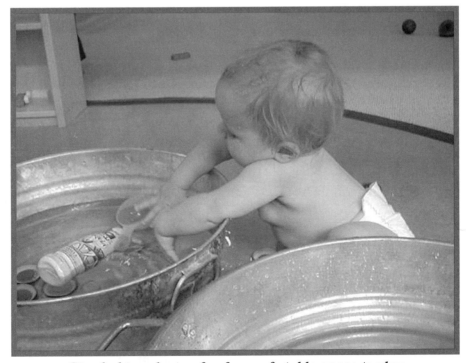

Give babies plenty of safe, comfortable space to play.

What children are like	How adults can help
Children's muscles grow stronger and coordination improves	
Young infants have many complex reflexes (natural reactions): They search for something to suck; they hold on when they are about to fall; they turn their heads to breathe better; and they avoid bright lights, strong smells, and pain.	Watch to see which reflexes babies use.

· · · · · · ·

Babies put their hands and every object into their mouths. They begin to reach for everything.	Safety first: Give babies items that are too large to be swallowed and that can be chewed on safely: rubber dolls or animals, soft plastic household items, plastic or fabric books, fabric toys. Keep objects within babies' reach. Wash toys often so germs don't spread. Offer new items as babies lose interest.

· · · · · · ·

Near the end of this age range, babies love to hold onto and let go of objects again and again. They look at things closely.	Give babies items that can be dropped without harm.

· · · · · · ·

Very young babies begin to lift their heads. Later they hold them up. Within the first few months babies roll over. Later they sit up without support. They soon can transfer objects from one hand to another. As they near the age of 8 months, they may begin to creep or crawl.	Safety first: **Before** babies are ready to try to sit up or roll over, make sure they will not hurt themselves when the day arrives. Never leave babies unattended. Roll babies gently back and forth so they feel comfortable with the motion. As soon as babies begin to try to creep or crawl, babyproof every area: cover electrical sockets, latch doors, close off stairways. However, give babies plenty of comfortable space to crawl—a carpeted floor is especially good.

What children are like	How adults can help
Children learn to communicate Babies cry to tell you they are in pain, hungry, or distress. Sometimes it is difficult to figure out why they cry.	Respond quickly but calmly to cries. If you make babies wait, they will cry more when they are older. Try to figure out what might be making babies cry and comfort them.
Babies smile or coo (make vowel sounds) to get you to pay attention.	Smile and respond reassuringly.
Babies smile at voices. They look intently at faces.	Keep talking as long as the child is interested.
Babies use sounds and movements to express interest or to make things happen.	Pay attention to what babies tell you. Watch what they do. Some babies drop their food on the floor or push the bottle away when they are finished eating. On the other hand, if babies are showing pleasure, keep up the activity. This is how babies begin to associate sounds with language.
Older babies begin to babble (make consonant/vowel sounds), both when they are alone and when they are with other people. Later at this stage, they begin to combine babble sounds (bah-bah). They recognize their names, names of familiar people, and names of favorite objects. They may laugh heartily. They listen intently to conversations.	Baby talk is unnecessary. Children will imitate what they hear. Talk about everything using the child's home language in simple, clear sentences.

What children are like	How adults can help
Children become aware of the world Babies may use a pacifier or suck their thumbs.	Allow babies to suck their thumbs or to use a pacifier to comfort themselves.

· · · · · · · ·

Infants will follow a slowly moving object with their eyes.	Hold a bright or black and white object within babies' view and move it slowly from side to side. Hang mobiles above cribs. Hold baby on your lap and look at books together.

· · · · · · · ·

About midway during this period, infants will reach for and then begin to hold onto toys.	Provide toys babies can hold—rattles with handles, spoons, bracelets.

· · · · · · · ·

When older babies drop a toy, they will look for it briefly.	Play babies' favorite game: "Drop and Pick Up Toys." Talk while you play.

· · · · · · · ·

At around 8 months, infants can identify objects from various viewpoints. They will be able to find a toy when they watch you hide it under a blanket.	Move babies around to different viewpoints and heights—different rooms, on the floor or cushions, in a crib, and carry them. Play "Peek-a-Boo" with toys hidden by a diaper or blanket.

· · · · · · · ·

Children solve problems and use tools Babies notice their own hands.	Talk with babies as they look at their hands.

· · · · · · · ·

Young babies can grasp a rattle when they can see both their hand and the rattle.	Put toys within babies' reach.

What children are like

How adults can help

Within a few weeks, babies hit or kick something to make a sight or sound continue.

Hang bells or other objects that make noise above babies' legs so they can kick them.

. . . .

Babies use movement to show you what they want: If they are riding the horse on your leg, they might keep bouncing when they want you to continue giving them a ride.

Resume any activity when babies indicate they want to continue.

. . . .

Children express feelings

Tiny babies clearly tell you when they are uncomfortable (*they may cry or wiggle*) or when they are happy and comfortable (*they smile, have a contented look*).

Pay attention to what babies tell you and follow through to continue the pleasure or get rid of the discomfort (*change the diaper, feed the baby*).

. . . .

Babies soon show they prefer to be with the person who usually takes care of them (*mother or other primary caregiver*) by kicking, smiling, or waving their arms when that person approaches.

Show how delighted you are to be with the baby!

. . . .

When babies are uncomfortable, most can be comforted by familiar adults.

Find out what comforts each baby best.

. . . .

Babies in the middle of this age range smile at people. They enjoy social contact.

Give babies the chance to know people of many ages and cultures. At the children's eye level, hang realistic pictures of families, pictures of people who look the same as and different from the children and families in the group.

What children are like	How adults can help
Babies make belly laughs.	Babies think lots of things are funny. Experiment to find out what.

· · · · · · ·

Babies fuss when they no longer have a favorite person or toy.	Always say goodbye when you leave a child and make sure parents say goodbye when they leave. This builds trust. Gently explain why the person left, that they will return, and that you understand. Then move on to a new, interesting activity.
	Offer a new toy to replace the one that is missing.

· · · · · · ·

By the end of this period, babies show several emotions: pleasure, anger, anxiety or fear, sadness, joy, excitement, disappointment, exuberance.	Talk with babies about their feelings. Notice how each baby expresses feelings just a little differently.

· · · · · · ·

Sometime around the age of 7 months, many babies become afraid of strangers (*stranger anxiety*).	Help parents understand this is a normal reaction and should be treated as a sign that the baby is growing up and learning more.

Other developmental accomplishments for children birth to 8 months . . .

These are just a few accomplishments to watch for as children develop and learn. The ages tell you about when to expect typically developing children to begin to demonstrate these accomplishments.

Crawlers, waddlers, and walkers (8 to 18 months)

What children are usually like at this age	How adults can help promote children's learning and development
Children show interest in others	
Children may be unhappy when they are with people they don't know well.	Gently introduce strangers. Use as few substitute caregivers as possible in programs.
Babies get to know each other over toys during play.	Some toys are more fun when two children play—rocking boats, balls, toy telephones. Have enough of each toy so children don't have to share.
Waddlers use actions to ask you to do something they want (*hand you a wind-up toy, bring you a book*).	Have toys that adults can use with children—books, dolls, musical instruments. Do what the child asks you to do.
Older waddlers begin to show a great deal of interest in children their own age.	Give children plenty of time to get to know their friends while they play.
Babies listen intently to everything you say.	Use language you want children to repeat: speak in their home language, no baby talk, no offending words.
Children become more aware of themselves	
Babies recognize their own names.	Use children's names often.

What children are like	How adults can help
Babies love to look in mirrors—they smile at themselves, watch themselves move.	Place unbreakable mirrors securely on the wall at children's height.
Older waddlers know they can make things happen. At the same time, they are not yet aware of what it means to be responsible for their own actions.	Tell and show children what happened as a result of what they did. "When you dropped this book, it fell on Kendra's foot. It hurts when a book falls on your foot. How can we help Kendra feel better?"
Almost-toddlers begin to show they have a strong sense of self. They try to direct the actions of others and frequently say "no" to make sure they have some say about what happens to them.	Give children two good, real choices of things they like: "Would you like some green beans or a piece of cheese?"
Older children begin to identify parts of their bodies.	Talk with children about parts of their bodies. "See what strong legs it takes to climb up our mountain!" Use fingerplays and songs with actions that include body parts. Talk and sing in the children's home languages. Ask parents to show you simple games from their culture.
Near the end of this age range, children begin to use me, you, and I when they talk.	Use these words correctly when you talk with children. Show pleasure at new words. Accept children's grammar without correcting them—just repeat it using the correct words.

What children are like

How adults can help

Children's muscles grow stronger and coordination improves

Older infants sit well in chairs, but want to do so only for a short time.

Provide comfortable, stable, child-sized chairs. Children enjoy figuring out how to get up and out of chairs.

· · · · · · ·

Babies begin to pull themselves up and to stand while holding onto furniture.

Have sturdy, securely anchored low tables, shelves, chairs, sofas, and other furniture for children to hold onto while they cruise.

· · · · · · ·

Waddlers begin to walk when they hold your hand. Then they walk alone.

Hold babies' hands when they walk. Rejoice at the early steps!

· · · · · · ·

Waddlers begin to throw objects.

Keep plenty of soft balls handy to roll, push, drop, and throw.

· · · · · · ·

Climbing up stairs on all fours is a great accomplishment during this period. Going down is more difficult.

Climbers with stairs on one side and a slide down the other are great.

· · · · · · ·

Older infants can hold a marker and scribble on paper.

Offer children wide, water-based markers and large sheets of plain paper.

· · · · · · ·

Almost-toddlers can stoop, trot, and even walk backward for a few steps.

Have enough open space for children to move around in. Go outdoors, too. Give children different surfaces for walking: carpet, grass, linoleum, sand.

What children are like

Children learn to communicate

Waddlers understand many more words than they can say. They will look toward objects when you say their names or do actions when requested (*if they feel cooperative*). Some children may be learning more than one language.

Older babies create long babbled sentences. Soon they use two or three words clearly.

They shake heads no.

Babies are interested in picture books. They point to objects.

Older children in this age range use sounds instead of crying to get your attention.

How adults can help

Talk with children at every opportunity. Check to see which words they understand. "Where is the piñata?" "Who can find the ball?"

Discuss with parents how you can best support their child's acquisition of two languages.

Carry on a conversation with babies—take turns talking.

Respect children's "no" when possible.

Provide bright, colorful board books with pictures of familiar objects. Read them together. Ask baby, "Where is the . . .?" Let the baby take the lead.

Notice how each child uses a different way to get you to listen or come. Be sure to respond as quickly as possible.

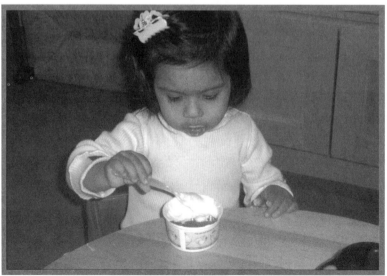

Allow children to feed themselves with a spoon as much as possible.

What children are like	How adults can help
Children become more aware of the world	
Waddlers carry blocks and try to stack them.	Provide blocks in various shapes and sizes.
If you hide a toy under one or two diapers while babies watch, they can find the toy.	Play hiding games.
These babies are persistent in looking for a hidden toy.	Play searching games.
If a ball rolls under the couch, babies of this age walk around the couch to get the ball.	Make sure your play area has a table or sofa for something to roll under. Have lots of balls to chase and find.
Waddlers help you dress them by pushing their foot into shoes, their arms into sleeves.	Take time to give children the chance to help dress themselves.
Children solve problems and use tools	
These older babies continue to move a wind-up car even when it has wound down, or search for the winder on a music box.	Have a few wind-up toys. No battery-operated ones, though. Child-propelled ones are best.
Waddlers bring a stool to reach something.	Use a low, lightweight stool.
Children this age push away things they don't want.	Pay attention to what children want or don't want. Respect their preferences.
Finger foods are great for self-feeding.	Serve bits of fruit, crackers, little chunks of meat, and as many finger foods as possible.
Children creep or walk either to get something or to move away from something they don't like.	Notice what children like and don't like.

What children are like

Older children are even more help in dressing themselves.

How adults can help

Let children do everything they can to dress themselves, but don't let them get frustrated with little buttons, buckles, or snaps.

· · · · · · ·

Children begin to feed themselves less with their fingers and more with a spoon.

Allow children to feed themselves with a spoon as much as possible.

· · · · · · ·

Children begin to drink from a cup without spilling all of it.

Keep a sponge handy. Use cups with lids to start. Only put a little bit of liquid in the cup.

· · · · · · ·

By the end of this period, most children feed themselves with a spoon.

Don't interfere when children are learning new skills such as feeding themselves with a spoon—it may take longer, but children have to do it themselves if they are going to figure it out.

· · · · · · ·

Children express feelings

Children are affectionate with loved ones. They hug, smile, run toward, or lean against favorite people.

Use lots of hugs. Respond warmly to their affection.

· · · · · · ·

Older babies are usually upset when they leave their primary caregiver.

Come up with a ritual that will help ease daily separations. Perhaps first say "good morning" or "buenos días" to the teacher, hang up coats, then walk to the door together, and wave goodbye from the window.

What children are like

Babies begin to show they are angry at people or things. They show their negative feelings by crying, hitting, and grabbing, for example.

How adults can help

Respect children's anger and negative feelings and help them find constructive ways to deal with them. "You are really mad because you can't play in the water longer. I know you loved it so much. Here is a towel to dry your hands and arms... Let's see who is playing in our hideaway—I hear footsteps on the ramp. Do you?"

• • • • • • •

Waddlers and walkers are so proud of their new accomplishments.

Clap hands and be excited along with the children when they learn a new skill.

• • • • • • •

These older babies show how intensely they are attached to their parents.

Give children time to show affection.

• • • • • • •

Children approaching toddlerhood assert themselves.

Continue to offer real choices so children begin to feel they have some control over what happens to them.

Other developmental accomplishments for children 8 to 18 months. . .

These are just a few accomplishments to watch for as children develop and learn. The ages tell you about when to expect typically developing children to begin to demonstrate these accomplishments.

What children are usually like at this age

How adults can help promote children's development and learning

Children show interest in others
Toddlers know you are watching them.

Talk with children about what you notice. "I see how easily you put those beads on the string. Would you like some other shapes to string?"

· · · · · · ·

Children this age often get upset if other people are in the way when they want something immediately.

Talk with children about their feelings. Help them find other ways to get what they need. "I know you want to push the fire truck, but Nicole has it now. Shall we ask her if she will be done soon? Or would you like to play with the ambulance?"

· · · · · · ·

At this age, children are just beginning to see that other people have rights and privileges. Sometimes they may share. Most of the time they won't.

Always treat children and co-workers respectfully. Share with others. Children learn to treat others by watching and listening to what you do and say.

· · · · · · ·

Playing with other children becomes more fun.

Make sure the day has plenty of time for children to play together if they choose to do so.

· · · · · · ·

The benefits of cooperation are evident for the first time: together children can lift a heavy laundry basket, for example.

Encourage activities that require cooperation—rolling balls, carrying a basket of toys, setting the table for snack.

Toddlers and 2 1/2-year-olds (18 months to 2 1/2 years

What children are like	How adults can help
Children identify with others of the same sex, age, and race.	Help children be proud of who they are. "How wonderful that your eyes are dark brown! And Marina's are bright blue."
Children are becoming increasingly aware of others' feelings.	Help children be aware of how what they do affects other children. "Tasha is worried that you will take all the clay and she won't have any left to play with. How can we work it out so you both can play with the clay?"
Children at this age begin to show some ability to regulate their own behavior in their relationships with others and in meeting their own needs.	Commend children when they begin to self-regulate. "Jason, how kind of you to wait until Rashad is finished washing his hands."
Children who are almost 3 years old enjoy activities with two or three other children for short periods of time.	Keep group times short and involve children actively: do fingerplays, read short stories, play simple group games (*"Ring Around the Rosie"*). Select some in each of the languages spoken by children in the group. Don't expect all children to join or stay in the group the entire time.

Children become more aware of themselves

Toddlers frequently say "NO!"	Keep your requests to a minimum. Be prepared to accept "NO!" Offer choices that do not include "NO!" "Which would you like to wear, your red sweater or your blue sweatshirt?"
Toddlers feel very powerful and creative. They want to explore everything.	Give children appropriate chances to have some say about what happens to them: offer choices of good things to do or eat. Provide activities that guarantee children's success. Have plenty of things to explore, indoors and out.

What children are like

How adults can help

Children begin to define themselves as good/ bad, attractive/ugly, and other notions about their value as a person.

Always focus on children's positive qualities. Sometimes their behavior is not acceptable, but the children are learning self-regulation. Help them regulate their behavior by explaining, "Here, we don't hit other children. We talk about how we can solve our problem." Never say, "You're a bad boy." Children live up to (*or down to*) our expectations.

. . . .

During this period, children begin to control their own behavior.

Support children when they try to regulate their behavior. Point out how proud they feel when they do.

. . . .

Toddlers use names for themselves and others.

Use children's names frequently.

. . . .

By now, children usually can identify six or more of their body parts.

Continue to use fingerplays, songs, mirrors, and dress-up clothes to help children naturally learn parts of their bodies in their home languages.

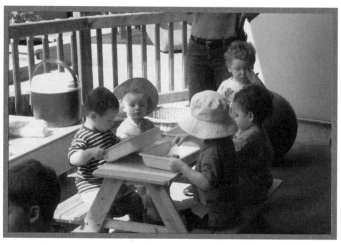

Continue to offer new toys, activities, people, and events for children to learn about, and give them words to grow their vocabularies

What children are like	How adults can help
Children's muscles grow stronger and coordination improves	
Toddlers scribble with markers or crayons.	Provide sturdy, watercolor markers and crayons. Offer large, blank sheets of paper.
Children at this age walk up and down stairs. They soon will jump off the lowest step.	Have a set of steps for children to practice walking up and down them.
Twos love to kick balls. They stand on one foot. Older twos may begin to stand and walk on their tiptoes.	Schedule plenty of time for children to work on these skills during play. Use a rubber ball. Play soft music for children to walk on tiptoes.
Toddlers thread large wooden beads on shoestrings.	Tie a knot at one end of the shoestring so beads don't slip off. Demonstrate how to string the beads.
Most twos can draw a shape that looks like a circle and control their scribbles.	Patterns and models of circles are unnecessary. Watch children's own drawing and see circles begin to appear.
Older children in this age range walk up stairs with one foot on each step.	Take pride with children when they master steps.
Older 2-year-olds begin to use scissors.	Use blunt-end children's scissors. Make sure some are left-handed. Show children how to carry them. Remember, children's first attempts to cut will be difficult and frustrating—do not expect children to cut on lines they draw until they have had lots of practice at about age 4.

What children are like

How adults can help

Late in this stage, children begin to draw back and forth with a crayon and they name their drawings.

Place blank paper on the floor for children to draw on. Never draw models for children to copy.

· · · · · · · ·

Sometime during this period, most children will develop daytime toilet control.

Help children learn to use the toilet when they are interested and when their bodies are ready. Keep the experience a positive one that children can be proud of. Never punish or humiliate children for toileting accidents.

· · · · · · · ·

Children learn to communicate

Around the age of 2, children may begin to speak in sentences. They usually prefer their home language, but will understand and speak other languages if they have meaningful interactions with speakers of the other language.

Use more words and longer sentences when you talk with children. Listen for new words. Encourage children to be bilingual by using language in speaking and labeling artwork, for example.

· · · · · · · ·

Toddlers sit for a short while to listen to a story.

Tell or read stories to three or four children with a flannel board or picture book for all to see.

· · · · · · · ·

As many as 200 words may be in a toddler's speaking vocabulary. Children learning two languages at the same time become aware that the languages are separate.

Continue to offer new toys, activities, people, and events for children to learn about—and provide words to grow their vocabularies. Use both languages in a natural way.

· · · · · · · ·

Children at this age begin to tell stories and play pretend games.

Invite children to tell some stories that begin "Once upon a time..." Encourage children's pretend play by providing everyday props such as kitchens, clothes, miniature people and animals, and small vehicles such as buses and boats. Select typical items from several different cultural groups.

What children are like	How adults can help
The uses of many household items are familiar to most children in this age range.	With a small group, begin cooking experiences: put cheese on crackers, cut fruit for a salad, break lettuce for tacos.

· · · · · · ·

Children's sentences become longer and more complicated as they approach the age of 3. They begin to talk about what happened during the day.	Make what you say interesting and engage each child in conversation. Listen and respond to what children say!

· · · · · · ·

Children become aware of the world

Toddlers can identify some objects by touch.	Use a large, soft bag with three familiar objects inside. Have children put their hands in and figure out what they are holding without looking. Encourage them to use their home language.

· · · · · · ·

Children begin using words about time, such as *tomorrow* and *yesterday.* Toddlers may ask "Is today tomorrow?"	Talk briefly with older twos about what happened yesterday and what you plan to do tomorrow.

· · · · · · ·

Group members figure out who is missing.	Ask the children to figure out who is absent. They usually just tell you anyway.

· · · · · · ·

Toddlers become increasingly independent: "Me do it!" "¡Yo puedo hacerlo!"	Give children many opportunities to do things themselves—wash tables, put mittens out to dry, park tricycles. They may need reminders to follow through.

· · · · · · ·

Older 2-year-olds dress themselves by putting on hats, socks, or slippers.	Allow time for children to dress themselves as much as they can.

What children are like

How adults can help

Children solve problems and use tools

When children this age play with a ring-stacking toy, they don't even try objects that have no holes.

Give children items in addition to the rings and see what they do with them.

. . . .

Children can sort objects into two groups (*such as hard and soft or green/verde and red/rojo*).

Use real opportunities to sort (classify): "We need a pile of knives and a pile of forks." "This shelf is for cars and that shelf is for trucks."

. . . .

Toddlers can help dress and undress themselves.

Be patient while children learn to dress—soon it will take less of your time.

. . . .

Children express feelings

Toddlers frequently are aggressive.

Help children control their own anger and aggression. Keep them safe from hurting themselves and never allow children to hurt each other.

. . . .

Children in this age range shift moods rapidly. One minute they are stubborn, the next minute they are cooperative.

Wait for children to calm themselves. Gently hold them if necessary.

. . . .

Fears of the dark or monsters may appear for the first time.

Help parents understand that imaginary fears are natural at this age. Suggest ways to work with fearful children. A children's book, talking, dramatic play, or other techniques may help.

. . . .

During this period, children begin to have more control when they express emotions.

Compliment children about how grown up they are acting when they express their emotions appropriately.

What children are like	How adults can help
Children are increasingly aware of their own feelings and those of others.	Continue to treat everyone with respect and to comment on what you are doing. "Let's get all of our puzzles put on the shelf so that we are ready to sing when Mr. Adams joins us."
Twos are proud of what they make and do.	Put children's names on their artwork. Hang children's work at their eye level. Notice when children concentrate, work hard, or stick to a task for an especially long time.
As they near age 3, children talk more about their feelings. Their feelings are often expressed in pretend play (*playing house, for example*).	Set up familiar play settings—medical offices, grocery stores, and other places children know. Have props common in their cultures for them to use.
Children at this age begin to develop a true concern for others.	Continue to show your concern and commend children when they are considerate of others. "How thoughtful of you to tell Jamie you are finished at the easel."

Other developmental accomplishments for children 18 months to 2 1/2 years. . .

These are just a few accomplishments to watch for as children develop and learn. The ages tell you about when to expect typically developing children to begin to demonstrate these accomplishments.

What children are usually like at this age	How adults can help promote children's learning and development
Children show interest in others	
Young threes prefer to play alongside another child or with one or two others.	Have many individual activities and materials children can do side by side. Also offer some things that require cooperation.
• • • • • • •	
Friendships are beginning but are often short-lived, especially early in this age range. Sometimes they center on silly activities.	Support children's friendships. One good way is to help children treat each other as friends.
• • • • • • •	
Threes may share when given the opportunity. Sometimes they can wait for a short while for a turn.	Allow sharing to develop spontaneously. Forcing it will **not** work. Children share when others are generous with them and when they do not feel the need to protect their possessions. Keep the need to wait to a minimum.
• • • • • • •	
Threes are increasingly less willing to hold an adult's hand while walking.	Keep an alert eye so children do not dart or wander away from you outdoors.
• • • • • • •	
Older threes are affectionate with younger children. They may begin to select special friends in their own age group.	Give children opportunities to play with children from a wide range of ages.

Young preschool children (2 1/2 to 4 years)

What children are like

How adults can help

Children become more aware of themselves

During this year, children develop a firm sense of their sex, age, race, language, and culture.

Share children's pride in who they are. Respect each child. Incorporate their home language, cultural objects, and familiar activities as a natural part of every day.

· · · · · · ·

Threes can spend fairly long times at tasks they choose: play in sand, build with blocks, paint, follow an obstacle course.

Plan the schedule to allow large blocks of time for independent play. Offer a wide range of activities. Expect children to repeat activities again and again.

· · · · · · ·

Children this age will test their skills. Sometimes they are cautious and at other times they may overestimate their abilities, especially if they are in a group with older children.

Adult supervision, especially on the playground, is essential. The area should be as safe as possible and positive rules should be set up.

· · · · · · ·

Threes are beginning to develop some self-regulation ability. They may still be easily frustrated.

Help children become more aware of how their behavior affects others and how friends treat each other. Eliminate as many frustrating situations as possible *(do not expect children to wait quietly in line or sit at tables doing what you want them to do)*.

· · · · · · ·

Young preschoolers are very proud of their achievements and begin to feel independent.

Share in children's pride. Allow time for children to be independent—to dress themselves, clean up, prepare snacks.

· · · · · · ·

The ideas of ownership and sharing are beginning to be understood.

Respect children's personal possessions and constructions. Compliment children when they share. Point out how good it feels to share with friends.

What children are like

How adults can help

Young preschoolers can brush their own teeth and hair, unbutton and unzip clothes, and wash their hands and faces.

Reserve enough time for children to take care of their personal needs. Teach proper hand-washing procedures and other self-help skills.

• • • • • • •

Children's muscles grow stronger and coordination improves

Toileting accidents may happen occasionally, especially at night. Food and art supplies sometimes get spilled.

Treat accidents matter-of-factly. Have extra clothes on hand. Ask children to help clean up the mess and to change their own clothes.

• • • • • • •

Threes love to use their large muscles. They become stronger and their coordination improves greatly during the year. They can jump, paint with a one-inch brush, begin to alternate feet when climbing stairs, do a forward somersault, kick a ball, hammer nails, and build increasingly higher towers.

Provide climbers, tricycles, balls, and lots of space and time to run, jump, and gallop. Demonstrate new skills or provide assistance as children take on new challenges.

• • • • • • •

Small muscle coordination increases. Drawings are more deliberate. Threes can lace shoes, button, and zip. They may begin to scribble their name or make the first letter.

Toys such as pegboards, beads to string, and construction sets are essential. Children's drawings are more controlled Occasionally, threes will give names to their artwork. Write the name in the child's language.

• • • • • • •

Children learn to communicate

Children can say their own names, express what they want using "I can . . ." and indicate when they need help or don't know something.

Allow lots of time for children to talk and express their needs and wishes and talk with each child every day.

Unit 2

What children are like

How adults can help

Three-year-olds frequently ask, "What?" "Who?" "Why?" and "How come?" They use language to solve problems and figure out how the world works.

Give clear, understandable explanations to children's questions. Use the child's home language whenever possible. Expect children to talk a great deal to each other and with you. Encourage bilingualism. Use one language at a time. Limit translating. Talk to children in a second language at a little higher level than they talk to you.

• • • • • • •

Vocabularies grow rapidly. Threes use words to describe and explain. If they hear other languages, they will increasingly become bilingual.

Provide lots of conversation opportunities for children to use language in culturally relevant ways: poems, nursery rhymes, recordings, games, stories, field trips.

• • • • • • •

At this age, children begin to understand how words can be spoken and then written down to be read again.

Have children tell you a story that you write down for them. They can then draw pictures to illustrate if they want. Sometimes children will draw first, then ask you to write their story.

• • • • • • •

Children at this age can listen to longer stories and pretend to read themselves. They can predict what might happen in the story and connect it to their own life experiences.

Read aloud to small groups (4 to 6 children) every day. Talk with children before, during, and after story. Gradually increase the length and complexity of stories you read and tell.

• • • • • • •

Children begin to recognize musical melodies, match a few tones, and move in reasonably good time to music.

Provide many musical experiences in which children participate by singing, playing, and dancing. Select music from many cultures.

• • • • • • •

Children become aware of the world

Three-year-olds are curious. They want to experiment with cause and effect. They take things apart with glee.

Provide children with materials to manipulate: blocks, sand and water (*with cups to pour and other tools*), puzzles, things that come apart.

What children are like

How adults can help

They draw figures with heads and bodies.

Provide open-ended art materials so children can express their own ideas of what things look like.

- - - - - - - -

Dramatic play becomes more involved. Frequent themes include work and family.

Add new props for dramatic play: office items, other dress-up clothes. Take field trips to expand children's experiences within and beyond their own cultures. Include pretend people (*with tan, brown, black, and white skins*) and animals in the block area.

- - - - - - -

Children at this age cannot yet distinguish real from pretend. Fact and fantasy are interrelated.

Frightening stories or television programs may be upsetting. Talk with children about what could happen and what is just pretend. Reassure them that you will keep them safe.

- - - - - - - -

Children begin to recognize the names of some letters or numerals especially those in their own names, and the names of the friends.

Teach letters and numerals intentionally and frequently. Write children's names on their artwork and label their cubbies. Use the child's home language. Read recipes, address Valentines, count for table setting, make lists, notice the time, talk about birthdays—these ways make letters and numbers real. Sing the ABC song.

- - - - - - -

During this period, children become increasingly aware of likenesses and differences.

Offer a wider variety of objects and ideas for children to compare: four or five different measuring cups, dolls with realistic ethnic features and skin colors, food with a variety of colors and shapes. Begin to talk with children about how unfair it is to treat people differently just because of their skin color or language.

What children are like

How adults can help

Children may become more aware of immediate time.

Begin to remind children that they have only five minutes until it is time for some new activity. Talk about what you plan to do tomorrow or did yesterday.

· · · · · · ·

At around this age, children can put their own toys away if they are supervised as they do so.

Invite children to help clean up together so they can find things when they need them the next time.

· · · · · · ·

Children solve problems and use tools

Children want to do everything possible for themselves: dress, eat, go to the bathroom, brush teeth, wash hands. They may need assistance, however, with more complicated tasks.

Watch children and give them time to take care of their own needs. Dressing is more difficult than undressing. Ask whether children need assistance.

· · · · · · ·

They can do puzzles with between 5 and 10 pieces.

Make sure you have puzzles with 4 to 12 pieces available so children can select the puzzle that best matches their skills.

· · · · · · ·

Threes can choose from two or three alternatives. They can choose what they want to do during choice time.

Give children real choices: "Would you like to listen to a tape or build with the table blocks?" Be open to their suggestions for activities.

· · · · · · ·

Threes can usually count as high as 5 or 10, and can count from 3 to 5 objects.

Provide opportunities for children to count small groups of objects if they are interested: "Let's see, how many shoes do we need to put on this doll? ... Uno ... dos ... We need two shoes. Dos zapatos."

What children are like	How adults can help
Children are increasingly able to use tools: draw with markers or crayons, use cookie cutters with clay, hammer nails into soft wood, play simple musical instruments, balance blocks. They may name what they are making.	Rotate tools and equipment available. Select **real** carpentry tools and **real** musical instruments (*maracas, tambourines, bells*) so children can use them successfully. (*Real ones last much longer too.*)

• • • • • • •

Children express feelings

At this age, children may cry, suck their thumbs, hit, or use other toddler-like behaviors when they are afraid or upset.	Never ridicule children for immature behavior. Comfort them and give them the chance to get themselves under control before returning to the group.

• • • • • • •

Children this age have a delightful sense of humor.	Watch to see what your children think is funny and use these ideas to make your classroom or home a joyful place to be. Silly songs, funny faces—what delights your children?

• • • • • • •

Three-year-olds can be very affectionate.	Provide lots of hugs and kisses every day, just as you do throughout the early years.

Other developmental accomplishments for children 2-1/2 to 4 years. . .

These are just a few accomplishments to watch for as children develop and learn. The ages tell you about when to expect typically developing children to begin to demonstrate these accomplishments.

What children are usually like at this age

How adults can promote children's learning and development

Children show interest in others
Preschoolers love to play together with two or three others—with blocks, at the sand or water table, in pretend play. They also still need time alone.

Provide lots of small group, child-directed activities. Have a quiet, private space where children can go to be by themselves. Limit whole group activities to 15-20 minutes.

• • • • • • •

Children are developing real compassion for each other. Friendships are more lasting. At the same time, prejudices may arise unless children are helped to appreciate each other and to recognize what is fair for everyone. Children gradually have fewer disagreements and are quick to apologize for their behavior.

Continue to be compassionate with the children and to compliment them on their ability to understand how others feel. Support friendships. Treat children with respect so they will do the same with others. Talk about differences and differently abled people in an honest, non-frightening way to help children appreciate how each person has unique qualities. Make culture a daily part of classroom experiences. Choose bias-free books. Model the behavior you expect from children. Encourage children to stand up for what is fair.

Older preschoolers (older 3-year-olds to 5-year-olds)

What children are like

Sharing and taking turns are becoming more common. However, preschoolers may also be bossy at times and call each other names and criticize each other. At times children use their growing language ability in an aggressive way, "You can't come to my birthday party!"

. . . .

Children become more aware of themselves
During this period children may be silly, boisterous, and use shocking language.

. . . .

Preschoolers are quite independent and have definite preferences. They want to do things that interest them.

. . . .

Children are easily discouraged and enjoy receiving praise.

How adults can help

By the end of this period, children can be expected to willingly take turns and share IF adults are generous with them and allow them to share as they are ready. Create opportunities for cooperation. Continue to demonstrate how to treat people in a friendly way.

Explain "In our program we are all friends. Friends are kind to each other. We use only friendly words." Use children's humor: Riddles and nonsense words may be fun. On the other hand, don't reward the use of bathroom language by giving children who use it lots of attention. Explain that those words are not used in the program because they offend or hurt people's feelings.

Provide many opportunities for success. Help children develop a sense of pride in their language and heritage as well as their own actions and accomplishments.

Allow children to handle responsibilities they are capable of: pour their own juice, wash their hands, hang up their coats, and other similar tasks. Respect children's preferences. Support their internal motivation to do well—rewards are not needed beyond children's own sense that they are trying and making progress (*awarding stars or candy for good behavior, for example, is unnecessary*). Encourage success and talk to each child individually every day.

What children are like

Older preschoolers are gaining greater ability to regulate their own behavior. They can wait for short periods of time. They grow in respect for each other's belongings.

Children in this age range are increasingly able to follow a leader or act as a leader.

Children near the end of this age range usually know their first and last names, left and right, their address, and their phone number.

Children's muscles grow stronger and coordination improves

During this period, children test their rapidly improving physical skills. They are proud of their abilities.

Large-muscle skills are expanding and becoming more refined. Skipping and hopping may appear. They are good at riding tricycles. Skills are usually used as part of a game. Children become able to bounce and catch a ball, walk backwards, jump over a low obstacle, balance on one foot.

How adults can help

Continue to help children control their own behavior. Plan the day so waiting is kept to an absolute minimum, not just because waiting is difficult for children but because it is a waste of their time.

Children can be leaders and followers naturally throughout the day—during dramatic play, outdoors, on field trips, and during music, for example.

Use natural opportunities to help children learn about themselves—play games, talk, write letters or notes, look at pictures of the people who came before them, have children sign their names on artwork.

Offer many increasingly difficult large- and small-muscle activities and ample time to pursue them. Keep competition to a minimum—make any comparisons friendly and focus on how well every child did.

Allow plenty of time for children to use their large-muscle skills: obstacle courses, sawing, large hollow blocks. Demonstrate new physical skills and provide just the right amount of assistance as children try out new challenges on their own.

What children are like

How adults can help

Small muscles continue to be more coordinated. Children's artwork begins to resemble real objects. Most children can make a drawing that looks like a person with facial features. Children can use scissors, glue, small beads, and paintbrushes with more skill. They can cut with a knife and string small beads. Near the end of this period, they start to tie shoes—usually the final step in being able to dress and undress independently.

Continue to offer a variety of art materials and blank paper. Never use coloring books or drawings for children to color. Give children opportunities to tell you about their artwork. Let children cut what they choose rather than trying to follow lines you draw for them. Do more elaborate cooking and woodworking projects. Provide smaller items for older children to use such as doll clothes with tiny buttons and sewing cards. Use more difficult finger plays.

· · · · · · · ·

Children in this age range can do puzzles with 10 to 20 pieces.

Set out puzzles with a wide range in the number of pieces. Floor puzzles like an alphabet puzzle may provide a good challenge for older children in this age group.

· · · · · · · ·

Construction skills become increasingly refined.

Have a variety of construction toys—small plastic blocks, interlocking shapes of various types, unit blocks, and hollow blocks. Introduce sewing (*with large yarn needles, yarn, and nylon net or burlap*) and other small-muscle skills to older children in this age range.

· · · · · · · ·

Children have usually settled on a preference for using their right or left hand.

Have left-handed scissors. Help children learn how to hold and use markers and other writing instruments properly. Never force children's hand preference.

What children are like

How adults can help

Children learn to communicate

Interest in written and spoken language increases. Children learn letters and words and are curious about print. They begin to match letters with those in their names and other words they want to write (Mom or I love you). In bilingual programs, they use both languages with ease.

Provide a print-rich environment with lots of books, magazines, telephone books, and signs in several languages for children to use. Respond to children's questions about letters and words. Write down the stories children tell you. Older children can write their own when you help them with spelling. If older children notice that certain letters have certain sounds, encourage them to try their own spelling—and don't "correct" it. Use upper and lower case letters appropriately when you write. Keep paper and pencils or markers in every area of the room for children to use.

· · · · · · · ·

Vocabularies are growing with every experience. Sentences become more complicated. Children understand more words than they say. They are persistent in asking, "Why?"

Provide lots of materials and experiences for children to learn new words and see new outlooks: field trips, props, songs, visitors, puppet stories. Be sure to help children see how many varied ways there are to find answers to questions: asking people, looking in books, experimenting.

· · · · · · · ·

Conversations become long and involved.

Allow lots of time for children to talk among themselves and with you about what they are doing: dramatic play, art activities, outdoors. Try to engage children in conversation with about five turn-taking exchanges.

· · · · · · · ·

Children enjoy making up their own stories which are usually a mixture of make-believe and real.

Encourage them to tell their own stories.

What children are like

Older preschoolers can retell long stories quite accurately.

Some children at this age, who have learned English as a second language, may want to only speak English to the point of rejecting their home language. They are able to pick up on biases surrounding them about their language, culture, or skin color. They may feel like they have to choose between speaking English or their home language and culture.

How adults can help

Give children a chance to use the flannel board, puppets, or other dramatic play methods to recreate stories. Encourage children who wish to do so to retell stories to the group. Watch that the stories do not contain stereotypes or distort the facts (*such as presenting only the viewpoint of the new settlers at the first Thanksgiving*). Encourage children to talk about the past, future or imaginary events.

Provide positive models of people speaking their language and of their culture in the program activities. Communicate with parents about the need to support home language.

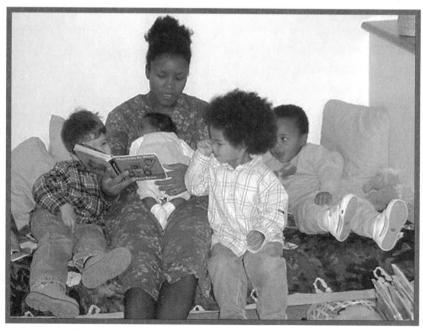

Help children understand how people are alike and different. Each of us is special and valuable.

What children are like

How adults can help

Music becomes more sophisticated: Children like singing games, want to dramatize songs, and make up their own songs (*often silly ones*). They are increasingly able to sing melodies on pitch and move in time to the beat.

Offer an ever-wider range of musical experiences including lots of songs with words in other languages, more complicated actions, and more real instruments from several cultures.

• • • • • • •

Children become aware of the discrete sounds that make up spoken language and can be manipulated.

Engage children in rhyming and alliteration games, songs, fingerplays, and other activities that draw attention to the sounds of language to promote phonological awareness.

• • • • • • •

By the end of this period, children may want to copy or write their own names, other important words, and even stories. Through these experiences they take important steps in learning to read.

Keep paper and markers or pencils handy. Let children write whenever they are interested. Never force them to write or trace letters. Help children sound out words they are trying to write.

• • • • • • •

Children become aware of the world
Preschoolers want to use real adult things.

Offer real objects for children to use: tools, money, ways to carry things (*briefcases; straw, paper, or fabric bags; baskets*), eating and cooking utensils, typical clothing, and similar everyday objects from several cultures.

• • • • • • •

Preschoolers may want to save all of their artwork and other projects and increasingly are able to carry over projects and topics of study from one day to the next. Children write for real purposes such as messages to friends.

Have children write their names on their work. If a block construction is prized, for example, they can make a sign asking others to leave it standing for a day or two. Make the sign using as many languages as are spoken by children in the program. Plan projects that engage children's thinking.

What children are like

Children at this age become curious about differences and similarities in people and their lifestyles. They generally choose friends of their own sex.

How adults can help

Help children understand how people are alike and different: eye color, hair, clothing, where we live, what we eat, members of families. Each of us is special and valuable. Discuss what is fair and accurate (*for example, sharing, standing up for what's right, songs drawn from a specific culture*) and what isn't (*playing cowboys and Indians, stereotyped drawings in books or on greeting cards*). Decorations and materials all through the room should include art, music, and other authentic everyday objects from a variety of cultures.

• • • • • • •

Interests of preschoolers expand to include topics such as transportation, adult jobs, science, dressing up, and different forms of music.

Add new topics as children express interest.

• • • • • • •

Preschoolers are still trying to understand what is real and what is make-believe.

Talk with children about what could happen and what is just pretend. Halloween masks may still be too frightening for some children.

• • • • • • •

Children want to take more responsibility for doing errands. Older 5-year-olds may be able to cross all but the busiest of streets by themselves if they have practiced the proper procedures with an adult over an extended period of time.

Give children more responsibility as they are ready. Follow safe crossing procedures. Perhaps set up streets for pedestrians and riding vehicles on the playground.

What children are like

How adults can help

Children solve problems and use tools

Preschoolers are increasingly able to figure out how things work and fit together. They are curious and want to try different ways to do things. They can sort objects using more than two categories. Cutting and pasting become favorite activities.

Bring in all kinds of objects for children to explore: an old toaster with any dangerous parts removed, a clock, hole punchers—anything safe for eager learners. Ask children to think of a variety of ways to solve problems: "What ideas do you have for using these yogurt tops that Kai's mother saved for us?" Involve children in making repairs. Stock up on paste and glue!

• • • • • • •

Children usually are able to resolve differences and negotiate conflicts between themselves with words.

Encourage children to use words to work out problems that arise during play. "Meaghan, you and Sadao both want to use the funnel in the sandbox. What solution can you two agree on?"

• • • • • • •

Children are naturally interested in shapes, colors, and textures.

Use the names of shapes and colors in natural ways: "What shape of blocks do you need to make a ramp for your truck?" "Your blue shoes match the blue in your shirt. See how they are alike?" Provide lots of textures through cooking, woodworking, clay and finger paint, and clothes for pretend play, for example.

• • • • • • •

Children learn to count at least up to 20 and may be interested in printing numbers. They begin to compare sizes and weights of objects and can identify basic shapes.

Continue to encourage the use of number and quantity in real experiences such as measuring, distributing or dividing items, and matching. Count and compare in each of the languages spoken by the children in the group.

What children are like

How adults can help

Typewriters or computers, woodworking tools, and other items to use for hands-on projects are of great interest and children develop skills to use them well. Projects may extend over several days.

Introduce more complicated cooking projects, new carpentry tools, a cash register, and other items as children are ready to use them. Take care to save their projects from day to day.

• • • • • • •

Children express feelings

Preschoolers still have intense feelings: fear, joy, anger, love. They may still need an adult to help them manage their strong feelings.

Accept children's feelings and help them find a safe way to express them. "You are really angry that your beautiful tower was knocked over. Let's sit here for a while until you feel calm enough to talk with the children who destroyed it." Children's books may help them see how others have faced and resolved problems such as divorce, moving, death, disabilities, learning a new language, a new baby in the family.

• • • • • • •

Children ages 4 and 5 are easily encouraged or discouraged. They may show off and demand attention.

Provide lots of opportunities for children to be successful and take leadership roles.

• • • • • • •

Children at this age usually are able to say goodbye to their parents with little difficulty if they have had previous group experience.

You may even need to remind children to say goodbye—often they want to plunge right in to the day's activities.

Other developmental accomplishments for older 3-year-olds to 5-year-olds. . .

That chart of developmental accomplishments contained a wealth of information. Much of it you may already have known. It is a good reminder, though, about how children's bodies change, that children learn a great deal from their experiences, that adults are key to helping children learn about the world, and that how adults treat children can make a big difference in how children treat others.

Perhaps you noticed in this chart that early childhood professionals focus on what children **can** do rather than what they can't do yet. It is important to see the accomplishments of toddlers, for example, rather than focusing on the skills they have not yet acquired.

Children need to practice, to consolidate what they have learned, and to have many real experiences with a wide variety of people and objects. From now on, you will think in terms of what children can do and how you can make the most of that particular day for that particular child. Be sure you are familiar with the **range** of development for every section on the chart. If you work with 5-year-olds, this information points out just how many things children have learned in a few short years! If you work with infants, look through the next section as a reminder of how quickly they will change.

If you haven't already done so, go back to the developmental chart. Lots of items are missing. Fill in at least two developmental accomplishments in each age range that are particularly important to you and the cultural groups you work with.

When you are finished, show your additions to your Advisor as part of your next conference. Later, we will look in some detail at how you will use all this information to answer questions you have about children and how you work with them.

Why you need to know about typical development

Information about how children develop is used for many different purposes. All teachers use information about typical child development so they can predict what kinds of environments, experiences, and materials will be safe, healthy, interesting, achievable, but also challenging for most of the child within a given age range. Some professionals use child development knowledge to help spot potential developmental problems. These highly trained early childhood special educators, physicians, therapists, and psychologists have specialized skills to identify and help children who are not developing typically. We will talk later in this unit about how to make use of their assistance.

Other professionals also use this information to help parents understand their own children. Pediatricians, for example, often give materials to new parents so they will know what to look for and how to help their children develop and learn.

Schools and libraries also have books and pamphlets about children's development and learning, some written for parents, and others written for professionals. You should become familiar with some of these for they will always be important to your work. Even after you become a CDA, you will continue to build your own knowledge about children's development by reading professional literature. Because we learn more all the time from research on children's development and learning, it is important for your knowledge to be current. And as you work with families, you will always be ready with ways to help them understand their own children.

Whenever you see pamphlets or articles about the way children develop and learn, read them. Also try to find material written in languages other than English. Find relevant ones that would be useful to parents in your program and add them to your Resource File. Think about how these other resources are similar to and different from your CDA materials and other professional literature.

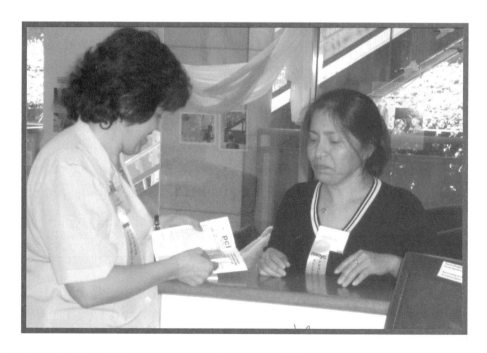

Read professional literature as much as possible so you continue to build your knowledge of children's development.

How do you collect information about each child's development and learning?

In order to be a good teacher, you need to know about children's patterns of learning and development in general. You use this information to prepare the environment and plan curriculum for the group. But you also need to really know the children in your group. You need to know what they can do, their interests, their strengths and needs, how they think, and what skills they are learning. You need to know about their languages and cultural heritages to make experiences meaningful for children. Once you know each child well, you can combine all you know to adapt curriculum and teaching, to assess children's learning and developmental progress, and to evaluate your own work.

Know what range of behaviors to expect. Help children continue to make learning and developmental progress.

There are many ways to learn more about individual children. We have included several practical methods here. You can adapt each of these to fit your style and your questions about children. Try each method at least once to get a feel for how it works. You will use these methods many times in your CDA Seminar and each day as you teach young children.

Every day, observe how . .

√. children show interest in others

. children become more aware of themselves

x· children's muscles grow stronger and coordination improves

. children learn to communicate

· children become aware of and learn about the world

k· children solve problems and use tools

· children express feelings

You observe children in your group

What a thrill it is to see a child's first steps! To watch a child learn to cut with scissors! To enjoy playing with a child who can throw and catch the ball! To see the pride when a child writes her name for the first time!

A big part of your day is spent observing children's development and learning. You probably even take pictures of what happens. Your program probably requires written progress forms. You most likely save some of the children's artwork or writing samples to show parents at your next conference. Perhaps you keep a diary of some of the fascinating things children have said or done.

Now that you are on your way to becoming a **professional** early childhood educator, you will want to begin to use these and other methods to more **systematically** record what you observe.

Your notes will help you answer questions about whether your children are making progress, what their strengths and needs are, how well you teach, and whether children achieve the learning goals you have for them. As you talk with your CDA Field Advisor, ask questions about your observations.

Whenever new children join your group, you will need to find out what they can do, what they like, and much more about them. Every fall, or whenever you have a new group, you will need to take notes about each child so you can choose the right experiences and materials to provide. As a teacher, you will constantly study children to see whether they are developing and learning as expected. You will always need to record what children do.

There are several ways you can take notes and organize them. The method you use depends on what you are trying to figure out. You need to match your questions with the best way to find the answers. Here are some

Ways to study children

- Keep a diary of your observations.
- Write about a specific incident.
- Record information on a chart.
- Interview children.
- Use formal assessment tools.

ways you can keep track of what children do. Perhaps you have other methods that work for you.

Read through the next sections, and try out four techniques for studying children. Then select one recording tool that will be helpful to you in answering a specific question you have. During the next conference with your Field Advisor, you can talk together about your experiences in using these observation tools.

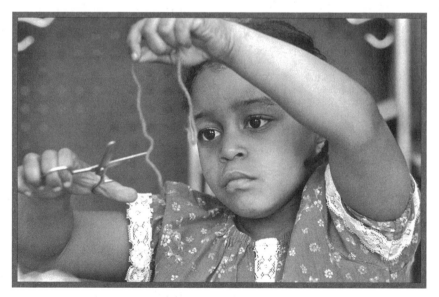

As a teacher, you will constantly study children to see whether they are developing and learning as expected.

Keep a diary

Each day, jot down something special about at least two of the children in your care. Use a small notebook for each child, a three-ring binder, or notecards—whatever suits you. Just write down the day and what happened like this:

March 4 – Today Brandon (20 Months) Crawled through the tunnel on the playground for the first time. He had been watching two other children coming out of the end for about 5 minutes before he did it himself.

May 15 – Allison poured her juice without spilling a drop. She's been trying so hard all month.

December 5 – Jamal (4 years, 5 months) wrote his J for the first time when he signed in.

When you look back on your notes, you will see just how much children learn when you're together. When you compare children's ages and skills with the information on the chart, you might see areas to emphasize. Or you might get some ideas for new experiences you need to plan or to pick up on children's interests.

As a first step, think about two of the children in your care and write here what they did today.

Date: ___11/1___

Who did what? (MW) identified identified & verbalized first letter of name on the alphabet chart

Date: (N.L.)

Who did what? (N.L.) built a structure in blocks & added people to the building

You have just started an informal diary! In this next week, decide how you want to organize your notes and begin to keep your diary every day. After a week, look back to see what you can learn about these two children's development or what you need to change in your teaching.

Continue to make daily notes for a full two weeks. Bring your diary to your next meeting with your Advisor so she or he can check your progress and answer any questions. You will use your diary notes to complete the exercises in Part 4 of this unit.

Write about a specific incident

Keeping track of what happened at certain times can help you answer specific questions about children's behavior. Many teachers find it helpful to occasionally sit down with a pen and paper, observe children, and write down details about what they see happen.

Perhaps you want to see what happens when you place 5-month-old Lindsay, sitting in an infant seat, in front of a mirror for the first time in your family child care home. You might write something like this:

September 2, 11 a.m. - Lindsay (5 months) turns her head toward the mirror right away. She reaches out with her arms and waves them around. Smiles. Kicks her feet. Watches herself for at least 5 minutes.

As children grow older, your observations may include more than one child. For example, a 4-year-old boy, Seth, seems to fight a lot when he is in a small group. Your notes about what he does with a group might read like this:

January 12, 9:30 a.m.: Seth, Melissa, and Brandon in the block corner.

Melissa: "Let's make a river with boats."

Brandon: "OK. Here, the river can start on this side." He takes the longest blocks from the shelf and places them on the floor.

Melissa carries more blocks and puts them next to Brandon's.

Melissa looks up to see Seth watching them: "Hey, Seth, don't you want to play boats with us?"

Seth does not answer her. He slowly walks over to the shelf with the boats. He picks up a barge, climbs onto the riding truck, and then rams into the river.

Brandon screams: "Seth, DON'T DO THAT! You are messing up our river!" ...

(*Note: Do you want to jump in and rescue the river before Seth demolishes it? It is tempting, but by now you know that whenever possible children should be given the opportunity to solve their own problems. Teaching problem-solving strategies will be discussed in more detail in Unit 4.*)

By writing down several brief samples of just what happens in your classroom with Seth and the other children, eventually you may be able to piece together why he acts this way, and what you can do to help him be a more friendly player.

When you write down examples like this of what you see, be sure to

1 Note the date and time.

2 Include the names of all the children involved.

3 Write where the incident happened.

4 Jot down what children said and exactly what they did. Try not to use words that jump to conclusions about why children behave the way they do. For example, in the situation above, instead of writing that Seth didn't want to play or that he was mean, we wrote what he **did**.

5 Do not get involved—just watch (*unless someone or something is about to get hurt, of course*).

Write a description of an episode with the children in your care: Choose a particular child to watch or choose a learning center to observe. Take your pen and paper, and watch quietly on the sidelines. Write down what happens here:

Date and time: _____11/22_____

Place: _____Block Area_____

Children: _____N. L.   M. C._____

What the children said and did: _____

Building a block structure and said it was a school. "look at the rooms and people."

You may need to collect several of these observations in order to practice writing about exactly what happens. Save your notes so you can discuss the observation with your Field Advisor.

Use a frequency chart

You want children to take advantage of all the learning opportunities you offer. But do children ignore some activities and use other areas all the time?

The only way you can know for sure is to keep a count, to find out how frequently or infrequently children behave in certain ways. For this purpose, you use what is called a frequency chart. For example, if you want to know how many children use clay or paste each day, keep a pad handy, and make a mark whenever a child enters that area:

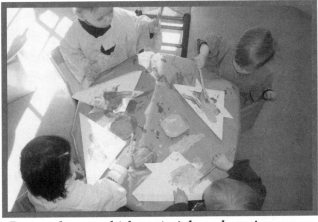

Do you know which materials or learning areas are most popular in your program?

WEEK: September 25

ACTIVITY:	M	T	W	T	F
Clay	II	I	IIII	III	II
Paste	III	II	HHT	II	IIII

Do you know why so few children used these art materials on Tuesday? And what made them so appealing on Wednesday? Did you put out some new magazines to cut or bring in some fancy cookie cutters?

What materials or learning experiences do children seem to ignore in your program? Or which ones seem the most popular? Use this chart to find out:

WEEK: _____

	M	T	W	T	F
ACTIVITY: puzzles					

Based on what you saw, how can you make the less popular activities more appealing? Or should they be replaced with more engaging or challenging materials?

I noticed some materials should be cycled more. Some children were bored w/ the puzzles, sooner than others.

Try out your ideas if you get a chance.

Another type of tally can help you see which experience each child uses. Sometimes children get in a rut and do the same thing every day. To find out whether children are playing in a variety of areas, use a chart like this:

Each time these children did these learning experiences:

WEEK: April 25

CHILDREN: Nikki   Sergio   Chaka

LEARNING
EXPERIENCE:

Learning Experience	Nikki	Sergio	Chaka
Read Books	I	II	IIII
Blocks	III	I	II
Do Puzzles	HHT I	I	HHT
Pretend Play	III	HHT I	I
Games	II	III	I
Easel	HHT	I	III
Water Play	IIII	II	

What might this information tell you about each of these children? Do some prefer to play alone? Which one likes messy things? Who prefers to play in groups?

Are there some children in your group who seem to do the same things day after day? Pick two or three children and keep track of what they do. **Fill in this chart to record what these children do for a week.**

WEEK: _____

CHILDREN: M.C.   M.W.

LEARNING
EXPERIENCE: M.C. dominantly stays in dramatic play or sand/water table.
M.W. consistently remains engaged at computer

What does this information tell you about these children? Who needs to be encouraged to branch out into other areas (*maybe girls are reluctant to play with trucks*)? Are some different or more difficult materials needed (*perhaps more materials are needed in the child's home language*)? **Use what you are learning to improve your teaching, and discuss what you have learned with your Advisor.**

Interview children informally

Did you ever just sit down and chat with a child in an effort to learn something about the child? You can learn so much just by casually talking together!

Sometimes you might be fairly direct about what you would like to know. If you are direct, ask questions that require more than a yes, no, or a "right" answer—but don't pry or your conversation may come to a sudden halt.

Better yet, pick up on children's cues and make comments children can respond to:

"You seem to be having trouble finding something of interest to do this morning." "You brought your doll to school today."

Choose a comfortable place and see what you can learn so you can be a better teacher. With reluctant speakers, try waiting five seconds or so for their response. This strategy—called "wait time"—actually encourages children to talk. Be sure to talk with children. Don't interrogate them.

As you talk, you may find out all kinds of things: what is bothering a child, where she or he would really like to visit on the next field trip, or discover an idea that is confusing for the child. A conversation might go something like this:

Date: October 28

Child interviewed: Alexandra, age 3

Question: Alex will soon be having minor surgery. How can you help her deal with this potentially frightening experience?

Conversation: "Alex, when you have finished looking at your book, please come sit next to me for a few minutes." Alex continues to read for a few minutes, then brings the book with her. "That must have been a good book you were reading—you had it for a long time," you comment.

"I know—I was looking at the pictures."

You want to know more, so you elaborate on your comment. "They must have been special pictures. You were concentrating hard."

"It's about a hospital. I'm going to a hospital."

"It is only a few days until your operation," you note. "This weekend I get to visit the hospital," she volunteers.

You ask, "What kinds of things will you see there?"

And so the conversation continues.

Based on what you discuss, you may want to put out some medical props in the pretend play area. Perhaps talking with the children about Alex's absence will help them understand her situation. Maybe after the surgery the children could take a field trip to a clinic, or a nurse could talk with them about ways to stay healthy. You need to know a lot about your children to select the most appropriate and positive learning experiences. You may learn more than you expect when you really listen to children in this way. Children may tell you personal things about their families, may announce what they bought for a birthday gift, or may reveal that a parent dislikes someone at work.

As a professional you must keep any information confidential, unless you suspect child abuse. Your suspicions of child abuse or neglect must be reported (*see Unit 3*). Always respond with respect to whatever children say.

In addition to talking, you might ask children to do a specific task. This can also give you information about their skills or understanding.

For example, you might give a toddler a puzzle with more pieces than have been available. If the child completes the puzzle with only a bit of struggling, it could be time to put some of the easier puzzles away. Or you might ask a child to build a block model and ask another child to make a building just like it. That could help you see how well she can use objects in space.

Think about what questions you have, and whether you might find an answer by interviewing or asking children to show you what they can do.

Think of a question about a child that might be answered through an interview. Write the question here:

Are you ready to be a big sister for the new baby?

Then think about what questions you might ask or what learning experience might give clues about what you would like to know to be a better teacher. Write how you could talk with the child here.

Ask the child about what big sister does to help and what she will teach the baby.

When you have a chance, conduct your interview and jot down what happened.

DATE: *2/15/11*

CHILD: *R.W.*

EXPERIENCE OR QUESTIONS FOR THE CHILD:

Did your mom have the new baby? Whats the baby's name? How have you been a helper to the baby?

CHILD'S RESPONSES/SOLUTIONS:

"Yes, the name is spiderman"
"I give her smiles"

What did you learn about this child? How can you use this in your teaching? Use what you have learned to improve your work with the child.

Now that you have tried out four different ways of studying children, pick one you would like to demonstrate to other CDA Candidates.

· **Choose a question that you have about a child or children.**

· **Study the question using any technique you think is appropriate.**

· **Prepare to share your example in your CDA Seminar. You should be able to tell the group what you did, how you did it, and why you chose the specific technique.** (*Be prepared to answer questions, too!*)

You use formal assessment tools

Before we leave the topic of ways to study children, there is one other important topic to know about—the use of standardized tests with young children. There are many kinds of standardized tools including the many types of checklists, tests, and rating scales used to evaluate children's abilities and progress. When used properly, these can be helpful in answering questions about development and learning. They are especially important in helping identify children with exceptional talents or with learning or physical disabilities.

Standardized tools are measures that have been carefully developed to have two characteristics: reliability and validity. Reliability means that the tool is likely to get the same or similar results when it is used by different people or when it is used on different days. Tests that have reliability provide more accurate results. Validity means that the tool measures what it is supposed to measure. For instance, a test that it is supposed to measure a child's psychomotor development should not really be a measure of the child's language comprehension. You can see that reliability and validity are very important characteristics. Without them, the results obtained from a test are either inaccurate or meaningless.

When tests are standardized, the developers write manuals that describe the purposes and groups for which the test is intended. Standardized tests or any measure for that matter *should always be used only for their intended purposes and always used with caution,* just as you use the developmental chart in this chapter with care. Some tests or checklists simply aren't accurate. Some don't consider childrearing differences among cultural groups, languages, and income levels.

Before you use any checklist, ask some questions about it: What is it for? How is it supposed to be used? What will the results be used to do? Why was this checklist or test selected? What training do you need to use and interpret it properly? Is it standardized?

If you have any questions about a child's development and learning that you can't answer, it is not a good idea to guess. It is best to refer the child to a specialist who knows about the issues. Specialists are trained to select the best type of test for each child.

If you work in a program where developmental checklists or other screening instruments are used, **collect some samples to bring with you to your CDA Seminar. Find out how** they are used so that you can discuss them in Seminar.

The more you know about children, the more valuable your own observations—made with one of the methods you have just used—will be in planning your curriculum and teaching strategies. Become increasingly familiar with these and other appropriate ways to observe children and record their behavior. **Choose one sample of your favorite observation tool for your Professional Resource File. Put in two copies—one blank and one filled in with a sample observation (*anonymous*).**

PART 4

How do you use information to teach appropriately?

Tamile, 5½ months, is just beginning to sit up steadily. You need to find some good places to let her feel she is part of the action.

At 14 months, Andrew insists on feeding himself. How can you be sure the finger and spoon foods are healthy foods?

It seems as if every toddler in your group wants to do everything for themselves. What responsibilities can they handle?

None of your 3-year-olds will sit still for a story. Why?

Nikki is almost 5 and soon will be a big brother. How do you help him feel good about it?

Your day is filled with problem-solving opportunities just like these—how do you help children become the best person they can be? You can make it happen. You know that children learn best through play and other teacher-guided small group experiences. You know the general characteristics of children at that age. You know what your particular children have mastered and what new challenges they need to continue to make progress.

You need to offer children good choices. Children usually ignore items that are "old hat" for them—toddlers rarely pick up teething rings, for instance. Children may also ignore a toy that is too strange. Instead, they generally choose an activity that looks interesting and yet not too difficult.

In good programs, children choose what they're going to do many times every day. New children who are not used to having choices about what to do may be overwhelmed. You will need to help them learn how to make good choices. For example, you may offer a more limited choice between two good options at first until they are comfortable making their own selections during free choice time.

Often children want and need to *practice* what they have already learned. A baby who has just mastered step climbing will do it over and over again. Preschoolers will write their names several times on a page just for the joy of being able to do it.

Sometimes children need and want to *try something new.* They always seem drawn to the fresh dough clay, the new dump truck, or the book you just checked out from the library. Novelty—but not too much—often appeals to children. You probably have seen a child who would rather play with the box than the toy inside.

On the other hand, children may not use an easel or a bowling game if they have never seen one used before. Children also are generally more willing to try new things when they know they usually are successful in what they do. Children are also more likely to do something on their own that they have seen done by the teacher. For instance, they will return to look at a book that the teacher read to the class, or will act out the story in the dramatic play area. Sometimes they will need you to model the use of a new material or demonstrate a new skill, such as how to make real clay hold together.

List something new that someone in your group tried this week:

T.H. tried a new small group activity.

Using your daily diary notes, what are some of the children in your group practicing?

Children in my group are practicing sharing & conflict resolution.

As you observe and teach, you will see it's true: Children learn best when teachers are clear about their learning goals, prepare the environment with the right materials, provide a variety of child-initiated and teacher-guided learning experiences to help children achieve the goals, and adapt their teaching strategies to help each child make progress.

At other times children will be ready to *combine something familiar with something new.* An older toddler who has enjoyed drawing with markers may be intrigued with some brightly colored chalk. A preschooler who has mastered hammering nails may want to start to saw some boards. A 5-year-old who has been writing his name may want to write a list or a story.

What did you see a child do this week that combined something old with something new?

A child started to write other students names at the writing table.

To plan learning experiences for children that are achievable but also challenging, and adapt your teaching strategies for each child, you:

1. consider what you know about child development and learning, and your goals for children,

2. observe children to see what they can do,

3. figure out what they will be moving on to next,

4. prepare the learning experiences and materials children need, and

5. plan how you will guide and/or direct the learning experience (*time to allot, questions you will ask, showing how to use something for the first time, number of children who can participate at one time*).

You use this way of thinking many times each day. In fact, the process is so important it even has a name. As a well-informed teacher, you decide what is **developmentally appropriate** for children—what experiences are achievable but also challenging and contribute to children's development and learning.

To plan appropriate learning experiences, you:

1. consider how children develop and learn, and your goals for children,

2. observe children to see what they can do,

3. figure out what they will be moving on to next, and

4. plan the materials you need and

5. how you can guide and/or direct the learning experience.

What happens if an activity isn't developmentally appropriate—challenging but achievable? You have wasted the child's time, your time, and the materials. Children may be bored because there is no challenge and do the activity half-heartedly or walk away. Or they may become frustrated and give up because the experience is not achievable. They may take out their frustration through disruptive behavior. Children won't achieve the goals you have for them.

What happened with your group this week that probably was not developmentally appropriate?

I feel that read a book that was to long and advanced for the age group.

What learning experiences did you offer that were challenging but achievable for your children?

We used strawberries in the basket to understand less and more.

It is not easy to decide what makes a developmentally appropriate experience for children. Much depends on the individual children, as well as on whether the experience is meaningful in the context of their culture. Most of the rest of this book will help you find solutions to questions you have about what is developmentally appropriate for children.

You are probably not sure about some experiences or discipline techniques, for example. Write a few of your concerns here.

You can look for the answers to your questions in the coming units, and by talking with your Field Advisor and Seminar group.

Every day you plan how to spend your day with children. For every activity or interaction, ask yourself: *is this developmentally appropriate for these children? Is this experience contributing to children's development and learning?* These are probably the most important questions you can ask as a teacher. There are many experiences and strategies that are appropriate for young children. There are also many common projects and techniques—worksheets, coloring books, and drill, for example—that are less appropriate.

You use this information to evaluate children's development and learning, and your work

Sometimes you want to confirm that children are flourishing. They are delightful, curious children who seem healthy and happy.

At other times you are concerned that a child may be lagging behind. Or a child's behavior seems stalled at a younger level.

Sometimes you are sure children have disabilities or other special needs that have gone undetected.

In all these cases, you can use your knowledge of child development and your observations of particular children to help you decide what to do next.

When children are doing well, you will want to share the good news with their families. If you suspect a problem, you may want to first discuss your concerns with your supervisor or the program director. Your notes will help you explain why you think the child should be referred for further testing or screening.

There are probably one or two children you work with who seem to be doing exceptionally well. You will want to provide learning experiences that continue to challenge them. You may have others in your group who seem to have some type of problem.

Which children will you concentrate on first as you begin your systematic observations?

I will concentrate on children who need the extra challenge to be further engaged.

What type of record keeping will help you find out what you want to know?

Observation and formal assessment tools will help me determine what I need to know and provide the evidence for my next step.

We will first look at keeping track of children's successes. Then we will examine how you can use assessment to find out which children have some type of problem.

Follow up on children's experiences

Your observations of children can help you decide whether you are really doing a good job and how you can improve even if things are going well.

Look back on your diary. Did you write mostly positive things or did you see mostly problems?

I showed an objective balance of what the child was successful in and unsuccessful.

Do any patterns show up—such as do the children have a hard time sitting still when you have them together as a group?

A particular child shows difficulty in concentrating during large group.

Are some learning centers or materials ignored while others are always in great demand?

Yes, there are popular areas of activity while other areas have little activity such as the library and at times the art area.

Take a good hard look at what you felt was so important that you wrote it down. Congratulate yourself on things that went well. Where were you successful?

I created a box for a child use when she seems disinterested in large group. It contains paper and new words. She likes to write words.

All children have different abilities. With a few exceptions, most children can benefit from attending the same program. This strategy is called inclusion.

Ask yourself how you can make the children's hours with you an even more beneficial experience. What areas seem to need improvement?

Finding newer materials for sand/water Table. A more attractive library for children to read.

You may have expressed some concerns about one or more children's physical, intellectual, social, or emotional development. Let's look now at how you, your program director, and the children's parents can work together to identify any disabilities.

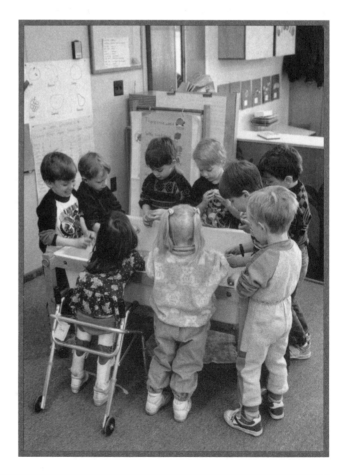

Screen children for possible disabilities

Parents are usually the first to notice a problem with their own child. Sometimes, however, the caregiver may be the first to suspect a problem. Regardless of where the concern first comes up, it is important to work openly and honestly with the parent, and to rely on the help of experts in deciding what to do.

Every community has services for children who have mild, moderate, or severe problems or disabilities. These individuals or agencies usually also have expertise in diagnosing disabilities.

Some offer screening services for programs for young children. Some organizations may be willing to check annually each child's hearing, dental, and sight problems. These kinds of health screenings should be done each year, regardless of whether you suspect any problems.

Most early childhood programs now conduct screening of young children as the first step in a process of identifying children who may be at risk of a developmental or learning problem. Standardized screening tools are brief and require relatively minimal training to administer. They are not designed to diagnose a child's problem. Rather, the results of developmental screening identify those children who are in need of a more systematic assessment using multiple sources of information before diagnosis of a possible problem can be made. That diagnosis will involve administration of other standardized assessment tools and tests by qualified specialists, involvement of the child's family, and other requirements that are part of federal laws governing the rights of children with disabilities and special needs.

Find out the names of agencies to contact for expertise in developmental and/or learning disabilities if you should ever need assistance for a family in your program. In most areas, the agency is the local school district. List the phone numbers and include information about each agency or service in your Professional Resource File for easy reference. (The Internet is the easiest place to find this information.) Your Field Advisor will assist you if you need help, and you will share your resources with other CDA Candidates during Seminar.

Teachers' observations of children and/or information parents give you in a conversation or conference usually helps you decide when to call in expert help. Your daily records and special observations, and those parents make, also help determine what type of screening is needed.

So always take care to keep dated notes, to record information accurately, and to keep your notes organized. Then, when a problem is suspected, you can provide your program director or other expert with good solid observational information from which to start the diagnostic process. Screening will be the first step in that process.

If developmental problems are identified early, and appropriate intervention occurs early, you greatly increase the child's chances for overcoming the problem and going on to future successes.

Just as you are likely to play a role in spotting a possible developmental disability, you are also likely to work with children who have already been diagnosed as having disabilities. All children with developmental challenges have a legal right to attend an appropriate educational program. At one time, it was believed that children with disabilities should all be in separate classes. Today, however, we realize that all children have different abilities. With a few exceptions, most children can benefit from attending the same program.

This strategy is called *inclusion*—children with disabilities and/or special needs are enrolled in the same program where their typically developing peers would be found. That way, children can learn in the least restrictive environment. Inclusion is required by federal law because research has found that not only do children with disabilities and special needs develop and learn better in inclusive settings, but their typically developing peers benefit as well. If you work in Head Start or nearly any other program with large numbers of children, yours is probably already an inclusive program. If you are a family child care provider, you may have already served a child with special needs in your group.

There is a large body of specialized information to help you make good decisions about working with these children. Some will be discussed throughout *Essentials*, but most of it you will gather on your own as the need arises with individual children.

Much of *Essentials* contains ideas you can use to improve your work with children. Before we look at some specific questions—let's see if what you have already learned can help you decide how to answer some typical questions parents will ask you about your program.

PART 5

What questions can you expect about what you do?

Parents want their children to have the best experiences they can, especially in their early years. When parents first visit, or after their child has been enrolled, they may ask questions like the ones that are listed here.

Other staff may also ask you to explain what you do. Think about how you would respond to these questions. You will find answers in the next few units of this book and in the videos.

1. Why do you plan for children in your program to play so much?

2. How do you get children to share?

3. Why do the boys and girls use the same bathroom?

4. Why does each child need a cubby?

5. Why do you insist parents always say goodbye to their child—even babies?

6. Why are meals served group style?

7. Where are the coloring books and worksheets?

8. Aren't you just wasting learning time when you change diapers or wait for children to dress themselves?

9. How do you get children to respect other cultures/languages, people with disabilities, different ages, and the opposite sex?

10. Will my child get confused learning two languages at once?

11. How do you make children sit still for stories or show and tell?

12. How do you help children learn the alphabet?

13. What do you do to teach children counting skills?

14. How soon can you toilet train my child?

15. Why do children go off by themselves or do things in small groups? Why don't you teach everyone something at the same time?

16. Why don't you do the same things with children every year? It's so much work to think up new activities.

17. Aren't you just a baby sitter?

18. Will my child be ready for kindergarten?

You can probably think of other similar questions. Write them here.

_____

_____

_____

_____

_____

If you don't find the answers to your questions here or in the videos, talk with your CDA Field Advisor or bring them up when you join your CDA Seminar group. See if together you can find out what is developmentally appropriate for the group of young children you teach.

By now, you should have watched the videotape to accompany Unit 2. Keep thinking about the questions in the Viewer's Guide. You will probably want to come back to this unit and its accompanying video to refresh your memory again and again throughout your teaching career.

This marks the end of your second unit of early childhood study toward your CDA Credential. Turn back to page 457 and check off your progress—this unit was really a giant step forward!

Now, let's deal with some specifics about curriculum planning and teaching. The next unit will review how to set up a safe, healthy learning environment—your CDA Competency Goal I.

Resources for more information

Albrecht, K. & Miller, L.G. (2000). *The comprehensive toddler curriculum.* Beltsville, MD: Gryphon House, Inc.

Bredekamp, S. & Copple, C. (Eds.) (1997). *Developmentally appropriate practice in early childhood programs. Rev. Ed.* Washington, DC: National Association for the Education of Young Children.

Chandler, P. (1994). *A place for me: Including children with special needs in early care and education.* Washington, DC: National Association for the Education of Young Children.

Colker, L.J. (1995). *Observing young children: Learning to look, looking to learn* (Video and trainer's guide). Washington, DC: Teaching Strategies.

Dodge, D.T. & Heroman, C. (2000). *Building your baby's brain: A parent's guide to the first five years.* Washington, DC: U.S. Dept of Education. Distributed by Teaching Strategies. Spanish edition also available: *Cómo estimular el cerebro infantil.*

Dombro, A., Colker, L., Dodge, D.T. (1997). *The creative curriculum for infants and toddlers.* Washington, DC: Teaching Strategies.

Jablon, J.R. Dombro, A.L. & Dichtelmiller, M.O. (1999). *The power of observation.* Washington, DC: Teaching Strategies.

Korelek, D., Dodge, D.T. & Pizzolongo, P. (2004). *Caring for preschool children. 3rd edition.* Washington, DC: Teaching Strategies.

Lally, J.R., Griffin, A., Fenichel, E., Segal, M., Szanton, E.S. & Weissbourd, B. (2003). *Caring for infants and toddlers in groups: Developmentally appropriate practice.* Washington, DC: Zero to Three.

McAfee, O. Leong, D. & Bodrova, E. (2003). *Basics of assessment: A primer for early childhood educators.* Washington, DC: National Association for the Education of Young Children.

Meisels, S.J. with S. Atkins-Burnett. (1994). *Developmental screening in early childhood: A guide (4th ed.)* Washington, DC: National Association for the Education of Young Children.

Meisels, S.J., Dombro, A.L., Marsden, D.B., Weston, D.R. & Jewkes, A.J. (2003). *The Ounce Scale: An observational assessment for infants and toddlers birth to 3 1/2 years.* Pearson Early Learning. Online at http://pelcatalog.pearson.com. Also available in Spanish.

Miller, K. (2001). *Ages and stages: Developmental descriptions and activities, birth through eight years. Revised edition.* Telshare Publishing Co. Distributed by Redleaf Press, St. Paul, MN.

Mulligan, S., Morris, S., Miller Green, K. & Herper-Whalen, S. (1999). *Child care plus+ curriculum on inclusion: Practical strategies for early childhood programs.* Child Care plus+, 634 Eddy Avenue, The University of Montana, Missoula, MT 59812. www.ccplus.org.

Sandall, S.R. & Schwartz, I. S. (2002). *Building blocks for teaching preschoolers with special needs.* Baltimore: Paul H. Brookes Publishing Co. Distributed by Redleaf Press.

Segal, M., Masi, W. & Leiderman, R. (2001). *In time and with love: Caring for infants and toddlers with special needs, 2nd ed.* New York: Newmarket Press. Available from www.zerotothree.org.

Segal, M. (1998). *Your child at play: Birth to one year. Discovering the senses and learning about the world.* New York: Newmarket Press. Available from www.zerotothree.org.

Segal, M. (1998). *Your child at play: One to two years. Exploring, learning, making friends and pretending.* New York: Newmarket Press. Available from www.zerotothree.org.

Segal, M. (1998) .*Your child at play: Three to five years. Conversation, creativity and learning letters, words, and numbers.* New York: Newmarket Press. Available from www.zerotothree.org.

Segal, M. (1998). *Your child at play: Two to three years. Growing up, language, and the imagination.* New York: Newmarket Press. Available from www.zerotothree.org.

Ways to set up a safe, healthy environment to promote learning

"NO! Don't touch that glass jar. You could break it."

"Which cookie would you like for snack?"

"How many times have I told you to stay away from those stairs?"

"Are you sure you want to draw? I'll have to get the crayons out of the cupboard for you, then."

OR

"These plastic stacking cups are for you. What can you do with them?"

"You may put these raisins on your celery stuffed with cream cheese if you like."

"Our rocking boat turns over like this so you can climb up and down the steps."

"All of the markers, crayons, and paper are here on this shelf. Help yourself whenever you are ready to use them."

Child care can be a risky place for young children. The highest risks are from injury and infectious disease. With proper attention to safety precautions and supervision, most injuries in early childhood programs are preventable. And although it is inevitable that young children will get sick at times, proper hand washing and other measures can not only prevent illness but also promote health and nutrition. Adults' knowledge and practice of correct safety and health procedures is absolutely essential. No amount of good curriculum or positive interaction will compensate for an environment that is not safe.

But effective early childhood programs do more than keep children safe and healthy, they promote children's learning in all areas, including health. Children learn wherever they are. They learn from what they do and see. They learn from what they eat and smell. They learn the languages they hear spoken. They learn how to treat others by the way they are treated. <u>Your attitudes influence</u> their attitudes.

How you set up your classroom, your family child care playroom, your play yard, or any space you use with the children makes a big difference in what children learn about themselves, about other people, and about the world around them.

If you want children to be safe and healthy ... you need to make their play areas safe, all of you must practice good hygiene, and you must serve only nutritious foods.

If you want children to feel good about themselves and their friends ... you must give them plenty of opportunities to succeed and to play in harmony.

If you want children to enjoy learning ... you select appropriate toys, arrange materials in an appealing way, and encourage children to be curious.

In this unit of your CDA early childhood studies, you will look objectively at **where** and **how** you work with children. Much of what you do most likely already works well. You probably would like some things to work better. Maybe your room arrangement seems to encourage children to run. Perhaps you or the children in your program get sick frequently. Maybe children become bored easily with the materials you have.

We will help you identify what works, and what doesn't, in all types of programs for young children. Unless you are a family child care provider, you may not be responsible for all these items, but you do need to know there are a lot of things to think about when you teach. This unit, like this competency goal, addresses three aspects of the environment:

safety, health, and learning. The first part of this unit will help you create a safe environment. Then we will outline good health and eating practices. Finally, we will give you some guidelines for planning the learning environment, how to plan your schedule, arrange and decorate your room, and buy new learning materials. Throughout this unit, we will suggest appropriate teaching topics and ideas for children's learning experiences, too. The videos for Unit 3 will help you see how programs in many different settings can successfully apply these concepts.

Your goal should be to create an enjoyable, challenging and age-appropriate place for children to learn.

As a result of this unit, we expect you to make changes. Whatever you change, your goal should be to create an enjoyable, challenging, and age-appropriate place for children to learn. Not only will the children benefit, but teaching will also be much more pleasant when the children are happily engaged in learning.

You will need about three weeks to complete your study of Unit 3. During this time you must:

1. Prepare for conferences with your Field Advisor to discuss four topics (*keeping children safe, staying healthy and well-nourished, planning environments that promote play and learning, and choosing appropriate learning materials*).

2. Complete four assignments (*take a pediatric first-aid class, complete the nutritional values chart, sketch space arrangements, and complete the Environment Checklist*), and three entries for the Professional Resource File including your first aid certificate.

3. Complete four assignments for Seminar (*identify uncomfortable topics, prepare meal/snack plans, revise space arrangements, and rate children's books for cultural relevance and anti-bias*).

What you learn in this unit will help you feel confident when you demonstrate your knowledge and competency for Goal I: To establish and maintain a safe, healthy, learning environment.

PART 1

How do you keep your children safe?

Safety is not an option. It is essential in any good program for young children. For example, falls onto hard sources are one of the leading causes of serious injury and even death for children in child care centers. Nothing is more serious than children's safety.

Look at your copy of your state and local regulations for your program. Most of those standards probably deal with safety. Refresh your memory by reading every safety requirement you must meet.

Go sit on the floor in the middle of the children's play area. Pretend you are a child. How does it feel to be so short? Can you reach everything you want to play with? What can you get into that you shouldn't be able to?

Crawl around the room and sit in each area. As you do so, write down what you see that doesn't work very well for young children. Maybe the puzzles are on such a high shelf that the pieces always fall out when a child takes them down. Are the sockets covered? Can children get at dangerous substances easily? Are your knees getting dirty? Are there small objects that babies or toddlers could choke on? **Make a list here of every-thing that is a potential danger or nuisance to children.**

Metal edge of whiteboard, open running space w/ trippable items.

Now go out to your playground, back yard, park, or wherever you take children to play outdoors. Sit on the ground and look around for possible hazards. Write down what you see.

Throughout this chapter are sections of a checklist for you to use. As you go through it, you will put a check next to items that describe your facility or program. Those without checks will be the areas you can work to improve.

Your Field Advisor will verify that you have accurately completed all sections of the checklist.

An excellent resource that includes more detailed checklists is: *Healthy Young Children: A Manual for Programs*, (2002, NAEYC) edited by Dr. Susan S. Aronson, a pediatrician who specializes in childcare issues.

✓ Environment checklist: Safety

This first part of the checklist contains some of the most basic safety concerns, practices that research demonstrates prevent injury. If you didn't notice each one of these items during your first survey, go back and look again.

Put a check next to items that de-scribe your program. Add anything else you feel is particularly important for safety in your program. Your location, climate, or ages of the children make a difference. Refer to this checklist often just to be sure you haven't overlooked something.

_____ Your program meets every state or local requirement for a safe program.

✓ Adults protect children from them-selves and each other—children may not hit, bite, or otherwise hurt people or things.

✓ All injuries and any first aid you give to children are reported to the appropriate staff (in a center) and to the children's parent

Safety indoors

✓ The floors are clean and in good repair. Floors are smooth and have non-skid surfaces. Rugs are skid-proof.

✓ All areas are well lighted. Regular lighting is bright enough for good visibility.

✓ There is enough space for children to move around without constantly bumping into eachother. Your state requires _____ square feet of usable indoor space per child. Your program has _____ square feet per child.

✓ Furniture and toys are sturdy enough to withstand constant use by children.

✓ Furniture, toys, and materials are appropriate for the age of the children (*child-sized chairs and tables, blunt-end scissors*).

✓ Furniture, toys, and materials are in good repair—no sharp edges or points; no peeling paint, splinters, or loose parts.

✓ Safety covers are on electrical sockets. Electrical cords are out of children's reach. Electrical cords are placed away from doorways and traffic paths. Electrical appliances are out of children's reach except when under close supervision (*such as cooking*).

_____ Radiators, ovens, fans, and space heaters are out of children's reach.

_____ Tap water temperature is 120° F or lower.

✓ There are no openings in any pieces of active play equipment between $3^1/_2$ and 9 inches that could cause head entrapment.

✓ Dangerous substances (such as toxic plants, balloons, plastic bags, cleaning products, matches, and medicine) are not accessible to children. Poisons and medicines are stored in a locked cabinet. Adult handbags are stored out of children's reach.

✓ You require a parent's signature to give medication. You maintain a log of when which medicines were administered to which child.

✓ Smoke detectors are located properly. You check them monthly to be sure they work.

_____ Fire extinguishers are easy to reach. You practice how to use them at least once a month.

✓ Emergency evacuation procedures are posted. You practice how to leave the building quickly with the children at least once a month. Diagrams and pictures are used to make procedures clear. Instructions are in every language spoken by any staff member or parent.

✓ Emergency telephone numbers are located next to each telephone. One telephone is in the room where the children play most. Symbols or other languages are used on the list so any parent or staff member can easily locate a number.

_____ Easy entry and access is available for people with disabilities including staff, children, or parents. Handrails are securely mounted at child height.

✓ Room arrangements, equipment, and furniture are adapted as needed so children with disabilities can participate in as many activities as possible.

✓ Children can come and go from your center without major safety concerns: there are no steep steps, parking is nearby and ample. Pick-up and drop-off procedures clearly designate how supervision of children is ensured during exchange.

_____ If your program uses buses, they are regularly inspected, drivers are well trained, and safe procedures for loading and unloading are followed.

Ways to set up a safe, healthy environment to promote learning   105

✓ Children are always supervised by adults —indoors, on the playground, in the yard, on walks and field trips. Every child is accounted for at all times by a supervising adult. Some method of assuring that no child is hidden or missing from the group is used. You anticipate potential problems and take steps to avoid them.

✓ Children are only released to author-ized people. Parents must sign a list of those who are authorized.

✓ Children know indoor safety rules. They are taught these rules in a way that does not frighten them. They are helped to un-derstand why the rules are necessary. Pictures, demonstrations, and children's primary languages are used when explaining rules.

✓ A well-stocked first-aid kit is easy to get to in an emergency, and is taken on field trips.

In addition, if you care for babies or toddlers:

____ Babies are never left unattended on a diaper-changing table, in their bath, or in a wading pool.

____ Cribs have all their slats. Slats are no farther than 2 $\frac{3}{8}$ inches apart or less (*2 inches apart in Canada*) and have snug-fitting mattresses.

____ Cribs were made after 1978 (*no lead paint*).

____ Crib sides are locked at highest set-tings for naps.

✓ Sleeping surfaces are firm. Soft bedding materials, pillows or heavy blankets are not accessible to infants when they sleep.

✓ Babies are always put down to sleep on their backs.

✓ Toys are too large for children to swallow. Toys are not hung across the cribs of infants who can sit up.

____ Rattles, pacifiers, or other objects are never hung around an infant's neck.

____ Highchairs, swings, strollers, and other equipment are sturdy, clean, and in good repair.

____ Infant walkers are not used.

____ Bottles are never warmed in a micro-wave oven (*because of the uneven temperatures that may result*).

____ Stairways are accessible only to adults.

Other indoor safety checks for my program:

_____

_____

_____

_____

Safety outdoors

____ Children have enough space to run around without bumping into each other or the equipment. Your state requires ____ square feet of outdoor space per child. You have ____ square feet of outdoor space per child.

_____ The play area is free of debris. It is fenced and/or located away from traffic. There are no poisonous plants growing in the area. There is no standing water. Sand is covered when not in use to keep animals out.

_____ Traffic patterns are set up so children are not likely to run in front of or behind moving equipment such as swings. Fall zones do not overlap.

_____ Equipment is clean, sturdy, and in good repair.

_____ Surfaces underneath indoor and outdoor play equipment that children can climb are covered with impact-absorbing material according to the critical height recommendations of the Consumer Products Safety Commission. Critical height is the highest point that a child can climb to. (See _Healthy Young Children_, 2002, p. 193.)

_____ The following surfaces are not used under indoor or outdoor climbing equipment: asphalt, concrete, soil or hard-packed dirt, grass, turf, linoleum, or carpeting.

_____ Impact-absorbing surfacing material extends at least 6 feet beyond all sides of climbing equipment.

_____ Equipment is securely anchored.

_____ Children have a variety of types of equipment to use for different types of play: riding toys, climbing apparatus, sand to dig in.

_____ A variety of surfaces are available, hard _(for riding vehicles)_ and soft _(grass for running and rolling)_.

_____ Children with disabilities can use most areas of the playground.

_____ Shade is available.

_____ Children know the rules for playing safely outdoors. Rules are explained with dia-grams, pictures, demonstrations, and in children's primary languages.

_____ When crossing streets, children must be accompanied by an adult. Everyone uses appropriate crossing precautions.

_____ When children ride in cars or buses, they use age-appropriate safety seats and/or belts. You have a policy that parents are expected to use these daily.

_____ An adult monitors each area of the playground at all times. Teachers do not use outdoor play time to talk among themselves. Unauthorized adults on the playground are asked to leave immediately.

Other outdoor safety checks for my program:

_____

_____

_____

_____

_____

You make safety a daily experience

Safety is much more than a hazard-free environment. Safety is what happens every day. This means setting some developmentally appropriate rules for children's behavior and teaching children how to be responsible for their own safe behavior.

Set up a few safety rules

Most likely you already have safety rules for children to follow in your program. **Write your rules here:**

_____

_____

_____

_____

Here are some tips about safety rules. **Compare these guidelines to your own rules.** Rules work best when they are stated in terms of what children should do, when there are just a few rules, and when they match the ages and competence of the children in your group.

If you put rules in terms of what children **should** do, children are much more likely to follow them.

Look back at your rules. How many tell children what to do (*rather than what not to do*)? _____ Do you often have trouble getting children to follow your rules? _____ If so, could it be that they don't know what they are supposed to do?

It is also important to have only a few important safety rules so children don't feel overwhelmed with too many. These are some basic rules that many programs for young children find helpful:

- We walk indoors.
- We take good care of our bodies.
- We are kind to other people.
- We take good care of our things.

These rules will need to be adapted to the ages of the children in your care. Younger children may need specific rules such as these:

- People are for loving. People are not for biting or hitting.
- We climb on the cushions and the climber, not on the sofa.

Somewhat older children may need specific rules such as these:

- Tricycles are only for riding on our playground roads. We never crash tricycles into anything.
- Sand is for sifting and pouring. Sand hurts when you get it in your eyes.

Older preschoolers will probably welcome the opportunity to set up some of their own rules. They might include this rule:

- One person may walk on the balance beam at a time.

If you work with older children, tell them you are thinking about rules. Ask them to make suggestions for rules that will help everyone in the group be safe. Write some of their suggestions here.

_____

_____

_____

_____

Children also need to know why a rule is necessary. Discuss with children why your group has rules. Children will surely ignore the rules if they don't know why the rules are needed. Even when children can tell you why it's not safe to stand on chairs or climb on tables, frequent reminders may be necessary.

Sometimes posters with pictures will work for preschoolers.

Use safe behaviors (good manners)

Of course, all the rules in the world and the safest equipment will not prevent every accident. **You also need a lot of common sense and a careful watch over children.**

Perhaps a child drops a bit of a banana on the floor. You notice it and ask the child to clean it up before someone slips. Another child can watch that no one else steps in the mess while it is being cleaned up.

Or you see that a bolt on the steering wheel on the playground is loose and the steering wheel wobbles. You tighten it up or ask the person responsible to do so before any more children are allowed to use it.

You must constantly check the environment and children's behavior. There really is no such thing as an accident. Accidents are actually preventable injuries!

Most of all, not only do you set rules, but you follow them, and you always use safe behavior yourself. You buckle up when you ride or drive in your car. You pull electrical cords from the socket by holding the plug, not the cord. You cut away from yourself when you use a sharp knife to make carrot sticks for snack. You **don't** go dashing across the street with a note a parent left behind! Children follow your example. When you do something safe—such as carrying scissors by the blades and walking slowly, for example—you point out to the children what you are doing and why. It won't be long until children will remind you when you are being unsafe.

Incorporate safety into the daily curriculum

Fire Prevention Week. Mr. Yuk. Community helpers. These are familiar topics for teachers of young children.

But how effective is it to talk about fire safety just one week each year? Children are constantly growing and learning new things. Safety needs to be a natural part of their daily lives. Children need to try out safety ideas in their play all the time—driving a fire truck, pretending to be doctors, or playing captain of a boat, for example.

While you may want to emphasize a topic for a week or two, you certainly want safety to happen in your group every day. Whenever you teach safety—which is constantly—keep these general guidelines in mind:

- Your purpose in teaching safety should be to **help children learn safe behaviors.** Fear is not a good teacher. Children shouldn't be taught in ways that intentionally frighten them. Instead, you want children to learn what to do to take care of themselves and their friends and family.

- The topics and the way you present them should **make sense to children.** Before you decide how to teach about a topic, talk with the children to find out what they already know. Ask open-ended questions such as: Who knows why we ...? What would you do if ...? Some topics are very abstract, such as electricity, yet children can learn how to be safe around electrical cords and appliances. They will learn more about how electricity works when they are older.

- Activities and materials should **be as**

realistic as safely possible. Children need to sit in safety seats and use safety belts. They need to cross streets again and again in the company of an adult. They need to use a disconnected telephone to practice pushing the buttons for the emergency number. Then, when children listen to stories, watch movies, and talk about being safe, these activities will make sense because children remember their **real** experiences.

Here are some specific teaching tips on favorite and appropriate safety topics for young children. **For each topic, jot down other ideas you have so you can share them later with your CDA Field Advisor.**

Everyday safety. Even the safest program has potential hazards for active children. A high tower of blocks crashes down on someone's head. Paint spills beneath the easel and someone slips. Toddlers fall down repeatedly as they learn to walk.

How do you reduce these risks? You always think how to make your home or classroom a safer place to be. You watch children and see what happens, then make changes. Perhaps a height limit needs to be set for block structures. Maybe soap flakes will thicken the paint so it doesn't drip. A flatter carpet might be safer for toddlers to practice walking. Always keep your eyes and ears open for safety's sake!

List some of your everyday concerns for indoor safety:

_____

_____

_____

_____

_____

Fire safety. Fire fascinates children. Its colors are pretty. It crackles. No wonder fires kill or injure thousands of children every year.

How do you help children learn to respect fire? Birthdays are good times to bring up fire safety in a natural way. Why do adults light the birthday candles? What happens to the match and candles after they burn?

Fall is a good time to talk about fire safety, when families rake leaves, light fireplaces, and heat their homes. Summer, too, with bonfires, fireworks, and barbecue grills, offers yet another opportunity.

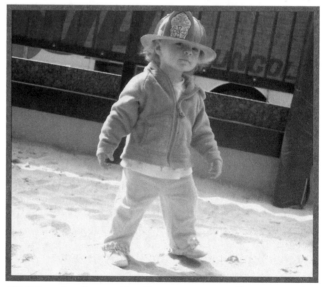

Children's dramatic play is an excellent way for them to work through their ideas about fire.

Preschoolers can learn to give matches they find to an adult so younger children won't accidentally start a fire. They can learn not to touch anything that has a fire in or near it—a stove, kerosene heater, campfire—so they won't get burned. They can learn and practice how to STOP, DROP, and ROLL, should their clothing catch on fire. They can memorize and practice phoning your local emergency number. Children of all ages can follow your program's procedures for a fire drill.

Children's dramatic play is an excellent way for them to work through their ideas about fires. The block corner should have a fire truck. Add some old pieces of hose, a medical kit, a blanket, and other similar props to the dramatic play area and let children explore their ideas about what happens in a fire.

If their play seems limited to siren noises, help them expand their play by asking questions such as "And then what happens when the firefighters arrive? What equipment do firefighters use?"

A visit to the fire station can be fun and a learning experience for children. If you plan it with the children's development in mind, this popular field trip is appropriate for preschoolers.

Talk with the firefighters ahead of time about the general principles of teaching about safety to young children. Ask whether children can climb into the driver's seat of a fire truck, try on boots and a helmet, or attempt to lift a hose—*real* experiences.

Your primary emphasis, however, should be on what children and grown-ups do to be safe with fire and why they do it.

In addition to your fire department, there may be other local resources for teaching fire safety. Perhaps the school PTA, your library, or a civic organization has a program or some books. Be sure to use only the parts of them that seem appropriate for young children.

Select stories that include men and women from various ethnic groups as firefighters.

A word of caution is in order here.

Many businesses, civic groups, and community leaders have teaching ideas, sometimes even complete curriculums, for teaching about safety topics. Many of these curriculums are not appropriate for young children. Some may try to scare children. Others may consist primarily of lectures or coloring books, rather than real experiences. Many fail to recognize that children learn best through active involvement.

You must rely on what you know about how young children learn when you select these materials. You may want to use only one or two good parts of such material.

Make a list here of other appropriate ideas you use to help children be fire safe.

_____

_____

_____

_____

_____

Crossing streets safely. Accidents involving motor vehicles are the leading cause of death for young children. You know how quickly a child chasing a ball can dart into the street. From the time children begin to crawl you can introduce ideas about keeping safe wherever there are cars or trucks. Find out what the children in your group know—just take a walk and see what children want to do when you approach the street. Then you will know where to begin.

Here are some things young children can learn about crossing streets:

- Walk only on sidewalks (*or in the opposite direction of traffic on the edge of the road if there are no sidewalks*).

- Always cross streets with an adult.

- Watch for cars about to leave the curb.

- Stop and look for cars coming from all directions before crossing streets or alleys.

- Take frequent walks to practice safe street crossing procedures.

Children may also enjoy using toy cars and miniature people as part of their pretend play. If crossing guards or police officers are familiar, children enjoy wearing orange belts or vests to play street crossing on the playground. As always, emphasize what children should do and make the experiences real. Then, when children are in elementary school, they will be ready to learn to cross streets by themselves.

Add your ideas for teaching street safety here.

_____

_____

_____

_____

_____

Safety seats and belts. Every state has regulations about child safety restraints. It is the LAW that every parent and teacher use the proper restraints for children—and themselves.

Despite such laws, children are often injured in low-speed accidents around town, because adults too often find excuses not to use proper restraints. Holding a child in your lap is no protection at all—in fact, it will only cause more injury in case of an accident, because the adult's heavy body would crush the child or the child would be thrown out the window.

How do children learn to be safe when riding in a car, van, or pickup truck? By parents and teachers giving them the experience of using a proper seat for every ride. Children who are expected and accustomed to riding in these seats do so willingly.

Infant seats face to the rear. Toddler seats face forward. There are special car booster seats for preschoolers. All of these seats are held in place with the car's safety belt. The child is held in place either by the car's belt (*on booster seats*) or by a separate belt system attached to the seat. One of the biggest problems, however, is that too many people do not properly install children's safety seats.

Your first step, then, is to make sure all the children regularly ride in safety seats. Next, bring the experience of safety seats into the programs. You may want to borrow a seat or find one at a garage sale. Make sure it is the right type for the children in your group. If you are a family childcare provider, you may need more than one for children of different ages. Put the seat in your play area so children can sit in it and see for themselves how good it feels to be safe.

Make sure your program's policy specifies that children arrive and leave in safety seats. Make sure your program's field trip policy includes a statement such as the one here: *Whenever transportation is provided for children in this program, they will be properly restrained. Adults driving or riding in the vehicle will also be properly restrained.*

Water safety. Children can drown in just a bit of water—a kitchen sink, wading pool, or toilet, for example. Although young children are never waterproof, even if they can swim, we can help them know what to do to be safe around water. Babies and toddlers need constant supervision and should never be left alone in a bath, at the beach, at a classroom water table, or even near a five-gallon bucket.

Toddlers and young preschoolers can make sure an adult is watching before they climb into a wading pool or splash in a big puddle. They can learn to walk (*not run*) near water.

Young children love to play boat. They can fish, search for treasure, or sail away to a sunny island. Build on this interest. They

can learn to buckle up in life preservers before they climb into a boat.

Older preschoolers can also learn what to do if they see someone who needs help in the water. Show children where to find lifeguards or other adults.

Check with your Red Cross or other water safety group in your community to find out what resources they have to help you teach children water safety.

Make a list here of water safety behaviors you can incorporate in your teaching.

_____

_____

_____

_____

Electrical safety. Most of us don't understand how electricity works, but we certainly should know and share with the children the need to be cautious with it.

As you watch and listen to the children in your group, you will probably see that crawling infants and curious toddlers would stick their fingers or anything else into a socket if they could. Therefore, every socket must have a safety cover.

Preschool children are still not capable of using electrical appliances alone, but with proper supervision they can learn how to plug something in and remove it from the socket. They can learn how to keep their fingers on the dials when they turn on the radio or television. They can learn not to touch electrical appliances that get hot—curling irons, heaters, electric skillets, toasters. Cooking projects are excellent times for helping children learn electrical safety when using appliances.

Write down some of your ideas for teaching children electrical safety.

_____

_____

_____

_____

_____

Care with hot and cold. Most children have probably accidentally been burned and will tell their friends how much it hurt. Others may have had their fingers stick to an ice cube or a frosty window. Start with children's experiences as a base for helping them figure out what things are too hot or too cold to touch.

Use warm and cool items that are safe to touch so children can feel the difference. For example, at lunch children could feel how warm their pizza is and how cool their milk is—take advantage of what naturally happens in the classroom.

Weather plays a big part in children's lives because it determines what they wear and what they play outdoors. Young children, especially infants and toddlers, will require sunscreen and hats to avoid burning even when they are outdoors for short periods of time. Shade should always be available on part of your outdoor play area so children can play in comfort in the summer. Drinks of water should be offered frequently.

In the winter, frostbite is a danger in cold climates. On bitterly cold, windy days you may need to stay indoors and find some vigorous games or activities. Usually children, even infants, can go out to play for at least a few minutes, though. Make sure they are warmly dressed but not so bundled up that they get hot and sweaty if they are active.

Older children may enjoy dressing up in clothes for hot or cold weather—in the opposite season. What fun a picnic at the beach would be in the middle of the winter! Doll clothes and dress-up clothes can also be seasonal.

What other ways do you have to help children understand hot and cold?

_____

_____

_____

_____

_____

Riding vehicles (_tricycles, low bikes, scooters_) safely. Another major cause of accidents for young children are cars in driveways that run over children who are riding or skating. Children are usually so short the driver cannot see them, or the child appears suddenly from behind a tree or another car.

Every good early childhood program has an assortment of riding vehicles. While your riding area is well supervised and away from traffic, children can still learn riding precautions to use when they ride on their own sidewalks.

Some programs even set up a miniature road with stop signs to help children develop good driving skills! At the very least, you will want children to learn not to drive their vehicle into another person or object.

Children should learn what to look for when a car is about to move: a driver climbs in, the engine goes *vroom*, lights may come on. With practice, while taking walks or riding on the sidewalk, children can identify these vehicles, and explain what they need to do to be safe around them: stop at every driveway or alley to look for a car that might move, never ride up a driveway unless an adult is with you. This topic is another excellent one to involve the children's parents and other community resources.

What kinds of activities can you think of to help children stay safe when they ride?

_____

_____

_____

_____

Poison and medicine safety. In every program for young children, both poisonous substances and medicines should be kept in a locked cabinet. Although you store these dangerous substances the same way, you handle discussions about them in two entirely different ways.

Poisons are presented as chemicals that are dangerous for your body—they can make you feel awful or even die. Children cannot always know what is dangerous, so they should be told, in the language most familiar to them, never to put anything into their mouth unless they ask an adult first.

Medicines, on the other hand, are chemicals that help our bodies get well when we swallow or apply the right amount. Children should never be misled into thinking medicines (*or vitamins*) are treats. Rather, if children have difficulty swallowing pills or liquids, mix them with drinks or food. The emphasis should always be on getting or staying well by taking good care of our bodies.

When children must be given medicine, it should be given to them by a teacher who speaks their primary language, with whom they feel comfortable, and according to written instructions from parents. The dosage and time of administration is written immediately on the child's medical record.

Children can also learn poison and medicine safety while playing doctor or hospital. Provide a variety of types of props: a stethoscope, bandages, crutches, prescription pads—whatever you can find that will allow children to pretend.

You and your program's health consultant probably have several other suggestions to help young children avoid poison and accept medicine when it is prescribed. **Write those ideas here.**

_____

_____

_____

_____

Playground safety. Children need to use playground safety every day. The design of your playground can either make it easy or difficult for children to be safe. The safety of the equipment, how securely it is anchored, and the depth of cushioning material cannot be compromised. The checklist earlier in this unit is a good place to start to identify areas where standards need to be met. Whenever possible, change the playground to make it safe rather than coming up with another rule for children.

Even when the areas are as safe as possible, your constant attention is needed on the playground. This is no time to socialize with other teachers.

Playground rules are used every day, not just on special occasions, so it is essential that children understand why you have the rules. Explain rules clearly, in children's primary language, when they are first introduced.

Each time you talk with a child about a rule, gently remind her or him about the reason. "Rachel, sand is for digging. Sand is not for throwing. It can get in people's eyes. Sand hurts our eyes very much."

List some ways your playground safety could be improved.

_____

_____

_____

_____

_____

Safety—and strangers. This topic is a broad one. It can cover everything from what a child should do when lost in a store to reporting abuse. No other topic arouses so much emotion. We all want children to be safe from physical or emotional abuse, but we don't want them to be so scared they avoid making new friends or refuse to talk with someone they can trust, either.

Much of what you decide to do about this topic will depend on your community and the feelings of the parents of the children in your program.

As a professional, your role is to help children grow up to become adults who feel good about themselves and who can make wise decisions. The tone of your voice, your posture, and what you say and do will all affect children.

Helping children know what to do when they are lost is a fairly simple problem compared to some of the other issues that fall in this category. Generally it is sufficient to read a good children's picture book that shows how a child handles the problem: Find a person who works in the store. Ask a police officer, zoo worker, or security guard for help. Stay where you are and wait for your parents to find you. After the story, children may want to act out what to do, draw pictures, or dictate stories about a time when they were lost.

Many materials have been developed to help children know what to do when approached by a stranger who makes them feel uncomfortable. An additional focus is needed, however, for we know that the greatest danger to very young children may actually be from people they know who abuse them either physically or emotionally.

Therefore, your primary goal will be to help children feel cared about, protected, and free to be honest about their feelings when they talk with you. They must know that they can trust you to take good care of them.

As part of this process, you can do and say things to inspire children's confidence and build their self-esteem. For example, you want children to be proud of their bodies and their functions, so you never make them feel ashamed of themselves. Dressing and using the toilet are excellent times to help children begin to learn proper names for their body parts. You can also help preschool children understand that the parts of their bodies covered by their swimming suits are private.

In addition, even young preschool children can begin to learn the difference between good touches and uncomfortable touches. They can learn how to say no to those touches that make them feel strange. Children also need to be told what to do when this happens: tell an adult that they trust. Children are not responsible for their own safety; adults must be responsible for keeping children safe and secure.

Select carefully from the children's books, videos, puppets, and other curriculum materials that are available so you choose only those that are appropriate for young children and sensitive to the cultures of the families with whom you work.

This is one topic you may want to discuss at length with your supervisor, the director, your licensing worker, or your CDA Field Advisor.

List here some of the concerns you have about how to help children deal with these harsh realities of life:

_____

_____

_____

You also need to know what to do if you see signs of potential child abuse or neglect. Knowing what those signs are and what to do about them will be discussed in Unit 4, Part 4 of *Essentials*. For now, it is important to know that each state requires that educators report any possible case.

Become familiar with the law and your program's policies concerning your responsibility regarding reporting suspected child abuse or neglect. **Find out how to report your concerns, and write the name and number here:**

_____

_____

_____

_____

_____

_____

Copy this information on your emergency telephone list, if it is not already there. Also add it and a copy of your program's policy regarding your responsibility to report child abuse to your Professional Resource File.

If the suspected case of child abuse or neglect is confirmed, you will want to seek the advice of a professional, such as a social worker or psychologist, about how to help the child and family handle such a delicate situation.

Now that we have covered some basic safety themes, are there others you have used or plan to use? **Make a list of them here:**

_____

_____

_____

_____

You are prepared for emergencies

What would you do if a child in your program:

- choked on a sandwich?
- fell and hit her head?
- was stung by a bee?
- got cut badly on a tricycle?
- burned himself on a hot pan?
- complained of ear pain?
- had a seizure?
- chewed on some plant leaves?

Old home remedies, common sense, and a first-aid kit are not enough.

As part of your training to become a CDA, you are expected to take a pediatric first-aid course (that includes treatment for a blocked airway and providing rescue breathing for infants and children) so that you will know what to do for these and other common types of accidents.

Contact your local Red Cross or other group and enroll in a class as soon as possible. You will be required to submit a copy of your certificate of completion to the Council before you can complete your CDA assessment.

Keep a record of your class and the original certificate in your Professional Resource File.

Record the dates of your class here:

_____

You are prepared for disasters, natural and otherwise

Safety is not something to take for granted. In addition to the issues covered here that apply to all programs, each geographic area has the potential for natural disasters such as floods, hurricanes, earthquakes or tornadoes. So every early childhood program needs disaster preparedness plans that are understood by everyone and practiced regularly.

Unfortunately, in our world today some of our worst disasters are not "natural"; they result from terrorism or criminal behavior. Therefore, emergency and disaster preparedness must include plans for dealing with such horrible incidents. An excellent model emergency preparedness plan was developed by Bright Horizons Family Solutions and is made available for any early childhood program through their website at www.brighthorizons.com (in the resource section). Programs may use and adapt this plan as long as they cite: Ready to Respond: Emergency Preparedness Plan for Early Care and Education Centers, Bright Horizons Family Solutions.

Just as terrorism and disasters put children at physical risk, they also threaten children's psychological safety and security. An exceptionally well-written booklet is available to help you help children in a post 9/11 world. The booklet, _What Happened to the World? Helping Children Cope in Turbulent Times_ by Jim Greenman

(2001), can be downloaded for free from the website: www.brighthorizons.com or purchased from NAEYC. A facilitator's guide is also available.

PART 2

How do you and your children stay healthy and well nourished?

You have probably heard a lot about how infectious diseases spread easily in group care for children. While outbreaks of illness can happen, children and teachers in good group care programs can improve their chances for staying well. How?

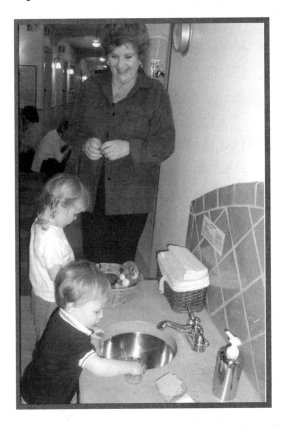

Children's health must be protected by the adults who care for them. Parents and staff share this responsibility.

You, the parents, and the children all work together. These are the main steps you must take:

Prevent illness and promote health

- Make sure all children are properly immunized. Keep child and staff health exam records current. Promptly and properly report contact with contagious diseases.

- Keep the environment clean. Clean and sanitize areas for diapering, toileting, and eating, as well as toys and furniture.

- Require correct hand washing procedures for adults and children.

- Serve only nutritious foods.

Just as you did in the last section on safety, you need to locate your state's regulations and/or Head Start Program Performance Standards for health and food service. Keep your copy handy and refer to it as you work through this unit.

Use the next four sections of the environment checklist to think about the primary ways in which you maintain a healthy environment. If you work in a group program, you probably are not in charge of some of the items listed, but you do need to know about them. If you are a family childcare provider, you are responsible for each one. Within each section, you will find ideas to present these health topics to children.

You monitor immunizations, health exams, and report diseases

Adults, who care for children, must protect their health. Parents and teachers share responsibility for preventing the spread of illness and promoting health.

Start your study of this critical aspect of child care by checking which points in the following list are already followed in your program. Add others that are especially appropriate. Then, look at the items you have not checked. This is where you can begin to improve children's health—and your own.

✓ Environment checklist: Immunizations, health exams, and diseases

_____ Your program complies with all state, local, and program regulations regarding child and staff health.

_____ When you contact parents about children's health, you share information in their primary language.

_____ Children are immunized according to the schedule recommended by the American Academy of Pediatrics before they are admitted to your program.

_____ At least once a year, you check children's immunization records to be sure they are current. Boosters as needed are recorded.

_____ Before children are enrolled, they have a health exam. You use the form provided by your licensing agent or another similar form. The form is signed by a health care professional. The health record includes any health conditions (*allergies or disabilities, for example*) and emergency contact information.

_____ Health exams are repeated each year either on the anniversary date of the child's enrollment or some other convenient date.

_____ Your program keeps a copy of all health exam records.

_____ Your own health exam is repeated each year. You keep a copy in your program records.

_____ Whenever you or a child in your group is exposed to a contagious disease (*pinkeye, impetigo, or chicken pox, for example*) you immediately report it to your supervisor (in a group program) or make a note of it (*in family child care*).

_____ You give parents information in their primary language about the incubation period, symptoms to watch for, and health care when a contagious disease is reported.

_____ You watch for signs that children may not be feeling well as they arrive and throughout the day.

_____ You and the children use a tissue once and then discard it in a closed container.

_____ Your program has a written policy about when sick staff and children may and may not attend. This policy conforms to the recommendations of the American Academy of Pediatrics (see p. 7-8 of *Healthy Young Children*). When you or the children are sick, you make no exceptions to this policy. This policy is given to parents upon enrollment. It is written in the parents' preferred language.

_____ You refer parents to medical services when appropriate. Whenever possible, the referral is made to a provider who can speak their language.

Other health practices appropriate for my program:

_____

_____

_____

_____

_____

_____

_____

_____

Some of us remember polio outbreaks or whooping cough. How fortunate we are that children can now be easily and quite safely immunized against these and other dangerous and contagious diseases such as measles and mumps. These diseases are not harmless childhood illnesses; they can cripple and kill,

but they are all preventable. Parents generally are very cooperative about scheduling immunizations and health exams. All children must be immunized against vaccine-preventable illnesses. Each January, the Centers for Disease Control and Prevention, the American Academy of Pediatrics, and the Academy of Family Practice jointly publish a new schedule of recommended vaccines. This schedule is available online at the websites of the Centers for Disease Control (www.cdc.gov) and the American Academy of Pediatrics (www.apa.org).

Comfort children who are ill

Sick children are cause for alarm in families. Parents are naturally concerned about their child's health, but also, children who are ill often cannot attend child care. As a result, parents often are forced to miss work, use leave time, and sometimes take a cut in their pay.

Too often, sick children are excluded from childcare programs unnecessarily. As Dr. Susan Aronson points out in *Healthy Young Children* (2002, p. 7), "There are only three reasons to exclude an ill child from a child care setting:

1. The illness prevents the child from participating comfortably in the program's activities, as determined by the childcare provider.
2. The illness makes the child have a greater need for care than the caregivers can manage without compromise to the care of other children in the group.

3. The child has a specific condition that is likely to expose others to a communicable disease."

When children must stay home because of illness, be sensitive to the parents' needs, too. Explain that in the long run keeping sick children at home usually means fewer sick days for everyone. Since it is difficult to make other child care arrangements on short notice, if possible, keep a list of caregivers willing to provide sick child care.

Your program's policy for excluding sick children needs to be carefully set and reviewed often to keep it up to date with medical advances and as in tune with parents' and children's needs as possible.

Sometimes when a child is ill, you become frustrated. Perhaps your biases about children's families come up: Lice, scabies, worms, and other conditions may seem to you to be a result of poor parenting or inadequate health care. Discuss any concerns you have about dealing with parents with your health consultant or licensing representative. Learn all you can about these conditions—and you will find that children from all types of homes can suffer from them. Stay well informed about common childhood diseases so you can concentrate on taking good care of children who do not feel well.

How do you help a child who becomes ill during the day? Just as you always do, you treat the child with dignity, handle any messes matter-of-factly, and offer as much comfort as you can. While you wait for the parent to arrive, you probably will want to give the child a place to rest away from the others in the group. Sometimes a child will want to stay close to you—perhaps resting her or his head in your lap. Try to provide as much comfort and attention as you can because, besides not feeling well, sick children are sometimes frightened.

Other children in the group will see how much comfort you provide. They will be reassured that they too will be cared for well should they get sick. Children treat each other as kindly as you treat them.

Your health is extremely important, too. Working with young children is exhausting. The stress is constant. Runny noses, diarrhea, and earaches are almost daily occurrences. Be sure you take good care of yourself: Get plenty of rest, eat well, wash your hands regularly, and stay calm!

What health areas do you want to improve in your program? List them here and follow through as soon as possible.

utilization of basic ointments

Dramatic play is an excellent way to help children learn about their health. Be sure you have plenty of props so they can relive their own experiences with being examined, immunized, and bandaged. Find some children's books, in English and other languages, to read together about what medical workers do. Field trips to a neighborhood clinic or a pediatrician's office might be helpful, too.

You keep the environment clean

Cleanliness is essential if you and the children are to stay healthy. If your environment is clean, dry, and filled with fresh air you greatly improve your chances of staying well. **Check each item on this list that applies to your program.**

✓ **Environment checklist: Keep the environment clean**

_____ Your program meets all state and local requirements for sanitation.

_____ If you prepare and store food, all state and local regulations are met.

_____ Indoor and outdoor areas are clean, dry, and well lighted. Natural light is let in whenever possible.

_____ Preschool children are expected to clean up their own spills, paper scraps, and other minor messes. You supervise their efforts.

_____ You use paper cups or child-sized drinking fountains for drinking water.

_____ Trash is emptied daily.

_____ Clean and sanitize bathrooms daily with bleach solution (*see page 125*).

_____ Spills of body fluids (*blood, urine, vomit, feces*) are cleaned with bleach solution. You wear disposable gloves when contact with blood or blood-containing fluids is likely, or when cleaning surfaces contaminated with blood or body fluids.

_____ You assign individual cubbies for children's personal belongings. If possible, each child keeps an extra set of clothing in her or his cubby (or you keep an extra set on hand). Each piece of clothing is labeled with the child's name. The child's name is easy to see on the outside of the cubby, and is written in both English and the child's home language.

_____ Dress-up clothing and accessories are washed or replaced weekly.

_____ Children's bedding is washed weekly. Only one child uses bedding between washings.

_____ Cots, cribs, and mats are washed whenever they are soiled. They are labeled with children's names.

_____ You ventilate indoor spaces with fresh air daily.

_____ Indoor heat and humidity levels are comfortable and healthy.

_____ You know where to find information on how to clean the environment in the event lice or other similar problems are discovered.

List your resources here:

_____

_____

_____

_____

_____

If you care for infants or toddlers:

_____ Infant equipment is cleaned with bleach solution (*see page 125*) regularly.

_____ Toys that infants put in their mouths are washed with bleach solution (*see page 125*) after each child's use.

_____ Bottles are never set down on the floor.

_____ Children's wet or soiled clothes are sealed in labeled, individual plastic bags so parents can launder them.

_____ Disposable diapers are thrown away in a covered container that can be opened with a step pedal and lined with a plastic bag, and is emptied daily.

_____ Cloth diapers are used only for children who are unable to use disposables; they are sealed in individual labeled, plastic bags for parents to launder them.

_____ The diaper-changing area has one of these two types of covers:

1. a plastic cover that can be washed with bleach after every diaper change, **or**

2. a paper cover that is discarded after every diaper change.

_____ Several changes of clothing are available for children who are learning to use the toilet.

Other hygiene practices appropriate for my program:

_____

_____

_____

_____

If you did not check every item in this section of the checklist, take steps to make your program a healthier place to be. You may need to meet with your director to share this information and work out a plan to improve the cleaning in your program. Unless these guidelines are followed, you, the other staff, and the children are at risk for spreading illness.

Bleach solution for disinfecting surfaces

Add 1 tablespoon of bleach to 1 quart of water
(¼ cup of bleach per 1 gallon of water) .

- Mix a fresh solution each day.

- Use it to disinfect surfaces that have been cleaned.

- Dispense from a spray bottle that you keep out of reach of children.

- Wet the entire surface until glistening and leave solution on the surface at least 2 minutes. Dry with a paper towel or allow to air dry.

Preschool children can certainly help you in your efforts. You can label their cubbies with their name and a picture they can easily identify. This way, they can put their belongings away by themselves. They can use sponges and water to wipe up their own messes. They can put their trash in the wastebasket when they finish eating. They can change their wet clothing and put on dry clothes. These are good health habits they will use the rest of their lives.

List some other similar responsibilities preschool children can take to keep your area clean:

_____

_____

_____

_____

You take good care of yourself, other staff, and children

Many other good personal habits are also a part of your daily routine. Let's look at what you and the children can do to take good care of your bodies—and increase everyone's chances of staying well.

✓ Environment checklist: Children and staff take good care of themselves

_____ Everyone should wash hands at the following times:

· **Upon arrival** for the day or when moving from one childcare group to another.

· **Before and after** eating, handling food or feeding a child; giving medication; playing in water that is used by more than one person.

· **After** diapering, using the toilet or helping a child use the toilet; handling bodily fluid (mucus, blood, vomit) from sneezing, wiping and blowing noses, from mouths, or from sores; handling uncooked food, especially raw meat and poultry; handling pets and other animals; playing in sandbox; cleaning or handling the garbage.

_____ Use liquid soap, running water, rubbing, and paper towels to dry your hands and turn off faucets (*see the poster on page 127*). Hand lotion is readily available for staff.

_____ Teach children and adults to sneeze and cough away from other people and toward the floor—or if someone is crawling on the floor, "give germs the cold shoulder" by sneezing or coughing on your own shoulder.

_____ You all brush your teeth after eating meals. Individual toothbrushes are labeled. Brushes are stored in an open container. Bristles do not touch each other.

Wash your hands properly and frequently.

Use liquid soap and running water.

Rub your hands vigorously for at least 10 seconds.

Wash everywhere:

- backs of hands
- wrists
- between fingers
- under fingernails

Rinse well.

Dry hands with paper towel.

Turn off water using a paper towel, not your clean hands.

Help children learn the proper way to wash their hands too.

Reprinted with permission from: Aronson, S. (ed.) with Spahr, P., *Healthy Young Children: A Manual for Programs, 4th Edition*, 2002. p. 12.

_____ At least one rest period/naptime is provided for older toddlers and pre-school children.

_____ Children are shown how and expected to use good toilet habits: wiping properly, lifting and lowering the seat, aiming well.

_____ Children do not share personal items. They use their own hairbrushes, combs, and hats.

_____ Children and adults wear clothing appropriate for the weather.

_____ Children play outdoors at least once in the morning and once in the afternoon.

If you care for infants or toddlers:

_____ You wash your hands after diapering each child and before and after feeding a child.

_____ You follow the specific procedures for changing diapers (*see pages 132–133*) **every time** you change a diaper. Post procedures in every language spoken by the staff and parents.

_____ Children take naps on their own schedules—they sleep when they are tired.

_____ Children who are learning to take responsibility for using the toilet are treated with respect. They are never shamed or made to feel like failures when they have accidents.

Other self-care procedures appropriate for my program: _____

_____

_____

_____

Teaching good personal habits

During their early years children are developing good personal habits to use all of their lives. They are learning to be proud of their bodies and their skills. Nearly every minute of every day will be an opportunity for children to learn and practice how to take good care of their bodies.

Hand washing. Many people are lazy about hand washing—it seems like such a bother. But did you know that hand washing is the *one best way* to prevent the spread of disease? It's true.

Hand washing is the first line of defense against infectious disease. Washing your hands thoroughly is more effective than anything else you do to keep the environment clean because so many types of diseases are spread by touching infected areas and then touching parts of your body or food.

If you wash your hands frequently and properly, children will follow your example. You simply **must** wash your hands often—especially in the winter, when it will seem as if you are wiping a runny nose every minute. Use lots of hand lotion and keep telling yourself how well you and the children will stay. Once you learn and practice proper hand washing techniques, you will never again be comfortable not washing your hands when necessary.

"This is the way we wash our hands to stay healthy! Bubbles, lots of rubbing, rinsing, and dry with a towel." Children love to play in water, so with guidance about the correct technique, teaching hand washing is relatively easy! Then just be there to supervise each time children wash their hands.

What else can you do to get children involved in hand washing? _Turn handwashing into a song / puppet skit._

Tooth brushing. Most children think it's fun to brush teeth—if the adults who teach them make it fun. And how good it feels afterward!

Be sure you and the children brush teeth after snacks as well as meals, especially if you eat sweet or sticky foods such as dried fruits or cheese. After your group finishes eating, make it part of your daily routine to brush your teeth.

You can use a sanitized, styrofoam egg carton, turned over, with holes punched in each hill, to store the brushes. Each child must have his or her own toothbrush, labeled by name and never shared! Store brushes so they stay clean and open to the air. The bristles should not touch any surface. Brushes should be replaced as they get worn or after someone has been sick. Cartons can be replaced weekly. Ask parents to save them for you.

A sink is not necessary for brushing teeth and can be difficult for a group. Instead, give each child a paper cup of water to wet the toothbrush, take a mouthful of water to swish and then spit the water back into the cup (Aronson, 2002, p.75).

Young children need to take good care of their baby teeth. If you work with older preschoolers, you even may get to share the delight of those first loose teeth. There are some excellent children's stories to read together about losing teeth. Maybe you will want to make a poster to record children's teeth lost or take pictures of those toothless grins. Remember, this is one clear sign that children are growing up.

Children are naturally interested in their teeth. You can find lots of ways to help children care for their baby and permanent teeth. Look at teeth in the mirror. Make a papier-mâché model tooth and use a large brush to practice brushing. Carve a jack-o-lantern with lots of strong teeth.

Find a dentist who is especially good with children and take a field trip to her or his office to help children feel more comfortable when they go for their checkups.

Children can also learn that what they eat can help keep their teeth healthy: drink lots of milk, avoid sweets and sticky things. Work with parents to encourage them to help children take good care of their teeth.

Professional organizations for dentists and hygienists sponsor a variety of activities. Find out what is available in your community. Select materials and activities that are appropriate and non-stereotypic for young children.

If possible, try to locate professionals in this field who are from some of the cultural groups or speak the language(s) of the children in the class.

List some special activities that you want to do with your children to help them learn to take good care of their teeth.

Get plenty of rest. Most children have such a good time playing that they don't want to take a nap. Infants, on the other hand, can fall asleep in the midst of the wildest commotion. Infants should always be allowed to sleep whenever they need to—adjust your schedule to theirs rather than expecting babies to adjust to you. Always put babies down on their backs to sleep and check on them at least every five minutes if they are in a separate room. Don't rely on a baby monitor to supervise sleeping babies.

Watch toddlers and preschoolers, and try to follow their natural nap schedule as much as possible as well.

A good schedule for early childhood programs alternates quiet and active times throughout the day. Children need both.

After a busy morning, children are usually ready to take it easy for a while. Generally, naps will take place sometime shortly after lunch and a trip to the bathroom. Lights can be turned out to get children in the mood. Some teachers like to read a soothing story or play soft music. Some sing quietly or gently rub children's backs to calm them.

What soothing techniques have you found work best for you and your children?

_____

_____

_____

_____

_____

If you are a family childcare provider, or even on the staff of many programs, naptime may be your only break. Be sure you get some rest, too!

Diaper changing. Diapers are a fact of life if you care for even one infant or toddler. Follow the steps on pages 132 to 133 **every time** to make it a safe and sanitary procedure.

How you treat children during diapering is also important. Don't view diapering as drudgery or lost time. Instead, look upon it as a special close time for just you and the baby. Be playful and talkative. Explain what you are doing with the baby in gentle tones. Play "This Little Piggy." Point out the names of body parts: "What strong legs you have. You can really kick them hard." Use the child's home language whenever possible during these important times. Right from birth, children will begin to learn to respect their bodies and to feel good about themselves—if that is your attitude. Diapering is one of the best ways to make sure children learn pride in their bodies.

Toilet learning. Few milestones of life have received as much attention as learning to use the toilet! Most parents are eager to no longer have the expense and hassle of diapers. They want to brag to their friends about their child's early toilet habits. No wonder they are in a hurry for their child to learn to use the toilet. You and the child's parents must work closely together during this critical period. Cultural groups handle this life transition in various ways, so sensitivity to families and regular communication are especially important.

Notice we call it toilet learning, not toilet training. That is because children learn to use the toilet just as they learn everything else: They show interest, their bodies are mature enough, and loving adults set the stage for positive events.

Sometime between the ages of 2 and 3, most children want to be dry. Their interest is easy to notice. They may follow others to the toilet or even walk into the bathroom on their own. Watch for children who stay dry for several hours and/or who indicate they are going to the bathroom by making a face, noises, or standing in a certain way. Your observations will give you the information you need to decide when a child is ready. Ask parents to help you look for signs.

Learning to use the toilet is a big step for children and parents. Few things you do with children require as much coordination and cooperation with parents. Few stages are treated with such high expectations.

Unless a child's body is ready, successfully learning to use the toilet is very difficult. Physical, intellectual, emotional, and social maturity—and practice—are all necessary.

When children are "ready," they can learn to use the toilet independently. But what is often their biggest hurdle? Their clothes. Buckles, belts, buttons, tights, zippers—what a struggle! It's no wonder children end up putting on new dry clothes each time they go to the bathroom! You may need to ask parents to choose clothes that are easy for a toddler to take off quickly. Sweat pants, shorts, and clothes with elastic waists are great.

When clothes are no problem, children quite readily learn to lift the lid, sit down, wipe themselves, get dressed, and flush the toilet. Children may need to watch you demonstrate with a doll or see how a friend does it, but before long they remember every step. There are also several good children's books that you might read with one or two children at a time.

Potty chairs are probably the easiest for children to learn to use because of their just-right size. But potty chairs must be washed and sanitized after each use, which makes them difficult to use in a group care situation. Slightly older children may benefit from a step stool firmly placed in front of the toilet. Select the type of arrangement that works best for the children, given the space and time you have.

How you set the stage for children to feel good about toileting makes a big difference. You have surely heard parents say things to their children such as "You bad boy. You got your pants wet twice today!" or "What a mess you made. Why do you create so much work for me?"

If you were a child, how would these comments make you feel? Not worth much. A failure. Not what we want children to feel when they are growing up!

If you have ever made a child feel bad for having wet or soiled pants, resolve never to do it again. Instead, think of ways you can support children during this major challenge of their young lives. Most parents will follow your example. Explain to those who are less sensitive to their children's needs that the process will probably take longer and children may have other problems unless you both help children feel good about toileting.

How to change a diaper

Diapering and toileting carry distinct health risks to children and adults. Diligence in frequent, proper handwashing and good personal hygiene habits are the first line of defense against the spread of infectious diseases caused by fecal contamination. The following steps to diaper changing are provided as a daily reminder:

1. Get organized.

- Before you bring the child to the diaper changing area, wash your hands and gather what you need: a nonabsorbent paper liner large enough to cover the changing surface from the child's shoulders to beyond the child's feet, a fresh diaper, clean clothes (if you need them), wipes removed from the container for cleaning the child's bottom, a plastic bag for any soiled clothes, disposable gloves (if they will be used), and a dab of any diaper cream (if the child uses it) on a corner of the disposable paper

- Put on the disposable gloves, if you use them.

2. Avoid contact with soiled items, and always keep a hand on the child.

- Carry the child to the changing table, keeping soiled clothing away from you. Be sure to keep a hand on the child.

- If the child's feet and clothing cannot be kept out of the diaper during the changing process, completely remove the child's shoes, socks, and those clothing items so the child does not contaminate them with the contents of the diaper.

- Put any soiled clothes in a plastic bag, and securely tie it to send the soiled clothes home.

3. Clean the child's diaper area.

- Place the child on the diaper change surface, and unfasten the diaper but leave the soiled diaper under the child.

- Use disposable wipes to clean the skin on the child's bottom. Remove stool and urine from front to back, and use a fresh wipe each time. Put the soiled wipes into the soiled diaper or directly into a plastic-lined, hands-free, covered can.

4. Remove the soiled diaper without contaminating any surface not already in contact with stool or urine.

- Fold the soiled surface inward

- Put the soiled diaper into the covered, plastic-lined step can.

- If reusable cloth diapers are used, put the soiled cloth diaper and its cover in a plastic bag or into the plastic-lined, hands-free, covered can to give to the parents or the laundry service without dumping or rinsing contents.

- Check for spills under the child. If there are any, fold over the disposable paper under the child's feet so that a fresh un-soiled paper surface is now under the child's clean bottom.

- If gloves were used, remove them and put them into the plastic-lined, hands-free, covered can. Whether or not gloves were used, use a disposable wipe to clean the surfaces of the caregiver's hands and another to clean the child's hands, and put the wipes into the plastic-lined step can.

5. Put on a clean diaper and dress the child.

- Apply any necessary ointments or creams to the child's diaper area.

- Note and plan to report any skin problems such as redness.

- Slide a fresh diaper under the child, adjust and fasten it. If pins are used, place your hand between the child and the diaper when inserting the pin.

6. Wash the child's hands, and return the child to a supervised area.

- Use soap and water at a sink to wash the child's hands, if you can. If a child is unable to stand and is too heavy to hold safely for handwashing at a sink, use the following method for handwashing:

  (a) Wipe the child's hands with a damp paper towel or a clean disposable wipe.

  (b) Discard the towel or the wipe into the plastic-lined, hands-free, covered can.

7. Clean and sanitize the diaper changing surface.

- Dispose of the paper liner used on the diaper changing surface into the plastic-lined step can.

- Clean any visible soil from the changing surface with soap and water or detergent and water.

- Spray a sanitizing solution to wet the entire changing surface (e.g.... one tablespoon household bleach to one quart of water. Mix fresh daily.)

- Put the spray bottle of sanitizer away and leave the bleach sanitizer on the surface for at least two minutes. The surface can then be wiped dry or left to air dry.

8. Wash your hands and record in the child's daily log.

- Wash your hands using soap and running warm water.

- Use a paper towel to turn off the water faucet.

- Use hand lotion to keep your hands from becoming dry and chapped.

- Record in a daily log what was in the diaper and any problems such as diarrhea, an unusual odor or blood in the stool, or any skin irritations. Report as necessary·

Reprinted with permission from: "How to Change a Diaper Instruction" from *Keeping Healthy Parents, Teachers, and Children* brochure (adapted from *Healthy Young Children: A Manual for Programs*), 2003

What words should you use when you talk about toileting? Some experts suggest you use only *urinate, bowel movement,* or other technical terms. Very few parents feel comfortable with these words. You and each child's parents need to agree on the general method of toilet learning. In addition, you need to respect the parent's wishes for what they want to call toileting functions: *peepee, tinkle, go potty, poop . . .* the list is practically endless.

Try to be flexible and accept anything that is not offensive. Children in a group will generally all start using the same word—one that is fun to say, perhaps.

On the other hand, how do you handle crude language? Talk privately and calmly with the child: "We don't use words like that here. Those words offend some people." Then, if you don't pay much attention to such language it will be used less often.

Because toilet learning is so often abused by adults, let's review some things that an early childhood professional would never do when helping children learn these important self-control skills:

NEVER rush a child.

NEVER shame a child.

NEVER tease a child.

NEVER punish a child.

Instead, encourage toilet learning when children are mature enough. Help them feel good about their bodies and growing up. Praise and encouragement are much more effective than ridicule.

Dressing. How grown up children feel to be able to get undressed and then dressed by themselves! Even before their first birthdays, babies delightedly pull off their own socks and shirts. They can push their arms through sleeves when they get dressed, too.

Children love to take clothes on and off—especially off. Give them plenty of opportunities with dress-up clothes that have large buttons, big zippers, snaps, and ample space to squirm around in. Buckle boots or large-laced work shoes are intriguing. Clasps on purses are fun to latch and unlatch.

You can probably think of many more everyday objects from many cultures that give children the practice they need with dressing. You certainly do not need to make or buy special boards or books for this purpose.

The changing seasons also offer many opportunities to talk about weather, clothing, and what we each do to stay well. Rainy days, snow, wind—children love the variety in weather. Be sure you all go outdoors at least once in the morning and once in the afternoon. The fresh air is good for your health and invigorating to the spirit.

As children grow, make sure they take increasing responsibility for dressing themselves. Each day you go outdoors. Paint smocks may need to be hooked and unhooked. Finger plays such as "The Mitten Song" are perfect to assist toddlers as they gain these valuable self-help skills. Be sure you allow ample time for children to get themselves ready. And have hooks labeled with names for each child's coat and hat or swimming suit and towel.

Never do for children what they can do for themselves—and be sure to encourage children to help each other whenever possible. Dressing is an excellent way to learn cooperation.

The Mitten Song

Thumbs in the thumb place
Fingers all together.
This is the song we
Sing in mitten weather.

—Mary Louise Allen

List some new dress-up clothes you want to add so the children can practice dressing:

_____

_____

_____

_____

Ask parents whether they have any of these items they could donate.

Body image. Everything you do with children is intended to build their self-confidence, to lead them toward more skills, and to foster their love of learning. Children's own bodies are one of the most fascinating learning tools you have.

Each child grows each day. Children love to look at their baby pictures and pictures of their families. Hang some on the wall at the children's eye level. Together, notice how children look a lot like their parents, grandparents, or others in their ethnic group. But don't overplay family resemblance if your group includes children who are adopted. Make charts to mark children's gains in weight and height. Children love to play with younger friends and help them learn new skills. In the process, the older children see just how much they really can do.

Two areas of child development that often are cause for discomfort with adults are children's growing awareness of themselves as girls or boys and masturbation. Sometimes children hold their genitals when they need to go to the bathroom. They are always curious about other children's bodies. Their curiosity is natural and healthy.

In good early childhood programs, young girls and boys share bathrooms because of the opportunity it presents for them to feel comfortable with other children and with their own sexual identity.

Bathrooms are excellent places to learn how our bodies work and what parts of our bodies are called. Help children feel good about their bodies. Talk about them in a natural tone.

Older children may compare their bodies. In one childcare center, a boy bragged, "Ha, ha, I have a penis and you don't!" The 5-year-old girl quickly countered, "Yes, but I have a vagina and I can have babies when I grow up."

Children need to feel good about being a boy or being a girl. Help them see that each has its advantages. And that men and women can be parents, have jobs, and do household chores.

You will have many other natural opportunities to help children feel strong and competent as boys or girls. If necessary, encourage girls to use blocks and boys to nurture baby dolls or pets. Never assign tasks that require strong muscles, for example, to only boys. Cooking experiences are shared equally. Read only books in which boys and girls are viewed as equals. We'll talk more about this important issue of sexism in Part 3 of this unit.

Sometime during their first few months children discover how good it feels to touch their bodies. Masturbation during the early years is usually nothing to be concerned about. It is best to gently remind children who masturbate to do so in private.

If a child masturbates so frequently that many opportunities to play or rest are missed, you may have cause for concern. Bring your concerns to your supervisor or health consultant. Your observations about the child will be essential in determining how to handle any problem.

If you are embarrassed to talk about children's bodies with them, to help them feel good about being a boy or a girl, or to see a child masturbating once in a while before falling asleep, for example, **discuss your feelings with your CDA Field Advisor.** You will need to be able to deal with these topics comfortably in order to be a good teacher. Young children should never be made to feel ashamed of themselves, and they will pick up your attitudes.

List any topics you want to discuss about children's bodies that make you feel uncomfortable:

_____

_____

_____

_____

You will have a chance to discuss these further during Seminar.

You eat healthy foods

In good early childhood programs, we not only want to prevent injury and illness, we want to promote health. One of the best ways to stay healthy and to feel good is to eat the most nutritious foods. Let's see how to fix and serve healthy snacks and meals in your program to contribute to children's overall health. Even if children only are in your group for a morning snack, it should be a nutritious one that helps them eat a balanced diet for the entire day.

Why waste your money on sugar, salt, and other chemicals that don't contribute to children's healthy development? Sodas, cookies, and other treats do not promote growth lifetime of being undernourished and overweight.

Use this next section of the environment checklist to improve the quality of the foods you serve in your program.

✓ Environment checklist: You eat healthy foods

_____ You meet all state or program requirements for food service preparation and selection.

_____ You keep a list of children's food allergies in a prominent place and written in all languages spoken by parents and teachers.

_____ You plan snacks in advance. You see snacks as part of children's overall daily nutrition.

_____ You try to offer a wide variety of fruits, vegetables, proteins, milk products, and breads.

✓ Environment checklist: You eat healthy foods

_____ If you prepare meals for the children, you plan the menu in advance. Each meal includes a fruit, vegetable, protein, milk, and bread.

_____ You post the menus, in as many languages as needed, for parents to see.

_____ The foods you serve represent a wide variety of cultural preferences. You frequently serve favorite foods of families in the program. You respect dietary restrictions and parent preferences.

_____ If children bring their own lunches, you store lunches properly until they are eaten. You send leftovers home so parents will know what their children ate.

_____ You serve only real, 100% juices (no soft drinks, no sugary substitutes).

_____ Vegetables and fruits are fresh whenever possible.

_____ You select foods that are low in sugar, salt, and other added chemicals. You read and compare labels so you can choose those with the most food value.

_____ When canned fruits are used, you select only those packed in juice, not syrup.

_____ You serve child-sized portions. You prepare foods with lots of appeal to children: finger foods, colorful combinations, different textures.

_____ Plates, cups, and utensils are scaled to children's size. Glass is never used.

_____ You adapt utensils and menus as needed to help children with disabilities feed themselves as easily as possible.

_____ You encourage children to try a bite of a new food. They are never forced to clean their plates.

_____ You never use food as a punishment or as a reward.

_____ You serve meals group style. All of you eat the same thing. Children are given as much time as they need to finish eating.

_____ Meals and snacks are pleasant times for friendly conversation.

_____ Children help prepare and cook food as often as possible.

_____ You model and expect children to use appropriate table behaviors: pleasant conversation, saying "please" and "thank you," and other manners specific to their culture.

_____ Foods are never wasted by using them as art materials.

If you care for infants or toddlers:

_____ You engage in practices that encourage and support mothers to breastfeed their babies. You follow any directions given by the child's parents or medical care provider regarding breast milk, formula, or solid foods.

_____ Infants are always held in an inclined position when they are given a bottle. Bottles are never propped. You use feeding time to develop a close, warm relationship.

_____ You tell parents what their children ate during the day.

_____ When children begin to sit in a high-chair or at a table, you feed each child individually. Children are never fed as if they were a production line.

_____ You help children learn to feed themselves by offering finger foods as they are added to the child's diet. You expect messes and do not criticize the child for making a mess. Ample time is allowed for self-feeding.

_____ Children learn appropriate table behavior as they are able.

_____ You do not serve food that babies or toddlers could choke on.

Other nutrition practices appropriate for my program:

_____

_____

_____

_____

Learn principles of good nutrition

Food contains vitamins, minerals, and other substances that contribute to healthy growth. No vitamin pill can take the place of a wide variety of naturally good foods! One of the best sources of current information about food and nutrition is your county Cooperative State Research, Education and Extension Service.

Locate their website to find information on nutrition for children.

Find materials in several languages if you need them. If you have any children who are vegetarians, request information about the special requirements to prepare nutritious foods for vegetarians. You will probably be astounded at how much information is available on this and other websites listed in the resource section.

Post the information on your bulletin board for parents. Keep these materials in your personal files so you will use the ideas often. **Write the website address here and add it to your Professional Resource File as well.** Cooperative State Research, Education & Extension Service:

_____

As you noted on the checklist, meals should always contain a fruit, vegetable, source of protein (_meat or cheese, for example_), bread, and milk. Snacks should always contain at least two of these items, and should contribute to the child's complete daily nutritional needs. The list below of especially good foods will help you get started with your selections.

You should get into the habit of reading labels, too, because even prepared foods which seem quite similar can be very different in food values. You may be astonished at what is contained in different kinds of food.

Dietary Guidelines for Young Children

The U.S. Department of Agriculture (USDA) and the Department of Health and Human Services (DHHS) publish dietary guidelines for all Americans, age 2 and older. A *Food Guide Pyramid for Young Children* that is a daily guide for children 2 to 6 years is available online at **www.usda.gov/cnpp/KidsPyra/** or from the USDA Center for Nutrition Policy and Promotion, Food Guide Pyramid for Young Children, 1120 20th St, NW, Suite 200, North Lobby, Washington, DC 20036.

When planning meals, use the Food Pyramid to decide the types and portions of food you provide for young children. Also use the guidelines as a basis for nutrition education of children and parents.

Select three or four items that you typically serve for snack. List the items on the chart on page 140. Read the labels and write down the per-serving levels of these common ingredients. Your Field Advisor will verify that you have completed this exercise.

Especially good foods

These foods are some of the best sources of balanced nutrition within each category. Young children should have one food from each category at each meal and one food from any two categories for snack.

Protein—Fish, poultry, meat, cheese, eggs, tofu

Grains—Whole grain, enriched breads, crackers, Melba toast; starchy vegetables (*peas, beans, corn, potatoes*); corn tortillas, breads; whole grain, enriched, cereals without added sugar; rice

Milk—Milk, cheese: cream, ricotta, hard, cottage; yogurt

Fruit—Bananas, nectarines, melons, cherries, berries, oranges, apricots, grapefruit, peaches, tangerines

Vegetables—Broccoli, cauliflower, spinach, carrots, Brussels sprouts, tomatoes, lima beans

FOOD Guide PYRAMID
for Young Children

WHAT COUNTS AS ONE SERVING?

GRAIN GROUP
1 slice of bread
1/2 cup of cooked rice or pasta
1/2 cup of cooked cereal
1 ounce of ready-to-eat cereal

VEGETABLE GROUP
1/2 cup of chopped raw or cooked vegetables
1 cup of raw leafy vegetables

FRUIT GROUP
1 piece of fruit or melon wedge
3/4 cup of juice
1/2 cup of canned fruit
1/4 cup of dried fruit

MILK GROUP
I cup of milk or yogurt
2 ounces of cheese

MEAT GROUP
2 to 3 ounces of cooked lean meat, poultry, or fish.
1/2 cup of cooked dry beans, or 1 egg counts as 1 ounce of lean meat. 2 tablespoons of peanut butter count as 1 ounce of meat.

FATS AND SWEETS
Limit calories from these.

Four-to 6-year-olds can eat these serving sizes. Offer 2-3-year-olds less, except for milk. Two to 6-year-old children need a total of 2 servings from the milk group each day.

U.S. Department of Agriculture
Center for Nutrition Policy and Promotion
January 2000
Program Aid 1651

Nutrition comparison of typical snack foods

Names of four typical snacks

1. _Cereal Bar_ 2. _Cheese & Crackers_ 3. _fruit_ 4. _Yogurt Graham Cracker_

**Per serving
levels of:**

Protein _____ _____ _____ _____

Carbohydrates
(*sugar/starch*) _____ _____ _____ _____

Fat _____ _____ _____ _____

Iron _____ _____ _____ _____

Vitamin C _____ _____ _____ _____

Vitamin A _____ _____ _____ _____

Sodium (*salt*) _____ _____ _____ _____

Calories _____ _____ _____ _____

Which one offers the best nutritional value?

_____

_____

_____

_____

_____

_____

Next time you purchase foods or plan menus, check the labels first. Avoid large quantities of sugar, salt, and fat. Try to select whole grains, enriched flours, fresh fruits and vegetables, and other foods that offer the most nutrition for the money and the calories. Don't be misled by "health food" or "natural" claims—read the label and compare nutrition.

Here are some good ideas for snacks and lunches to get you off to a good start. Ask parents for suggestions to be sure you include familiar ethnic foods. Special provisions will need to be made for infants just beginning to eat solid food and for children who have allergies, special food requirements, or dietary preferences. See whether parents can regularly come in and prepare foods from their culture with children. **Practice meal and snack planning by adding your favorite ideas to this list. You will share them with the others in your CDA Seminar.**

Meals and snacks are pleasant times for friendly conversation.

Yummy snacks

Celery stuffed with low-fat cream cheese
Fruit juice

French toast squares
Apple slices

Orange sections
Bagel quarters

Carrot sticks
Yogurt dip with cinnamon or orange juice

Melted cheese
French bread squares or tortilla chips

Banana milkshake
Graham crackers

Deviled eggs
Broccoli trees

Your ideas:

_____

_____

_____

_____

_____

_____

_____

_____

Favorite lunches

Macaroni and cheese

Broccoli

Baked apple with raisins

Milk or juice

English muffin pizza

Green beans

Peach slices

Milk or juice

Chicken taco with corn tortilla (*chicken chunks, lettuce, tomato, shredded cheese*)

Banana

Milk

Tuna melt (*whole-wheat bread, tuna, melted cheese on top*)

Greens

Melon chunks

Milk

Scrambled eggs

Stewed or sliced tomatoes

Orange slices

Milk

Your ideas:

_____

_____

_____

_____

Teach good habits with food

Your example is your primary teaching tool. If you eat healthy foods, have a positive attitude about trying new foods, and use appropriate table manners, the children in your group will soon follow suit.

Too often, children see parents or teachers gulp down a cup of coffee and a donut for breakfast, for example. Or we may reach for something in front of the children instead of asking to have it passed to you. All of us have bad habits either in what or how we eat.

List some of your bad food habits here.

_____

_____

_____

_____

_____

Each week, choose one bad habit to get rid of, and then do it. You are only hurting yourself and the children you care for with your behavior.

Instead, resolve to set a good example for children.

Every person needs three healthy meals each day. Children need between-meal snacks. And babies need to eat whenever they are hungry.

If children arrive at your program without breakfast, talk with their parents. Find some way to work it out so children eat breakfast either before they come or after they arrive. Some parents will send food, others may be willing to pay you an additional fee if you provide breakfast. Children and adults need to get their day off to a good start with a nutritious breakfast. Many good early childhood programs such as Head Start provide breakfast.

You may be eligible to be reimbursed for the food you serve. Does your program qualify for the Child Care Food Program? _____ Find out by contacting your licensing agent or state department of agriculture or education. Use local resources, too, to make sure you don't skimp on food to try to save money.

Your enthusiasm for good food will be contagious, but don't overdo it either, or children may wonder why the big deal. When children help prepare foods, they are often more willing to try them for the first time. They love to slice, spread, stir, and dip foods. How foods look and feel in their mouths make a difference too. Have a variety of colors, shapes, temperatures, and textures.

Sources for food. Few children have an opportunity to learn where these foods come from—except the grocery store! Young children can get to know so much by visiting farms (*in the winter, spring, summer, and fall*) to see cattle, vegetable crops, fruits, dairy cows, grains. Watch dairy cows being milked. Visit a butcher shop. See grains ground into flour. Dig some potatoes. Shop at ethnic markets. Give children plenty of chances to see many types of food in different stages of growth and preparation.

Build on these field trips by growing plants outdoors in a small garden or in a sunny window. Read lots of books about foods.

List at least four places you can take children to help them better understand where their food comes from:

_____

_____

_____

_____

If possible, plan a field trip to each of them during the best seasons.

Settings for mealtimes. The atmosphere you establish at snack and mealtimes is very important. Doesn't a meal with candles and romantic music (*or whatever your favorite setting*) always taste better?

When children work with food, these are some things children learn. **Add others that you can think of to this list:**

- choose healthy foods from many cultures (*health, social studies, self-esteem*)

- write lists and read recipes (*languages and reading*)

- shop and spend money wisely (*mathematics, economics, consumer education*)

- measure, time, and divide foods (*mathematics, sharing, cooperation*)

- see how food changes when it is cooked, is mashed, or is mixed with other things (*science*)

- _____

- _____

- _____

- _____

We so often take eating for granted. Don't. Think about what you want children to learn. What attitudes about foods do you want them to have? Here are some appropriate goals for older toddlers and preschoolers when they eat. **You may have other goals as well. Add them to the list.**

- Children are encouraged, but not forced, to taste at least one bite of new foods. Sometimes they are surprised and like it!

- Children enjoy talking informally with their teacher and friends. Don't ask boring questions such as "What color are the peas?" or "What shape is the bread?" Instead, have a natural, pleasant conversation about topics the children bring up.

- Children become familiar with foods from many cultures, especially those of their friends in the group. Welcome a new child on the first day with a favorite food (*ask the parents for suggestions when the child enrolls*). Regularly serve typical foods from a variety of cultures—don't limit this opportunity to a few special occasions.

- Children serve themselves child-sized portions and are expected to eat only until they are full. Group style meals are more relaxed. Never force children to clean their plates. Give children the time they need to finish.

- Children learn respect for others at the table (*by saying "Please pass. . .," "Thank you," and using other courtesies appropriate for their culture*).

- _____

- _____

- _____

- _____

Talking about food preparation and eating is an important part of any early childhood program environment. These curriculum areas are just two of the many opportunities you have to plan, set up, and guide children to ensure that the environment promotes learning. Now let's look at some others—how you schedule your day, set up your home or classroom, and choose materials for children.

How do you plan an environment that promotes play and learning?

What do children love to do more than anything else? PLAY! And how do children learn best? PLAY!

Children's play looks so simple, but it isn't. Children's play doesn't just happen. Teachers have vital roles in supporting and enhancing the value of children's play. You set the stage for children to learn through play. They need time to try out their ideas. They need a comfortable area in which to play. They need real things—good toys and equipment that they can use independently. And most of all, they need an adult who knows how to make all of the pieces of the environment, the people, and the action fit together. Let's see how you make it possible for children to learn through play.

You select appropriate learning experiences

We have already talked in general about how important it is to plan learning experiences that are appropriate for children's development, and experiences that provide just the right amount of challenge for each child. Now we will look at how a professional early childhood educator plans what will happen each day. Let's start with the framework within which you structure each day.

Establish a schedule

Every program—half day, full day, home, center—needs a schedule. Not a rigid one. Not one that is ignored. But one that helps lend a sense of predictable rhythm to the day for you and the children.

Some of you work in programs where your schedule must be coordinated with others, perhaps so you can share playground space. Family child care providers, on the other hand, can probably set their own time frame.

Use this section of the environment checklist on page 147 to evaluate your schedule. As you have done before, continue to add any points to the checklist that are especially important for your program.

Children pursue their interests...discover how the world works...communicate with others...see how to act like other people...practice familiar skills and learn new ones...cooperate and solve problems. — They learn by doing.

Play Today?

You say you love your children
And are concerned they learn today?
So am I — that's why I'm providing
A variety of kinds of play.

You're asking me the value
Of blocks and other such play?
Your children are solving problems.
They will use that skill everyday.

You're asking what's the value
Of having your children play?
Your daughter's creating a tower;
She may be a builder someday.
You're saying you don't want your son
To play in that "sissy" way?

He's learning to cuddle a doll;
He may be a father someday.

You're questioning the interest centers;
They just look like useless play?
Your children are making choices;
They'll be on their own someday.

You're worried your children aren't learning;
And later they'll have to pay?
They're learning a pattern for learning;
For they'll be learners always.

—Leila P. Fagg

© 1975, National Association for the Education
of Young Children. Reprinted by permission
from *Young Children*, January 1975, p. 93

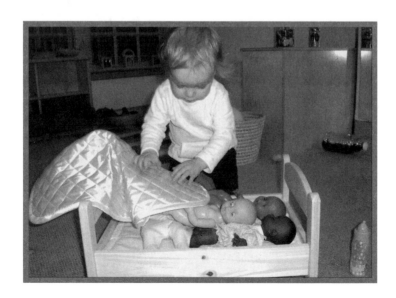

✓ Environment checklist: Schedule

_____ You have a daily schedule. It is written in the home languages of the parents and teachers, and posted for parents and children. You occasionally refer to the written schedule as you work with the children.

_____ Your schedule is coordinated with all others who are affected by it or who share space with you.

_____ Children are aware that you follow a basic routine. They are told before it is time to change from one activity to another so they have time to wind up what they are doing.

_____ Children play outdoors at least once in the morning and once in the afternoon.

_____ Your schedule alternates between active and quiet times.

_____ You plan time for both individual and small group activities. Most activities involve individual play or groups of two to four children.

_____ You plan for child-initiated and teacher-directed learning experiences.

_____ Whole group times for children, 3 to 5 years old, are kept short (10 to 20 minutes), are used to build a sense of community, and actively involve children as much as possible.

_____ The schedule is flexible to allow for children's needs and to take advantage of good learning opportunities when they come up.

_____ The schedule balances large-muscle and small-muscle activities.

_____ You plan for frequent, large blocks of time during which children have opportunities to choose what to do from many options you've provided.

_____ You plan blocks of time for teacher-led activities (_morning meeting, music, introducing a new piece of equipment_).

_____ You balance the use of two or more languages when teaching a second language, providing for the use of both first- and second-language development strategies.

Other schedule considerations for my program:

- transitions
- quiet places in room
- Labeled structure
- Proximity control

Here are two fairly typical schedules for older toddlers and preschoolers, one for a morning part-day program (*a similar sequence could be followed in the afternoon*), the other for full-day childcare. Both of these schedules demonstrate how you put the ideas in the checklist into action.

Typical part-day schedule

8:45–9 a.m.	Children arrive, greet parents
9–9:45	Choice time—play and small group/individual activities/reading
9:45–10	Large group times
10–10:30	Outdoor play
10:30–10:45	Toilet, snack, brush teeth
10:45–11:30	Small group activity/play
11:30–11:45	Review day, prepare to leave

For an afternoon-only program, a similar sequence could be followed.

Typical full-day schedule

7–9 a.m.	Children arrive, greet parents, breakfast/reading books/play
9–9:15	Morning meeting/ daily plan/ sharing/finger plays
9:15–10	Choice time/play/small group and individual activities
10–10:15	Toilet, snack, brush teeth
10:15–11:00	Outdoor play
11:00–11:30	Small group activity/story/music
11:30–12	Clean up, toilet, lunch
12:30–1:15	Outdoor play/games
1:15–1:30	Toilet
1:30–3	Nap/rest/quiet play for older children
3–3:30	Toilet, snack, brush teeth
3:30–4:15	Outdoor play
4:15–7	Play/small group reading/leave for the day

For a program using more than one language with the children, additional scheduling considerations may be needed. If there is going to be a balance of the two (*or three!*) languages being modeled by the adults, specific times for them to occur may need to be planned. Although the specific strategy for any program should be determined by the needs and language backgrounds of the children, language usage should not be haphazard. The strategy might be flexible during the day or you may actually set aside times of the day or entire days to focus more on one language during that time.

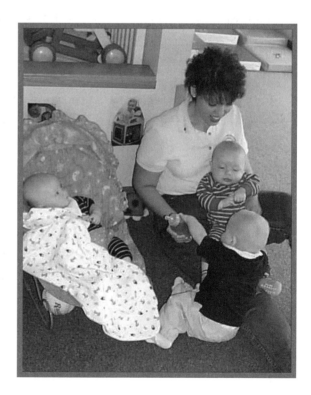

If you work with infants, your schedule will be much looser, but you will still want to establish some predictability.

Typical bilingual part-day schedule

8:45–9 a.m.	Children arrive, greet parents	Los niños llegan, recibe a los padres
9–9:15	Music, story sharing	Musica, compartiendo, cuentos
9:15–10:00	Play in areas	Juego en las areas
10:00–10:15	First language Small group time	Primera lengua Tiempo de grupo pequeño
10:15–11:00	Outdoor play	Juego afuera
11:00–11:10	Second language Small group time	Segunda lengua Tiempo de grupo pequeño
11:10–11:40	Wash hands Lunch	Lavado de las manos Almuerzo
11:40–12:00	Toilet, leave	Hora del baño, salida

If you work with infants, your schedule will be much looser, but you will still want to establish some predictability. You will want to keep three factors in mind:

- each baby's personal rhythms for eating and sleeping,

- infants' tendency to play alone or alongside another child, and

- length of time babies can maintain interest in an activity.

A full-day schedule for infants might be like this:

Typical infant program schedule

8–9 a.m.	Arrival, say goodbye to parents
8–9:15	Play/lap book reading
8–10	Diapering/bottles
8:30–11	Naps/individual play/diapering
10:30–12	Outdoor walk/play
11:30–1	Diapering/lunch/mid-day bottles
12:30–2:30	Naps/individual play/diapering
2–4	Bottles/outdoor play/diapering
3–5	Naps/songs/lap book reading/play/diapering
4:30–6	Play/bottles/leave

These schedules are just samples to give you some ideas. Regardless of the children's ages or the setting in which you teach, you probably need to juggle the availability of staff, children's needs, playground use limits, and many other factors. What are some of them? , No outdoor
, G.M.w/ no equip.

First, young children want to be on the move. They like variety. Neither infants, toddlers, nor preschoolers should be expected to spend too much time in one place or on one activity. Not in line. Not in the highchair. Not on a carpet. Not at the table. They like and need to be involved. They want to be in on the action, not just a watcher. Infants nearly always head for the action, either with their eyes or by crawling or walking.

Toddlers rarely pay attention in a group for more than four or five minutes. Even preschoolers function best in small groups. While 4-year-olds might stay alert in a group of 10 or 12 children, they rarely pay attention for much longer than 10 to 15 minutes. Small groups make it easier for children to listen and provide opportunity for each child to talk.

Second, young children get frustrated with rigid time restrictions. Because they need to be active, plan how you can help them make smooth transitions from one activity to another in your schedule.

Children like to be involved and in on the action, not just watch.

Don't waste their time by insisting they stand in line to wash their hands, sit until everyone is absolutely quiet for a story, or wait while all the children get ready to go outdoors. If at all possible, break into small groups to avoid these time-wasters and help children move on to the next activity. Keep children involved in all of the daily routines.

Third, young children need individual attention. Be sure each day has time for you to talk with every individual child in the family's primary language. Greet the child personally, talk throughout the day about what the child is doing or thinking or feeling, and say goodbye at the end of the day. Small group times provide opportunities for interactions that address developmental skills at the child's individual level.

After you have considered all the factors, **write your preferred schedule in the space that follows. Use the codes to help you see how your schedule is balanced. Discuss your schedule with your Advisor.** Depending on how different it is from the one you follow now, you may want to gradually make changes. If you work in a group program and want to make some schedule changes that will affect other staff, check with your supervisor and the other teachers first. And talk about any changes with the children—preschoolers especially quickly come to expect that one activity will follow another.

My preferred daily schedule

In the column labeled *type of activity,* use these codes to indicate what is happening during that time:
A—children are active, Q—children are quiet, C—children initiate activity, T—teacher directs activity.

Time	Activity	Type of activity A Q C T
8:15-8:45	Greet Child/Table Activities/circle Intro	AC
8:45-9:00	Bathroom/Washing Hands	
9:00-9:30	Breakfast	
9:30-10:30	Introduce group Act. / Choice time	
10:30-11:00	Gross Motor	
11:00-11:30	Group Story/Wash Hands/transition to Lunch	
11:30-12:00	Lunch	
12:00-12:30	Bathroom/Wash hands/Toothbrush	
12:30-2:00	Nap	
2:00-2:30	Bathroom/transition Activities	
2:30-3:00	Snack/Table Activities	
3:00-3:30	Circle Time/small group activity continue.	
3:30-4:00	Individualization/Library	
4:00	Dismissal	

Plan for the day

Now you have a good idea of how to structure the children's day. How do you decide what happens within that day? How do you decide what you want children to learn and what experiences you plan to support that learning? This is called *curriculum planning.*

Children learn not only through play—but they also learn from every other event, most planned but many spontaneous: The janitor who comes to replace an overhead light, the snake that one child brings to visit, a friend who just learned about moving to another town.

Of course, you can't leave the whole day, or even a few minutes, to the chance that something exciting might come up. Use this section of the checklist to help you think about how to plan curriculum — what happens during your day with children.

✓ Environment checklist: Curriculum planning

_____ Your program has a written curriculum that describes the goals for children's learning and development, and the materials, experiences, and teaching strategies that you will use to help children achieve the goals. Your goals are realistic and keep in mind cultural, language, and individual differences and special needs.

_____ You choose learning experiences and teaching strategies that help children reach those goals. In addition, you pick up on interests children have expressed, and on skills they are working on.

_____ You frequently ask yourself about whatever you've planned: What are children learning by doing this?

_____ You choose topics that help children gain understanding of themselves, each other, and people of various ages, sexes, and cultural groups. Stereotypes are never portrayed. Cultural diversity and cooperation are always promoted. Children learn about cultures and languages daily, not just on holidays or as a tourist might, but through real experiences with real people and things. Children learn to identify what is fair and to stand up for their rights and the rights of others.

_____ You plan curriculum that helps children feel good about themselves, their families, their culture and language, and their friends. You appreciate and plan for individual differences of all kinds.

_____ You encourage children to ask questions, experiment, and figure out things on their own.

_____ You ask lots of open-ended questions (What would happen if ...? or Why did this ...?) rather than questions that have one correct answer.

_____ You encourage children's creativity. Models, coloring books, and patterns are avoided. Children's artwork is expected to be unique.

_____ Most activities for children involve real, hands-on experiences.

_____ Most activities busily involve children. At times, children learn from demonstrations, but time spent watching is limited.

_____ If television or videos are used, programs are selected for their appropriateness for children. You talk with the children about what they see and hear. Television/videos are used for a very limited time each day.

_____ Children work individually or in small groups most of the time. Preschool children (3 to 5-year-olds) gather in larger groups for 10 to 15 minutes.

_____ Children learn to appreciate beauty and diversity in the world around them (art, nature, music, literature) through daily, culturally authentic activities.

_____ If something more interesting happens, you do not force children to continue with what they are doing, but give them an opportunity to learn from whatever is going on.

_____ You take advantage of resources within the community: story hour at the library, puppet shows, community fairs, ethnic neighborhoods, to acquaint children with the interesting things and people around them.

_____ You present activities with enthusiasm to build children's interest and curiosity. You have a playful, cheerful attitude. You demonstrate respect for all peoples.

_____ You move about the room and observe and interact with children as they play.

Children and their work are treated with respect and interest. Instead of asking, "What is it?", you engage children in conversation about their work and play.

_____ You support children's play rather than interfere and dictate what they do. For example, you show children how to use new materials appropriately, help children expand on a topic by offering ideas or props, ask open-ended questions to extend children's thinking (*"Why do you think ...?"*), write names on artwork, and pick up ideas from children's play to plan other experiences that extend children's learning.

_____ You see every minute of the day as a learning opportunity: for example, when children are diapered, snacks and lunch, and dressing; disagreements between children; everything that happens.

_____ Field trips are well organized: You have permission slips from each parent, you carry a first-aid kit with you, adult chaperones are recruited, you visit the place first and talk with the staff to ensure the children's safety and that appropriate activities will be offered, children are prepared for what to expect by talking and thinking about the trip in advance, rules are reviewed in children's primary languages, safe transportation is arranged, follow-up activities are planned so children can build on what they have learned.

Other curriculum planning considerations for my program:

_____

_____

_____

_____

_____

_____

_____

_____

_____

_____

_____

Each of the items on the checklist is a component of a good, developmentally appropriate program. They are so important that each of these ideas will keep coming up throughout this book, in your CDA Seminar, and in your teaching. Watch for them and make changes in your program as you keep learning more about what is best for young children.

Hang up the poster at the end of this unit to remind yourself to ask:

> ## ✳ What are children learning by doing this?

Support children's play and learning during choice time

All through the day, you coordinate, supervise, and guide children's learning experiences.

You set up the room or your home, help children choose what they want to do, talk with individuals or groups to support or expand their play, stay alert for any problems that may need your presence, and make notes about individuals and activities. You walk about the area, sit occasionally with a small group, and are constantly aware of what all the children are doing.

In good programs, the teacher prepares the environment and materials before the children arrive and several times throughout the day. During play times, children can select what they want to do. If children have a difficult time choosing their own activities, the teacher suggests things that would seem to be of interest based on what she already knows about them. She shows them how to use any unfamiliar equipment and materials.

While children play, the teacher moves about the room, stopping to chat with a group who are building with blocks, or watching a child engrossed in drawing at the easel. Perhaps some children are having a disagreement. The teacher observes but does not interfere unless they reach a standstill or someone is about to get hurt. If necessary, she intervenes to teach problem solving and negotiation strategies.

This style of teaching not only illustrates what **to do**, but also what **not** to do.

- Talk to individual children; do not lecture to the entire group for long periods of time.

- Provide good choices; do not choose children's activities for them all of the time.

- Encourage children's own writing and drawing; do not use work sheets, workbooks, coloring books, or other seatwork.

- Support and extend play; do not interrupt or interfere with children's play.

- Prepare transitions in advance; do not make children wait or line up.

- Be available and responsive to children; do not carry on a lengthy personal conversation with another teacher. Do not ignore the children. Do not leave the children unattended.

You will learn more about effective early childhood teaching in Units 4 and 5 and in the videos that describe developmentally appropriate practices. But for now, it is important to know that early childhood education is built upon your understanding of each child, the social and cultural context, and child development in general.

You have been observing children and getting to know them for a few weeks by now, so you probably have a good idea of what the children in your group can do and what their interests are. Perhaps you have found out what materials are used often and which are ignored.

On the following pages, summarize what you know about each child's abilities, interests, and any concerns you have.

You will use this information in this unit and in the next two to plan curriculum, to decide how to arrange your home or classroom, to choose the best learning materials, and to make decisions about daily learning experiences as well as accommodations for children with special needs. Use additional paper if you need it and put a copy of one week's plan in your Professional Resource File.

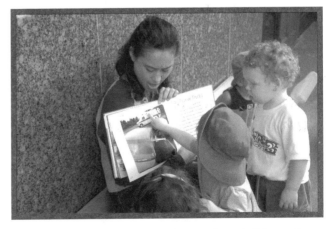

What do you know about the children in your group? What topics interest them?

What do you know about the children in your group? What topics interest them?

CHILD'S NAME: _____

Abilities: _____

_____

Interests: _____

_____

Concerns: _____

_____

CHILD'S NAME: _____

Abilities: _____

_____

Interests: _____

_____

Concerns: _____

_____

CHILD'S NAME: _____

Abilities: _____

_____

Interests: _____

_____

Concerns: _____

_____

CHILD'S NAME:_____

Abilities:_____ .

_____

Interests:_____

_____

Concerns:_____

_____

CHILD'S NAME:_____

Abilities:_____

_____

Interests:_____

_____

Concerns:_____

_____

CHILD'S NAME:_____

Abilities:_____

_____

Interests:_____

_____

Concerns:_____

_____

CHILD'S NAME: _____

Abilities: _____

_____

Interests: _____

_____

Concerns: _____

_____

CHILD'S NAME: _____

Abilities: _____

_____

Interests: _____

_____

Concerns: _____

_____

CHILD'S NAME: _____

Abilities: _____

_____

Interests: _____

_____

Concerns: _____

_____

CHILD'S NAME: _____

Abilities: _____
_____

Interests: _____
_____

Concerns: _____
_____

CHILD'S NAME: _____

Abilities: _____
_____

Interests: _____
_____

Concerns: _____
_____

CHILD'S NAME: _____

Abilities: _____
_____

Interests: _____
_____

Concerns: _____
_____

CHILD'S NAME: _____

Abilities: _____

_____

Interests: _____

_____

Concerns: _____

_____

CHILD'S NAME: _____

Abilities: _____

_____

Interests: _____

_____

Concerns: _____

_____

CHILD'S NAME: _____

Abilities: _____

_____

Interests: _____

_____

Concerns: _____

_____

CHILD'S NAME:

Abilities:

Interests:

Concerns:

CHILD'S NAME:

Abilities:

Interests:

Concerns:

CHILD'S NAME:

Abilities:

Interests:

Concerns:

Writing down what you know about each child is hard work! But it is essential to help you be a better teacher. For now, we will focus on learning goals and children's interests to select some topics to concentrate on in the next few weeks.

Look back over your list. If you teach preschoolers, there is a good chance that their interests include such topics as: themselves, their families and communities, dinosaurs, money, people who help us, animals, their names or other words, plants/food, transportation, water, letters and numbers, drawing and writing, books.

Toddlers often are interested in climbing, pushing, dumping, colors, dressing, stacking things, their bodies, and messy things.

Infants and waddlers are interested in things such as rocking, sliding, crawling, dropping things, squishing things, watching themselves in mirrors, and making things happen (over and over).

List below any topics that are of interest to more than one child or topics that you know several children would be curious about.

insects, instruments

Think about your learning goals for children. Keep your children's interests in mind as you go through the next two sections of this unit. Think about how you might set up your room so children can investigate these ideas and achieve your learning goals. You might begin a list of materials for children to use, too. For example, you have a goal that preschoolers learn the alphabet. Think of ways you can use their interest in their own names to achieve that important learning goal. And add lots of writing materials, magnetic letters, alphabet puzzles and books to the environment as well.

You arrange and decorate the space

You probably have one primary room where children in your care spend most of their time. You may also have rooms for sleeping, eating, and perhaps a special bathroom. Some programs are housed in churches, some in child care providers' own homes, some in schools, and some in spaces designed especially for young children.

Whatever your space is, even if it works well, improvements can usually be made. So few early childhood educators have ideal environments that we will assume you probably would like to make yours work better for your group. Perhaps it is noisy, or children seem to run a lot indoors, or some areas never seem to attract any children.

The design of and/or lack of space does make a difference in children's behavior.

What areas in your space seem to work well?

Blocks, sand/water

What problems have you noticed in your teaching environment?

Certain areas can be a high traffic area, need proximity control.

This section of the environment checklist will help you think about some of the basic principles involved in designing a space for young children.

✓ Environment checklist: Use of space

_____ All state and local safety requirements are met (*fire exits, windows, floor coverings, flammability, see earlier checklists.*).

_____ Your space is flexible so you can meet the needs of children or adults with physical or other disabilities.

_____ You can monitor children's activity in every area.

_____ Indoor areas are bright, well lit, and appealing.

_____ Your space is designed to encourage a wide variety of age-appropriate, culturally relevant activities.

_____ You give each area outdoors a specific purpose: vehicle riding, swinging, climbing, sand.

_____ You organize the room into learning centers that promote specific types of activity: table toys, dramatic play, blocks, library/reading, science, art/messy activities (*clay, paint, water, sand*), private thinking space, music, large muscle, or other appropriate areas.

_____ You group quiet activities together and noisy or messy activities together.

_____ You place related activities near each other: blocks and small transportation toys, for example.

_____ You have enough play areas so that children spread throughout the space without crowding.

_____ Some areas are hard (*tables, chairs, vinyl floors*) while others are soft (*pillows, rocking chair, carpet*).

_____ You have varied the areas so that some contain activities that have one obvious use (*climber with slide*) while other areas are more complex (*large hollow blocks*).

_____ You have made clear pathways for children to walk from area to area without walking through the middle of busy spaces. Furniture is used to mark off play spaces and pathways.

_____ Your pathways are short. You have no long hallways that invite children to run or yell.

_____ You frequently observe children to see how they use the space and make adjustments as children's skills and interests change.

_____ If your program is in your home, you arrange your space so that the space and belongings of family members are private and treated with respect.

_____ Your primary play space is convenient to sleeping areas (*especially for infants*), bathrooms, and outdoor exits.

_____ Labeling of areas or objects is done in English and the home language of the children. Different colors are used for different languages to reinforce that they are separate language systems.

Other space considerations in my program:

- Appropriate equipment/supplies is at child level

If these points help you see where you might change something, try it. You can always move everything back the way it was. Keep experimenting. Watch the videotape for this unit to help you evaluate your learning environment.

When you are fairly satisfied with your room arrangement, draw a rough sketch of your primary teaching space. Note doors and windows. Include major pieces of furniture. Mark the name of each learning center. Talk with your Field Advisor if you have any questions.

You will use this floor plan again in your CDA Seminar. And in case your ideas change as you learn more, we have included another page for you to draw a revised plan later.

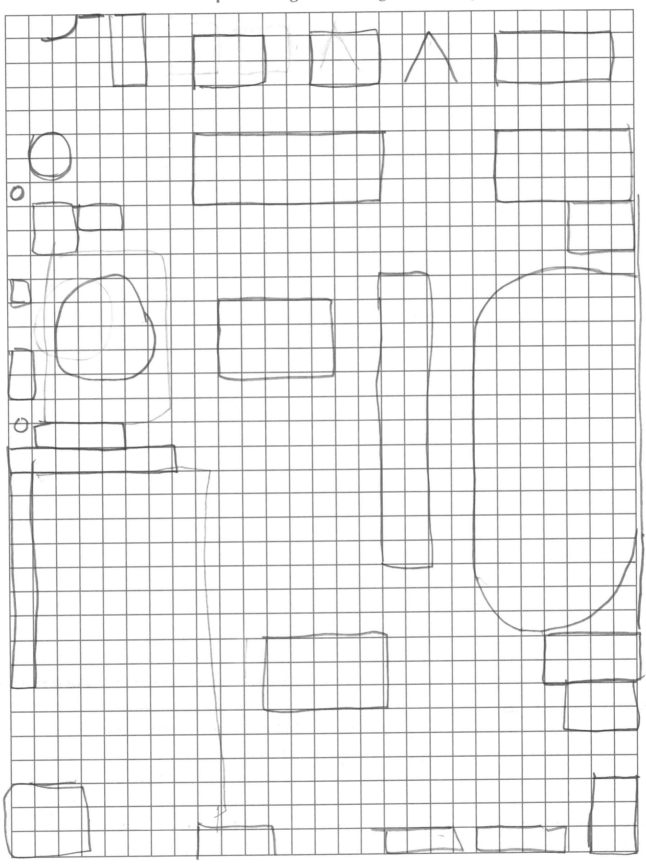

Floor plan designed for seminar

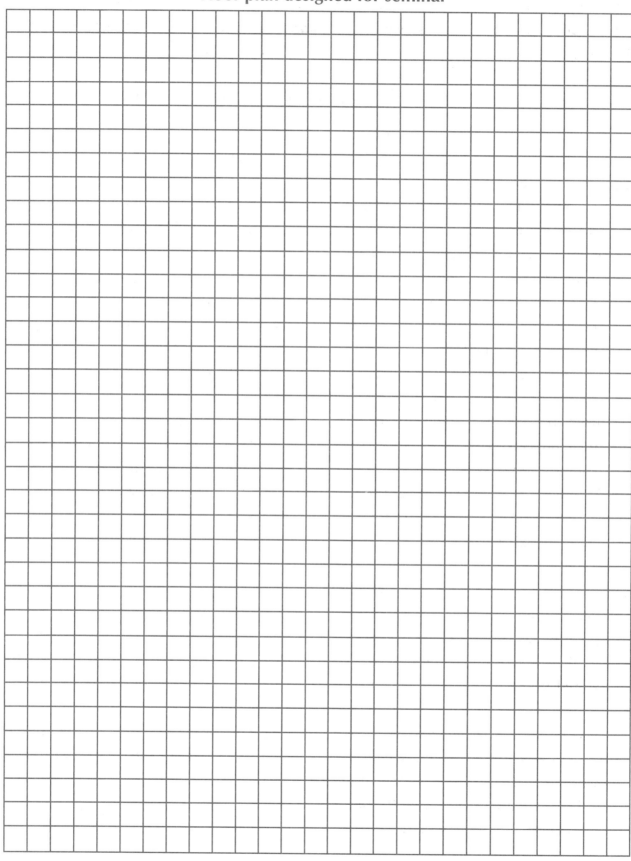

Unit 3

Once your basic use of space is determined, you select the furniture and storage equipment for children's materials. Your observations of children will help you determine what should work well for them.

✓ Environment checklist: Furniture and storage

Floor plan designed through self-study

_____ All furnishings are sturdy, safe, and the appropriate size for the children in the group.

_____ Furnishings are adapted as appropriate to meet the needs of children or adults with physical or other disabilities.

_____ If children of different ages are in the same group, table and chair sizes are varied. Partitions or tables are used to help older children protect their projects from intrusion by younger children.

_____ Infant areas include rocking chairs, mirrors, and other age-appropriate items. Children can crawl and walk about easily.

_____ You use low, open shelves for children's learning materials. Blocks, paper, puzzles, science materials, markers—learning materials are stored where children can reach them easily.

_____ You expect toddlers and preschoolers to return materials to the shelf where they found them. Every shelf is labeled with pictures and/or words in children's home languages.

_____ You never use toy boxes: fingers, heads, or arms can get caught; toys get lost and broken easily; children have difficulty finding what they want; and they never develop the habit of putting their toys away where they belong.

_____ Most of the furniture can be moved by one adult so that it can be rearranged easily. Large items are on casters or rollers with locks.

_____ You store preschool items with small parts (tiny plastic building blocks, for example) in unbreakable containers.

_____ Children can move chairs up to a table if they wish to sit down.

_____ Additional supplies are stored elsewhere rather than taking up valuable program space (_in closets, under beds, in the basement_).

_____ Toys and materials are rotated (_some put away, others brought out_) as children's needs, skills, and interests change.

_____ Special furniture is available to meet the needs of children with disabilities.

Other furniture and storage checks for my program:

_____

_____

_____

_____

_____

_____

_____

_____

With all these ideas fresh in your mind, this is a good time to "go shopping." Look back at what the children in your group are interested in, can do, or soon will be doing (_pages 156-161_).

Pull out some of your school-supply catalogs or borrow some from your director, public library, or family child care network. Look through the catalogs. Identify (_or cut out pictures of_) one or two pieces of furniture that you think would be good additions to your program. Explain why.

_____

_____

_____

_____

If your budget is tight (_and whose isn't?_), think of ways you could find, make, or improvise something similar. What could you do to get these items without spending a lot of money? Would a parent who is a carpenter be willing to make one if you supply the lumber? What about going-out-of-business sales, yard sales, secondhand shops, or consignment stores? Your CDA Field Advisor may be able to help you think of alternatives, too.

In addition to how the space is used and the furniture you select, the way you decorate your space can determine how welcome children feel. In fact, these seemingly small touches can make a big difference in the kind of atmosphere you create for children.

First impressions can be lasting. Just poke your head in the door of someone else's classroom or family childcare home. What is the first thing that strikes you?

_____

_____

_____

_____

_____

_____

The environment checklist includes some pointers for decorating your teaching space, whether it be in your home or in another building.

✓ Environment checklist: Decorations

_____ Your teaching space sets a warm and welcoming atmosphere.

_____ All pictures, posters, signs, and accessories reflect and celebrate diversity within your program, community, and country: culture, ethnic groups, age, sex, language, family, and abilities.

_____ Children's artwork is hung at their eye level. Most of the room is decorated with their work. Each child's work is individual (_no two look alike_). A wide variety of work is posted—not just what you consider to be "the best."

_____ Pictures of children and their families are hung about the space at the children's eye level.

_____ Children's names are prominently displayed everywhere appropriate. It's clear who belongs in this classroom.

_____ Posters, pictures, plants, baskets, and other accessories are pleasing to look at.

_____ They radiate beauty and come from or authentically show many cultures.

_____ You avoid too many cartoon and other "cute" or commercial characters—children see enough of them elsewhere, and many of them depict stereotypes. Instead, you aim for variety with some photographs and some drawings of real people.

_____ The environment is not littered or cluttered with too much print or too many pictures.

Other decorating points for my program:

_____

_____

_____

_____

_____

_____

Take a look around your teaching area and think of some things you can do to enhance it. When is the last time you added something new? Are your posters dog-eared because they have been used year after year? Ask parents to bring in their old magazines. Find some new pictures. Choose some based on the children's interests you've observed. Hang children's latest artwork and writing samples.

Write here what you did to enhance your teaching area.

- Create a comftorable, spacious library
- Have 2 places to have circle, which provides diff. teach opportunities.

_____

_____

You choose appropriate learning materials

By this time, you probably have some new ideas about changes in your space, furniture, and decorations. Now let's look at what fills your shelves and how appropriate the materials are for the children in your group.

When we talk about learning materials, we mean all of the toys, books, writing materials, art supplies, puzzles, games, climbers, riding toys, and other equipment that children use.

This next section of the environment checklist corresponds with the chart of developmental accomplishments in Unit 2. Make sure you have at least some toys and materials in each category for each age range you teach. We have left lots of space for you to fill in other appropriate learning materials—there are far too many to list everyone's favorites here.

✓ Environment checklist: Appropriate learning materials

_____You select a range of materials that are appropriate for children from 6 months younger than the youngest child in the group to 6 months older than the oldest child. A broader range is provided if any of the children have disabilities or other special needs.

_____Popular toys are available in duplicates, or even threes, so children can use them without waiting.

_____Toys and materials are intended for children to **use** them, not to watch toys perform. There are no battery-operated toys.

_____Children can choose from a wide variety of different types of materials that offer a balance of activities:
- small muscle/large muscle,
- quiet/active,
- short interest/extended play,
- cause-and-effect/creative,
- unlimited possibilities/one or a few solutions,
- messy/neat,
- loud/quiet,
- indoors/outdoors, and
- pretend/real.

_____You make sure all toys, pictures, books, posters, and other materials authentically demonstrate acceptance of children's sex, family, race, language, and culture. You use the criteria in "Ten Quick Ways to Analyze Children's Books for Racism and Sexism" to evaluate all materials _(see pages 176-179)._

If you work with young infants (_birth through 8 months_):

Until children can move around by themselves, they do a lot of looking and listening, and rely on you to give them a change of scenery. Toys go straight to their mouths, so nothing should be so small they could swallow it. Infant toys have one or more of these qualities:

_____ Bright or contrasting colors (*board books, pictures*).

_____ Interesting designs (*people's faces, mobiles, pictures, books, blankets*).

_____ Movable parts (*people, mobiles, balls, fish*).

_____ Shiny, reflective surfaces (*unbreakable mirrors on the wall at children's eye level, small ones to hold*).

_____ Noisy parts (*rattles, balls, voices, pots and pans, squeaky toys*).

_____ Tactile surfaces (*people, spoons, texture balls, cloth and rubber dolls or animals*).

_____ "Chewable" materials—but not to be swallowed (*teething rings or beads*).

Teachers can also participate personally in infants' activities:

_____ Talk, sing, recite poems, play "Peek-a-Boo" and "This Little Piggy," move them from place to place for different views, and most of all—hold babies.

_____ Hold babies for lap book reading.

Other good toys for infants:

_____

_____

_____

_____

_____

_____

_____

If you work with crawlers, waddlers, and walkers (*8 to 18 months*):

At this age, children are delighted to be mobile. Their language skills are growing rapidly. They can increasingly use their hands to make things happen. Toys for this age have these qualities:

_____ Safely allow children to crawl over, under, and through (*obstacle course of large cushions, empty boxes*).

_____ Low items to hold on while walking (*low table, cushions*).

_____ Give chances to balance, rock, climb (*rocking chair, climber, steps/slide combi-nation, carpeted climbing space, rocking horse*).

_____ Can be held and manipulated (*cars, trucks, planes, boats, cardboard books with round edges, dolls, large cardboard blocks, unit blocks, puzzles with two to four pieces*).

_____ Make noise or do something when manip-ulated (*knobs to turn, buttons to push, squeaky toys, telephones, balls, maracas, bells, piano, pounding benches, stacking toys*).

_____ Allow first opportunities to scribble (*watercolor markers in dark colors and large blank pieces of paper*).

_____ Allow children to copy familiar behaviors (*purses, dolls with ethnic features and skin colors, cradles, dishes and pitchers, steering wheels*).

_____ People who speak children's home languages to play games, talk, sing, and read with.

_____ Things to push or ride (*low riding vehicles that are steerable but have no pedals, toy lawn mowers, pretend baby strollers*).

Other good toys for crawlers, waddlers, and walkers:

_____

_____

_____

_____

_____

If you work with toddlers and 2-year-olds:

Toddlers and 2-year-olds are becoming increasingly independent. They are more aware of others and like to imitate them. They are becoming more familiar with their community. They can do lots of things with their fingers and hands. They are very active. Therefore, toys for children at this age have these qualities:

_____ Come apart and go back together (*puzzles with four to six pieces, sorting toys, large plastic building sets, stacking boxes or dolls*).

_____ Can be dumped and refilled (*buckets of spools or beads, containers with pieces inside*).

_____ Sometimes require cooperation (*balls, wagons*).

_____ Require finer motor skills (*spools or beads to string, blunt-end scissors, clay, tempera paints including brown and black with wide brushes at easels, watercolor markers, sturdy crayons, large sheets of paper, finger plays*).

_____ Allow for jumping, throwing, kicking (*climbers, balls, lots of space*).

_____ Can be pushed, pulled, or ridden (*low-riding vehicles that steer and have pedals, pull toys, shopping carts, large trucks*).

_____ Let children pretend (*dress-up clothes and accessories, medical props, baby care items, play food and appliances, dolls, small realistic vehicles, rubber animals*).

_____ People who speak the children's home languages to read with, say poems, sing songs (*picture storybooks, recordings*).

Other good toys for toddlers and 2-year-olds:

_____

_____

_____

_____

If you work with children aged 2½ through 3 years old:

Children at this age sometimes seem like toddlers and at other times very grown up. Much of their play is alone or with one or two other children, and they sometimes share. They are curious, are learning more about language, and are very active. Toys and materials for children this age allow them to:

_____ Try out and practice new skills (*dress-up clothes, watercolor markers and large sheets of paper, tempera paints, blunt-end scissors, clay dough, finger paints, paste, and glue*).

_____ Use numbers and letters in real situations (*you write down the stories they dictate, they distribute napkins for snack, you write their names on artwork, follow simple recipes, make lists and labels, read picture books that have simple stories*).

_____ Play alone or with one or two children (*small tables so children can work side by side with puzzles, pegboards, beads, art, table blocks, more dramatic play props, zoo and farm animals*). Rarely use large group activities.

_____ Do lots of running, jumping, pushing, pulling, galloping, riding (*balls, tricycles, large cardboard blocks, obstacle course, climber*).

_____ Explore cause and effect (*blow bubbles; unit blocks; sand and water with scoops, funnels, and cups; toys that come apart, latch, open, and/or close; rhythm sticks, drums, tambourine; construction sets with fairly large pieces*).

Other good toys for children from 2½ through 3 years old:

_____

_____

_____

_____

_____

_____

_____

If you work with older preschoolers (*older 3-year-olds through 5-year-olds*):

Preschool children are increasingly able to plan what they want to do and carry out their plans. Their dramatic play is much more involved. They can play together in small groups for as long as 30 minutes or more. Early literacy and math skills are growing daily. Friendships are more stable and they can take turns. Preschoolers are very aware of their gender, culture, and abilities. These are some of the qualities of toys for preschoolers:

_____ Allow children to play together cooperatively (*large sets of unit blocks, dramatic play props for many different settings such as restaurant, office or vet, simple board and card games, puppets, large empty boxes*).

_____ Give opportunities to write and use letters and numbers for meaningful purposes (*you provide writing materials for children to write their own messages; you write stories or letters children dictate in their preferred language; children make lists, label projects; typewriters/ computers; more complicated recipes, shopping, cash register*).

_____ Children can expand upon their own ideas (*more art materials such as crepe paper, collage materials, chalk, papier-mâché, tape, markers and crayons of all colors; carpentry with hammer, nails, saw, and soft wood; more real musical instruments such as guitar, recorder, harmonica; cameras*).

_____ Help children acquire early literacy skills (*provide a print-rich environment, an inviting library corner with a large selection of books clearly displayed, all kinds of storybooks and nonfiction books, audiotapes of books in children's home languages, child-made books, and books in learning centers throughout the classroom related to the topic of study such as construction books in the block area*).

_____ Help children learn more about people and cultural diversity (*various peoples depicted properly in music, art, nonfiction and storybooks, pictures, foods*).

_____ Use more small muscles (*tiny plastic construction sets; sewing cards; sewing with burlap or nylon net, yarn, and yarn needles; puzzles with many more pieces*).

_____ Still have lots of activity (*roller skates, balance board, Frisbee, plastic bat and balls, riding vehicles, beanbags, bowling pins*).

Other good toys for preschool children:

_____

_____

_____

_____

_____

_____

As you look at this list, dollar signs may have flashed before your eyes! How can you possibly afford so many things?

The best toys for early childhood programs are those that can be used in more complex ways as children gain new skills. Unit blocks are a good example. Children can play with them from infancy through the elementary years. Although they are very expensive to buy, they don't wear out. Blocks are a good long-term investment.

You want to get the most for your money. Consider the life expectancy of major purchases. If you buy better quality riding vehicles, for example, they will last much longer than cheap imitations.

Children will use dramatic play items (*ethnic dolls, doll beds, kitchen appliances*), musical instruments, and many other items for years. Your cost actually may be far less for popular toys that span children's ages or for well-made toys that hold up under hard use.

Careful thought should be put into smaller purchases too. Slightly thicker paper may be a better investment because it doesn't tear so easily. Children will be more successful when they draw or paint. And remember, many toys are common household objects (*pots and pans, measuring cups, funnels*). Many art supplies are discards (*meat trays, paper bags, fabric scraps, egg cartons*).

How do you put what you've learned into practice?

Now it is time to apply all that you have learned so far in your CDA early childhood studies.

Look over everything you have in your classroom and begin to weed out those items that are inappropriate. What would you remove?

1. _____
2. _____
3. _____
4. _____
5. _____

Write down three things you can do to improve the quality of materials in your classroom.

1. _add interesting things to water (shaving cream)_
2. _new & comfy furniture._
3. _____

Children often tell us when activities are inappropriate. Remember when you did a tally of which activities were most and least popular (*page 85*)?

Now, think about the three most popular and the three least popular activities. Then try to figure out why children do or don't choose them, based on the activity qualities in the checklist. Are they appropriate for the

children's ages? Have they been around, with no variation, for too long? Have you unwittingly encouraged only a few children to take part (*such as suggesting carpentry for boys more often than for girls*)?

Three **most popular** activities:

1. _Sand/water_
2. _Art_
3. _Dramatic Play_

Why?
- _Senses stimulated_
- _Role play w/ fake food_
- _Interactive/creative_

Three **least popular** activities:

1. _Library_
2. _Table Toys_
3. _Blocks_

Why?
They are less messy

Next, evaluate the books you provide for children. List five children's books that you regularly use in your group. Using the criteria in the following "Ten Quick Ways to Analyze Children's Books for Racism and Sexism," rate your books. *Circle "O" for OK*

---

or "S" for stereotyped next to the titles on your list. Jot down why you decided they were OK or stereotyped and be prepared to discuss your opinion with your Advisor.

1. O S _What Color is your underwear?_
2. (O) S _Froggy Learns to swim_
3. (O) S _Brown Bear, Brown Bear_
4. O S _____
5. O S _____

Ten quick ways to analyze children's books for racism and sexism

Both in school and out, young children are exposed to racist and sexist attitudes—expressed and in other med~ perceptions un~ about people of ~ as reality. It is di~ to convince chil~ titudes. But if a c~ detect racism and se~ can proceed to transfer the p~ areas. The following 10 guidelines are offered as a starting point in evaluating children's books from this perspective.

Build a book list:
10 books consisting
- _feelings_
- _colors_
- _family_
- _divorce_

of Puerto Ricans, the switchblade-toting, teen- ~ of women, the completely ~ demure, doll-loving ~ mother. While you ~ es in the blatant ~ iations which in ~ ule characters

DORYX®
(coated doxycycline hyclate pellets)

~here are non-White ~ustrations, do they look just like European-Americans except for being tinted or colored in? Do all faces of people of color look stereotypically alike or are they depicted as genuine individuals with distinctive features?

- **Who's doing what?** Do the illustrations depict people of color in subservient and passive roles or in leadership and action roles? Are males the active "doers" and females the inactive observers?

1. Check the illustrations

- **Look for stereotypes**. A stereotype is an oversimplified generalization about a particular group, race, or sex, which usually carries derogatory implications. Some infamous (overt) stereotypes of African-Americans are the happy-go-lucky, watermelon-eating Sambo and the fat, eye-rolling "mammy;" of Latinos, the sombrero-wearing peon or fiesta-loving, macho bandito; of Asian Americans, the inscrutable, slant-eyed "Oriental;" of Native Americans, the naked savage or "primitive" craftsman and his squaw;

2. Check the storyline

The Civil Rights Movement has led publishers to weed out many insulting passages, particularly from stories with particularly from stories with African-American themes, but the attitudes still find expression in less obvious ways. The following checklist suggests some of the subtle (*covert*) forms of bias to watch for.

- **Standard for success.** Does it take "White" behavior standards for a person of color to "get ahead?" Is "making it" in the dominant White society projected as the only ideal? To gain acceptance and approval, do non-White persons have to exhibit extraordinary qualities—excel in sports, get A's, etc.? In friendships between White and non-White children, is it the non-White who does most of the understanding and forgiving?

- **Resolution of problems.** How are problems presented, conceived, and resolved in the story? Are people of color considered to be "the problem?" Are the oppressions faced by people of color and women represented as causally related to an unjust society? Are the reasons for poverty and oppression explained, or are they accepted as inevitable? Does the storyline encourage passive acceptance or active resistance? Is a particular problem that is faced by a person of color resolved through the benevolent intervention of a White person?

- **Role of women.** Are the achievements of girls and women based on their own initiative and intelligence, or are they due to their good looks or to their relationship with boys? Are sex roles incidental or critical to characterization and plot? Could the same story be told if the sex roles were reversed?

3. Look at the lifestyles

Are people of color and their setting depicted in such a way that they contrast unfavorably with the unstated norm of White middle-class suburbia? If the group in question is depicted as "different," are negative value judgments implied? Are people of color depicted exclusively in ghettos, barrios, or migrant camps? If the illustrations and text attempt to depict another culture, do they go beyond oversimplifications and offer genuine insights into another lifestyle? Look for inaccuracy and inappropriateness in the depiction of other cultures. Watch for instances of the "quaint-natives-in-costume" syndrome (*most noticeable in areas like costume and custom, but extending to behavior and personality traits as well*).

4. Weigh the relationships between people

Do the Whites in the story possess the power, take the leadership, and make the important decisions? Do people of color and females function in essentially supporting roles?

How are family relationships depicted? In African-American families, is the mother always dominant? In Latino families, are there always lots and lots of children? If the family is separated, are societal conditions—unemployment, poverty—cited among the reasons for the separation?

5. Note the heroes and heroines

For many years, books showed only "safe" people of color as heroes and heroines—those who avoided serious conflict with the White establishment of their time. Racial and cultural groups today are insisting on the right to define their own heroes and heroines based on their own concepts and struggles for justice.

When people of color do appear as heroes and heroines, are they admired for the same qualities that have made White heroes and heroines famous or because what they have done has benefited White people? Ask this question: Whose interest is a particular figure really serving?

6. Consider the effects on a child's self-image

• Are norms established that limit the child's aspirations and self-concepts? What effect can it have on African-American children to be continuously bombarded with images of the color white as the ultimate in beauty, cleanliness, virtue, etc., and the color black as evil, dirty, or menacing? Does the book counteract or reinforce this positive association with the color white and negative association with black?

What happens to a girl's self-image when she reads that boys perform all of the brave and important deeds? What about a girl's self-esteem if she is not "fair" of skin and slim of body?

In a particular story, is there one or more persons with whom a child of color can readily identify to a positive and constructive end?

7. Consider the author's or illustrator's background

Analyze the biographical material on the jacket flap or the back of the book. If a story is about people of color, what qualifies the author or illustrator to deal with the subject? If the author and illustrator are not members of the group being written about, is there anything in their background that would specifically recommend them as the creators of this book?

Similarly, a book that deals with the feelings and insights of women should be more carefully examined if it is written by a man—unless the book's avowed purpose is to present a strictly male perspective.

8. Check out the author's perspective

No author can be wholly objective. All authors write out of a cultural as well as a personal context. In the past, children's books have traditionally come from authors who are White, European-American and who are members of the middle class, with one result being that a single ethnocentric perspective has dominated American children's literature. With the book in question, look carefully to determine whether the direction of the author's perspective substantially weakens or strengthens the value of his/her written work. Are omissions and distortions central to the overall character or "message" of the book?

9. Watch for loaded words

A word is loaded when it has insulting overtones. Examples of loaded adjectives (*usually racist*) are *savage, primitive, conniving, lazy, superstitious, treacherous, wily, crafty, inscrutable, docile,* and *backward.*

Look for sexist language and adjectives that exclude or ridicule women. Look for use of the male pronoun to refer to both males and females. While the generic use of the word "man" was accepted in the past, its use today is outmoded. The following examples show how sexist language can be avoided: *ancestors* instead of *forefathers; chairperson* instead of *chairman; community* instead of *brotherhood; firefighters* instead of *firemen; manufactured* instead of *man-made;* the *human family* instead of the *family of man.*

10. Look at the copyright date

Books about people of color and their lives—usually hastily conceived—suddenly began appearing in the mid-1960s. There followed a growing number of "minority experience" books to meet the new market demand, but most of these were still written by White authors, edited by White editors, and published by White publishers. They therefore reflected a White point of view. Only since the late 1960s and early 1970s, has the children's book world begun to even remotely reflect the realities of a multiracial, multicultural society, and to reflect feminists' concerns.

The copyright dates, therefore, can be a clue as to how likely the book is to be overtly racist or sexist, although a recent copyright date, of course, is no guarantee of a book's relevance or sensitivity. The copyright date only means the year the book was published. It usually takes a minimum of one year—and often much more than that—from the time a manuscript is submitted to the publisher to the time it is actually printed and put on the market. This time lag meant very little in the past, but in a time of rapid change and changing consciousness, when children's book publishing is attempting to be "relevant," it is becoming increasingly significant.

Are the books you listed appropriate for children, or do some of them perpetuate stereotypes and myths about people?

Save one sample of a book that is stereotyped to discuss with the other Candidates in your CDA Seminar. Read the OK books to the children in your care, if the books are age-appropriate.

Books—and other materials—that do not convey a respect for sex, age, race, abilities, language, culture, and families should only be used with preschoolers and/or their parents as special examples to spark a discussion about how pictures and stories are fair or unfair to some people. See the resource list for several books that provide suggestions of ways to help children and adults recognize and counter biases.

Use these criteria every time you choose books, posters, games, dolls, and other materials. Don't waste your money on items that perpetuate myths or inaccurate generalizations about people's heritage or abilities.

Based on the work of the Council on Interracial Books for Children, Inc. Out-of-print.

Pretend you have $400 to spend on new learning materials for your classroom. Using all the information you have about children's interests, the most and least popular activities in your program—how would you spend it?

Now let's go shopping again! You know where you would like to make some improvements.

ITEM

Cost

Why children in my group would benefit

ITEM

Cost

Why children in my group would benefit

ITEM

Cost

Why children in my group would benefit

ITEM

Cost

Why children in my group would benefit

ITEM

Cost

Why children in my group would benefit

ITEM _____

Cost _____

Why children in my group would benefit _____

_____

ITEM _____

Cost _____

Why children in my group would benefit _____

_____

ITEM _____

Cost _____

Why children in my group would benefit _____

_____

ITEM _____

Cost _____

Why children in my group would benefit _____

_____

ITEM _____

Cost _____

Why children in my group would benefit _____

_____

ITEM _____

Cost _____

Why children in my group would benefit _____

_____

Well, you are on your way to being a great teacher of young children! You are making the kinds of decisions that teachers must make and you are making them based on your own observations and understanding of the needs of the children in your own group. You have set up a splendid teaching area equipped with excellent materials.

If you have not already done so, be sure to see the video that accompanies Unit 3. Think about the questions raised in the Viewer's Guide and talk about them with your Field Advisor if something is puzzling to you.

Now we will turn from a focus on **where** to **what** happens in your interactions with children. Be sure to check that you have completed Unit 3 in your self-study section on your CDA progress record.

What are children learning by doing this?

Resources for Planning a Safe and Healthy Environment

American Academy of Pediatrics, American Public Health Association, and National Resource Center for Health and Safety in Child Care. (1992). *Caring for our children— National Health and Safety Performance Standards: Guidelines for Out-of-Home Child Care Programs (2nd ed.)* Available for purchase at www.naeyc.org. Electronic versions available for free download at http://nrc.uchsc.edu.

Aronson, S.S. (2002). *Model child care health policies (4th ed.)* Washington, DC: National Association for the Education of Young Children.

Aronson, S.S. (Ed.), compiled with P.M. Spahr. (2002). *Healthy young children: A manual for programs (4th ed.)* Washington, DC: National Association for the Education of Young Children.

Bright Horizons Family Solutions. *Ready to respond: Emergency preparedness plan for early care and education centers.* Available for free download at www.brighthorizons.com.

Caring for our children, 6 video set. Titles: *Standards and you; Basic caregiving; Ready for anything; Setting up for healthy and safe care; Keeping it in shape; and Illness in child care.* (1995). Washington, DC: National Association for the Education of Young Children.

Child Care Nutrition Resource System, Website for U.S. Department of Agriculture's Child Nutrition Programs, www.nal.usda.gov/childcare/index.html.

Early Childhood Committee of the Pennsylvania Chapter of the American Academy of Pediatrics. (Revised 1999). *Preparing for illness: A joint responsibility for parents and caregivers* (brochure). Washington, DC: National Association for the Education of Young Children.

Farish, J.M. (2003). *When disaster strikes: Helping young children* cope (brochure). Washington, DC: National Association for the Education of Young Children.

Greenman, J. (2001). *What happened to the world? Helping children cope in turbulent times* (booklet). Cambridge, MA: Bright Horizons Family Solutions. Available at www.naeyc.org.

Keeping healthy: Parents, teachers, and children (brochure). (1999). Washington, DC: National Association for the Education of Young Children.

Safe, active play: A guide to avoiding play area hazards (video). (1997). Washington, DC: National Association for the Education of Young Children.

Resources for Planning the Learning Environment

Alvarado, C. et al. (1999). *In our own way: How anti-bias work shapes our lives.* St. Paul, MN: Redleaf Press.

Bronson, M.S. (1995). *The right stuff for children birth to 8: Selecting play materials to support development.* Washington, DC: National Association for the Education of Young Children.

Brown, J.C. & Oates, L. (2001). *Books to grow on: African American literature for young children* (brochure). Washington, DC: National Association for the Education of Young Children and National Black Child Development Institute.

Copple, C. (Ed.). (2003). *A world of difference: Readings on teaching young children in a diverse society.* Washington, DC: National Association for the Education of Young Children.

Curtis, D. & Carter, M. (2003). *Designs for living and learning: Transforming early childhood environments.* St. Paul, MN: Redleaf Press.

Derman-Sparks, L. and the A.B.C. Task Force. (1989). *Anti-bias curriculum: Tools for empowering young children.* Washington, DC: National Association for the Education of Young Children.

Derman-Sparks, L., Gutierrez, M. & Day, C.B. (1989). *Teaching young children to resist bias: What parents can do* (brochure). Washington, DC: National Association for the Education of Young Children.

Dodge, D.T. & Kitterege, B. (2003). *Room arrangement as a teaching strategy. Rev. ed.* (video). Washington, DC: Teaching Strategies. Also available in Spanish: *La nueva organizacion del salon como estrategia educativa.* D.T. Dodge.

Greeman, J. (1988). *Caring spaces, learning places: Children's environments that work.* Redmond, WA: Exchange Press.

Hill, D.M. (1977). *Mud, sand, and water.* Washington, DC: National Association for the Education of Young Children.

Isbell, R. & Exelby, B. (2001). *Early learning environments that work.* Mt. Rainier, MD: Gryphon House.

Jalongo, M.R. (2004.) *Young children and picture books, 2nd ed.* Washington, DC: National Association for the Education of Young Children.

Koch, T. & Kamberg, M.L. (1997). *Tips from Tina: Help around the house—Hundreds of practical ideas to make family child care easier and more fun.* St. Paul, MN: Redleaf Press.

Pelo, A. & Davidson, F. (2000). *That's not fair! A teacher's guide to activism with young children.* St. Paul, MN: Redleaf Press.

Rand, D., Trent Parker, T. & Foster, S. (2001). *Black books galore! Guide to great African-American children's books.* New York: John Wiley & Sons. Available from Redleaf Press.

Reading Is Fundamental. (2003). *Literacy-rich environments* (Three detailed posters depicting literacy-rich classrooms for toddlers, preschoolers, and literacy-filled family child care homes). Available from www.naeyc.org.

Rogers, C.S. & Sawyers, J.K. (1988). *Play in the lives of children.* Washington, DC: National Association for the Education of Young Children.

San Fernando Valley Child Care Consortium; A. Godwin & L. Schrag, Cochairs. (1996). *Setting up for infant/toddler care guidelines for centers and family child care homes (Rev. ed.)* Washington, DC: National Association for the Education of Young Children.

Schon, I. (2002). *Books to grow on: Latino literature for young children* (brochure). Washington, DC: National Association for the Education of Young Children.

Skeen, P., Garner, A.P. & Cartwright, S. (1984). *Woodworking for young children.* Washington, DC: National Association for the Education of Young Children.

York, S. (2003). *Roots and wings: Affirming culture in early childhood programs. Rev. ed.* St. Paul, MN: Redleaf Press.

Positive ways to support children's social and emotional development

HOW WONDERFUL IT IS to see children who genuinely care about others ... who are persistent when they learn new skills ... who celebrate their successes ... and who have loving adults to help them deal with their strong emotions!

At every age and at all times, children need adults to help them be secure, loving, self-motivated, successful people. They will be better prepared to deal with life's challenges and problems.

Much of the time, children are a joy to be around. They want to please us, they try hard, they are loving and generous. Sometimes children's behavior can be frustrating—they bite, scream, don't pay attention, or are afraid of monsters.

> Two 3-year-olds both want to play with the same toy and one hits the other. Mr. Olesen says to the children nearby and to the child who hit, "It's so important to let people know how you feel—so important. Use words to tell him how you feel.... Yes, tell him instead of hitting."

> Lakeisha (*18 months*) sees her friend Paige fall. She rambles over to Paige, pats her gently on the back, and says, "OK, OK."

> Three preschoolers are making French toast. Yuichi wants to flip his piece over, but he is quite awkward at it. Ms. Silva shows him how to hold the turner, slide it in under the bread, then turn his wrist and the spatula to flip the toast.
>
> Yuichi lifts a piece out of the pan and puts it on a plate. He tries to turn the next piece of bread, and, after some difficulty, manages to flip it. Yuichi and Ms. Silva smile at each other.

In this unit we will talk about how to encourage cooperative, friendly behaviors, and how to deal with the natural, sometimes difficult behaviors children engage in every day.

First we will think about what kinds of people we want children to be—not just today, but tomorrow, in elementary school, and as adults. These goals are based on research demonstrating the importance of social skills and emotional self-regulation for later success in school and in life. Positive social-emotional development is an essential task of the early years of life, requiring considerable adult support. Then we will talk about guidance and discipline—what teaching strategies work to support children's self-regulation and long-term healthy development, as well as how to deal with children's difficult, challenging behaviors when they occur.

The years from birth to formal schooling are the optimum time to lay a foundation for healthy social and emotional development. Building positive social skills and emotional relationships while children are very young is certainly much easier than trying to intervene later to correct negative behaviors.

Word list

Anti-social—Acting in ways that hurt (feelings or physically) other people.

Cognitive—Thinking or intellectual development.

Oppositional—When two people cannot cooperate or agree.

Pro-social—Acting in ways that help people get along better.

Regress—Go back to less mature behaviors.

Reinforce—Encourage a behavior through praise or attention.

Timelines

You will need about three weeks to complete Unit 4. You have four tasks to complete:

1. Prepare for conference with your Field Advisor to discuss topics (*what kind of people we want children to be, plan the environment to prevent problems, act in consistent positive ways with children, supporting families and culture, use a positive approach with challenging behaviors, dealing with difficulties, helping families cope with life's stressful events*).

2. Complete two assignments (*observe children at play and develop plans to build social and emotional skills*) and three entries for the Professional Resource File.

3. Complete five assignments for Seminar (*explore culture you grew up in, expand knowledge of other cultures and lifestyles, identify ways to deal with everyday expressions of bias, develop techniques for staying calm when children are out of control, and learn procedures for reporting child abuse*).

4. View the accompanying videotape using the Viewer's Guide.

Finally, we will look at some of the typical challenges children face as they make friends, figure out who they are, and grow up. And we will see how you can help children handle extreme stress—new babies in the family, separation and divorce, disabilities, hospitalization, death, and abuse.

PART 1

What kind of people do we want children to be?

"What a bad boy you are!"
"That's a good girl."

When we say things like this to children, what are we really telling them?

Not much. And a lot.

When we aren't specific about what was bad or good, we are labeling **the child** as bad or good. And before we know it, most children will begin to live up to our labels.

Children are neither bad nor good. Their **behavior** may range from appropriate to not appropriate, and even that depends on the situation.

Picture a child running and making fire engine noises. That behavior is entirely appropriate on the playground or in the back yard. It may be fine in the basement of your family childcare home or in the all-purpose room. It is not appropriate at the library.

Successful teachers do not think of children's behavior as either bad or good. They look at children in a different way. They realize that all through childhood, children are learning to regulate their behaviors according to the requirements of the situation. Our first step in knowing how to help children learn to regulate their own behavior is to know how they learn and develop. Then we can give a lot of thought to the kind of people we want children to become.

You understand what children are like

As we saw in Unit 2, many people around the world have studied children. We know how development occurs and how children's experiences affect their behavior. Based on this knowledge about children, we can make wise decisions about how we interact with them.

Know individuals

Babies radiate their own personalities. They tend to act in certain ways. Some infants are easy, some difficult, and some a little of both. Young children may be outgoing and friendly, withdrawn and quiet, or somewhere in between. All through life, individual differences account for some of our behaviors.

Know age-related expectations for children's behavior and development

Many behaviors are related to children's development and somewhat predictable. For example, most infants struggle with separation anxiety. The notorious "terrible twos" are an important stage of development for toddlers. You are already familiar with these from your study of the chart of developmental accomplishments/expectations in Unit 2 and from your experience with children.

Recognize cultural differences.

All development and learning occur in and are influenced by social and cultural contexts. So it is not enough to know about development in general. Teachers must also be aware of cultural variations in the way children acquire and demonstrate their learning.

These three areas of knowledge are interconnected. From her knowledge of child development, a teacher will expect that a baby uses crying to communicate emotions, but each individual baby has her own particular set of cries that are well known to her primary caregiver. And depending on the culture in which the child lives, a baby's cries may be responded to immediately or the baby may be given time to learn to self-comfort.

Turn to the section(s) of the chart that includes the ages of the children in your group. Look at the three parts that deal mostly with social and emotional development: *children show interest in others, children become more aware of themselves, children express feelings.*

Think about your experiences with children at this age. In your own words, write one paragraph describing some other typical social or emotional behaviors:

Children are developing the ability to share and take turns. Children understanding how to react to the feelings of their peers.

Know how to treat children

Much of children's behavior is learned. They copy the way they have seen other people act: relatives, neighbors, friends, or characters on television shows or in movies. They might learn to yell, hit, and criticize. Or they might calm themselves down, talk about their feelings, and solve problems constructively.

Most of the time, young children act the same way they are treated. Your attitude, discipline strategies, and the way you plan the learning environment can make a tremendous difference in what children are like.

Jeffrey always hits when another child doesn't give him what he wants immediately. You've seen his mother hit him when he doesn't instantly obey her.

Dhruv quietly moves about the room and works independently. His father is an engineer who spends many hours in his home workshop.

Two children in the group flit from activity to activity, use loud voices, and usually play superheroes. They watch lots of cartoons on TV.

Maria is always able to keep herself busy. While others are bickering over toys, she can be found sitting and looking at picture books. You can see that Maria has done this many times before.

These examples point out why you and the children's families need to work together to provide the kinds of experiences that lead children to become happy, well-adjusted people.

You have goals for children

All families have hopes and dreams for their children. Those dreams should enable their children to become all they can be—happy, productive members of our society.

Each time you talk with children's families, you learn a little more about what they hope for their children. They probably selected your early childhood program because you share many of the same goals for their children.

Perhaps you want children to ...

... feel proud of themselves, their families, and their culture.

... feel competent and confident.

... be curious—eager to learn and try new things.

... gain increasing ability to regulate their behavior in different situations.

... be fair, kind, cooperative, friendly people.

... sense that their talents, language, and learning styles are respected.

... feel secure but not overprotected.

... feel part of a community.

... know they can talk about their feelings. They trust adults who listen and understand.

... develop their own inner strengths.

Each family and cultural group emphasizes slightly different areas of development. Add to this list some other goals you share with the families of children in your care.

Perhaps you want children to ...

- to be persistent in accomplishing tasks
- over come difficulty and challenges
-

At times families have expectations for their young children that you do not think are in the children's best interests. Perhaps they want their child to read before the age of 3 or expect their 12-month-old to learn to use the toilet. Maybe they want their child to start preparing for the Olympics at the age of 4.

These parental goals may be the result of unrealistic expectations or they may reflect different cultural values from yours. Later on in *Essentials*, we will discuss ways of comfortably talking with families and negotiating differences in goals for children so that everyone benefits.

Gain a healthy self-concept and self-esteem

Every child is unique. Children need us to help them see what wonderful individuals they are—their own special looks, skills, personalities, tempos, likes, and dislikes. By helping children be happy with who they are, and who nobody else can be, we strengthen their sense of value as a person.

Children's self-concept—their stable perceptions about who they are despite changes in their behavior—is being built throughout early childhood. Self-esteem—their sense of worth as a person, is also developing.

Most early childhood educators are aware of the importance of positive self-concept. But too often, this understanding gets translated into making books about why "I am Special". Children's self-esteem doesn't develop from such trivial activities. It comes from being truly valued by people who matter to the child such as parents and teachers. And self-esteem develops gradually over time as children take on and succeed at ever more challenging tasks.

Think about your own self-esteem. When you feel good about who you are and what you are capable of doing, you are ready to take on almost any challenge.

Children are no different. Children with positive self-esteem know from their own experiences that they are capable, loving, and fun-to-be-with people. Self-esteem is the key to self-confidence!

Be confident as learners

Did you ever watch a baby beam when she first claps her hands, or a toddler glow when he zips his coat? Children have a natural pride in what they can do. When children know they are able to do things, they are motivated **from inside** to try more new things. Confident, competent children become competent adults. Success leads to more success.

In contrast, if children feel like failures, they rarely have much interest in anything. Their feelings of competence can be easily damaged if we don't notice and support their successes.

Curious and eager to learn

Children's first group experiences influence how they feel about learning and school. In their early years, if they are often bored, unchallenged, or frustrated by tasks much too hard, by the time they get to elementary school, they are less likely to be motivated to learn.

However, if they can be curious, find delights in books written in their own language and that contain pictures that look like them, are given a chance to try out ideas, play and laugh together, solve their own problems, and feel loved and welcome, they will be eager to learn all through their lives.

Teachers of young children set the stage for children to be eager to learn. Your attitude, the experiences and materials you plan, and the way you treat children can make learning a positive experience—one that children will want to continue.

Be capable of self-regulation

Discipline.

Punishment.

These are the words most often used to describe what we do to make children "behave" or "be good." As we have already seen, children themselves are neither good nor bad; their behaviors are just appropriate or inappropriate, depending on the time and place.

Our goal is for children to be able to regulate their own emotions and behavior according to the circumstances. Why? So they don't need an adult hovering over them to enforce every rule or to punish them for the least infraction. You probably have seen children who shake in fear when they have broken a rule. Or who lie about what they did because they are afraid of the punishment. Or perhaps worst of all, children whom adults and other children don't want to be around because they are always out of control. These children have probably not been taught how to self-regulate or they have been punished in ways that don't help them develop healthy forms of emotional control and ways of expressing feelings.

As a professional, you look at children's current and long-term development. The process for learning self-regulation takes times. Children need lots of adult guidance and patience—some more than others.

But the rewards are many: Children become teenagers and then adults who feel good about themselves, are trustworthy, can make reasonable decisions, and are a joy to know! When you teach self-regulation you make an investment in children's futures.

Help children
want to control themselves
by finding appropriate ways
for them to express their feelings.

Build caring relationships with other people

Children learn to love because they feel loved. They feel safe and secure, physically and mentally protected by those who care about them. Children need to feel lovable before they can love others. The ability to form human relationships is essential for healthy development. And loving relationships help protect children from the negative effects of societal risk factors such as poverty and violence. Children also **learn** through relationships. Those relationships begin for babies with their parents and other family members and then extend to other people, including their caregivers and teachers. Children need these relationships to learn language and a host of other things about how the world works.

Have a positive sense of their own identity

We've talked about how children are unique individuals. But children are also members of groups. Groups pass on their language and culture, the obvious and less than obvious rules that tell us how to behave.

Many people aren't even aware of their own culture and how much it influences the way they see the world. Some families understand the importance of helping children feel good about their cultural identity and learning to speak their home language. Unfortunately, some cultural groups have been historically discriminated against in our society and some families may even try to cover up their heritage. They don't share their roots with their children. They may feel it is better not to teach children their home language, but speak to them in English instead, even though it makes communication difficult.

But children's healthy development depends on their having a good sense of their identity and that includes their cultural, linguistic, religious, racial, and ethnic identities.

Feel secure

The security blanket that the cartoon character Linus carries around makes the point clear, children need to feel secure. Consistent relationships with people along with familiar things give them secure feelings. When they feel secure, they can do new and different things.

Kyle and his mother are spending his first day in preschool together. At first, Kyle sits with his mother, watching the other children.

He spots some children playing with airplanes, looks tentatively at his mother, and then walks toward the activity. He stands and watches. When a child says, "Do you want to fly this plane?" Kyle looks back at his mother, who smiles. He reaches for the plane.

Throughout the morning, Kyle occasionally walks back to his mother, who reassures him and comments on what he is doing. Then he returns to his play.

Kyle feels secure that this mother is there on his first day. He needs occasional reassurance from her, but he neither clings nor ignores her presence. All children need something familiar to feel secure until they are ready to explore on their own.

Cooperate with teachers and other children

Kindergarten teachers often say that children's ability to cooperate with their teachers and other children is one of the most important indicators of their readiness for school. Cooperation is needed for children to successfully play together whether they are building a firehouse or pretending to be veterinarians. Cooperation is also important because there is much that children can learn from each other. And of course, any time a group of people occupy the same space such as in a classroom, rules of behavior must be observed requiring that children know how to get along with each other, solve problems when they arise, function independently, and make friends.

Trust others

Growing up is so hard. Children need at least one understanding adult who can **really** listen to what they say. Someone who will not criticize, scold, judge, or turn off children's ideas. Children need someone with whom they can share their joys, their fears, and their dreams. They need someone they can count on to follow through on promises, someone who will treat children with respect.

You will undoubtedly be one of those people. Learn how to be a good listener and how to respond to children's work and thoughts.

All of these features of long-range social and emotional development blend together to build children's **inner strength**—their ability to use their own resources to get as much out of life as possible, both now and as they mature. Let's now look at how we can make all of these goals for children become a reality.

PART 2

How do you guide children's development of inner strength?

Children do not naturally acquire social competence and emotional self-regulation. They need caring adults to patiently teach these skills and many opportunities to practice them.

In this section of *Essentials*, we will concentrate on positive, specific, research-based ways to help children learn to regulate their own behavior and get along with each other. These ways work. They help children learn valuable social skills and emotional control. When you use these teaching strategies, you will feel good about yourself as a teacher. The children will feel good about themselves. And even skeptical parents will soon begin to see the value of this positive approach. Children will begin and continue to use prosocial behaviors that will last all their lives.

When teachers encounter discipline problems with children, they inevitably want a quick fix. They want someone to "fix" the problem child so that they can get on with teaching the curriculum. But there are no effective quick fixes. In early childhood classrooms, teaching children self-regulation and social skills is a big part of the curriculum.

There are four basic steps in teaching with this child development-based type of discipline. These steps come from The Teaching Pyramid: A model for supporting social competence and preventing challenging behavior in young children *(see page 196.)*

This Pyramid was developed by two federally funded research centers: the Center on the Social and Emotional Foundations for Early Learning, and the Center for Evidence-based Practice: Young Children with Challenging Behavior *(see Resources)*.

First, you must lay a strong foundation by building positive relationships with children, families, and colleagues. Second, you eliminate as many problem-causing situations as possible by engaging in classroom preventive practices. That is, you start by "fixing" the environment to prevent challenging behaviors. Then, you focus on your behavior as a teacher and act in consistent positive ways ("fix yourself", so to speak). You use effective social and emotional teaching strategies so the children learn how to behave in positive ways.

After attention has been paid to these first three steps, discipline problems will be fewer. However, it is likely that you will still encounter some children who exhibit particularly challenging behaviors. That's where the fourth step comes in – then and only then, do you try to "fix the child." You employ intense individualized interventions with those particular children to help them learn self-regulation and acquire social skills.

STEP 1: Establish positive relationships with children, families, and colleagues

As we have seen throughout this book, positive relationships are the foundation for all development and learning. In terms of children's social and emotional development, when you have a positive relationship with a child, your influence will be greater. Children pay attention to the adults they care about and try to be like them. Positive relationships also build healthy self-concept and self-esteem. Children with positive self-concept are less likely to engage in negative, challenging behaviors. Specific suggestions for establishing relationships are described under Step 3.

STEP 2: You plan the environment, curriculum, and schedule to prevent problems

Many common behavior problems can be eliminated with thoughtful attention to how the physical environment, space, and time are organized for children. Children who have many interesting, intellectually engaging things to do and learn about are less likely to misbehave. They're just too busy. Too often, teachers get it backwards. They think that first they have to get the children to behave before they can engage them in play and learning. But actually, if children are engaged in interesting play and challenging projects, fewer problems occur.

The Teaching Pyramid
A model for supporting social competence and preventing challenging behavior in young children

Reprinted with permission. Young Children Article — The Teaching Pyramid: A Model for Supporting Social Competence and Preventing Challenging Behavior in Young Children, 2003, Vol. 58/No. 4/Pg. 49.

Whenever children build with blocks, someone always rides a tricycle through and bumps into the building.

Caitlin grabs the doll from Joshua. Soon Pallavi yanks it away from her.

Children wander aimlessly about the room during free play. When you suggest a puzzle, they begin half-heartedly, and then dump the pieces on the floor.

While you read the story, several children fidget, loudly lift the Velcro strips on their shoes several times, and then get up and leave.

You probably have had similar incidents happen with children. And you may have already figured out the reason. Why do you think children misbehaved in these examples?

Block wrecking: Upset that a peer is using blocks that he had earlier.

Doll grabbing: Child is upset that the doll she put down for a nap was picked up by another peer.

Puzzle dumping: Frustrated w/ not being able to complete puzzle

Story fidgeting: Distracted by neighboring peers or has a short attention span.

Often, children are not the cause of the problem at all. The environment, the schedule, the curriculum, or your expectations can cause conflict and disruption. We often unwittingly plan the day or set up the materials in ways that invite children to behave inappropriately. Let's explore how to avoid doing this.

Identify toys and materials

Children often fight over toys. If dolls are a popular item, for example, having enough dolls so infants and toddlers don't need to share will prevent conflicts. Your money will be better spent on duplicates of favorite toys than on lots of items children ignore.

Even preschoolers, who are becoming more able to share, need enough duplicates of toys to keep up their interest and avoid long waits for a turn. Children will share when they don't feel the need to protect things and when generous adults share with them.

The children in the example probably dumped the puzzles because the clinking sound they made on the floor was more interesting than the puzzles. Perhaps they had done the puzzles many times already. Maybe the puzzles were too easy or too hard.

Rotate toys so children always have a varied selection. Just put some (*that are too familiar or too easy*) away for a while and bring out others. Select those that provide just the right amount of challenge.

Be alert to children's boredom and skill levels. Think up interesting, new activities with different materials. Many things you use will be discarded items that cost nothing: egg cartons, packing chips, computer paper. Just make sure everything you offer is respectful of people and of the children's individual ability levels.

Which toys and materials in your program frequently cause problems? What could be done to reduce the problem?

Blocks, computer, and
Dramatic play materials.
I have a staff member ~and~ to
interact properly w/ child. Have
a ~timer~ timer to fairly allow everyone
~opportunity~ opportunity.

Discuss your ideas with your CDA Field Advisor.

Make good use of group times

Most teachers seem to think circle time, sharing time, show-and-tell, or some other whole group gathering is the only time children are learning because an adult is directing what happens.

But your experience probably has been that many group times are spent telling children to sit down, to pay attention, and to PLEASE stop playing with their shoes!

Circle time, long transitions, stories, and other large group times often cause a problem for young children. Until children are about 3½ years old, stick to smaller groups. Four or five children are enough. Even with preschoolers, you will find more behavior problems the larger the group and the more time they are asked to sit still and pay attention.

Group times are useful for building a sense of community and feelings of belonging. If you want preschoolers to gather together, make the time short, keep the children involved, and don't be offended if children's attention wanders. If children wander off, use this behavior as a clue and reevaluate the appropriateness of the group activity.

Read stories to *small* groups so children can sit on your lap or next to you. Then you can informally talk about what happened, children can see the pictures, and they will experience stories as a pleasant, warm time with their teacher. Children's librarians can assist you in choosing stories that are of the right interest level and age level (see pages 319-320.) In addition, they are a good resource to locate related items that can embellish a story session. Short songs, finger plays and games that tie the session together provide a means of introducing some "active" time into a seemingly quiet time. What a great way to build a love of reading!

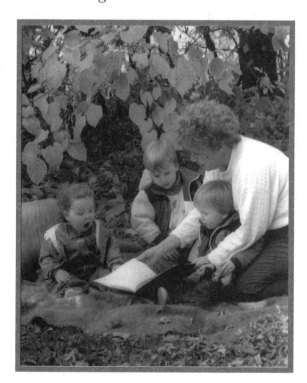

Read stories to small *groups so children can sit on your lap or next to you.*

Ways to make group time more appropriate for preschoolers

Before circle:

- **Schedule** it to avoid distractions. Between other more vigorous, individual activities is best.

- **Plan** for children to move into and out of circle in an orderly way. (Gather children quickly so they don't have to wait, use open-ended activities such as finger plays while children gather, set up activities for a few children to go to at a time when they leave.)

- **Select** very interesting activities appropriate to children's development.

- **Plan** the order of activities so you can vary the pace.

- **Anticipate** problems. Sit near children who have the most difficulty.

During group time:

- **Watch** to see what the children do and change your plans accordingly. If no one is paying attention, skip to something more interesting.

- **Tell** children how you expect them to behave and why.

- **Give** clear, simple instructions about what children are to do next.

- **Keep up** the momentum: show enthusiasm; whisper; use mystery, suspense, or humor; bring out props. Don't spend your time telling children to sit or listen. Do something so appealing they will want to be there.

- **Comment** on appropriate behavior. Ignore minor distractions.

After group time

- **Think** about what worked and what didn't. Don't make the same mistakes twice.

Note: Adapted from "Getting Past Two Little Pumpkins" by O. McAfee, *Young Children*, September 1985, 40(6), 27. Copyright © 1985 by National Association for the Education of Young Children.

Reprinted with permission.

What have you found makes group time successful?

Having a clear plan outlined, w/ materials accessible, and clear reminders for expected behavior.

Discuss your ideas with your Field Advisor.

Follow Oralie McAfee's excellent suggestions (*see page 199*) for ways to have a more appropriate circle time with preschool children.

If you want to have a celebration—plan a picnic, a special visit by parents, or some other event. Children can decorate, fix refreshments, and perhaps everyone can join in to sing "The Wheels on the Bus" and some other favorite songs.

Organize space

One of the best ways to prevent behavior problems is to carefully organize the space so that children can do their best. You probably had no trouble figuring out why the trike-riding children kept knocking down the block constructions: The block area was most likely in a traffic path!

As you saw in Unit 3, you can arrange your classroom or your family childcare home play areas in ways that protect children's activities. When the area works well, you make it much easier for children to control their own behavior in appropriate ways.

What changes can you make in your space that will help direct children toward more appropriate behaviors?

Placing a cloth material to cover the face of the block shelf to prevent behaviors during circle.

Watch for indications your actions have worked and discuss what happened with your Field Advisor.

Here are some tips on ways to make sure your environment doesn't cause clashes over the use of space:

- **Organize the area to separate activities.** Eliminate long pathways so children aren't tempted to run. Use physical barriers to show where running or bike riding should end. Place noisy activity areas (*pretend play, vehicles, blocks*) near each other so quieter activities (*reading, writing, art*) are not disturbed.

- **Arrange spaces in ways that help children understand how it should be used.** Label children's cubbies and clothes so things don't get lost. Mark shelves with pictures and/or words so children can return items to their proper place.

Minimize transitions

Many behavior problems occur during transition times: getting ready to go outside, preparing for meals or nap, moving from choice time to group time, moving from the classroom to the large muscle room. Most of the time, problems arise because young children are expected to wait with nothing to do during these transitions (such as sitting quietly with their hands folded until all are served lunch!) Most young children are very clever at creating interest during boring or uninteresting situations. Lots of times, what teachers see as misbehavior is just the child trying to find something interesting to do.

Don't set children up for failure this way. Make sure that the number of transitions children experience during the day are kept to a minimum. Warn children before the transition is to occur ("Five more minutes until cleanup time.") Engage children in singing songs, doing finger plays, or telling stories during times when waiting can't be avoided. Most of all, examine your time schedule to be sure that children have ample time to engage in play and projects and minimal time is wasted waiting for the next activity.

STEP 3: You act in consistent, positive ways with children

Equally important to planning materials, activities time, and space to avoid problems is **how we act** with children. In this section, we will describe ways to build a personal relationship with each child, how to support children's families and cultures, and how to teach children social skills and emotional self-regulation.

How you treat each child—how you communicate your acceptance of them as individuals—is the key to being a successful early childhood educator. Nothing else you do for children will make them want to please you or will have as much impact on their sense of themselves as capable and loved human beings, now or in the future.

All of the strategies described here are based on research about the effects of various approaches on children's development. Don't just do what comes naturally, or teach the way you were taught. Practice these interaction strategies until they become automatic.

As you do, you will feel good about yourself, for you will be using the most up-to-date, effective, and child-oriented methods for helping children learn to discipline themselves for the rest of their lives.

Build a personal relationship with each child

There are so many things you can do to create a predictable, secure setting and thereby help children learn to regulate their own behavior. Besides being necessary for becoming self-disciplined, positive relationships between adults and children are one of the basic building blocks for children's overall healthy social and emotional development.

Remember, you foster children's trust in you and people in general each time you interact with them! All of the following strategies for interacting with children help build that trusting relationship and feeling of security as well. Each contributes to children's long-term development of a sense of acceptance and well being.

Be there.

Young children, especially babies and toddlers, need reliable adults. Use substitutes infrequently. Your presence definitely gives the children a feeling of security and convinces parents that their children have consistent, reliable care.

Of course, there will be days when you are absent for illness, vacation, or other business, and substitute care has to be arranged. If at all possible, introduce your substitute on a day when you are there. Give children time to get to know the person. Then tell children in advance who will be taking your place if you know you will be absent.

Greet children and family members warmly.

Let children know you are happy to see them and that you look forward to an enjoyable day together. Let families know their children will be safe and happy in your care.

"Hi, Kristy! I'm so glad you are here today. We missed you while you were sick. How do you feel now?"

It is often hard for children to say goodbye and to be away from their loved ones. Respect those feelings. Their separation difficulties may be especially strong after weekends, vacations, and illnesses and at certain times in their development.

When children are reluctant for their parents to leave, say things such as this:

"I know you had such a wonderful weekend. You really enjoyed so much time with your family. Now it is time for them to go to work. Dad will be back to pick up this afternoon after nap. Let's both wave goodbye out the window."

During the day you will want to talk with children frequently about their families. Display photographs of their families near the diaper-changing table, on the children's cubbies, and in other conspicuous places.

Talk about what Mother, Dad, or other family members are doing while the children are with you. If you try to avoid the topic, children will wonder why you are ignoring their favorite people! Don't use the excuse that it will make children too sad or lonely. They have a right to miss their loved ones.

> Never say, "Be a big boy now. Don't cry. The day will be over before you know it." Treat children's feelings with respect. Their feelings are **real**.

In addition to saying hello with every arrival, you need to be sure to say goodbye when children and family members leave. Often, children are as reluctant to go home as they were to say goodbye in the morning—they are having such a good time! Family members may even need reassurance that this reaction is typical and that their children are not rejecting them—just that they have chosen such a good program for their children.

Plan to make this transition from program to home as smooth as possible. If all the children leave at the same time, your schedule can be planned so activities end together. Everyone says goodbye as their parents pick them up or they get on the bus.

If children leave at different times, select open-ended activities for the last part of the day. This way, children can save what they are working on for another day or can easily leave the activity without disrupting a group or missing something special. Art activities, construction toys, books, table toys, individual projects, and even outdoor play usually work well at the end of the day.

If a child is coming into an already established program, before the child's first day, ask parents to visit the program with the child. This gives the child a chance to look around, find the bathroom, and feel more comfortable about you and the environment.

On the child's first day, ask the new child and parent to arrive early. That way, the other children join the new child instead of the other way around. As the other children arrive, you can more gradually introduce the newcomer.

Keep children's needs a priority. Be especially responsive to the needs of babies by cuddling and picking up on their cues about their schedule. Talk with them softly in their home language if possible to give them a chance to get used to your voice. Move gently and slowly so children can adjust to you. Watch the baby to get a feel for her or his personal style. Show older newcomers their cubbies and where to hang their coat or store their lunch. You might also ask another child, perhaps one who is fairly outgoing, to be the new child's guide for the day or week. Give the newcomer a brief review of the day's schedule so she or he knows what to expect:

"First we all choose what we would like to play with, then we have a morning meeting, then we work on projects and play, then we play outdoors, and when we come in we have lunch."

Then the new child can get involved in an activity so the other children join her or him. During the day, you may want to point out that:

"After we play outdoors this afternoon, your mother will be coming to pick you up."

Small things can mean so much to show new children they are welcome. Have their names already on their cubbies and cots or cribs. Hang their family photo with the rest of the children's.

Display books with characters that look or talk like they do. Skip nametags unless everyone is new. If everyone is new, ask the children if they could wear their nametags for just that day—most will want to when given the choice.

Learn children's names immediately, signaling that you want to establish a relationship. Frequently call new children by name, especially during those first difficult hours. Talk about what the children did during the day before they came to your program, using their home language whenever possible. Talk about their old and new neighborhoods—express a genuine interest in children's lives by listening rather than prying. Post pictures of their families. Display their artwork and writing attempts.

Use your observation skills to learn more about children's strengths, needs, and interests so you can plan more appropriately for each one. Be sensitive to children's own pace and unique personality—some will plunge right in, while others may need a week or two to feel more comfortable.

What strategies do you use to make children feel welcome on their first day in your program?

Have items that are theirs w/ their name on it. Place their pictures from home visit in the room.

Show affection.

Use a warm tone of voice and snuggle and hug. Be generous with affection and touch, tailoring it to children's individual styles and their cultural preferences.

Make sure you treat all children with respect: Use children's names often. Speak in children's home languages whenever possible. Never say "Hey, you!" or use nicknames that belittle children.

Do not back away from children you find unappealing in some way. Talk with a trusted co-worker to try to help you overcome any feelings of dislike you may have for a child. These are the children who may be most in need of a caring relationship with you, their teacher.

Show that you enjoy children's company. If you don't want to spend time with children, or are feeling burned out, take a vacation. Children are too vulnerable to be cared for by someone who doesn't have their heart in their work.

Be sensitive about how you show affection to young children by knowing what is culturally appropriate. In some cultures, certain types of touch or eye contact, for example, may not mean the same thing as it does in your culture. Find out about the families in your group. Then use the positive ways they use with their children.

Show children affection in the tone of your voice and by snuggling and hugging. Be generous with affection and touch, tailoring it to children's individual styles and their cultural preferences.

Be sure you help children know the difference between touches that feel good, and touches that make them feel uncomfortable. Help them understand that it is OK to say "Stop!" or "Don't do that anymore!" to an adult who makes them feel uncomfortable.

Make eye contact in culturally appropriate ways.

When you talk with children look at them in their eyes, unless they are taught by their culture not to do so. Get down to their level. Bend your knees, sit on the floor, or sit in a chair.

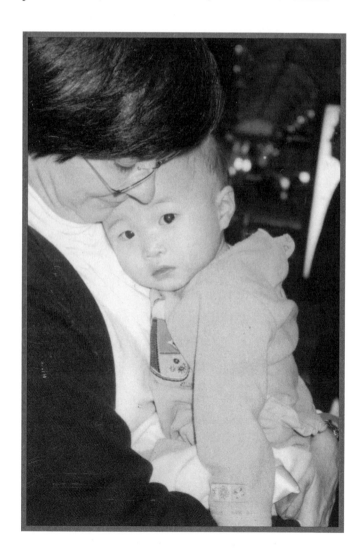

Never yell at children from across the room or outdoor play area **unless it is an emergency.** Remember the story about the boy who cried "Wolf!" If you yell at children all the time, they will soon tune you out and then when it really is an emergency they will keep right on ignoring you.

Start today to use this simple, but very important, teaching technique of getting down to the child's level to make eye contact.

Respond quickly.

Be sensitive to children's requests for assistance. An infant's cry should never be ignored. Go as quickly and calmly as you can to find out what is wrong or what the baby needs. Babies cannot be spoiled by too much attention. In fact, if you respond quickly to babies' cries when they are very young, they tend to cry less often and for shorter times when they are older. Respond calmly and lovingly.

Babies also are helped to feel secure in your care when you adapt to their schedules, then gradually guide them into more regular eating and sleeping patterns. Never make infants wait to eat if they are hungry or wake them up just because it's time to do something else, for example. Be sensitive to each baby's own rhythm.

It is sometimes difficult to respond appropriately when children either do not have the language skills or do not know what the problem is. Many times their cry for help is silent or comes out through antisocial behavior—biting, hitting, or withdrawal, for example.

Sometimes you will have to use observation,

talk with parents, and the process of elimination to figure out why the child is crying or acting in unacceptable ways. We will look at some typical causes for misbehavior later in this unit.

With older children, it may be is easier to figure out what's wrong because when they need help they usually ask for it. Familiar requests for help are "I can't . . ." or "This isn't working." Sometimes they show frustration by stopping before completing a project.

Whenever or however children ask for help, keep this key question in mind: **What can I do to help the child regulate her or his own behavior?**

If you solve the problem by doing it yourself, children may feel like failures. They begin to expect someone else to solve problems for them. They lose the chance to figure

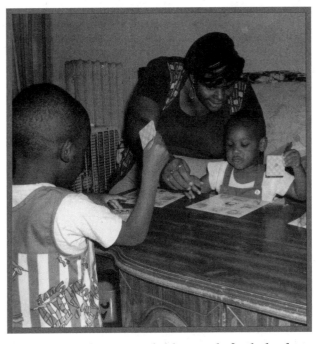

Whenever or however children ask for help, keep this key question in mind: What can I do to help the child regulate her or his own behavior?

something out for themselves. They certainly won't learn to think about what they are doing, to try several solutions, and to feel successful for having figured it out on their own.

Instead of taking over, give children an opportunity to take the next step on their own. Ask them what they are trying to do: "What did you want to do with the saw?" Or comment on what you see, supplying words that describe emotions: "You seem to be frustrated with your progress, but I know you can figure this out."

Once you know the child's goal, you can help get to a solution, often by asking more open-ended questions to get the child to think through the steps involved. Questions with yes or no answers rarely are helpful. Instead, ask open-ended questions such as "What is giving you difficulty?" or "What do you think you need to do first (or next)?"

If the child seems to be at a real loss, you might suggest some solutions in the form of questions: "What do you think would happen if you tried a thinner piece of wood?" "How about using the vice to hold the wood?"

Children learn to cope with frustration best when they do as much as possible themselves and stick with something until they find a solution. Don't interfere with the learning process. Instead, find a way to help children figure out how to solve their problems. This technique works for all types of problems, including resolving disagreements between children.

Use this space to write down an example of how you supported a child who was figuring out a solution to a problem.

_____

_____

_____

_____

Respect children's choices.

Children feel much more secure when they feel they have some control over what happens to them. They know they can make a difference, that they have some say in their fate, that someone has confidence in them—they feel trustworthy. Whenever a choice is possible, offer children **real** choices and accept their decisions. Just make sure that whatever the children choose, it will be a **good** choice! You wouldn't offer children a choice between chocolate ice cream or orange slices for snack, for instance. Nor would you offer a child the choice between wearing a swimsuit or a snowsuit to play outdoors.

Instead, the choices you offer should be appropriate, similar, and they should matter to the child: healthy foods, similar types of clothing, appropriate activities. Don't give choices where they don't really exist. For example, don't say, "Would you like to go outside now?" when you have no intention of letting a child stay in. Instead, you could offer a real choice: "We're all going outside now. Would you like to carry the jump rope or the hula hoop?"

The type and number of choices offered should depend on the child's maturity. Children can handle increasing responsibility as they grow older and gain practice in making decisions.

Let **infants** and **waddlers** choose which toy to play with or which color of sweater to wear.

Toddlers can select which activity to do or which fruit to eat for snack.

Older preschool children can select from three or four good options of what to do, eat, or wear.

Individual choices should also be part of your daily planning. Choice periods should include a variety of options for children to engage in play and other teacher-guided experiences. Some activities would focus on small groups (*reading, blocks, dramatic play, cooking*) while others would be more individual (*art, puzzles, books*).

Children's days should be filled with choices for them. Then they can select from among several activities you have planned those that best match their interests and skills. That is one way that they learn the important skill of decision-making. There is a special bonus in store for you when you offer children choices: **Children who feel they have some control over what happens to them usually will be much more willing to cooperate at other times.**

Two-year-olds have a reputation for always saying "NO!" But if you give them choices, rather than always insisting upon a specific behavior, children generally will be a lot less negative when something comes along about which they have no choice. If a toddler must wear a sweater to play outdoors, offer a choice: the red sweater or the blue sweatshirt.

Write here an example of a choice that you gave to a child and what the child did:

_____

_____

_____

_____

_____

Encourage self-help skills.

You don't want to rush children into too much responsibility, but the more things they do for themselves, the more they learn how to be in charge of their own actions. All through this book we have talked about appropriate self-help skills for young children: toileting, washing hands, brushing teeth, cleaning up spills, hanging up clothes, taking good care of and putting away toys, preparing food, and making choices.

Most children are eager to learn these skills and take responsibil͡ for their own behavior. Such skills incre ͡ ͡ of security because they kn͡ on themselves and they

Take every opportuni͡ tice these skills—don'͡

208

Let children perfect these real-life skills on real-life objects: children's own clothes or dress-up clothes, toys children use every day, meal times. Be sure to allow enough time for children to do it themselves.

Encourage children to help others learn skills, too. You have surely seen how catching it is when the first toddler learns to put on her coat. She lays it on the floor, collar toward her feet, sticks her arms in the sleeves, and flips the coat over her head and on! There is no easier or more fun way!

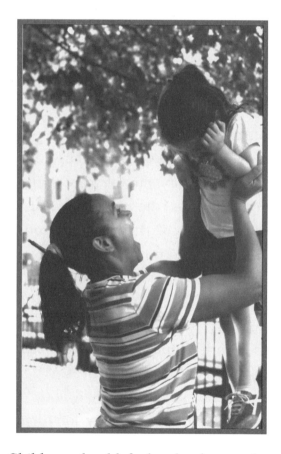

Children should feel valued everyday. They thrive on one-on-one contact and attention. Pay attention to each one during the day, and make it a point to talk with every child.

Know children as individuals.

Children should feel valued everyday. They thrive on one-to-one contact and attention. Pay attention to each one during the day, and make it a point to talk with every child. A brief statement of fact such as "Hi, Jocelyn. I see you are using the lotto game," can open up a whole conversation on topics the child considers important. Or ask the child about things that have happened in the past, will happen in the future, or are in their imagination.

How you interact with children lets them know how important they are to you. Perhaps you're all playing outdoors and a child kicks a ball. You enthusiastically note, "¡Qué fuerte pateaste la pelota!" "What a strong kick!"

Changing diapers, feeding infants, and other routines are perfect times for you and the youngest children to get to know each other better. While doing these tasks, you can describe what are happening, or recite rhymes, poems, songs and finger plays to the child, so the routine becomes an opportunity to build language. Never let children feel like they are just one of the forgotten crowd. If you have trouble remembering whether you have talked to each child during the day, keep a tally on a card in your pocket.

Notice children's successes. Positive attention is much more effective than negative attention if you want children to act appropriately.

Many times, children are so needy for attention that they misbehave—that is a sure way to make most people notice them. Instead, ignore inappropriate behavior (as long as no one is getting hurt) and catch children behaving appropriately!

"Casey and Nicole, you figured out a way to carry that heavy bucket full of water! The two of you are working so cooperatively. That's hard to keep walking together."

"Your baby looks so cozy all tucked in his bed, Rasheed. What a loving father you are."

"All the lids are on all the big plastic bottles! You got every one to match, Takenori and Ariel. You must feel so proud."

Children's self-esteem is given a big boost when you notice what they do. Sometimes this encouragement strategy is called **reinforcement**. When you comment on positive actions, you accomplish at least two things:

- You let children know which behaviors are appropriate: cooperation, sharing, finishing tasks, nurturing others, trying hard.

- You build their sense of pride for behaving appropriately.

Children live up to our expectations for them. Even the most difficult children will begin to regulate their behavior when they are given attention for acting appropriately. It won't happen instantly, but your efforts will be rewarded. Children will act more maturely.

Select one child in your group who could benefit from additional attention to successes.

During one week, keep a diary of all the things you did to help that child feel more successful.

When you finish, discuss your strategies with your Field Advisor.

Support children's families and cultures.

Our primary goals for children's long-term development include having a healthy self-concept and self-esteem as well as a positive sense of identity. These concepts can be fostered when children's experiences in your program are built on respect for the cultural values of their own families and other families.

As an early childhood educator, you have responsibilities to support children's healthy development regarding their families and cultures:

- **Children's individual development must be fostered within their own cultural group (*concentrating on their values and lifestyles*).**

- **Children must be taught to value diversity (*stressing individual and group differences and similarities, race, skin color, bilingualism, differing abilities*).**

- **Children must be taught to counteract bias and stereotypes.**

Foster children's development within their own cultures.

Perhaps you are puzzled about what a culture really is and why it is important to consider for young children's total development. While you will be looking at these issues in depth during your CDA Seminar, you can start getting ready now.

Instead of thinking about other cultures first, it may help you to understand culture better if you start by thinking about your own cultural group. Your cultural values and beliefs strongly affect how you work with young children.

Cultural group values and beliefs are expressed in the "typical" way things are done. Even though everyone in the group does not always do things the same way, culture can be thought of as general trends in thought and behavior that the members of the cultural group recognize, understand, and are familiar with.

What are some of the beliefs your cultural group holds ...

... about infant feeding: breast/bottle, time, introduction of solids, crying, how much infants should be held?

_____

_____

_____

_____

... about how to handle toilet learning? At what age? Should it be different in any way for boys or girls?

_____

_____

_____

_____

... about spanking? Who should do it? Who shouldn't?

_____

_____

_____

_____

_____

... about boys crying?

_____

_____

_____

_____

... about typical toys?

_____

_____

_____

_____

What are some other familiar practices that your cultural group sees as important in childrearing? **Ask your CDA Field Advisor to help you think of some and be prepared to discuss your ideas in your CDA Seminar.**

Childrearing practices are only one way to see differences between cultural groups. There are many others. Jot down some things your cultural group values in these areas. Add others that are especially important to you.

Language:

_____

_____

_____

_____

How you dress:

_____

_____

_____

_____

How you express affection:

_____

_____

_____

_____

Holidays you celebrate:

_____

_____

_____

_____

Art preferences:

_____

_____

_____

_____

Musical tastes:

_____

_____

_____

_____

What it takes to be pretty or handsome:

_____

_____

_____

_____

Who is considered smart?

_____

_____

_____

_____

Skin color:

_____

_____

_____

_____

How girls should act:

_____

_____

_____

_____

Now think about some stereotypes that people hold about your culture. Write those here:

_____

_____

_____

_____

Exactly what then is culture? And why is it important to understand in order to help children develop and learn? Because culture mainly consists of rules about how to give meaning to experiences—rules that are passed down from generation to generation. The rules tell us what values to hold and what ideas to believe in. All of the items on the lists here—and many more—are areas of behavior where cultural groups have rules or expectations about what is appropriate. Most cultures have

a long history, with roots in countries and civilizations that have grown and changed in response to resources and conditions.

Culture then is not just outward symbols like the way we dress or foods we eat, but rather a deep structure of how to behave. Cultural rules guide us in how to show respect, to whom respect is owed, our concepts of time and personal space, the value and goals of schooling, and in general, what kinds of people we want children to become.

Once you have a better idea of what cultural beliefs have influenced what you value and what you do with children, you will be better able to genuinely learn about culture in groups outside your own.

List all the cultural groups represented among the children you care for:

_____

_____

_____

_____

Your first step is to learn more about these cultural groups. How? You can talk with the children's families, read authentic materials (*good children's books are a great resource*), learn the language, listen to some new types of music, or visit a museum or library, for starters.

Begin immediately to find out as much about these cultures as you can, so you can use this information in your work with the children in your care. Before you can be an effective teacher, you need to learn as much as you can about the values, customs, struggles, contributions, and languages of children's cultural groups. It is essential to know these in order to make your program culturally comfortable for the child. You must understand, for example, how cultural characteristics are so fundamental to children's ability to make sense out of the world—that they simply can't be ignored in the everyday interactions in the setting.

The following material on educating culturally diverse children by Barbara T. Bowman offers some valuable ideas for you to consider.

Educating language-minority children

By Barbara T. Bowman

Why can't all Americans just speak Standard English? This plaintive question reflects the distress many citizens feel about the linguistic diversity in the schools. In many school districts, languages of Central and South America, Africa, and Asia mix with American dialects, creating classrooms in which communication is difficult. Across America, children are not learning essential lessons in school. In the next decade or two, the problem will become even more serious. Language-minority children will become the majority in public schools, seriously straining the capacity of those institutions.

In a nation increasingly composed of people who speak different languages and dialects, the old notion of melting them together through the use of a common language is once again attractive. Requiring all children to speak the same language at a high level of proficiency would make the task of educating them a good deal easier. Unfortunately, what seems quite good in theory is often difficult to put into practice. In this instance, the interrelationship of culture, language, and the children's development may make a common language difficult to obtain.

Culture, language and development

Differences in the ways groups think and act are more than a matter of using different words or performing different actions for the same purposes. Differences in cultures are more substantial than whether members of a community eat white bread, corn pone, or tortillas. The behavior of people varies, and the beliefs, values, and assumptions that underlie behavior differ as well. Culture influences both behavior and the psychological processes on which it rests. Culture forms a prism through which members of a group see the world and create shared meanings. And a group's culture is reflected by the group's language.

Child development follows a pattern similar to that of culture. Major structural changes in children, such as language learning, arise from the interaction of biology and experience. Such changes are remarkably similar in kind and sequence among cultural groups. But the knowledge and skills—the cultural learning—the child acquires at various ages depend on the child's family and community.

Learning a primary language is a developmental milestone and a developmentally appropriate educational objective. However, the uses to which that language is put are determined by the culture. As the ideas from a child's social world are brought to bear through the guidance of the older members of the community, children come to share meanings with their elders.

Classroom discourse presents children with the challenge of learning new rules for communication. The use of formal language, teacher control of verbal exchanges, question-and-answer formats, and references to increasingly abstract ideas characterize the classroom environment, with which many children are unfamiliar. To the extent that these new rules overlap with those that children have already learned, classroom communication is made easier. But children whose past experience with language is not congruent with the new rules will have to learn ways to make meaning all over again before they can use language to learn in the classroom.

When teachers and students come from different cultures or use different languages or dialects, teachers may be unaware of variations between their understanding of a context and their students'; between their expectations for behavior and the children's inclinations. When children and adults do not share common experiences and beliefs, adults are less able to help children encode their thoughts in language.

Teaching children from different cultures

Teachers facing the challenge of teaching children from different cultural communities are hard-pressed to decide what constitutes an appropriate curriculum. If children from some groups are hesitant to speak up in school, how can teachers organize expressive language experiences? If children from some groups are dependent on nonverbal cues for meaning, how can teachers stress word meaning? How can teachers test for mastery of the curriculum if children do not speak a standard language or use the same styles of communication? Cultural diversity makes it hard for teachers to assess each child's developmental status, find common educational experiences to promote growth, and measure the achievement of educational objectives.

Given the complex interaction between culture and development, is it possible to design a developmentally appropriate curriculum? If that question implies that the same curriculum can be used for all children, the answer must be *no*. However, the following developmental principles can provide a conceptual framework for teachers trying to bridge the gap between children's cultural backgrounds and school objectives.

Guidelines for teachers

First, **teachers need to learn to recognize developmentally equivalent patterns of behavior.** Before children come to school, they have all learned many of the same things, such as a primary language and communication styles. Although these developmental accomplishments may look different, they are developmentally equivalent. When a child does not respond to the social and cognitive expectations of the school, the teacher should look for a developmentally equivalent task to which the child will respond. A child who does not separate buttons correctly can be asked to sort car logos or other personally relevant artifacts. A child who does not listen to stories about the seasons may be spellbound by a story about an ice skater. Teachers with doubts about the development of culturally different children should assume that the children are normal and look at them again, recognizing that their own vision may be clouded by cultural myopia.

Second, **it is essential not to value some ways of achieving developmental milestones more highly than others.** Asa Hilliard and Mona Vaughn-Scott point out that because the behavior of African-American children is so different from that of their white peers, African-American children are often judged to be deficient, rather than different, in their development. Young children who speak languages other than English, or who speak non-standard dialects, are often reluctant to give up this connection to their group. When such children find that the way they talk is not understood or appreciated in school, they are apt to become confused or disengaged. And their rejection by the school presages their rejection of school.

Third, **teachers need to begin instruction with interactive styles and content that is familiar to the children.** Whether this entails speaking in the child's primary language, using culturally appropriate styles of address, or relying on patterns of management familiar to the children, the purpose is to establish a basis for communication. While fluency in a child's primary language may not be possible for many teachers, they can nonetheless become more adept at planning and implementing a culturally sensitive curriculum. Such a curriculum encompasses more than tasting parties, ethnic costumes, and shop-worn introductions to practices of people from different nations or racial groups. In order to teach such a curriculum, teachers must come to grips with their own ethnocentricity.

Fourth, **school learning is most likely to occur when family values reinforce** school expectations. Parents and other community members must view school achievement as a desirable and attainable goal if children are to build it into their sense of self. Interpreting the school's agenda for parents is one of the most important tasks for teachers.

Fifth, **when differences exist between the cultural patterns of the home and community and those of the school, teachers must deal with these discrepancies directly.** Teachers and children must create shared understanding and new contexts that give meaning to the knowledge and skills being taught. Learning mediated by teachers who are affectionate, interested, and responsive has greater sticking power than learning mediated by an adult who is perceived as impersonal and distant.

Sixth, **for children from different racial and ethnic groups, meanings of words, gestures, and actions may differ.** Assessment of learning outcomes presents a formidable problem when children misunderstand the teacher's requests for information or demonstrations of knowledge and skills. Formal assessment should be delayed until teachers and children have built a set of new meanings.

A developmentally appropriate curriculum can never be standardized in a multicultural community. But thoughtful teachers can use principles of child development to make the new context of school meaningful and to safeguard the self-confidence of children.

Help children experience and value diversity by getting to know lots of other people, preferably first hand.

Experience and value diversity.

The world, our country, and your community are diverse. Perhaps some communities are more diverse than others, but diversity surrounds us: Not only culture or race, but people also have minor or more visible disabilities, religious preferences, and live in different family groups.

Your role is to help children build on their experiences by getting to know lots of other people, preferably first hand, and to live each day in a way that demonstrates how rewarding diversity can be to each person.

You will also need to help children unlearn some of the stereotypes they have already formed.

There is a wealth of materials that can assist you in exposing children to all types of differences. These include books, artifacts, individuals, and materials.

The principle of valuing and accepting differences applies to every activity and conversation you have in your classroom or home. Your positive attitude about the value of people is essential if children are to gain a wider perspective about the world in which we all must live and work in harmony.

Look at the diversity within your community. What cultural groups will the children come into contact with? What other types of diversity will they experience both first-hand and through the media?

_____

_____

_____

_____

_____

As an early childhood educator, you must feel comfortable with your own attitudes about families who are different from the ones you grew up with, or who are different from those of the supposedly traditional nuclear family—a family with working father, mother at home with children rarely exists in the United States. Single parents, different custody arrangements, multigenerational families, and blended (*step*-) families are just some of the variations that nearly always are found in even a small group of people.

It is hard to do this by yourself, so **this will be one of the areas you work on in your CDA Seminar.** For now, we will see how you can integrate respect for children and their families—from many cultures, with disabilities, with various family members—into your daily work with young children.

Pictures of posters with African-Americans, European-Americans, Asian Americans, and Native Americans, showing both sexes, differently abled people, and all ages are an excellent start. Positive books about stepparents or living with grandmother are a good addition. Cooking foods of children's cultures is a beginning. Learning about how children celebrate holidays and special occasions in their homes is fine. Trying out crutches and playing with puppets that have disabilities are good ideas. They are not enough.

Children need to do more than spend one week a year crawling into a tepee in order to gain concrete ideas about Native Americans yesterday and today. They need more than one brief movie about elderly people who are active in their community to really get to know how people age. If children are to get an accurate picture of what being human is all about, they need more than a tourist approach. Children need to **live with diversity**.

To offer a balanced approach, you need to incorporate languages, real objects, music, art, and many other aspects of people's experiences into your curriculum. This way, you will establish an atmosphere in which diversity is accepted and celebrated as a natural part of life.

Bring diverse individuals into the environment as guests or volunteers. Perhaps someone who signs or uses cued speech can teach all of you some basic communication skills to use with the deaf. Or children can feel books prepared in Braille. Visit a library with a teletype service. See how a Braille typewriter works. With every experience, children begin to appreciate how many ways there are for people to communicate.

Label materials or children's constructions in more than one language. Use different color pens for each language. Provide books in a variety of languages. Read the stories to them, or invite a storyteller to bring a new dimension to the literature. Audio recordings also provide a new dimension to the stories and often have background sounds or music that provide additional depth. Recite poems in the language in which children feel most comfortable. Create finger plays. Perhaps the words will not be understood at first, but children will get the message that all languages are valued, not just English.

Languages. Language is children's window to figuring out the world.

Just try reading a story to a child using an unfamiliar language. You will get a puzzled look back. Using the same language that the child knows and understands is an essential part of every early childhood classroom.

Many children come to early childhood programs knowing languages other than English. Learning a second language during the early years is easier than later in life, but still requires a lot of effort and support from competent speakers of the language. Children learning a second language need help to feel comfortable in using their home language. They need help to strengthen that language at the same time they are becoming fluent in English. Opinions vary about the best way to achieve this. Some experts believe that translating everything doesn't work, because children soon learn to wait until they hear the language they know best and tune out on the other. Do some additional reading on this topic. Chapter 5 and the resource lists have more ideas about how to support second language learners.

If you don't speak the same home languages of the children in your group, what ways have you found to foster development of their home language?

_____

_____

_____

_____

Real objects. Dress-up clothing can come from many cultures. Ask parents to contribute garments from their culture if possible. Make sure anything you purchase is authentic, not just stereotypes of what people in that culture wear. Clothes should also be primarily what people wear every day, not what they wear only on special occasions. Be sure to include

---

Remember (*and remind parents too*) that the library is a wonderful resource. Children's librarians are trained in child development as well as literature and other resources. They can provide children and families a positive introduction to a whole new world of information—through toys, books, audio and video materials. Libraries are publicly funded and free to everyone! (*See pages 319-320.*)

---

many types of shoes and other accessories.

Also in the dramatic play area, you can incorporate models or pictures of ethnic foods, a variety of serving and eating utensils (*Native American baskets, chopsticks*), and different types of furniture (*futon, cradle, hammock, rugs*). Families can be composed of various members (*mother or father and child only, combined families due to remarriage, grandparents, roommates*). Crutches, canes, hearing aids, old glasses, and other devices can become as familiar as the doll cradle.

Dolls, puppets, and miniature people can portray people of both sexes from many cultures, and with varying ages and physical abilities. Every doll should have authentic features and clothing also. If you cannot find any to purchase, perhaps someone could make them. You may need to give some specific guidance to make sure they are appropriate for the cultures or physical abilities represented.

One often-overlooked aspect of culture is children's games. Every cultural group has its own games. Many games can be made with household objects or common items such as rocks. Some require no props at all, just a willingness to play. Preschool children enjoy games when the rules are tailored to their developmental abilities and the emphasis is on having fun, not on competition. Perhaps a parent or an elderly person in the neighborhood would be delighted to play some favorites with the children.

Most young children are very interested in various modes of transportation and construction. Select vehicles and tools from several cultures and time periods: sleds, boats, wagons, trains, rockets, shovels, and road graders.

If you are not sure where to locate books and other materials or to find some resource people to assist you, remember to check with your local library. Their job is to keep records of various community resources as well as collect and arrange many print and non-print materials. If you have not done so yet, now is a good time to visit your local public library.

Write down the name, address, phone number and hours of operation here.

_____

_____

_____

_____

_____

What kinds of objects can you add to provide a better balance of multicultural experiences for young children?

_____

_____

_____

_____

Share your ideas with your Field Advisor and the other CDA Candidates in your Seminar.

Music. Music from many cultures is marvelous for developing an appreciation for different types of instruments, rhythms, expressions, themes, and languages.

While recordings are useful, it is hard for children to visualize who is playing the music and what the instruments look like. Try to obtain real instruments, such as drums, different types of bells, stringed instruments, or shakers, from several cultures. Demonstrate how sounds are made. Older children might even enjoy creating their own instruments.

After children have lots of experience with real instruments, they will be able to identify sounds in recordings. Singing children's songs or folk songs in both the original language and English is a marvelous way for children to explore language and music at the same time. Parents or grandparents are often thrilled to be asked to share some of their favorite childhood songs with the group.

Children are intrigued with different types of dance. Ask willing families to teach children some simple ethnic dance steps. Take small groups to a local performance. Watch a video of cultural dances. Just make sure the dances are authentic, not just a stereotyped idea of the real thing. Also, help children see that people in any cultural group dance once in a while, just as the children do, and not every day.

Keep everything in context and as authentic as possible so children can put things in proper perspective.

What kinds of musical experiences do you need to add to assure more cultural variety?

_____

_____

_____

Talk about these ideas with your CDA Field Advisor.

Art. Children can also begin to appreciate how cultural groups express themselves through art. Museums and libraries are excellent resources for this. Don't limit your focus just to flat pieces or art from Western cultures.

Fabrics can be touched in clothing, rugs, hangings, pillows, or blankets. Preschool children can try their hand at simple weaving, quilting, and other textile arts. They are spellbound when they watch a sheep being sheared or wool being carded. Perhaps they could use food coloring to dye swatches of cotton. Compare the colors and textures of fabrics to children's hair and skin. What a wide array of beauty! The possibilities for using fabrics as a learning tool are limitless.

Carvings and sculpture—wood, stone, metal, and clay—can be handled and appreciated when you choose sturdy pieces. Children can try to use similar techniques: Children can carve soap with plastic knives. Younger children can collect rocks. Older children can begin to work with wood.

Commercial clay substitutes or homemade dough are fine, but children also need to experience the texture and feel of real clay. Dig it together if you can. Point out how the color of real clay is similar to some skin colors. After children have worked with clay for a while, try to find a potter willing to show how to use their potter's wheel. What a thrill!! Baskets, boxes, caned chairs, and pottery—all have intriguing cultural variations and children can use them, too. There are many other art forms like these that you will discover once you start talking with parents and seeking more information.

Painting can be done on paper, textiles, fences (*with water and a big brush!*), and faces. Many different types of media can be used: Craypas, crayons, tempera, finger paint, food coloring. Explore ways in which different cultures use the materials they have available to draw and decorate.

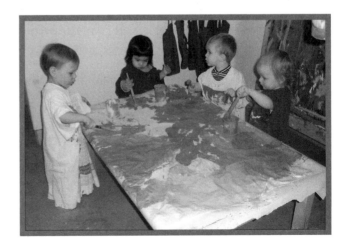

Painting can be done on paper, textiles, fences and faces!

How can you broaden children's art experiences to reflect many cultural variations?

_____

_____

_____

_____

What other ideas does your CDA Field Advisor have to suggest?

_____

_____

_____

_____

Everyday living requires many diverse types of cooperation and work. Help children see how much variety there is. Once you get started thinking in terms of what children are already familiar with, and how similar activities occur in different ways among different families, you will wonder how you ever left out or skimmed over such an important facet of children's education!

What have you done to include cultures, different life styles, and people with disabilities in your teaching environment?

_____

_____

_____

Be prepared to share your ideas about all the questions in this section with your Field Advisor.

Counteract bias and stereotypes.

Just as with all other behaviors, young children copy others' ideas and attitudes. They may unwittingly repeat stereotypes—untrue generalities, usually negative—they have heard or seen others express without fully understanding what they mean. It is important to help young children avoid these, even in their earliest experiences.

We all have biases—tendencies to favor or disfavor. In fact, every culture and family is biased toward itself—that's part of having a healthy self-concept, of being proud of who we are. However, as an early childhood professional, you must also be aware that because they cause you to prejudge people our biases can get in the way of doing your best with young children.

Good teachers spend a lot of time figuring out what stereotypes they hold about race, cultures, families, sexes, disabilities, or ages. Then we work to change our thinking. It's harder for some of us than others, especially when we have spent so many years cultivating our opinions.

What are some stereotypes or biases that you learned that you would like to change?

_____

_____

_____

You will discuss these in more detail during your CDA Seminar.

Stereotypes in the environment. Preschool children are forming important attitudes about themselves and others regarding sex and gender, age, abilities, and race. Unfortunately, stereotypes appear in every classroom, because they are so deeply embedded in our society. But there are strategies you can use to reduce the presence of these in your setting.

We have already looked at how to avoid children's books and other learning materials that contain biased attitudes about race and sex. These same ideas can be adapted to select classroom materials that avoid other stereotyped ideas about physical or mental capacity, family composition, and age.

The work of Barbara Sprung and Merle Froschl at Education Equity Concepts in New York has produced valuable resources for this effort, along with the Early Childhood Equity Alliance (www.rootsforchange.org.)

Look around your classroom or family child care home. What evidence do you see of stereotypes (*race, culture, family, sex, age, or disability*)?

_____

_____

_____

_____

_____

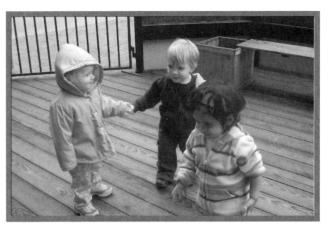

Children who get along well can use the same strategies they are learning now to share, negotiate, and solve problems as adults. Your example is the primary way children learn to be friendly and cooperative. You always treat children, their families, and neighbors or other staff with respect.

Interactions that reflect bias. You want children to learn to get along with each other better and to stand up for what is fair and right. Therefore, you need to notice when children's interactions reflect society's biases. If you ignore slurs and prejudices, children will perpetuate negative values and attitudes.

What if at Thanksgiving, a child asks whether the Indians are going to scalp people at your harvest feast? Or a child makes fun of another who wears braces on her legs? Or someone says girls can't play with blocks or boys can't cook? Or a child stares at an elderly neighbor on a morning stroll? Or a child comments, "Pink is my favorite color. Black is ugly." Children pick up stereotypes very easily from other people; in print from books, greeting cards, and advertisements; and from movies.

How do you deal with instances such as these? **This is one time when the principle of ignoring inappropriate behaviors does not apply.** You must take direct action to counteract these unproductive and erroneous ideas.

Your goal is to help children feel comfortable when they (1) stand up for themselves; and (2) insist that everyone respect the rights of others. Children need self-confidence and practice to develop these strengths.

Early childhood educators are irresponsible if we fail to prepare children to deal with the world's harsh realities. Just being around children from other cultural groups (*or sexes, or ages, or with disabilities*) isn't enough to ensure children will grow in their understanding of each other. Instead, we must show children appropriate ways to interact, teach them the truth about others, and involve them in solving problems based on what is fair.

Teaching children about what is fair is not something you set aside 10 minutes for each day. Questions and attitudes about differences between people come up frequently, and you can stimulate children's thinking even further by raising questions about physical and cultural differences and similarities, equipping your classroom with many objects that reflect diversity, and reading books about a variety of children and situations.

In addition, you will need to directly confront biases as they come up. How you deal with everyday expressions of bias such as these examples will be dis- cussed in your CDA Seminar. Think about how you would respond in each situation and make some notes here:

"You're a sissy because you play with dolls."

_____

_____

_____

_____

_____

Good early childhood teachers use an anti-bias curriculum:

Anti-bias curriculum is about preparing children for healthy, effective, cooperative, and peaceful living in a diverse, complex society and world. It is about strengthening children's self-identities and their abilities to respect differences and interact cooperatively with each other. It is about opening up choices. Consequently, anti-bias curriculum is also about challenging those conditions that prevent all children from achieving their full range of abilities and possibilities. This requires facilitating our own and children's critical thinking, problem solving, and developing skills for creating social change. In a word, anti-bias curriculum is about empowerment.

—*Louise Derman Sparks*

On a field trip, children stare at a person in a wheelchair.

_____

_____

_____

_____

_____

A child puts his fingers at the corners of his eyes, pulls his skin up, and brags, "Me Chinese brother."

_____

_____

_____

_____

_____

A new child shrinks back in fear from an African-American child when the group joins hands to play a circle game.

_____

_____

_____

_____

_____

List two or three other incidents you have experienced (like name calling) that reveal prejudice among children. How did you respond?

_____

_____

_____

_____

_____

Talk with your CDA Field Advisor about how you feel about your responses.

Responding to incidents such as these may be difficult for you. Perhaps you feel embarrassed to talk about prejudices with young children. Or perhaps you were raised to not notice skin color or disabilities because it wasn't "nice."

The following guidelines will give you the support you need to respond in ways that are comfortable for you and that are also professional:

- When a child is the target of bias, first offer comfort. Assure the child's safety. Listen to the child's concerns and express your understanding in a culturally appropriate way. Acknowledge the child's recognition that what was said or done was very unfair. Indicate you know how badly her or his feelings are hurt.

- Then talk with the child or children who hold the stereotypes. If a small group is involved, talk with each child individually, so you can get to know more about each child's thinking. If the entire group is affected (*as in the example with the wheelchair*), you may need to meet together.

- How you respond depends on the children's ages and the nature of the stereotype, but you never punish or ridicule the offending children. Instead, allow the children plenty of time to talk about the ideas, questions, or feelings that led to the incident.

  A simple statement such as "You think Adam is a sissy because he plays with dolls" can open up the conversation. As the child talks, you will have a better idea how to counteract the unfair attitudes. You will find more about talking with and listening to children in just a few pages from here, but we will provide some specific examples now because this is an area about which most people feel very uncertain.

- When you talk with children who have shown prejudice, you always relate what happened to people's feelings and what is fair.

  "It hurts people when you make fun of them. We don't make fun of people here. Each person is valuable."

  "Ideas like that are not fair to other people. In our school, we treat everyone fairly."

  "Friends don't treat each other like that. Friends are kind to each other."

- Sometimes you must explain history or a child's physical condition. Do it as accurately, fairly, and simply as possible so children can begin to understand and see it in context. Always reassure children that they are safe.

  "Native Americans were the first people to live here. Then strangers came and tried to take away their land. The Indians defended their homes and families. That was a long time ago. You don't have to worry about people being hurt like that any more."

- Children are often worried that they, too, could develop a disability. Again, assure the child's safety.

  "You are worried about your leg, too. But Anthony was in a bad accident. We are always careful. We will keep you safe."

When you meet with your CDA Seminar, you will practice other techniques to confront children's stereotypes.

Teach children social skills and emotional self-regulation.

It is not enough to demonstrate respect for children and their families. Teachers of young children must also help them learn to be friendly, cooperative, and to share, negotiate, and solve problems. These important skills prepare them for success in school and will also serve them well as adults.

Your example is the primary way in which they learn to be friendly and cooperative. You always treat children, their families, and neighbors or other staff with respect. Children will see you as a role model.

Foster children's friendships everyday.

Within your program, you establish an atmosphere that is warm and welcoming. You have only a few reasonable rules about behavior:

- We treat each other in friendly ways.

- We cooperate with each other.

- We take care of materials.

How do friends treat each other? They help each other, they talk pleasantly, they never hurt another person, they are kind and considerate, they are generous, they are courteous, and they offer comfort.

Ask the children in your group how friends treat each other. Have a large piece of paper handy so you can write down their answers. This is an excellent language experience as well. Jot down their responses here:

_____

_____

_____

_____

Watch and you will see children who treat each other in friendly ways—if they have seen adults act like that. A baby might pat a crying child on the back. Toddlers may offer a friend their truck when they are finished. Preschoolers can be eager helpers for each other and younger children. Just keep your expectations in line with children's development.

The atmosphere you establish sets a tone of cooperation rather than selfishness or competition. Although infants and toddlers primarily play alone or beside other children, rather than with them, they still can be cooperative at times.

Friendships begin to develop in infancy. Babies might roll balls to each other or coo and reach toward one another. A child who can crawl or walk might take a toy to a nonmobile child. Toddler friendships are even firmer. A toddler might sit with another to look through a book or play hide and seek on the climbing structure.

Preschoolers are increasingly able to work together and form lasting friendships. They can choose a theme and carry it out at length in dramatic play or with construction toys. They might dance together, or offer assistance to a differently-abled child on the playground, or pull each other in the wagon.

How do you foster friendly behavior and cooperation among children?

- Set up the environment to invite children to cooperate, play, and work together. Have enough space for three or four children to play in a small group. Set up enclosed areas such as lofts or climbers. Use double-width easels for children to paint next to each other or together. Establish teams to use computers or work together on a writing project like making a book. Pick interesting props to encourage dramatic play. Read books about cooperation, such as _Swimmy_ (Lionni, 1968).

- Provide toys that are more fun with two or more children: blocks, rocking boats, balls, wagons, jump ropes, stethoscope, bandages, telephones—there are hundreds of items. Choose large puzzles with enough pieces so two or more children can work together, and put the puzzle on a small table with two or three chairs.

- Play games that support doing things together such as "Ring Around the Rosie" (_everyone does_ the same thing) or bowling (*one child bowls, one is the pin setter, another keeps score*). Change the rules of games that seem too competitive—put out enough chairs for everyone to play "Musical Chairs." Just listening for when the music stops, finding a chair, and sitting in it is enough challenge for young children.

- Always be friendly and cooperative with children and other adults. Phrase directions and rules in a positive way: "Walk, please," rather than "No running." Help children see how their actions affect others. "When you dropped the briefcase, it hit Liliana on her foot. That hurt. She is crying. How can you help her feel better?"

- Notice when children are friendly and cooperative. Let them know how proud they should be of their behavior. "Garrett, you were so kind to help baby Jassmin with her mittens so we could all go outdoors to play. Her smile is telling you 'thank you'."

- Intervene to help unpopular children make friends. If there are children in your group who are neglected or even rejected by their peers, set up pairs with more popular children for some activities so the unpopular child can have a role model. Computers and games are an excellent way to help two children get to know each other better.

- Encourage children to use words (*rather than violence*) to find solutions to their disagreements. Help children feel good about their successes—and they will soon applaud others for theirs.

You can foster children's friendships every day

Here are some suggestions for encouraging cooperation:

- Set up the environment to invite children to cooperate, play, and work together.

- Provide toys that are more fun with two or more children.

- Play games that support doing things together.

- Always be friendly and cooperative with children and other adults.

- Notice when children are friendly and cooperative.

- Intervene on behalf of unpopular children.

- Encourage children to use words (*rather than violence*) to find solutions to their disagreements.

How do you encourage cooperation and friendly behavior with your group? What do you do to help unpopular children? List several of your strategies here.

_____

_____

_____

_____

_____

_____

Listen and understand.

Being a child is not easy, although it may seem like it on those days when everything goes wrong for us! Children are trying so hard to figure things out, to do what pleases others, and to grow up. Each child needs at least one adult who will listen attentively and understand how the child feels. Children who can find words to describe their feelings are well on their way to controlling those feelings.

Sometimes children are bothered by something and you don't know what. Sometimes they get into fights and give you two or more conflicting stories about what happened. Sometimes they are dealing with difficult times in their lives and need a comforting ear. In all these cases, we can help children resolve their problems by listening to them, supporting their feelings, and helping them work through the problem.

Really listening to children is not as easy as it might first appear. Many books have been written about how to listen to others. Listening is so important because you need to be aware of what children are thinking and feeling. Then, based on what you know, you can decide on the best action to help get the problem resolved. Lots of times, just listening is enough to help children work through their own difficulties.

We will cover some of the basics of listening here, and then in your work with children you can practice your skills. Don't wait to start using these techniques, though. It will feel awkward at first, and you might even be skeptical about the idea—but it does work,

you maintain everyone's dignity in the process, and children learn how to solve social problems on their own.

Encourage children to trust you. You already know how important it is for children to be able to trust you. Children need to feel comfortable when they talk with you. Bend over, squat, or sit on a low chair so you are on the child's level and give your full attention to the child. Avoid distractions. And keep any secrets (*unless you have a legal obligation to do otherwise, as in reporting child abuse*).

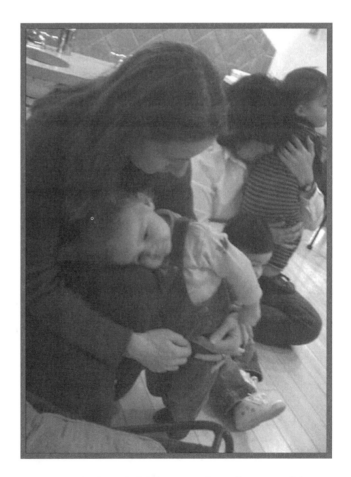

We can help children resolve their problems by listening to them, supporting their feelings, and helping them work through the problem.

Trust children to solve their own problems. Young children never learn to do things on their own like feeding and tying shoes if we do everything for them. The same is true of their ability to solve social problems. Most of the time, children are more capable than we realize. Unless we trust them to practice and occasionally make mistakes, they'll always be dependent on others to negotiate social situations.

Pay attention to what children say. When children have a disagreement, seem sad, or have done something inappropriate, it is very tempting to want to lecture, ask harsh questions, criticize, or give a lengthy explanation. STOP! You can't talk and listen at the same time. Say as little as possible so the child can talk. Keep the emphasis on finding out the truth about what happened and how the issue can be resolved.

Listen to both actions and words. Children use body language as well as spoken language to communicate.

These are the main principles of effective listening:

- Be someone children can trust.

- Let children do most of the talking.

- Pay attention to children's actions as well as their words.

- Accept whatever children say in a way that leads them to think more about the idea or solve the problem themselves.

- You guide what happens—you do not impose solution.

Tyler is mad. He stomps over to you. "Kimberly hit me!"

You take Tyler by the hand and walk calmly over to Kimberly.

"Kimberly, Tyler is angry. He says you hit him."

"I did not hit Tyler," asserts 4-year-old Kimberly. But her eyes are on the floor and she is squirmy.

The children's body language tells you there is more to the story. Learn to read what posture, eye contact, tone of voice, and other actions. Tyler and Kimberly are usually cooperative. Tyler rarely gets angry enough to stomp. Kimberly is usually confident. So something must be up.

Expand children's thinking. Talk further with Tyler and Kimberly:

"But Tyler says you hit him," you point out.

"Yes, she did, because I wouldn't give her the red marker," retorts Tyler.

You pause. Kimberly continues to look down and fidget, but says nothing. "Tyler says you hit him because he wouldn't give you the red marker," you repeat, and then wait again.

"Well ... I asked him nicely first and he said 'No'," admits Kimberly.

What did you do to encourage children to tell what happened?

- You stated Tyler's version of what happened.

- You included Tyler in the discussion and gave him an opportunity to explain.

- You gave Kimberly time to think and respond to what Tyler said.

- You restated Tyler's account with more details.

- You waited for Kimberly to think. She then admitted she hit Tyler.

Kimberly did not feel threatened or belittled in the discussion, so she eventually acknowledged her inappropriate behavior. Now it is clear what happened.

What happens next? But now what do you do? Scold Kimberly? Call Tyler a tattletale? Make Kimberly apologize? Put Kimberly in time out? Insist that Tyler give Kimberly the red crayon? NO indeed. You think about what children are learning in the situation. You think about your long-term goals for children. And then you ask the children what they think should happen now.

Does asking the children what should happen next seem unteacherly to you? Are you frightened that you are not in control of the children? You are still there to **guide** what happens, but you don't impose a solution.

If children express solutions, listen to what they say and try to use their ideas to help settle things down. This way, they certainly are learning to regulate their emotions and behavior, be responsible for their actions, and solve problems. Effective listening can work in many situations with children. You encourage children to state what happened or what they think. You give children time to respond. You keep the focus on the issue. The key is to keep children involved, not to take away from their feelings and actions by talking yourself.

You will use these listening skills many times each day. Begin immediately to practice, even though it may feel strange. The next time you really listen to a child, jot down some notes about how the conversation went. Record here what was said as soon as you can.

_____

_____

_____

_____

_____

Talk about what happened with your CDA Field Advisor.

Use social and emotional teaching strategies

Many children need us to directly teach them about emotions—anger, frustration, sadness, and happiness—and how to express them appropriately. Teachers need to help children identify their own feelings and those of other people. To correctly identify and talk about feelings, children need vocabulary—not just "happy", but more complex words like "excited, enthusiastic, surprised, or comfortable." Children can learn about emotions by talking about pictures, playing with puppets or other games.

The other strategies described earlier, such as helping children make friends, solve problems, and express anger appropriately are all important social-emotional teaching strategies.

STEP 4: You use a positive approach to help children with challenging behaviors.

Think about the basic skills we have just discussed to implement a positive approach to encourage children to develop self-regulation and social skills: you have developmentally appropriate expectations for children, you make sure the environment doesn't create problems, you build a positive relationship with each child, you build their concepts of themselves and their families, and you teach social skills and problem-solving.

Well, all these positive methods are fine, you say. But what do you do in a really tough situation where children are especially difficult or even completely out of control? Do you spank? Do you yell? Do you threaten? NO! You remain calm. You control your own anger. And you use similar, but more intensive, adult-structured strategies to help children learn to regulate and appropriately express their strong emotions and get along with other people. Intervene when children are out of control.

Sometimes a child engages in actions that are dangerous and hurtful to other people: running wildly, yelling, biting, hitting, pushing, kicking, spitting, calling names, using offensive language, and throwing tantrums, for example.

How do you handle explosive episodes? First, maintain your own control, regardless of what the children are doing. **Never allow yourself to act like a child.** Remember, we want to show children how to behave by acting the way we want children to act. That is why we never hit, bite back, spank, or otherwise lash out at a child.

While maintaining your control, you try to figure out what went wrong. Most challenging behavior results because a young child is trying to get something (such as your attention or a favorite toy) or to avoid something (such as taking a nap or sitting during circle time). Therefore, it is vitally important that the child NOT succeed in using unacceptable behavior to achieve a goal.

So as difficult as it sounds, you must not give attention to the negative behavior. Don't try to reason with a child who is out of control. You may need to stop the aggressive child from hurting anyone (you and the aggressive child included). If so, try to remain calm and use words, "I cannot allow you to hit. Hitting hurts. We don't hurt our friends."

Focus your attention first on the injured child, if there are any, and console him or her. Remember, all the children who are in the vicinity are watching what happens. During the entire episode, children are learning that you will protect them from others and help them control themselves.

As for the aggressor, you may need to physically restrain and leave the room with her or him until the child calms down. Do so gently and in a way that helps the child feel secure.

When the child has regained self-control and is able to talk coherently, you can begin to use your listening skills. You make it possible for children to retain their dignity, to trust you to be strong when they are out of control.

Sometimes children's behavior will make you angry. You may want to scream and take out your frustration on the child. But you are an adult and a professional early childhood educator. You have better ways to help children learn to control themselves. Your goal is always to look at the future and give children the opportunity to learn self-regulation in a positive way.

What are some techniques you use to calm yourself down so you can use professional techniques to help children regain their self-control when they are acting up?

What would you do if a child spit in your face?

> Pray, count to 5. Then clearly articulate the wrong in spitting.

Be sure to think carefully because you will be asked to share your ideas with your Seminar group—everyone is searching for ways to stay calm.

Teach, not punish.

Sometimes a more systematic strategy is needed when a child's destructive or hurtful behavior persists and disrupts the classroom. The goal of this approach is not just to control children's behavior now, but also to help them develop skills that contribute to long-term development.

Often, teachers and parents think first of how to punish misbehavior, perhaps by put-

ting the child in timeout or withholding a favorite food. Punishment stops the bad behavior for a short time, but does not teach the child what to do instead. Whenever you find yourself using the same punishment over and over, you can assure yourself that it is not working!

You probably are familiar with an isolation strategy called *time out.* Lots of people use it whenever a child behaves inappropriately. In most time outs, children are removed from the situation, usually asked to sit on a chair away from the others, and told to think about what they did. A time limit may be given (*"You can return to the group in five minutes."*), or children determine when they are ready to play in a more friendly way.

But what do children learn in this kind of time out? And what are its long-term effects? Children learn that they only have to wait a few minutes until the problem goes away. They may spend the time figuring out how to get

> Threats are not effective, can strike fear in some children's hearts and can ruin their sense of security with you.
>
> NEVER, ever threaten to ... flush the child down the toilet ... burn a security blanket ... lock the child in a closet ... or otherwise endanger anything important to the child. Children need to know you will protect them from harm, physical or emotional. That requires your acceptance of them, even when they misbehave. Remember, your goal is to help children learn self-regulation.

revenge. They usually have no opportunity to explain the situation from their viewpoint, so they may feel they were treated unfairly. They never even had a chance to negotiate or figure out a solution to the problem. And if they were bored or didn't like the activity, they found a sure way to get out of doing it!

Time out is usually just an easy way out for the adult. It is an escape for children, which doesn't help them learn what to do instead, and may even teach them things we don't want. Think for a minute about older children who are expelled from school because they are misbehaving. Often they don't want to be in school—and getting thrown out is just what they want! So if you are using timeout, let's explore some alternative strategies—that help children develop self-regulation skills that support long-term development.

One such approach guides teachers to carefully observe and analyze children's misbehavior.

· What usually happens before the behavior to trigger it?

· What is the specific behavior you're trying to correct?

· How often does it actually occur? Under what conditions is it most likely to occur?

· And then, what happens after the misbehavior?

· What are the usual consequences?

These questions are part of a well-researched strategy called ABC Functional Assessment, described in *Practical Ideas for Addressing Challenging Behavior* (Sandall & Ostrosky, 1999) and in *Meeting the Challenge: Effective Strategies for Challenging Behaviors in Early Childhood Environments* (Kaiser & Rasminsky, 1999).

"A" stands for "antecedent" or what comes before the misbehavior, "B" for behavior, and "C" for consequence. If we want to change a negative behavior, we first need to know the conditions when it usually happens (when it's time to get ready for lunch or when too many children try to engage in a popular activity).

Sometimes, just learning what usually comes before and leads up to a problem helps you solve it. You can anticipate situations where a child will probably encounter difficulty and redirect them to another activity. Or you can be available to assist an individual child during a necessary transition.

Redirect the activity.

Whenever possible, you want children to select their own activities, to follow their own ideas through, to figure out their own problems. There are times, however, when you need to firmly take the child by the hand and move her or him to something more productive.

Katie joins three other children at a small round table. They have been playing with the Legos™, have made some elaborate constructions, and the limit for that activity is three children. As soon as you see her enter the area, you walk over. The other children are reminding her that the area is full, but she doesn't look like she is ready to leave.

"Katie, the children are telling you there are already three people playing with Legos," you point out as you extend your hand. "Let's see what else you might like to do until they have finished. Would you rather use the unit blocks or work on puzzles?"

In this example, there are some important points. The children already knew the rules and used words to tell Katie. You respected what the other children were doing and didn't tell them to hurry, or ask one of them to leave.

At the same time, you gave Katie a clear signal that she must leave, but you did not force her to hold your hand. You offered two other acceptable choices that were somewhat similar to Legos. And you indicated that when the area was open she could play with the Legos. Katie may be disappointed, but she also learned that her rights would be protected in a similar situation.

You can use this same technique of redirecting in other situations where the child's efforts clearly are not being productive or are disrupting others. At times like this, you need to be firm so that children know you are serious, but you don't need to lecture or belittle children.

Dana (age 2½) rushes up to three other toddlers who are coloring. He grabs a handful of crayons, scribbles all over one of the pictures, and is reaching for the next one.

"No, Dana! Don't mess up our pictures," one of the children cries.

You rush to the scene. You firmly ask Dana to put the crayons back where they belong. Then you ask the children if they have anything to say to Dana.

"I am mad at him."

"He messed up Sarah's drawing."

"He isn't my friend."

"We don't want him to play with us."

Dana seems unfazed by the children's complaints. You offer him a choice of throwing pillows or hitting some clay until he is ready to talk. He chooses throwing pillows.

Later, when he has calmed down, you can listen to Dana and perhaps learn why he is acting this way. Does he need attention? Is he angry about something? Was he just bored? When you listen you may find out and can take steps to help him solve his problem.

When have you found it necessary to redirect children into a more productive activity? List one or two of your own examples here.

_____

_____

_____

_____

Talk with your CDA Field Advisor about your strategies and other ways you might have made the most of these learning opportunities.

Intervene with individual children.

For children with persistent behavior problems, redirection is not sufficient. You will need to analyze the situation more fully. Sometimes, we are so frustrated by children's negative behavior that we say things like, "He spits all the time." OR "He is always hitting."

Of course, those statements are exaggerations. It is physically impossible to do either one.

A more productive approach is to conduct a systematic observation of the negative behavior, actually count how often it occurs and record what usually triggers it. Then be sure to record what happens after the behavior.

With this information, you can begin to anticipate and change the situations that lead to misbehavior. For example, if the child hits others during transitions, make sure that you position yourself to help her prepare for the upcoming transition. Give the child your attention for being cooperative rather than disruptive.

Kaiser and Rasminsky (1999) point out that most challenging behavior is an attempt to get something, avoid something, or change the level of stimulation. Your analysis should help you determine what the child is trying to get (your attention or a toy); what the child is trying to avoid (taking a nap, sitting for story); or what level of stimulation the child is trying to change (boredom while waiting).

Find acceptable outlets to express feelings. Pretend play is a natural way for children to express and work out their feelings in a secure environment. Sometimes, though, feelings are so strong—anger is so overwhelming or sadness is so consuming—that children need additional outlets.

Find safe ways that will enable children to feel protected by caring adults. If children are angry and need to physically take out their frustration, they may find a release by hitting or throwing pillows or cushions. Sometimes they pound their fists on a soft pad or stomp around outdoors. Clay is wonderful for pounding with fists or hammers.

If children are sad, they may just want some private, quiet time. Or they may want to talk or write a letter. Or paint. Or read a book with you about a child facing a similar problem. Acting out stories is an excellent way to have children express a variety of feelings and understand the results of their behavior.

The better you know children, the easier it will be to help them channel their feelings into more acceptable behaviors.

Group play in the classroom can on occasion cause all of the children to act wildly. Monsters, fires, and other emotionally charged topics can lead to harmful aggression, shrieking, or other inappropriate behaviors. When possible, you notice that the play is escalating and de-fuse it before the children's feelings become overwhelming.

If it suddenly erupts, your actions will help children regain their control and calm down. Act calmly but firmly. You may need to hold a hand or two. Speak quietly. Move slowly. Perhaps turn the lights out to restore the quieter, playful atmosphere. Or maybe going outdoors will help children channel their energy more appropriately.

How you guide young children toward appropriate behavior:

1 Establish positive relationships with each child.

2 Plan to prevent problems with toys and materials, schedule, group times, and space.

3 Act in consistent positive ways with children

   • create a secure feeling

   • support families and cultures

   • help children become friendly and cooperative

   • solve problems with a positive approach

   • teach children to identify feelings and express them appropriately

4 Help children with particularly challenging behaviors to acquire social skills and self-regulation.

You use your professional judgment to decide what methods will be most effective, but you always remain in control of yourself. The better you know children, the easier it will be to help them channel their feelings into more acceptable behaviors.

What are some ways you have helped children express their strong feelings?

_____

_____

_____

_____

Work with a professional intervention team

A few children in your group may be identified as having moderate or even severe emotional problems that require additional professional support. In these cases, an intervention team will usually be available to work with the child. You as the classroom teacher need to be an integral part of that team, along with the child's family, and experts in early childhood special education. The team will develop an intervention plan that will guide you in selecting and implementing appropriate intervention strategies for the individual child. Although we will take more later about working with a team in your agency or in your community, remember that an important role for you will be to contribute first hand observations of children during the times they are in your program. The skills you are learning to make objective observations and careful records of children's behavior you will draw on over and over.

All through this unit, we have looked at positive ways to support children's developing ability to regulate their own emotions and behavior so they can lead happy, productive lives. You will use these strategies every day to help resolve typical developmental problems and to support children during stressful times.

Before we move on to some other aspects of social and emotional development, jot down any questions or ideas you have about children in your group who need some extra attention in one or more of the areas we have discussed. Write their names here, and list the strategies you intend to use to help them mature in a healthy way.

Self-concept and self-esteem _____

_____

Confidence and competence as learners

_____

_____

Curiosity and eagerness to learn _____

_____

_____

Self regulation _____

_____

_____

Cooperation _____

_____

_____

_____

Relationships with others _____

_____

_____

Security _____

_____

_____

Identity _____

_____

_____

Trust _____

_____

Inner strength _____

_____

Talk with your CDA Field Advisor about your questions and plans. Ask your Advisor to help you locate information about working with specific difficult social or emotional behaviors that you have encountered. Put the information in your Professional Resource File.

Teaching young children is filled with dilemmas. There are rarely any clear-cut answers, especially when dealing with unique situations. **List some here that you have found particularly troublesome. Raise them for discussion in your CDA Seminar.**

How do you deal with the difficulties of growing up?

Sometimes it seems as if children are full of surprises! Never knowing what to expect is part of why we find working with children so appealing.

At the same time, much of their behavior is really pretty predictable, once we understand how they develop and learn.

You expect developmental hurdles

In this part of your study about children's development, you will see how we guide children as they deal with some of the expected social and emotional hurdles of growing up.

These hurdles include separation anxiety, oppositional behavior, egocentricity, shyness and aggression, sexual identity, and fears. If these terms sound unfamiliar to you, you will soon see that they are professional shorthand for behaviors that are very familiar.

Much of what you already have learned fits in with what we discuss here, the widely held expectations of development and positive guidance methods that lead to self-discipline. Now we will build on what you already know, and try to put even more pieces of the puzzle of the whole child's development together.

Deal with stranger and separation anxiety

Jamie was such a darling baby. He cooed for his grandmother. He smiled at everyone in the grocery store. He didn't even mind when his parents left him with his family child care provider every day!

Then all of a sudden, he whimpered when he was handed to Grandma. He cried as he was pushed through the aisles of the grocery store. But worst of all, he wailed whenever Mom and Pop left him to go to work.

Grandma said, "Don't be strange, boy. I'm mad at you." Shopping was suddenly a chore. Leaving Jamie each day was pure torture for his parents—and a trying time for his child care provider as well.

What went wrong? Nothing. Absolutely nothing. In fact, everything went right. Most babies, sometime between the ages of about 5 months and 3 years, become frightened of strangers. Babies know the familiar faces, voices, and smells of their parents, and they have developed strong feelings for them. Not even their regular childcare provider—you—

can take the place of their family. This momentous intellectual and social achievement should be celebrated! Baby is learning about people and is securely attached to the most important ones.

Of course, even when you know that stranger anxiety is a natural part of development, there will be times when it is difficult for you as a caregiver. You must deal with crying children each morning and you need to advise parents about a very perplexing aspect of development.

For example, parents often ask when the best time is to enroll their son or daughter in childcare. Usually you will want to encourage parents to enroll their baby at a time other than the peak of the child's period of stranger anxiety. It is far more sensitive to the baby's feelings (*and the parents'*) if children are enrolled before they develop stranger anxiety or after they have passed its most intense period.

When the child is already in your care and begins to exhibit a wariness of strangers, YOU may be the stranger, even though the child has spent a great deal of time with you. Parents need to feel reassured that the tears and screams last only a few minutes after they leave, and then children settle down to have a happy day.

Don't assume parents will take your word for this, especially first-time parents. A phone call to dismayed Moms and Dads may help later in the morning. If the children are old enough, encourage them to talk or at least listen to the parent's voice on the phone.

Most of all you need to be warm, understanding, and loving each day while babies adjust to the change of care. Welcome children and parents warmly. Speak in the language with which they are most comfortable. Make sure they go through their usual morning ritual and say goodbye.

But when the parents must leave, be confident in helping them do so. If any of you hesitate, the child may think that crying will convince a parent to stay. Instead, help the baby get involved in something interesting.

Get out a bright ball, or a cuddly animal, or a musical toy. Sometimes a picture of children's families or a recording of parents' voices speaking in their home language will help ease the transition for the child.

You can help families deal with this puzzling stage. Suggest to parents that they give babies a while to warm up at their own pace with Grandmas, strangers, or babysitters. The parents can stay nearby during this "getting to know you" time. Soon most babies will be climbing into the visitor's lap.

Rather than criticizing children for their natural feelings (*"Don't be strange, boy. I'm mad at you."*), encourage parents to find a way to tell their child how proud they are that baby loves Mom and Dad so much.

This is one of many early opportunities to use a positive approach to childrearing. Even the most difficult situations can be handled in a positive way that supports children's long-term development.

How do you help infants feel less overwhelmed by separation or stranger anxiety when they arrive each day?

_____

_____

_____

_____

Tell your CDA Field Advisor how you handle these trying times.

Prepare for oppositional behavior

The "terrible twos." Everyone has heard of them. And most parents dread their arrival. Only those of us who know children and how they develop can really appreciate how wonderful the child's "NO!" can really be.

Our first step in dealing with 2-year-olds is to stop calling them terrible. How would you like to be labeled "thickheaded 30" or "fierce 40" or "flabby 50"? Such negative labels can damage children's self-esteem and may even be self-fulfilling (children become what we say they are).

Instead, look at this third year of life as one in which children are beginning to take control of their own lives. They want to act grown up. They assert themselves. They have opinions and preferences. They want to do things for themselves. Do these descriptions sound familiar? Yes, those are some of our long-term goals for children's development.

Children at this age are filled with opposites: They want to be independent and in control, but they need a clear set of limits or they will be overwhelmed. They want to be powerful, and yet constantly run into something they can't do alone. Their feelings are strong, so they need someone they can rely on to help them verbalize and manage those feelings.

Right from birth, the balance of power over who is in control starts to slowly shift from the adult to the child. At first, parents have all the power over everything children need. Then babies begin to hold their own bottles. Waddlers begin to walk where they want to go. And toddlers may refuse to eat their vegetables. Increasing self-regulation is a major part of growing up.

Many adults want to make sure their child still understands who is "the boss." With this attitude, the smallest incident can turn into a power struggle.

> Two-year-old David is contentedly rolling small balls of clay. You give all the children the five-minute signal before clean-up time, but when the time is up, David continues to play with the clay. When you ask him to put it away, he stubbornly refuses.

What should you do? You could force David to quit by putting away the clay for him and carrying him, kicking and screaming, outdoors to play. After all, you have a schedule and you want children to follow the rules. But what is David learning if you rip him away from the clay? He's learning that his feelings and interests don't matter.

Or you could threaten him, "Unless you put the clay away now, you won't be able to play with it tomorrow." But you already know that threats strike fear in children and don't help them develop long-term self-regulation. And "tomorrow" may be a meaningless concept to a 2-year-old.

What is a more professional approach? How can you avoid a power struggle and still respect the child and yourself? This is one possible solution:

"David, I can see that you are having fun with the clay. You don't look like you are quite ready to quit yet. Would you like to take it outdoors with you? Or do you want to leave it out on the table so you can use it again when we come back inside?"

Instead of rigidly sticking to your rules, you offer the child a choice. Either choice is a good one and will accomplish your goals (*get all children outdoors to play, respect children's interests, build self-regulation*). And best of all, the power struggle never even took place. Both you and David get what you need.

Offering choices was an excellent way to let children of all ages exercise their growing decision-making abilities. Offer good, real choices, like those in the example, and children can't go wrong.

Of course, sometimes you cannot offer a choice. You will still have to say "no" in some situations. But when you do, be firm and fair, and whenever possible, offer an alternative.

"No jumping from the sofa. You could hurt yourself. Your car could break if you land on it."

"Sofas are to sit on. These are our jumping cushions. How can you jump from the red one to the blue one?"

Twos will test limits, so make sure your environment is safe and your rules are reasonable and simple. Children will soon learn that they get to make choices frequently, that you mean business when you say "no," and that the environment is arranged for them to try out their skills.

As fate would seem to have it, most children also are ready to learn to use the toilet sometime during this period of strong negativism. These two developmental characteristics seem so incompatible. How can a child learn to use the toilet just when she or he is always refusing to do what adults want? No wonder toilet learning is a major—often-dreaded—event and a power struggle to get the child to do what the parents want!

On the other hand, when toilet learning is seen as something the child wants—to be independent and self-regulated—it clearly is a great match for the child's social and emotional development as well as physical development.

You and the child's family may be more prepared to use effective methods to help their child with this task.

In all of these and other similar situations, once you realize what is happening—children are growing up—you will see that twos are really pretty terrific!

If you teach 2-year-olds, what can you do to be more in tune with their development?

_____

_____

_____

_____

How can you help families look at the positive side of 2-year-old's negativism?

_____

_____

_____

_____

Your CDA Field Advisor will be interested to hear about your ideas.

Support children's play and social interaction.

Years ago, many people in our profession thought that infants and toddlers never played together or made friends. They claimed that very young children were not capable of showing sympathy toward or warm feelings about other children. They thought young children could only see things their way.

Now we know better, thanks to teachers like you, parents, and researchers who took a closer look at how children act in real situations. Children generally do see themselves as the center of everything, but occasionally they can relate to how others feel.

If infants and toddlers have been treated kindly, know each other, and are in an appropriate environment, you probably saw them giggle together . . . hold hands . . . share . . . offer comfort when the other has been hurt—sometimes. They definitely are beginning to relate to and understand others.

Young children are not completely egocentric. They are, however, naturally self-centered. They know their own feelings and wants best, and have little idea about how what they do makes other people feel.

How terribly important it is to understand children's natural self-centeredness and how it influences the way they play, make friends, and get along with each other.

Types of play. Children's play looks so simple—it's just what they want to do all day. However, play is really a very complicated process through which children learn about the world, each other, and themselves.

Most very young children are content to play by themselves. This is called **solitary play.** Babies gaze at themselves in mirrors, shake rattles, and watch the fish swim. Of course, older children and adults also occasionally enjoy time all to ourselves. Solitary play is what we do when we put together a jigsaw puzzle, read a novel, or tinker in the garage.

Watch a child of any age engaged in solitary play. What happens? How long does the child concentrate on the task at hand? Does the child talk to herself or himself or to others? What is the expression on the child's face like? Write a brief observation here:

_____

_____

_____

_____

Another typical form of play, one that is especially common during the late infant and toddler years, is called *parallel play*. Two children play side-by-side, for example in the sandbox or water table, each doing their own thing. At first glance they may appear to be playing with each other, but careful observation will reveal that they seem unaware of the other's presence. Older children and adults also engage in this type of play.

Find two or more children engaged in parallel play. What are they doing? How long do they continue? Are there any interactions between them? Write what happened here:

_____

_____

_____

_____

By the time children are preschoolers, we begin to expect more *cooperative play*. Children's social and intellectual development has matured enough so preschoolers can pretend to be someone else or stick with a game, sometimes for half an hour or more. In pretend play, each child plays a particular role (*bus driver, passenger, police officer*) but they all function together to pursue ideas on their theme. Or, with simple games, children cooperate to follow rules so that they are interacting together in one connected event. Cooperative play provides a good context for children to build self-regulation and an opportunity to learn from other children, especially expanding language.

Select a group of preschool children engaged in cooperative play. Write down exactly what happens here.

_____

_____

_____

_____

Your Field Advisor will verify that these observations are completed.

Children can learn to be friendly and cooperative in your program at the same time you are respecting these age-appropriate types of play. Although many of the toys and activities that programs tend to provide encourage cooperative play, all three types of play should be available to children.

Sometimes a child involved in isolated or parallel play needs to have you to protect her or his right not to be interfered with. You may need to resist the temptation to encourage children to play together or share toys and materials.

> Joshua is pouring water into and out of the containers at the water table. Riley comes over and starts taking over all the containers. You move in. "Riley, come with me to the other sink. I'll get you some containers of your own to use."

> Two children are in the dress-up area both preparing separate meals with separate menus for separate pretend families. You watch quietly, without encouraging the children to share. You only offer assistance if either child needs something.

There are plenty of opportunities to foster cooperative play as a way to help children build skills in making friends. But remember to balance them with opportunities for children to be at the center of their own world.

In Chapter 5, we'll describe effective teaching strategies for extending children's learning through play.

Help children make friends and get along

One of our long-term goals for children is to help them become friendly and cooperative. Yet developmentally, it takes a long time for children to be able to put others' needs ahead of their own. Don't always insist that they do. But when the opportunity arises, model cooperative behavior for them as a way to resolve disputes.

> "I can see that both Marilena and Robrett want to play with the wagon. You are both tugging on the handle. What can both of you do to use the wagon at the same time? Well, Marilena could pull while you ride, and then you pull while she rides. Or you could both get in and I'll pull!"

Also remember to catch children behaving appropriately! Let them know that you notice their growing skills.

> "Shannon, that was so generous of you to share your paint smock with Akua. We'll have to look some more to find hers."

> Si, nosotros podemos mirar el libro juntos. What good friends you are, Carlos and Craig. You are always thinking up fun things to do together."

When they are given enough positive experiences and lots of adult guidance and encouragement, children will learn to compromise and share freely as they mature.

Support shy children

New children in a program will generally be more reserved. Most newcomers take a few days to really settle in.

Some children just are naturally less outgoing than others, even when they have been in the group a long time.

How do you support these children's social and emotional development?

Shyness can result from one or a combination of factors. Some children seem to be shy because their parents are. Others are just less socially or intellectually mature for their age. Some are shy only in certain situations and more outgoing in others. We may also interpret certain cultural behaviors as shyness—some children may look down or pause before answering a question, for example. Unfamiliarity with other children's language may also make it difficult for children to interact easily with others. Before you become concerned that a child is shy, talk with the parents, learn all you can about the culture, and observe the child in many situations.

You can help shy children feel more comfortable in a group program by using all of the positive guidance techniques we have already discussed.

Manage superhero play

Children pretending to be superheroes poses a dilemma for many adults because it often results in dangerously aggressive play among children. Is it appropriate for children to imitate superheroes? Do superheroes just reinforce stereotypes? What are children really learning in this type of play? Why is it so popular?

Not surprisingly, this is not a topic about which early childhood professionals agree. Some argue that superhero fantasy play is overwhelming for young children because until children are about age 6 they do not always know what is real and what is pretend. They point out the negative behaviors associated with so many superheroes—violence, guns, and antisocial actions.

Others contend that superhero play—when it is well supervised—can help children feel a sense of power in a safe setting. They note that children can even handle fearful characters because the behaviors of the superhero are so limited by the role. Some superheroes even have admirable qualities—courage, honesty, fairness, and compassion.

Make superhero play manageable

- Help children recognize human characteristics of superheroes.

- Discuss real heroes and heroines.

- Talk about the pretend world of acting.

- Limit the place and time for superhero play.

- Explore related concepts—bats, space travel.

- Help children develop goals for superheroes—figure out a plan for a rescue mission or treasure hunt, for example.

- Help children de-escalate rough-and-tumble play. Provide a safety zone for those who do not wish to participate.

- Make it clear that aggression is unacceptable.

- Give children control over their lives in other areas.

- Praise children's attempts at mastery.

Note: Adapted from "Living with He-Man: Managing Superhero Fantasy Play" by M. J. Kostelnik, A. P. Whiren, and L. C. Stein, *Young Children*, May 1986, 41(4), 7. Copyright © 1986 by National Association for the Education of Young Children. Reprinted by permission.

And of course, as with all pretend play, children can learn to get along with each other, develop their vocabularies, solve problems, and find ways to cooperate through superhero play. If you support this position, turn to good literature in order to locate some superheroes. Classic stories like Johnny Appleseed, Paul Bunyan, and Pecos Bill can be read and acted out to provide children superhero play.

Because of its popularity on television and among commercial toys, it's unrealistic not to expect some superhero play in most programs for young children. There are ways that you can make such play more manageable. Some of these techniques, suggested by three experienced educators, seem to strike a balance between both positions.

Look at the ideas on page 246 on how to make superhero play more manageable. Decide for yourself whether you believe superhero play can be managed in a positive way with your group.

If you decide to include superhero play and help children control it, record an incident of this type of play. Write a paragraph about what happened here:

_____

_____

_____

_____

_____

What problems did you encounter when you tried to make superhero play more productive? What techniques did you use to resolve them?

_____

_____

_____

_____

If you decide not to include superhero play, write a paragraph explaining why.

_____

_____

_____

_____

Discuss your ideas and experiences with your Advisor. Then save your notes to share with others in your CDA Seminar.

Encourage pride in sexual identity

Frilly pink dresses and lace for baby girls. Baseball suits, racecars, and trucks for baby boys. Just look at the greeting cards or clothing for new babies! Long after women have made great strides towards equality, sexism still permeates our society. In fact, many people don't even know how to interact with a baby if they don't know its sex.

No wonder, then, that children learn what is expected of them as a boy or a girl—

behaviors, attitudes, or aspirations—from a very young age and from every person they meet and every experience they have. But if girls learn to be weak and act helpless, and boys learn to be powerful, emotionless, and in control, some of what they learn may limit their thinking about how to live their lives.

Although the options are decidedly broader for both men and women than they were just a few years ago, many teachers are dismayed to find that most boys are more aggressive, play more with blocks, and like to ride tricycles at great speeds. Many girls, on the other hand, still enjoy playing with dolls, dressing up, and making cakes in the sandbox. What are you to do?

It is not an easy task to help children be comfortable with who they are as a boy or girl and what that means in their lives. Many parents have very strong feelings about how they want their children to think and behave based on which sex they are: Girls grow up to marry and raise families while boys work, for example. Some ethnic groups are adamant about the differences between what proper behavior is for each sex.

This clearly is an area that requires working together with parents—or you may find yourself contradicting childrearing beliefs without even knowing it. It is always important to take into account parents' desires for their own children and to balance those with your broader professional responsibility to guide children toward the ability to function well in the real world.

If the two views disagree, sometimes you can only compromise by agreeing to have one set of expectations in your program while the parents have another set at home. You may already be doing this with some discipline techniques, and this may be another area in which you and parents agree to disagree.

Because one of your long-term goals is to help children feel good about who they are, understanding what it means to be a boy or a girl is an important part of that. You have seen how shared bathrooms enable children to appreciate similarities and differences in their bodies. Your comments and observations are an excellent way to help children feel proud of who they are and to learn more about their bodies.

"You are a girl. Your body is special. When you grow up you will be able to have a baby. You have special parts inside where a baby can grow, just the way you grew inside your mother."

"Boys have penises and girls have vaginas. Penises are outside boys' bodies and vaginas are inside girls' bodies. Both of your bodies have special places. And both of you also have arms, and eyes, and belly buttons!"

You also support children's self-esteem in other ways related to the fact that they are a boy or a girl.

"Christopher, you are such a good cook. You got the carrots so clean and then you cut them in sticks. Your friends will enjoy them so much. You are a boy who can be proud of his work."

"One of our most productive block builders has done it again. Angelica has built a really complicated apartment building. Maybe someday she will be an architect."

Interestingly, although children know very early which sex they are, it will not be until they reach the elementary school years that they come to realize that is what they will **always** be. Some girls, especially those who have been overprotected or who have been referred to as tomboys, may even say they want to be boys when they grow up! And some boys may wish they were girls, perhaps so they could have a baby.

You will need to listen for children's signs of wanting to be the other sex, and gently explain that becoming a boy (*or a girl*) is not possible.

> "Jessica, you will always be a girl. Girls can be carpenters, too, when they grow up."

> "You really wish you could be a girl so you could be a Mommy. Well, Brian, you will always be a boy. But you can grow up to be a Daddy and take good care of your children, too."

You have many other excellent ways to help children understand that boys and girls alike can do many things. Be especially careful about which children's books you choose to make sure that they do not portray sexist roles. There are many fine book selections that portray children and adults in a variety of roles.

Similarly, the posters and pictures you choose should show men and women, boys and girls, in a diversity of jobs. Stand firm that in your program girls can wear hard hats and drive trucks, and boys can put on aprons and play with dolls in pretend play. Point out how strong and capable children of both sexes are.

You may feel uncomfortable with some of these ideas yourself. List some issues here that concern you about the development of children's sexual identities, or note any disagreements about sex roles you have had with parents.

_____

_____

_____

_____

You will be able to discuss how you can resolve these questions when you talk with your Field Advisor.

Using the criteria in "Ten Quick Ways to Analyze Children's Books for Racism and Sexism" (*pages 176-179*), select five good children's picture books that portray boys, girls, men, and women in roles that support development of children's sexual identity. List those books here.

_____

_____

_____

_____

Introduce these books to the children in your care if you have not already done so. Your Field Advisor will discuss the reasons for your selections with you.

Cope with fears

Monsters. The dark. Dogs. A friend's Halloween mask. Thunder. Children may be frightened of so many things. Some fears seem logical; others don't. But understanding development helps us know what to do to help children cope with their fears.

We have already seen how, during one stage of infancy, many children are afraid of strangers—or even people they see fairly often.

Other fears may also be explained mostly by understanding child development. During the infant and toddler years, children still rely a lot on the surface appearances of things and often think that objects have life.

Anika (*22 months*) was watching her parents to get ready for a Halloween party. She seemed to enjoy it until Daddy put on his mask. Her face puckered up and she turned away, even when Daddy tried to reassure her by saying, "Anika, it's still me. There's nothing to be afraid of."

Brett (*30 months*) was playing happily outdoors when the family childcare provider began to drag the hose out to fill the wading pool. The hose snaked from its pile across the grass, and Brett went running away.

Nicholas (*age 1*) arrived earlier than usual at his family childcare provider's home. She was still putting on her makeup and didn't have her glasses on. He refused to go to her and looked very puzzled.

Preschool children are also generally afraid of other categories of things: monsters, the dark, or animals. Sometimes they are afraid because they have seen others be afraid. Sometimes they have had a frightening experience themselves—watching too many scary movies or being lost in the store. And sometimes they are just afraid for reasons we adults cannot comprehend.

Write down some of the things that infants and toddlers you have known seem afraid of:

_____

_____

_____

_____

_____

What are some common fears you have seen in preschool children?

_____

_____

_____

_____

_____

Most fears will disappear with time, as children develop a better cognitive understanding that people and things stay the same regardless of their outward appearance and that objects are not really alive.

In the meantime, you can help children cope with their fears by taking their fears seriously and reassuring children that we will keep them safe. Children need our calm explanations, even though they may not yet be quite ready to fully understand them.

It's not enough, however, to tell children, as Anika's father did, "There's nothing to be afraid of." For there is indeed something to be afraid of or the child would not have reacted in fear! Instead, acknowledge the child's fear in the language most comfortable for the child: "I can see this mask really scared you." Try to change the situation: "Here, let me take it off." Then reassure the child: "See, it's Daddy underneath. I just put on this silly mask for Halloween. I'm sorry it scared you."

Obviously, masked parties (*Halloween, Mardi Gras*) are not a good idea for most young children. Even some kindergarten children have trouble dealing with masks. If you celebrate these or similar events, stick to simple costumes and a touch of makeup. Meanwhile, play "Peek-A-Boo," "Hide and Seek," and other games that help children figure out how the world works.

Pretend play is a marvelous way to help children deal with their fears. With a few carefully selected and non-threatening props, they can play out the situations you know are scary for them. Let the children choose the play for themselves so they can feel in control of the situation. Most children can work through their fears by playing them out and channeling their aggression in safe ways during play with themes such as visits to the doctor or scary movies.

Reading books may help children see how others have coped with similar fears. One favorite is *Milk and Cookies* (Asch, 1982) about

a firebreathing dragon in the basement. Ask your librarian to help you find others related to the fears the children in your group have.

Children who are afraid of animals or other specific things may be helped by gradually introducing smaller, quieter replicas of the same item. For instance, you might help a child who is afraid of cats by doing several related things that gradually help the child adjust to more intense experiences over a period of time: put a cat puzzle together, look at pictures and books with cats, pet a stuffed animal that looks like a cat, take a walk through the neighborhood to look for cats, and perhaps finally actually touch one of the furry creatures. Never rush a child, and be sure to stop if the child indicates either with words or behavior that the experience is frightening. Sometimes a lighthearted approach works.

Four-year-old Tracy was afraid of sleeping in her own room. Her parents tried a night-light. That didn't help. They tried sitting with her while she fell asleep, but she would wake up when they left.

Finally, in frustration, her parents talked with her teacher about what might be the problem. Tracy's teacher suggested they talk with her about why she was having difficulty sleeping in her room. They did, and learned she was afraid a bad witch lived under her bed. The Tooth Fairy had visited her older sister and apparently this idea was translated into a bad witch for Tracy.

That night a few minutes before bedtime, Mommy and Tracy went to her room. Mommy bent over to look under the bed. "OK, witch," she said in a gruff voice. "It's time to get out of Tracy's room. She wants to sleep. SCAT!" Mommy playfully chased the invisible witch out the window. Together, she and Tracy waved goodbye.

Your listening skills are essential when you talk with children about what they fear. Questions such as "And then what do you think would happen?" or "What would you do if ....?" may help children figure out how to deal with the problem themselves. As always, try to stay away from questions that have just a yes or no answer, and use the child's home language.

Fears in general are another area in which you need to work closely with parents. Your support and their parents' understanding will help children feel protected. Together, you can help eliminate much of the stress of growing up.

Helping children and their families cope with stress using children's books

Separation causes great stress in children. Some separations may seem insignificant to adults but are real fears in children: going to bed (*leaving the family circle*); getting lost in a store; having a babysitter; going to school for the first time; staying overnight with family or friends; moving or changing schools; parents going on a trip (*business or pleasure*); child's illness or loved one's illness, particularly hospitalization; differences from peer group (*shy, thin, fat, tall, short, rich, poor*); a parent incarcerated; a parent in the armed service; divorce, abandonment, separation and the most stressful of all, fear of death (*the child's own or a loved one's*).

Children must be reassured that they will always be cared for. They are afraid they will be alone. Children are affected by the worries of the parents, especially if the parents act differently. Children need proper preparation for the separations listed above in order to minimize the stresses. Communication is extremely important and the ability to discharge their fears with a caring adult, such as a teacher, helps children to cope. Often the use of children's literature elicits discussion from even shy students because they can see that other children and/or animal characters have the same problems; the way those characters cope may give the children ideas for managing their own stress. It may, according to Fassler (*1978*), help them to see that they have already solved some of the problems the book characters have, and this gives the children a sense of power.

A few good children's books dealing with stress are listed below:

Bedtime: *Goodnight Moon, There's a Nightmare in My Closet*

Constancy: *Runaway Bunny*

Staying over: *Ira Sleeps Over*

Business trip: *Friday Night Is Papa Night*

Illness: *I Want Mama*

Divorce/Separation: *A Father Like That, Two Homes*

Death: *Freddie the Leaf; The Dead Bird; The Two of Them; My Grandpa Died Today; Sam, Bangs and Moonshine; Annie and the Old One; Bridge to Terabithia*

Reprinted by permission of M.L.H. Burger and the Association for Childhood Education International, 17904 Georgia Avenue, Suite 215, Olney, MD. Copyright © 1991 by the Association.

You support families dealing with life's stressful events

Children's lives are filled not only with developmental challenges, but also with stressful events—some major and others minor. Let's look at how you support children and families as they deal with some of life's stressful events: children's new brothers and sisters; divorce, separation, and blended families; disabilities; illness and hospitalization; death; and child abuse.

In all these situations, your primary goal will be to reduce stress as much as possible. At the same time, you will keep in mind children's long-term development, rather than applying a bandage approach.

As a professional, parents will often look to you for advice on these topics. Be prepared to give an informed response and know when to refer them to more expert help.

Prepare for new babies

When a new child enters a family, everything changes. An only child is no longer an only. The youngest child is now somewhere in the middle. And parents must adjust their time, resources, and energy to the new size of their family. What can you do to help parents make this experience a positive one for their young children? Young children are still developing their sense of time. Because 7 or 8 months away is really much too long a time for them to grasp, you probably recommend that parents wait a little bit to inform their other children about the new baby.

However, once their mother's body starts to change, and preparations for the arrival begin, children can and should be informed about the good news and included in the joyful changes. Adults' positive and sensitive attitudes help children feel accepted and involved in their growing family.

Many children become more interested in taking care of baby dolls when they learn a new brother or sister is on the way. Others have fun sorting through their toys, selecting those they have outgrown and putting them aside for baby. If a new baby means a change in sleeping arrangements for a young child, discuss these changes in terms of their growing up.

All during this process, children need to feel involved, to see how much they are growing up, and to feel that their needs are being met with respect. You can do this by talking about how wonderful it is to be a big brother or sister. Or point out how much children have grown since they were babies. Perhaps a mother is willing to bring her older baby in to bathe or diaper—children can see how lovingly these routines are done. Build enthusiasm for babies!

There are many good books for young children that can help them understand how babies grow in special places inside their mothers. Find some and list two or three of your favorites here and in your Professional Resource File so you can recommend them the next time a

parent asks. If possible, read them with your group:

_____

_____

_____

_____

_____

Just before the baby's arrival, remind parents to tell children, in simple, clear terms, what arrangements have been made for their care while mother is away. How frightening to wake up some morning and find a strange person there instead of your parents!

Once baby comes home, young children can contribute to the baby's care in developmentally appropriate ways. They can sing lullabies, bring a diaper or clean shirt, fold laundry, or listen for the baby to wake up—even toddlers feel so grown up when they have some responsibility.

On the other hand, children's own needs also must be met. And this is where your daily interactions can play such a big part. You can listen to children's concerns. You can make sure there are plenty of baby-related items in the housekeeping area. Your support, at a time when parents may feel overwhelmed, can be a major factor in giving families a good start together.

Preschool children who already have babies in their families may be a big booster for new siblings because they are so eager to share their experiences. In fact, children who do not have a baby may begin to encourage their par-

ents to have one because their friends have a baby brother or sister to love.

When these positive steps are taken, children are much less likely to feel jealous or left out. Occasionally, despite everything all of you do, some children will find it difficult to accept their changed place in the family. You can use your observations and knowledge of child development to know when to recommend parents or children to experts who can counsel them through such situations.

With most children, becoming a brother or sister is a wonderful event. You and their parents can work together to set a positive, loving atmosphere for the entire family.

What are some ways that you have found to be particularly effective in helping young children enjoy becoming new brothers or sisters?

_____

_____

_____

_____

Support separating, divorced, and blended families

Much as we wish it weren't true, marriages are not always successful. And after two parents no longer choose to live together, it is very difficult for them to keep their children's needs in perspective at a time when they are dealing with their emotions and deep disappointment in their own lives. Likewise, when parents find a new partner, it is sometimes difficult to make sure children still feel welcome and included in the new family.

Regardless of the situation—separation, divorce, or remarriage—forming a new family is a stressful time for everyone. Your strength and support can make it possible for the children to deal with these traumatic events in ways that reduce stress and contribute to their long-term development.

Children often blame things that go wrong on themselves. Knowing that, you and the parents need to make it clear to the children that they are in no way responsible for a family break-up. Tell them that the divorce is an adult problem, and that you will still all work together to take good care of the children. Children must be told again and again in the language that is most familiar to them that they are still loved and secure, even if mother and father no longer love each other.

Once in a while, parents handle arrangements for custody and visitation with only a few disagreements. Children are given the information they need to feel secure about where they will live, who will take care of them, and where they will go during the day.

But sometimes a friendly separation is not possible. Children must be told in a kind way that only mommy, or only daddy, will be taking care of the family from now on. They need to know how often, or even if, they will have any contact with their other parent. Covering up the truth or even lying will destroy trust between parents and children—and never will

children need to trust a parent more than at a time like this.

Similarly, when a parent is looking for and then finds a new partner, children may feel left out unless both partners make a concerted effort to continue to consider children's needs and feelings as well as their own. They need to know their parents still love them.

Children need to be included early in any new relationship. They should meet potential stepbrothers or sisters long before the wedding day. And of course, throughout the relationship, the parent must make a special effort to do things just with the children and without the partner.

In a remarriage, the stepparent may bring other children into the family. Children need to know where they will live, which room is theirs, and whether they can keep all their favorite toys or the family pet.

Even the youngest children deserve to know about arrangements like these that affect them. Urge parents to be sensitive to children's concerns throughout the breaking up or re-forming of a family.

As an early childhood teacher, your primary role will be to listen and understand the child's strong feelings, to lend some stability when everything seems to be changing, and to help children come to terms with what has happened through no fault of their own. Young children may need lots of cuddling and individual attention. They may need time to take out their anger in acceptable ways: pounding clay, hammering nails, or throwing pillows.

Most children benefit from knowing that other children have faced similar situations and have resolved them in a positive way. Many fine children's books deal with separation, divorce, and families formed by remarriage. Others focus on the wide variation in the types of families.

Find at least three good children's picture books about separation, divorce, remarriage, or blended families. List the titles below. For your Professional Resource File write a short summary of the book along with a description of how you would use it with a child or family. Book titles:

Sometimes children who have been through similar experiences can be a great support to their friends.

Sheryl, almost age 5, had never known her father, but had been part of a large extended family of aunts, uncles, cousins, and grandparents. When her mother decided to marry, Sheryl was understandably not enthusiastic. Her mother planned a big birthday party, in part to help Sheryl see that her needs would continue to be met in her new family.

Just before the party, Sheryl spent a day with Julie. Julie's mother had recently remarried. Julie explained how great it was to have two dads. She told about how thrilled she was to have a beautiful flower girl dress for the wedding.

Before the day was out, Sheryl couldn't wait for her mother to get married.

Children can be very resilient about new situations when their needs and feelings are handled with care and sensitivity. You can help maintain stability in children lives if you:

- **keep your expectations consistent**—do not condone misbehavior just because children are facing a difficult transition. On the other hand, be understanding if the child's behavior temporarily regresses.

- **give children the solitude or extra attention they may be missing at home**—some time alone with you or on your lap can work wonders.

- **give children many opportunities to feel successful and in control of other aspects of their lives**—compliment children for their efforts, offer choices children can handle, make your program a pleasant place to be.

- **encourage dramatic play or other appropriate activities for children to work through strong feelings**—children may want to rip paper, draw pictures of their family, or dance vigorously.

- **avoid taking sides with parents**—keep your commitment instead to the child's well being—you may be the only one who does so for a time.

- **don't let your own opinions about divorce affect your behavior**—you must act professionally regardless of your personal feelings.

Some other adjustments in your program routines may be required. When you schedule parent conferences, you may need to plan two for some children. If you prepare Father's Day, Mother's Day, or other holiday gifts, again, two gifts may be needed—one for the parent and one for the stepparent or grandparent. Make a special effort to include parents and stepparents in any events such as parent meetings, fundraisers, and other group gatherings.

You may also have some legal obligations concerning who will pick the child up and when. To protect everyone involved, it is essential that you have a signed form with the names of all people authorized to pick the child up. Don't depend on the child's word. Ask that parents inform you immediately if any court order or other legal action could affect these important arrangements. Do not get caught in the middle of a child custody fight. Get legal advice if you are in a difficult situation.

If either parents or their children seem unable to make positive strides in resolving their personal problems, you may need to suggest they consult the director of your program who can refer them to an appropriate professional. If you are a family childcare provider, you may need to recommend they obtain counseling.

Children who leave your group.

Infants become toddlers, toddlers become preschoolers, and preschoolers move on to kindergarten. As teachers, we have said goodbye to many children over the years. It never gets any easier.

Just as you do when a child moves away, you want to help children and their parents say goodbye to you. Although you don't want to extend the goodbye too long, a month in advance is not too soon for older preschoolers. Even infants and toddlers need at least a week or two to get used to the idea of being in another classroom or with another family child care provider.

You can be a great help to parents in keeping children in contact with one another. They will need the phone numbers and mailing addresses for their children's friends. Make sure it is OK with parents before you give out the information. As we have seen, these friendships can be quite close even during the toddler years.

Let families know how much the children have grown while they have been with you and that you will miss them. Your observation diary and portfolios of children's work will provide some excellent personal examples to use. If you weighed or measured children early in the year, repeat it at the end.

"I remember when you first came to our family child care program. You were just 14 months old and you barely could walk then. Now you can run, and jump, and ride a two-wheeler. You have grown up so much in just 4 years. And now you are going to begin kindergarten. Please stop by and visit us once in a while. We will miss you."

Remember, you and the children's parents are setting an example for children about how to say goodbye. Rather than avoid the pain, find positive ways to say goodbye and keep in touch.

Perhaps a picnic once a year for your program's alumni is appropriate. Or a potluck dinner would give the children who were together in a family childcare program a chance to renew friendships. Letters, photos, and drawings can be exchanged all year long.

All through their lives children will be saying goodbye. Start them off with some good strategies to deal with these stressful times.

What ideas do you have to help children say goodbye to you?

_____

_____

_____

_____

Assist with disabling injuries

We have already talked in general about working on a daily basis with children with disabilities, and you know how to locate resources for their families. We have also discussed bias and stereotypes about disabilities and you know how to address them in your environment. But sometimes, families and children experience sudden disabling injuries and require additional support from you.

Families may understandably be stressed when first facing a family member's disabling condition. Assistance from a medical provider or specialist will most likely be required.

Helping a child learn to adapt and accept a sudden parent or sibling disability will require some special forms of support, much like other family crises. Specialists are best suited to make recommendations to you.

However, if the situation is one where the disability affects a child enrolled in your program, you will base your strategies on principles of good early childhood practice.

In a good classroom, you already have books about and pictures of people who have different abilities. You may have dolls or puppets with a range of physical attributes. The dramatic play props include equipment such as glasses or crutches.

Children will feel comfortable enough to ask questions and express their concerns about people's abilities. You always treat children with respect and expect them to treat others that way. So most of your preparations for a child's re-enrollment (_or a new child's enrollment_) are already part of your daily interactions with children.

When a child who has been disabled is about to be enrolled, you need to talk to toddlers and preschoolers so they will be prepared in a way that is sensitive to everyone's concerns. Puppets or dolls with different abilities often work well when giving an explanation. For example, you might say something like this:

"Tomorrow, Nicholas will join our group. Remember how he likes to play with blocks and to ride tricycles? Nicholas was in an accident. Many doctors and nurses have helped him get better. You may notice that some of his skin looks and feels rougher than yours. That is where he was burned in his accident. We are so glad Nicholas will be here to play with us again. What can we do to help him feel welcome?"

Or, in the case of a child who has a disability from birth, you might explain the child's physical differences in this way.

"We are so glad that Marina will be in our class tomorrow. She loves to paint and play ball. Marina was born with very short arms. Our arms keep growing, but hers grow more slowly. That won't happen to your arms. Marina likes to do things by herself, just like you do. It will be fun to have Marina as a new friend."

Older preschoolers may have more questions once the new child arrives and they see the extent or particulars of their disability. Answer questions as truthfully but reassuringly as possible.

"Yes, Nicholas has many scars on his skin. He was burned in an unusual accident. We all are very careful here to make sure everyone is safe."

"You are worried that your arms might get short or stop growing. That won't happen. Marina's arms were this way even before she was born."

Keep your explanations brief, respectful, and use words children will understand. Never make children—the child with special needs or the other children—feel guilty or uncomfortable.

"These boys and girls have never met someone quite like you. They are curious and want to get to know you better. We all like to learn more about each other so we can be good friends."

One of your goals with children with disabilities will be to adapt to each child's needs by making changes in the environment, usually called appropriate accommodations. Remember, you want all children to participate as fully, and as independently, as possible in your activities. You may need to lower or raise a table, widen spaces between furniture, install ramps, or learn to sign. To adapt your program, you will need to talk with the child's parents, and other member of the intervention team. See pages 282-285 for specific suggestions for accommodations for children with special needs.

Because you are so in tune to needs of the children in your group, you may find that other children want to be overly helpful to those with disabilities. A few words to it may help them see how important it is for each child to be as independent as possible.

"Patrick is trying so hard to put his shoes on by himself. You feel so grown up when you put your own shoes on. Soon Patrick will have practiced a lot and he will be able to do it as easily as you do."

Parents of children with disabilities are learning to cope with additional challenges each day. As their child's teacher, you can provide them an additional support. Listen to their concerns and help them find appropriate solutions to any problems.

Sometimes they will have difficult questions. If you do not feel qualified, be sure to refer parents to your program director or another professional with more training in special education or medicine. You will discuss this more in your CDA Seminar.

What ideas do you have to create a classroom climate where children with disabling conditions can thrive along with the other children?

_____

_____

_____

_____

_____

Share your suggestions with your CDA Advisor.

Prepare for illness and hospitalization

Children's illnesses that require hospitalization come in three major forms: some are emergencies, some are scheduled procedures with an almost certain recovery, and others are long-term fights for life. In all three situations, as a professional you will be called upon to support children and their families. Your role will be to help eliminate as much stress as possible and to find constructive ways to deal with difficulties.

None of us can ever be prepared for an emergency. However, both before and after an emergency trip to a hospital, we can give children a sense of security that they will be well taken care of.

Play is an excellent vehicle for teaching young children, especially about emotionally stressful events. We need to provide a wide variety of props for children to act out medical care experiences: ambulances, stethoscopes, surgical masks, and prescription pads are essential in a good early childhood program. Children's ideas about medical care often come out through play and in their artwork.

Children's books are another excellent way to broaden their understanding about the people and equipment in a hospital. Be sure to present information in the languages with which children are most comfortable. Medical personnel, especially if they are parents of the children, can visit and describe what they do to reassure children about the normalcy of health care.

Children who are scheduled to enter the hospital should certainly have a visit beforehand. Some hospitals even have special tours for children. If possible, parents should be encouraged to use a hospital that supports their presence, night and day, and that has a staff that use the family's language. Hospitals have strange smells, strange people, always have the lights on, and are filled with unusual noises. No wonder children are so frightened without someone close to them right there.

Ask your Field Advisor to help you find out about policies of your local hospitals. Write down what you find out.

Orientation for children scheduled to enter the hospital:

_____

_____

_____

_____

_____

Rooming in for parents:

_____

_____

_____

_____

If you have a choice, which hospital seems most sensitive to children's emotional needs for security and trust? Write down the name of the hospital here:

_____

_____

_____

_____

On rare occasions, a child in your care may be terminally ill. Before you talk with the children about how very ill the child is, you need to resolve your own feelings. Only then will you be able to respond appropriately to children's anger or fear.

Talk with the parents and perhaps the medical care provider to better understand the illness and how to help the child and family. Medical opinion remains divided on whether children themselves should be told, but most experiences seem to indicate the child has some intuitive sense about impending death even if the adults are not forthright.

Use the information you have to make a wise decision about how much to tell the other children in the group. As always, your role is to help alleviate stress and not to create more.

Teach children about death

"Bang! Bang! You're dead," shouts a child on the playground. The victim drops to the ground and lies still for an instant. Then she gets up and begins chasing the criminal.

If only life were so simple: Someone who is killed in one movie soon appears again in another. Cartoon characters never die regardless of how many bombs are dropped on them or how many cliffs they fall from.

On the other hand, children's lives are often touched by real death—of a beloved pet, a grandparent, a neighbor, or even a close family member. They find a dead butterfly. They see a pile of motionless fur in the road. How confusing it must be when the dead animal or person doesn't leap up!

There are many reasons to have animals in the programs for young children, because children can learn so much: They can take responsibility for their care. Children can see first hand different animal's nesting habits, sleeping, and eating patterns. An animal's unfortunate death can be yet another vehicle to support children's learning and their emotional growth.

Through their real experiences with animals and people, children start to learn what death really means. They see that the dead one can no longer see, hear, feel, move, or breathe—and never will again. Children are curious about death. You can support their interest by caring for and studying animals, alive and dead.

The next step is not nearly so easy. Only when children have an understanding of what death means physically can they begin to deal with the emotional aspects of death. Children will ask whether they will die. Or whether their parents will die. How do you deal with such a difficult topic?

Erna Furman's ideas seem especially rooted in what we know about how young children develop and are extremely sensitive to the feelings of people as well. These recommendations are based on her work. They are primarily for older preschool children, as younger children cannot yet comprehend the finality of death.

You can deal with death best when you know what children are thinking and what their parents believe is the best approach. Some families choose to ignore the topic, others exhibit wishful thinking, some rely solely on religious explanations, and still others try to help children understand reality without overwhelming them.

Once you know the family's approach, you can then try to help parents understand that children are still developing a sense of time, that abstract concepts such as heaven are not yet meaningful to young children, and that children do have strong feelings about death. If it is a parent or sibling who has died, your support will be even more essential.

It would be dishonest to respond to the question "Will I (or you) die?" with "No" because eventually everyone dies. On the other hand, you cannot respond with a simple "Yes," or the child may believe it could happen instantly.

Instead, we should respond in a manner that tells the truth but also puts it positively in the context of time.

"Well, we will all die someday. But before then, you probably will grow up, and have a fine job, and love your wife and children, and even become a grandparent!"

Part of our role as teachers is to help children learn how to deal with strong feelings such as anger, sadness, and disappointment. We have already discussed appropriate ways to help children build their own strengths in these areas.

At the same time, we don't want children's strong feelings to be dulled so that they feel no pain in emotionally difficult situations. If a child did not react strongly to a death, we would be even more worried about her or his development. What if children didn't care if their cat died? Or if they seemed indifferent to someone's suffering?

You probably have already been asked by at least one parent about whether their children should be told of a grandparent's death, for example, or should attend the funeral. Let's see what the best way is to handle such situations, based on what we know about children's long-term emotional development.

You want children to talk with you, to trust you, to feel secure. Surely these goals are never more important than when you help a child face the loss of an pet or person. So you do want children to know the cause of death and to help them deal with their anger and sadness.

Children are curious about why things die. While you surely would not provide gory details, you might explain an animal's death like this.

"Brownie was a wonderful guinea pig for our class. He lived a long life and made many children happy. But his body was wearing out, because guinea pigs don't live as long as people do. His heart finally stopped beating and he died."

Be sure to answer children's questions about why someone died in as forthright a manner but as simply as possible. One of the best books about the topic is *When People Die* (Levete, 1998).

Dealing with the feelings about death is difficult. You may say something such as this:

"I am so sorry to learn of your grandfather's death, Tara. You and he shared so many good times together. It may be hard for you to talk about it right now, but I know you may want to remember some of your happy times with him. You can come to me whenever you would like to talk about him."

One way people come to terms with sadness, to ease the transition between life and death, is to have a funeral. Children often request funerals for dead pets.

Della was almost 5. Her 10-year-old goldfish was floating on the top of its aquarium. She found a box for it and asked her parents if it could be buried in the back yard. Fish was placed on a tissue and the box was closed. The family walked solemnly to the gravesite, which was marked by a large rock. The hole was dug, the box placed in it, and earth gently pushed over the top. Della carefully perched the rock atop the grave. Her parents had tears in their eyes—Fish had been with them a long time before Della was born.

Della paused for a second, and then skipped off merrily, asking, "Can we go buy my new shoes now?"

Weeks later, though, she still talked about Fish, and frequently went to the backyard to look at his grave.

Simple funerals such as this one are certainly appropriate for young children. Sometimes children want to sing their favorite songs. It is not unusual to hear "B-I-N-G-O" or "The Farmer in the Dell" at a pet's funeral.

Before deciding to take a young child to a formal funeral, however, encourage parents to think about what type of service it is and whether the parents feel comfortable with it, who will be available to comfort the child, and whether the parents feel the experience would be sensitive to the child's needs.

Long, emotional services would tax a young child beyond her or his limits. If the parents resent the child's presence (*perhaps not wanting to demonstrate their emotions in front of the child*) or feel that an open casket could upset the child, it might be better to make other arrangements.

However, if the service and events are not going to be emotionally upsetting but rather supportive of the family, young children probably should be invited to attend. Families need to join together in sharing their grief for and memories of loved ones. They can be a source of strength to each other and give children a real sense of belonging.

If children are excluded from the funeral, they may feel left out, especially if the person was someone very important to them. One child had the measles and still was upset that she was unable to go to her beloved great-grandmother's funeral. She was the only child she knew who even had a great-grandmother.

If the parents decide the child will not attend, be sure they make arrangements for the child's care appropriate to the child's feelings—a trip to an amusement park would not be a constructive way to help the child deal with the death.

Everyone in the family will be searching for ways to come to terms with the death long after the funeral. No one can rush the mourning process. On the other hand, if a child or parent seems stuck and unable to get on with life, or if the death was of a parent or sibling, you may need to refer the family for counseling.

Some of you may have strong beliefs—religious, cultural, or personal—that determine your thinking about how to handle death with young children. What are some of those beliefs that seem to conflict with what you know about child development and good early childhood practice?

_____

_____

_____

_____

List here any conflicts or questions you have about helping children cope with death.

_____

_____

_____

_____

Discuss them with your CDA Field Advisor.

Recognize signs of abuse

We talked briefly about your obligation to report potential child abuse in Unit 3. It may be your skill at detecting the signs of child abuse—physical, sexual, or emotional—that will bring the child safety and protection.

As a teacher, you see children almost every day. You are therefore in a good position to notice any changes in a child's behavior or physical condition. You also are very aware of how the parents treat their children and what stresses the family might be under.

You have a professional, legal, and ethical responsibility to report any *suspected* harm or potential risk of harm to a child.

Reporting your suspicions does not mean accusing or reporting the abuser. *It means reporting any signs on or about the child that may have been caused by abuse:* suspicious marks that could not have been caused by accident for example, or a child's report of abuse. Remember, your job is not to make accusations, nor to determine the guilt or innocence of anyone who might be involved. Get a copy of the requirements that the law makes of teachers for suspected child abuse reporting and put them in your Professional Resource File. **You will discuss at length in your CDA Seminar the reporting procedures in your community.**

Every program must have policies and procedures about what to do should a child in your group be abused. Most teachers find themselves in a state of shock or feel numb when something like this happens. If you have a plan to follow you can let it guide you.

Much of how you deal with the abuse of the child will depend on the circumstances. If the abuser is someone you know—a member of the family—for example, and/or the abuse has been going on for some time, the situation may be very difficult for you to deal with personally. You may feel guilty that you did not recognize that the child was being abused. You may be very angry that someone you know and trusted could take advantage of a child for whom you care so much. You may well feel emotionally overwhelmed yourself.

Abuse by a stranger may be equally chilling. You may wish you had done more to help children say "NO" to strangers. You may find yourself suspecting every stranger who walks past your outdoor play area. You may keep saying, "If only I had ...."

In addition, if criminal charges have been filed against a family member, you may have some legal obligations, especially in terms of who is authorized to pick the child up. If a stranger was involved, parents may demand additional security measures for their children when they go on field trips or play outdoors, for example.

Regardless of the situation, you will probably react with shock and disbelief, with horror and disgust, and with anguish for the child who is so dear to you. Despite your feelings, you must be in control as a professional.

Before you are confronted with a child abuse situation, find out where to get support in your community to help you, the family, and the child deal with the problem. Localities have a child abuse hot line, a family counseling center, or a child welfare agency with staff to assist families.

Write the name of the counseling/ child welfare agency and the phone number here and on your phone emergency list. Then you can find it easily if you ever need it. Add the agency name and phone number to your Professional Resource File.

_____

_____

_____

_____

Indicators of possible child abuse

Child

- bruises or wounds in various stages of healing

- injuries on two or more planes [*sides*] of the body

- injuries reported to be caused by falling but which do not include hands, knees, or forehead

- oval, immersion [*in hot liquid*], doughnut-shaped, or imprint [*hot iron or cigarette*] burns

- reluctance to leave school [*or child care program*]

- inappropriate dress for the weather

- discomfort when sitting

- sophisticated sexual knowledge or play

- radical behavior changes or regressive behavior

- child withdraws or watches adults

- child seems to expect abuse

- revealing discussion, stories, or drawings

Adult

- unrealistic expectations for child

- reliance on child to meet [*adult*] social or emotional needs

- lack of basic childrearing knowledge or skills

- substance abuse

Stress

- positive or negative changes—moving, new baby, unemployment, divorce

Note: From "Child Abuse and Neglect," by B. J. Meddin and A. L. Rosen, *Young Children*, May 1986, 41(4), 28. Copyright © 1986 by National Association for the Education of Young Children. Reprinted with permission.

As a teacher, your first responsibility must be to the child. Confidentiality about the case is an absolute must. In a center program, only your supervisor needs to know because of any possible legal consequences.

When the child returns to your group, you will need to continue to offer your support by giving more individual attention, or allowing the child time alone although under your careful supervision, or listening about the child's confusion.

On the other hand, you will not support the child's long-term development if you are overprotective or otherwise play favorites at the expense of the other children. You want the child to have time to deal with the situation but you also want the child to resume the usual activities in life as they are appropriate.

Some children's books deal with child abuse. Select one or two especially good books and list the titles here. Then you can obtain them without searching should you need to use them. If a child is abused, you will need to make a decision about whether to read the books to the whole group, to just the child involved, or to recommend them to the parents to read at home.

Discuss your selections with your CDA Field Advisor.

Although your efforts and those of the counselors involved will be directed toward helping the child return to a more secure life, you will at times be frustrated. Court proceedings can sometimes drag on for months. Children may have to relive their experiences before one or more juries or judges. Again, you can be a great support to the child during this harrowing time.

You may even be called to testify, perhaps to verify that the child is capable (*or not capable*) of taking the stand, is truthful, or to report on any observed changes in the child's behavior after the incident. If you become involved in this aspect of such a case, you must obtain legal advice immediately.

Most parents will rely on your support as well. Few family incidents are as upsetting as having a child abused. Your strength can help the family weather this storm. But your support alone is not enough. Almost without exception, abused children and their families need additional professional counseling. Work together with your program director, a social worker, psychiatrist, or other trained professional to help the family rebuild its strengths.

This is an excellent time to put all you have just learned into action. Refer back to your brief descriptive sketches that you did in Unit 3 for each child in your group. Right now you are especially in tune with children's social and emotional strengths and needs.

Look through your notes for any patterns that might give you clues about children who need additional support in their social-emotional development. List those children here, and begin to make a plan to work with them and their families to help children build on their strengths and address their needs.

CHILD'S NAME _____

Social-emotional concerns _____

_____

Support strategies _____

_____

_____

_____

CHILD'S NAME _____

Social-emotional concerns _____

_____

Support strategies _____

_____

_____

_____

_____

You have reached the end of the self-study portion of one of the most difficult parts of your CDA training. Why is social and emotional development such a difficult topic? Because so many people have so many different discipline methods. Because so many of us had parents who were not aware of how important our feelings were. And because so many of us had teachers who weren't aware of the role of culture in development. We can't always rely on our own experiences to make us good teachers!

We must all continue to improve how we teach by making changes in what we do. These changes might not always feel comfortable at first, but by using researched-based approaches to teaching, you will feel good about yourself, and children's long-term development will benefit.

You have much of the basic information you need to start to improve your teaching strategies. Mark your progress by checking the box in your CDA progress Record for this Unit.

Then continue to use this more research-based approach to teaching. And for the rest of your career keep learning more about children's social and emotional development. Researchers are always finding new, more effective ways to guide children's development. Keep up with your profession by reading and attending workshops or classes.

By the time you complete your CDA Professional Preparation Program, you will have a solid background in how to foster children's social and emotional growth. Much of what you will have learned also applies when you work to advance their physical and intellectual competence. We will now focus on those two aspects of children's development.

Resources for more information

Bredekamp, S. & Copple, C. (Eds.). (1997). *Developmentally appropriate practice in early childhood programs (Rev. ed.)* Washington, DC: National Association for the Education of Young Children.

Center on the Social and Emotional Foundations for Early Learning. Funded by the Child Care and Head Start Bureaus, U.S. Department of Health and Human Services. http://csefel.uiuc.edu.

Center for Evidence-Based Practice: Young Children with Challenging Behavior. Funded by the Office of Special Education Programs, U.S. Department of Education. www.challengingbehavior.org.

Chrisman, K. & Couchenour, D. (2002). *Healthy sexuality development: A guide for early childhood educators and families.* Washington, DC: National Association for the Education of Young Children.

Derman-Sparks, L. & the A.B.C. Task Force. (1989). *Anti-bias curriculum: Tools for empowering young children.* Washington, DC: National Association for the Education of Young Children.

Gartrell, D. (2004). *The power of guidance: Teaching social-emotional skills in early childhood classrooms.* Washington, DC: NAEYC and Delmar. www.earlychildhooded.delmar.com)

Greenberg, P. (1991). *Character development: Encouraging self-esteem and self-discipline in infants, toddlers, and two-year-olds.* Washington, DC: National Association for the Education of Young Children.

Honig, A.S. (2002). *Secure relationships: Nurturing infant-toddler attachment in early care settings.* Washington, DC: National Association for the Education of Young Children.

Huber, D. *Serving biracial and multiethnic children and their families.* (Video). St. Paul, MN: Redleaf Press.

Hyson, M. (2003). *The emotional development of young children: Building an emotion-centered curriculum.* New York: Teachers College Press. Available from NAEYC.

Jervis, K. (Ed.) (1984). *Separation: Strategies for helping two- to four-year-olds.* Washington, DC: National Association for the Education of Young Children.

Kaiser, B. & Rasminsky, J.S. (2002). *Challenging behavior in young children: Understanding, preventing, and responding effectively.* Allyn & Bacon. Available from NAEYC.

Kaiser, B. & Rasminsky, J.S. (1999). *Meeting the challenge: Effective strategies for challenging behaviors in early childhood environments.* Canadian Child Care Federation. Available from NAEYC.

Kissinger, K. & Krutein, W. (1994). *All the colors we are.* St. Paul, MN: Redleaf Press. (Picture books for preschoolers, in English and Spanish).

Lally, J.R., Griffin, A., Fenichel, E., Segal, M., Szanton, E.S. & Weissbourd, B. (2003). *Caring for infants and toddlers in groups: Developmentally appropriate practice.* Washington, DC: Zero to Three.

Levin, D.E. (2003). *Teaching young children in violent times: Building a peaceable classroom (2nd ed.)* Washington, DC: NAEYC with Educators for Social Responsibility.

Lieberman, A. (1993). *The emotional life of the toddler.* The Free Press. Available from www.zerotothree.org.

McCracken, J.B. (Ed.) (1986). *Reducing stress in young children's lives.* Washington, DC: National Association for the Education of Young Children.

Neugebauer, B. (1992). *Alike and different: Exploring our humanity with young children. Rev. ed.* Redmond, WA: Exchange Press.

Palmer, D. & Neugebauer, B., & Wolf, D. (1986). *Connecting: Friendships in the lives of young children and their teachers.* Redmond, WA: Exchange Press.

Riley, S.S. (1984). *How to generate values in young children: Integrity, honesty, individuality, self-confidence, and wisdom.* Washington, DC: National Association for the Education of Young Children.

Saifer, S. (2003). *Practical solutions to practically every problem: The early childhood teacher's manual. Rev. ed.* St. Paul, MN: Redleaf Press.

Sandall, S. & Ostrosky, M. (Eds.) (1999). *Practical ideas for addressing challenging behaviors.* Missoula, MT: Division for Early Childhood of the Council for Exceptional Children. Also available from NAEYC.

Sandall, S. & Ostrosky, M. (Eds.) (2001). *Teaching strategies: What to do to support young children's development.* Missoula, MT: Division for Early Childhood of the Council for Exceptional Children. Also available from NAEYC.

Slaby, R.G., Rodedell, W.C., Arezzo, D. & Hendrix, K. (1995). *Early violence prevention: Tools for teachers of young children.* Washington, DC: National Association for the Education of Young Children.

Stone, J.G. (1978). *A guide to discipline (Rev. ed.)* Washington, DC: National Association for the Education of Young Children.

Stone, J.G. (2002). *Building classroom community: The early childhood teacher's role.* Washington, DC: National Association for the Education of Young Children.

The Child Care Collection, Ball State University. (2003). *Acquiring self-regulation: Social and emotional development of infants and toddlers.* (Video). Available from NAEYC.

The Child Care Collection, Ball State University. (2003). *Communication and learning: Social and emotional development of infants and toddlers.* (Video). Available from NAEYC.

The Child Care Collection, Ball State University. (2003). *Making friends and getting along with peers: Social and emotional development of infants and toddlers.* (Video). Available from NAEYC.

Warren, R.M. *Caring: Supporting children's growth.* (1977). Washington, DC: National Association for the Education of Young Children.

Steps to advance children's physical and intellectual competence

AT THIS POINT in your CDA Early Childhood Studies, you are familiar with how children develop and learn: You know what it takes to set up a safe, healthy environment that supports learning. You know how important it is to interact with children in positive ways.

But you may still be asking yourself the question: "What do the children DO all day?"

In this unit we will combine all of what you have learned so far with many more specific, appropriate teaching strategies. Then you will be better prepared to promote children's social, emotional, physical, and cognitive development through play and other teacher-guided learning experiences. You will be prepared to plan what children do all day.

We will start by looking at what you want children to learn. Then we will focus on how children learn and what you need to do to be an effective teacher of young children.

PART 1

What do you want children to learn?

Pretend for a moment that Graham, Julia, Jerrod, and Maya are four children in your program. Think about some typical events that might happen.

"Wow! Look at that! The paint doesn't stick to where I colored. It only shows on the paper," exclaims Graham, a preschooler who has just discovered the wonders of crayon resist.

Julia, at 4-$\frac{1}{2}$, is enchanted by learning to write her name. She looks carefully through all the name cards of her friends and announces proudly, "Look! Jamie, Jordan, and Joey have names that start like mine."

Jerrod, 13 months old, stands at the bottom of the three-step climber with a slide. He lifts his leg and finally gets his knee on the step. He pulls up his other leg and perches his foot on the step. Then balancing carefully and holding on to the railings, he lifts himself and stands on the first step. He beams, wiggles his bottom in delight at his success, and begins to tackle the next step. He's on his way to the top!

Maya, a toddler, finds a basket of large wooden beads and shoestrings. She puts the basket on the floor, plunks down next to it, and picks a bright red bead and a pink shoelace.

First she tries to poke the end with the knot in it through the hole. But nothing happens. She looks around.

Her teacher is watching nearby. "What else could you try to get the lace through the bead?" she asks Maya. Maya tries another bead, but the knotted end still doesn't go through.

Then she grabs another shoestring, this time from the other end, and pokes it through the blue bead. Soon she has three beads on her string, and asks her teacher to "Make a necklace." Her teacher ties the beads loosely around her neck.

Timelines

You will need about three weeks to complete Unit 5. You have three tasks to complete:

1. Prepare for conference with your Field Advisor to discuss five topics (*goals for children's learning, planning physical activities, helping children communicate, promoting exploration and discovery, and planning curriculum*).

2. Complete two assignments (*identify learning goals for a specific activity area, and develop a sample weekly plan*) and three entries for the Professional Resource File.

3. Complete three assignments for Seminar (*prepare an interactive storybook reading with questions to promote vocabulary, examine pros and cons of using food in art activities, and think about ways to help children become more responsible citizens*).

Word list

Curriculum—A written plan that describes the goals for children's learning and development, and the materials, experiences, and teaching strategies to be used to help children achieve those goals.

Closed-ended question—Question that has one right answer.

Large-muscle—When children use their arms, legs, backs, and torsos. Generally is play that requires big movements.

Open-ended question—Question that could have many different answers (*these questions often begin with <u>why</u> or <u>how</u> or <u>what do you think would happen if . . . ?</u>*).

Fine motor—When children use their fingers and hands. Generally is play that requires small muscle coordination.

Transition—Times when children are finishing one activity and moving on to the next one.

If the parents of these children asked you what they were learning, how would you respond? Would you say, "Oh, Graham is just doing art," or "Julia is just playing a matching game since we don't teach reading." Or "Jerrod is just playing," or "Maya just loves to dress up"?

These answers are incomplete and inaccurate. They are only part of the picture of what these children are really doing and they don't acknowledge how much children are learning from these early experiences.

Sure, Graham was doing art. But he was also figuring out some of the basic principles of physics—that wax and water do not mix—and experiencing how exciting it can be to learn. He used his hands and fingers to draw and paint. And he was making his own discoveries. His self-esteem was bolstered, and he was eager to share his accomplishments with others.

Julia was applying her newly developed awareness of the alphabet to a meaningful situation. She has now learned the letters in her own name and is starting to observe the same letters in other familiar words like the names of her friends.

Jerrod was indeed playing and at the same time figuring out how to make his legs work together to climb steps. But he was also solving the problem of how to get to the top of the slide by himself. And he was thrilled to do be able to do it!

Maya was discovering how to string beads skillfully and she used what she made to decorate her body. But she also was picking up some new vocabulary *(through)*. She found, through trial and error, what really worked to get the string through the beads and she solved her problem herself—that's science in action. She is learning to ask for, and receive, help when she needs it.

Long-term goals for children's physical and intellectual development

Families and teachers want children to:

- **develop** strong, well-coordinated bodies;

- **gain** fine motor skills and eye-hand coordination;

- **develop** speaking and listening skills, and increase vocabulary;

- **learn** early literacy skills such as phonological awareness, alphabet knowledge, print awareness, early writing, and knowledge of and appreciation for books;

- **use** art, music, and movement to express themselves;

- **learn** early mathematics concepts, such as numbers and counting, patterns, and reasoning;

- **make** sense out of the world;

- **recognize** real problems and figure out solutions to them;

- **think** critically and logically, ask questions that lead to more questions; and

- **lead** well-balanced, productive lives.

Some of what these children learned did contribute to their physical growth. Some was related to their intellectual abilities. Some of it strengthened them as people. *As you can see, most learning doesn't fit into the neat little categories of either physical, cognitive, social, or emotional development—because in nearly every learning situation each area of development is involved. They all overlap.*

Children learn many different things from what seem like such insignificant happenings—you need to know what to look for and how to guide what happens. At other times, you will carefully plan learning experiences to lead to specific outcomes. But first, we must decide on what we want children to learn.

Being a teacher means giving a great deal of thought to what you want children to learn in your program. And it means taking into consideration what research says about the kinds of learning outcomes that predict later success in school and life.

In Unit 4, we listed some goals for social and emotional growth that families and teachers share for children now and all during their youth: to feel good about themselves, to be confident and competent, curious and eager to learn, self-regulating, friendly and cooperative, secure, and trusting.

Now let's add to that list with some specific goals for children's long-term physical and intellectual development. These are some of the other goals you share with families:

- **develop** strong, well-coordinated bodies;

- **gain** fine motor skills and eye-hand coordination;

- **develop** speaking and listening skills, the ability to communicate and understand;

- **learn** early literacy skills such as phonological awareness, alphabet knowledge, print awareness, early writing, and knowledge of and appreciation for books;

- **use** music, art, and movement to express themselves;

- **learn** early mathematical concepts such as numbers and counting, patterns and reasoning;

- **make** sense out of the world;

- **recognize** real problems and figure out solutions to them;

- **think** critically and logically, ask questions that lead to more questions;

and probably most of all—

- **lead** well-balanced, productive lives.

Please add any other broad goals that you, your program, or the families have for children. Think carefully about your own specific program and the specific cultural groups and families you serve. Perhaps learning English while continuing to develop their home language may a goal for some children in your program. If your program has written goals, such as the Head Start Child Outcomes, get a copy. Your Field Advisor will discuss them with you.

Your challenge is to work toward all these goals in developmentally appropriate ways. Let's see how to do that.

PART 2

How do children learn —and how do you teach?

Now that we've described goals for children's learning—**what** we want children to learn—we need to think about **how** children learn and how to teach. As a teacher of young children, one of the most important things for you to understand is how children learn. Most of us remember our school experiences as sitting at desks, listening to lectures, doing worksheets, or being part of a formal reading group. These kind of instructional techniques may be fine for older children and adults, but they do not work well for very young children.

How do young children learn?

Young children do learn a great deal about the world directly from adults. But as much as possible young children need to be active learners. They need to make sense of the world through their own first-hand experiences. And play is one of the best contexts to support young children's learning.

The National Academy of Sciences appointed two distinguished panels of scientists to review the research on early childhood development and learning. One report

focusing on the first three years of life is called *Neurons to Neighborhoods* (Shonkoff & Phillips, 2000). The other report, *Eager to Learn: Educating Our Preschoolers* (Bowman, Donovan, & Burns, 2000), describes learning for 3- through 5-year-olds.

The report about babies and toddlers is appropriately called, "Neurons to neighborhoods" because it describes how babies are born with millions of brain cells (or neurons) that get connected as a result of experiences during those early years of life. The research finds several things about learning and development for babies and toddlers:

- The critical importance of loving, caring relationships with adults—first parents and family members and then caregivers;

- The need for many experiences that enable the baby to safely learn about and explore the world through seeing, touching, hearing, tasting, and smelling;

- How the first three years of life is a critical period for language development; and

- The value of play to promote the learning and development of babies and toddlers.

Here are some of their findings from research about preschoolers' learning:

- Responsive adults are the most important influences on young children's positive development and learning. Positive teacher-child relationships promote children's social competence and academic learning.

- Supportive learning environments stimulate cognitive development—such environments actually build children's brains.

- Teachers and parents promote development when they create learning experiences that build on and extend a child's competence— experiences that are challenging but achievable, that is "developmentally appropriate".

- To provide such developmentally appropriate experiences, teachers must be sensitive to developmental characteristics, and individual and cultural differences among children.

- Cognitive, social-emotional, and motor development are interrelated, and necessary for early learning and later academic achievement. All areas require active attention during the early years of life.

These findings support some of what we've always known about early childhood development and also expand our earlier knowledge. For example, research about preschoolers finds that when they have had lots of opportunities to gain knowledge, preschoolers are actually more competent than we previously thought. But the key is providing good teaching and learning opportunities!

How should we teach babies and toddlers?

Throughout *Essentials*, you will find examples of appropriate ways of interacting with babies and toddlers to support their development and learning. To be an effective teacher of babies or toddlers, you must:

- Build a responsive, caring relationship with each child;

- Talk with individual children frequently, describing what is going on and responding to the child's attempts to communicate;

- Play with babies or toddlers using age-appropriate toys and materials;

- Use routine caregiving such as dressing, feeding, or diapering as opportunities to support learning;

- Provide lots of first-hand experiences for babies and toddlers to use all their senses to learn about their world—take walks, provide materials like water or play dough.

How should you teach preschoolers?

Research shows that the most effective pre-school programs—the ones that lead to positive learning outcomes for children—provide a balance of child-initiated/teacher-guided play and teacher-led, small group learning experiences. We use the phrase "child-initiated/teacher-guided play" for a reason. Because when the teacher is intentional in planning the play environment and providing choices for children, and then purposeful in supporting and extending the play, children benefit more from the play experience. Adult support of learning is especially effective within the context of children's play.

The National Academy of Sciences' Panel also concluded that one of the most effective ways to help young children achieve the goals you have for their learning is to develop and extend their interests. At this age, when children's attention spans and ability to self-regulate are still developing, you are more likely to engage them by tapping into their interests. So, if you want children to learn numbers, have them count whatever they care about whether it's snack crackers, animals, or blocks. If you want them to learn about print, read to them from books with characters who look like them or who do the things they do like going to school, preparing for bed, or having a new baby sister.

The National Academy of Sciences' Panel put it this way:

"How should teaching be done in preschool? Research indicates that many teaching strategies *can* work. Good teachers acknowledge and encourage children's efforts, model and demonstrate, create challenges and support children in extending their capabilities, and provide specific directions or instruction. All of these teaching strategies can be used in the context of play and structured activities. Effective teachers also organize the classroom environment and plan ways to pursue educational goals for each child as opportunities arise in child-initiated activities and in activities planned and initiated by the teacher" (Bowman, Donovan & Burns, p. 8.)

So good teachers tailor their teaching to the needs of individual children. They select from a range of teaching strategies depending on the learning goal and the needs of the child. The chart below describes a continuum of teaching behaviors ranging from least directive to most directive (Bredekamp & Rosegrant, 1995). All of these teaching strategies are appropriate sometimes, and none is appropriate all the time.

Continuum of Teaching Behaviors

Nondirective   **Mediating**   **Directive**

Acknowledge	Model	Facilitate	Support	Scaffold	Co-construct	Demonstrate	Direct
Give attention and positive encouragement to keep a child engaged in an activity.	Display for children a skill or desirable way of behaving in the classroom, through actions only or with cues, prompts, or other forms of coaching.	Offer short-term assistance to help a child achieve the next level of functioning (as an adult does in holding the back of a bicycle while a child pedals).	Provide a fixed form of assistance, such as a bicycle's training wheels, to help a child achieve the next level of functioning.	Set up challenges or assist children to work "on the edge" of their current competence.	Learn or work collaboratively with children on a problem or task, such as building a model or block structure.	Actively display a behavior or engage in an activity while children observe the outcome.	Provide specific directions for children's behavior with narrowly defined dimensions of error.

Source: Reaching Potentials Transforming Early Childhood Curriculum and Assessment, Vol. 2. Edited by Sue Bredekamp and Teresa Rosegrant. Washington, DC: National Association for the Education of Young Children, 1995, p. 21. Reprinted with permission from the National Association for the Education of Young Children.

Let's think about applying this continuum of teaching behaviors to the goal of helping preschool children learn early literacy skills.

Deborah Chang teaches 3- and 4-year-olds in a Head Start program. Among the Head Start Child Outcomes that she is working toward with her group are helping children learn letters and engaging them in early writing. To achieve these learning goals, among the strategies she uses is to provide daily sign-in sheets for the children and a writing area. Of course, the children are at very different developmental levels so she must individualize her teaching. Let's see how she uses the various teaching strategies to provide different levels of support for each child.

Acknowledge: Jose has Down syndrome and a relatively short attention span. He makes a recognizable J but loses interest and wants to move onto other things. Deborah says, "Jose, I see you made your J very clearly. You are learning to write your own name." On second thought, Jose begins to try his O.

Model: Katie has recently joined the class after being adopted from China. She is learning English as her second language and has many adjustments to make to her home and surroundings. When she arrives, Deborah greets her with a smile at Katie's eye level and says, "Good morning, Katie. I'm glad you're here. I'll sign your name for you on our chart."

Facilitate: Natividad is almost 5, but she has a very long name so it is taking her a while to master. She keeps mixing up where the I's go. Deborah comes up with an idea to make it easier for her. She points out that there is an I before and after the V and that the V is in the middle. That little bit of guidance is the key Natividad needs to spell her name correctly every time. She beams with pride at her accomplishment.

Support: Marco has been writing his first name successfully for several months. Deborah decides he needs help to continue to progress. She writes his last name on a special card just for him that he can refer to whenever he needs it.

Scaffold: Vivienne has mastered writing her name and the names of many of her friends. She loves to draw pictures and dictate to Deborah the story she wants to tell. Deborah decides she needs more challenge and wants to build on her letter knowledge to promote her early writing ability. When Vivienne describes her picture as "A flower for Mommy," Deborah draws four lines on the paper (one for each word) and writes: A — for ——. She says, "Can you write the rest of your story?" Vivienne soon gets the idea and writes in "FR" for flower and "MOM," a word she already knows.

Co-construct: Deborah knows that she has a small group of boys in her class who are very interested in dinosaurs but not especially interested in writing. She decides that by working with them on an investigation of dinosaurs, she can further her own goals of helping them learn literacy skills. She doesn't know much about dinosaurs herself, but sits down with the four boys. Together they list answers to questions: What do you know about dinosaurs? What do want to know about dinosaurs? How can we find out? They decide to visit the public library and also to explore the Internet. After several weeks, they each draw and write answers to the question, What did you learn about dinosaurs? Deborah is delighted to report that she learned as much as the boys!

Demonstrate: One of the learning outcomes for Head Start is for children to learn the concept of a "word"—a fairly abstract, challenging goal for young children, especially since we don't easily hear the breaks between words in speech. When Deborah reads a Big Book to a small group of children, she carefully points to each word as she reads. She draws the children's attention to the white space between the words. Sometimes, she counts the words in a line. She uses books that are familiar to the children such as *Good Night, Moon* by Margaret Wise Brown. During free choice time, she finds the children demonstrating this form of reading to each other.

Direct/Instruct: Deborah observes each of her children on a regular basis. She finds that most of the children are making adequate progress toward her literacy goals. She is concerned, however, that three of them—Ana, Eric, and Freddie—can only recognize one or two letters. Deborah plans several small group activities to focus their attention on letters. She doesn't try to teach all the letters at once. She starts with the letters they know and soon adds others. They all recognize A and E. So for about 10 or 15 minutes during free choice time, she plays an alphabet game like lotto or concentration with them. Once they recognize the letters, she introduces a new letter. She uses these small group opportunities to directly teach the alphabet to Ana, Eric, and Freddie.

Think about your own teaching. Which of these teaching behaviors are you most comfortable with? Which do you use most of the time?

_____

_____

_____

_____

_____

_____

Which of these teaching behaviors could you use more often? With which children would that teaching strategy be useful?

_____

_____

_____

_____

At times, you will need to modify your teaching, the enviroment, or your curriculum to support the development and learning of children with special needs. Here are ways to accomplish your goals for each child.

Do whatever is necessary to enable a child with a disability to function as independently and feel as secure as possible.

Modifications and Adaptations for Children with Special Needs

Adapted from *The Head Start Path to Positive Child Outcomes: A Guide for Education Leaders* (Head Start Bureau, 2003).

Teachers need to be intentional about supporting the learning and development of children with identified disabilities or special needs. Following are descriptions and examples of seven research-based types of modifications and adaptations (Hemmeter, Joseph, Smith & Sandall, 2002; Sandall et al., 2000; Sandall, Schwartz & Joseph, 2001; Wolery and Wilburs, 1994). Although these modifications were developed for children with special needs, some modification types are helpful for any child who is not making expected learning or developmental progress as well as for English Language Learners.

1. **Environmental support:** The teacher alters the physical or social environment, or time schedule/expectations to promote a child's participation, engagement and learning.

• For example, if a child has difficulty putting toys and equipment away during clean up—use pictures or symbols on shelves and containers. Make clean up a matching game.

• If a child has difficulty playing near peers—plan cooperative small group activities with engaging and highly motivating materials so that the child is in proximity with peers while engaging in fun activities such as murals, cooperative block structures, and so forth.

• If a child has no play partners—build friendships by seating the same peer next to the child every day at a planned activity such as small group or circle time.

• If a child does not participate in learning centers during free choice time—create a picture schedule for the child. The picture schedule can have pictures or symbols representing the various learning centers organized in a certain order (e.g., 1) art, 2) dramatic play, 3) blocks, etc.). The child should be taught to refer to the schedule each time she finishes an activity or engages in a learning center for a specified amount of time with a teacher to help the child learn how to play in that area.

• If a child has difficulty making transitions—just before the transition provide the child with a picture or symbol representing the area or activity that the child should go to next. The child could even take the picture or symbol card with him to the next area.

• If a child quickly finishes with an activity and then has difficulty waiting for the next activity—open one or two quiet centers (such as the book area or computer) after the activity and allow the child to leave the activity and go to one of the open quiet areas, when she is finished.

2. Materials or equipment adaptations: The teacher modifies materials or provides special equipment so that the child can participate as independently as possible.

- If the child has difficulty standing at an art easel—lower the easel and give the child a chair, or cut the legs of an easel and place it on a table.

- If a child's feet do not reach the pedals of a tricycle—tape wooden blocks on to the pedals.

- If a child's feet do not reach the ground in a regular child-size chair—place a stool under the table that they can rest their feet on it and stabilize their body. This stability helps children to more easily use their fine motor skills.

- If a child has difficulty using two hands to act on materials—stabilize materials using tape, Velcro, nonskid backing (such as bath mat appliqués) and clamps.

- If a skill or response required by a toy is too difficult for a child—modify the response. For example, if a child has difficulty turning the pages of a book, glue small pieces of sponge or Styrofoam to each page; this will separate each page making it simpler to turn the page.

- If a child doesn't choose the art center because actions such as gluing and pasting are still too difficult—use contact paper or other sticky paper as the backing for collages. The child only has to put things on the paper.

- If a child has a hard time grasping markers and paint brushes—add a piece of foam around the markers and paintbrushes to make them easier to hold.

- If a child shows minimal interest in the wooden blocks—wrap some of the blocks with colorful, shiny paper.

- If a child is not yet interested in storybooks—include photograph albums with pictures of the children. Make photograph albums of field trips and class activities.

3. Simplifying the activity: The teacher simplifies a complicated task by breaking it into smaller parts or reducing the number of steps.

- If a child is easily distracted when playing with manipulative toys such as puzzles, beads, and such—hand the pieces to the child one by one. Gradually increase the number of pieces the child has at one time.

- If a child is overwhelmed by activities such as cooking projects, craft projects and table games, and is rarely successful—break down the activity into its parts. Describe the steps in clear terms, "First we do (x) then we do (y)" etc. Draw pictures of steps to make it even clearer.

- If a child has difficulty understanding stories—use objects or flannel board pieces that represent characters or objects in the story. The child may make connections between the physical objects.

- If a child has a long walk from the car or bus to the classroom, and then dawdles, complains, and sometimes stops and drops to the floor—put photos, posters, or other interesting displays at strategic points along the way. Encourage the child to go to the next spot and describe the achievement, "You got to the baby elephant picture—can you find the baby lion?"

- If a child has difficulty with projects that have multiple steps—prepare the activity with the individual child in mind. Some children may do the entire project. Others may receive projects that have been started and they finish the last two or three steps.

4. **Using child preferences:** The teacher identifies and integrates the child's preferences for materials, activities, or specific people so that the child takes advantage of available opportunities.

- If a child tantrums and tries to leave large group times such as circle—let the child hold a favorite, quiet toy (i.e., teddy bear, blanket, etc.).

- If a child has difficulty making transitions form one area or activity to the next—allow the child to carry a favorite toy from one activity to the next.

- If a child does not come readily to circle time or other large group activities—begin large group time with a favorite activity such as blowing bubbles or singing that child's favorite song.

- If a child has difficulty engaging in new activities or learning centers, or perseverates (stays with one activity only) on one activity—incorporate the child's favorite toy into the learning center that they rarely go to. For example, if the child loves cars but never goes to the dramatic play area, create a "car wash" in the area.

5. **Adult support:** An adult intervenes or joins the activity to support the child's level of participation.

- If a child repeats the same play actions over and over without making any changes, use adult support. For example, a child at the sand table dumps and fills, and dumps and fills without seeming to pay attention to the effects of his actions. Show the child another way to dump and fill but make small alterations from the way that the child currently plays, such as hold the container up high while you dump it, or dump it through a funnel or short tube.

- If a child is not interested in books—have the parent(s) record a story and then let the child listen to the book on tape in the book area. The parent could also say a special hello to their child on the tape.

6. Peer support: The teacher uses peers (the other children) to increase a child's participation.

- If a child doesn't know how to select an activity or game from the computer menu—pair the child with another child who is familiar with operating the computer, and let the peer show the child how to select an activity from the computer menu.

- If a child is watching two children play and seems like he wants to join them—ask the two children to invite the child to join them.

- If a child doesn't know when and where to go during the transition to the playground—pair the child with another child who knows the routine and follows directions. Ask the children to find their partner and hold their partner's hand.

- If a child is learning to use English words or sign language to request food items at snack or mealtime—have another child hold the requested food (such as a plate of crackers). The child will need to request the crackers from the friend instead of always making requests of adults.

7. Invisible support: The teacher purposely arranges naturally occurring events within an activity.

- If a child is just learning to pour from a pitcher –let other children pour first so that the pitcher is not too full.

- If a child is a reluctant talker during group activities—give the child a turn to talk after another child who is particularly talkative. This gives the reluctant child ideas about what to say.

- If a child needs more practice on a particular gross motor skill such as walking on the balance beam—incorporate this skill into an obstacle course. Put a popular, fun, or noisy activity after the more difficult one. For example, let the children hit a gong after they walk across the balance beam.

- If a child has difficulty staying focused during small group activities—have her sit in such a way that distractions are minimized (i.e., away form the window and door, next to quieter children, etc.).

Now, on to what children do all day. And more about how you teach.

You enable children to develop strong, well-coordinated bodies and fine motor skills

Children's bodies develop when children are healthy and when they have lots of opportunities to use their large and small muscles in a wide variety of developmentally appropriate ways. How then, do you enable children to develop strong, well-coordinated bodies?

Play outdoors frequently

Even in the coldest of climates, children need to go outdoors every day for at least a few minutes. Children should be dressed properly of course, but since the fresh air is vital to their health, spend as much time as you can outdoors. Give children things to do while they're out. Older children can help carry tables and materials. Puzzles, blocks, paints, water play, dress-up clothes—everything can go out. Never restrict yourself to just "recess" or typical playground equipment outdoors. Meals and snacks always taste better on picnics. Read a story on a blanket under a tree. Think of every activity you do inside as a potential outdoor activity.

What activities have you never done outdoors?

_____

_____

_____

_____

Choose something from the list and as soon as possible, take it outside. Watch how children use the activity differently outdoors.

Balance active (*large-muscle*) and quiet (fine motor) play and other learning experiences

Children need lots of playtime each day—in fact, most of their day should be spent in play. During this playtime, children may choose from what the teacher has planned to do indoors and outdoors.

You provide the time, equipment, and activities that enable children to use their bodies, muscles, and brains in a variety of ways. For example, sometimes a toddler will want to use a table toy such as a puzzle or interlocking blocks. Other times that same toddler will want to jump around on the mats and cushions. Give them both choices.

Provide a wide range of activities and materials suitable for the children's development, to challenge but not frustrate them.

And of course, you adapt activities and materials for any children who have special needs. Perhaps a paintbrush will need to be attached to an arm or a brace. Maybe you need knob puzzles with a large number of pieces for a preschooler who has difficulty picking up small items. Do whatever is necessary to enable a child with a disability to function as independently and feel as secure as possible. See pages 282-285 for examples of modifications for children with disabilities.

Sometimes children have been ill, or overprotected, or find an activity too difficult, or were injured doing something similar. You don't push or force children to participate. You want children to feel competent and successful. You watch as their muscles develop and provide opportunities to practice newly mastered skills while providing a challenge to achieve skills they soon will be able to do.

Young infants.

For the first few months, infants' large muscles are developing at a rapid pace and their fine motor coordination also begins. Infants need space to kick, to roll over, to drop things, to bounce, to crawl, to balance themselves, to walk, to dance. They need spoons to grasp and chunks of food to pick up.

Eleven-month-old Brooke has discovered the wonderful taste and feel of cereal bits. Feeding herself is exciting. She crawls over to the cupboard and jabbers. As soon as her family childcare provider gets out the box, Brooke begins to pop the cereal into her mouth.

Newborns sometimes are comforted by being wrapped tightly, but soon they find out how glorious it feels to kick their legs and wave their arms. Happily play a baby's favorite game of dropping and picking things up—plastic measuring cups, keys, or toys. You can probably think of other safe ways to give young babies a feeling that what they do can make a difference in their environment.

As babies grow more mobile, you give them safe places to move about. Some areas are carpeted. You provide cushions to climb on and cardboard boxes to climb in. Empty diaper boxes make great wagons for pulling babies. They love to play "Pat-A-Cake" and ride the horse (*your bouncing leg*). Pounding benches, drums, and a small basin of water to splash in are wonderful for growing arms. Finger foods enable children to begin to feed themselves as their small muscles and budding teeth begin to work for them.

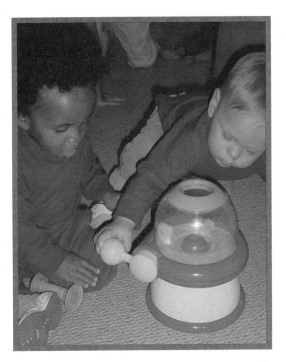

Provide a wide range of activities and materials suitable for the children's development, to challenge but not frustrate them.

You would not give an infant small beads or tiny plastic blocks. Why? Because infants put everything in their mouths and they could choke. Nor can you expect babies to draw with markers, turn the thin paper pages of a book, do intricate finger plays, or feed themselves with a spoon. But they can manipulate and "taste" board books and hear nursery rhymes and songs. Keep your expectations reasonable.

List some appropriate large- and small-motor toys and household objects that should be available for infants to choose from every day:

_____

_____

_____

_____

Discuss your list with your CDA Field Advisor.

Older infants and toddlers.

Toddlers' large muscles are still developing, but they are also beginning to coordinate their hands and fingers with more skill.

Emilia is engrossed with the clay dough. She takes a large hunk from the covered can, kneads the clay with her hands for a long time, and then plops it on the table. She rolls it by pushing hard with her arms, then picks off tiny chunks and lines them up carefully. "Look, I made cookies!" she exclaims to no one in particular. Then she picks up

her cookies and pokes them one at a time back into her ball.

So you provide toddlers with lots of places to run and climb; fairly low places to jump from; music for dancing; smaller items to fit together and take apart; sand and water to pour, carry, and sift; items to balance and dump and fit pieces together; things to push or pull; and the chance to feed themselves with spoons.

Ramps and steps with play areas below can provide hours of fun and challenge for toddlers. Slides, low bikes to pedal, wagons to pull, small shopping carts or lawn mowers to push—all are valuable for children's development. Open grassy areas give them space to run. Give a toddler a bucket of water, a three-inch paintbrush, and a wooden fence or the side of a building. Much of the typical toddler's day is spent in large-muscle activities, so both your indoor and outdoor play areas should center around these types of activities and equipment.

Toddlers also are developing finer muscle control. Puzzles with knobs make it easy for them to remove and replace the pieces. They like fitting things into containers and then dumping them all out again: Try a plastic ice cream container filled with screw-type jar lids—the clatter is delightful!

Large pieces of blank paper work well for scribbling and drawing with markers or crayons. At first, children will make random marks or move the crayon back and forth across the page just for the fun of it. But gradually their marks become more controlled and begin to resemble circles and lines. Clay is wonderful to roll and squish, as Emilia has discovered. Usually toddlers prefer to work on the floor or to stand at a small table for these activities.

Appealing books for toddlers have sturdy paper pages and bright pictures. More and more book publishers are paying attention to the needs of the younger child. "Board" books (*so named because their pages are made out of cardboard*) are available with colorful, bright illustrations of familiar objects. Some new ones on the market include books on colors, shapes, and letters. Action songs—"The Wheels on the Bus," "Johnnie Hammers with One Hammer," and a simple version of the "Hokey-Pokey"— are always hits. Toddlers love to put their hand into a mystery bag or box and try to guess what they feel with their fingers. Dress-up clothes have large buttons, snaps, or zippers so children can fasten them themselves and for others. Get large cardboard blocks (*or make some from empty milk cartons*). Begin with some basic shapes in unit and table blocks. Find

items toddlers can fit together, such as clean plastic bottles with their lids or egg cartons and colorful plastic eggs (*with surprises inside the eggs*).

Mealtimes will be messy, but young toddlers can begin to feed themselves with increasing skill—and they certainly won't learn unless you give them the chance to practice. Likewise, learning to use the toilet may result in a few accidents. That's part of life. Enlist children's help to clean up.

On the other hand, you do not expect toddlers to color between the lines, to use watercolors, to build with tiny plastic blocks, to draw on small sheets of paper, to make realistic looking art products, or to feed themselves thin soups. Why? Because toddlers' hands and fingers are not yet ready for such difficult tasks. Nor are their minds ready to deal with abstract paper-and-crayon tasks imposed on them. Match your expectations to their development.

All young children are much more interested in the **doing** rather than in coming up with an end product. Doing is real learning.

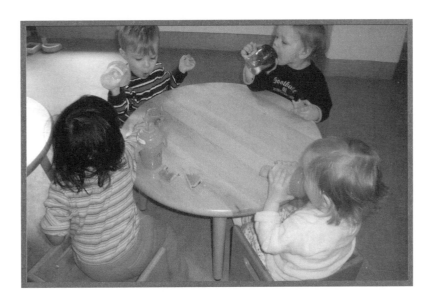

Mealtimes will be messy, but young toddlers can begin to feed themselves with increasing skill

List here some good activities that are always available for toddlers' large muscle and fine motor development. Remember to balance active and quiet play.

_____

_____

_____

_____

_____

Review these with your CDA Field Advisor.

Preschool children.

By the age of 3 or 3½, children's legs and arms are becoming quite well coordinated. They can use low riding vehicles with pedals easily and are ready to drive around increasingly difficult obstacle courses. Preschoolers can climb and swing their bodies in the air. They want to learn how to do forward rolls and other more complicated things with their bodies.

Jarrett chooses to paint at the easel almost every day. He gets his smock from the hook and asks a friend to button it in back for him. He makes sure there are at least four colors and four 1-inch brushes in the tray. Then he uses tiny strokes with the side of the brush to make intricate designs. Some days he will use broad strokes as well. Once in a while, he paints over everything and crumples up the paper. On other days, he puts his name on a corner of the paper and hangs it to dry.

Preschoolers also love to run and chase (play "Follow the Leader;" "Simon Says;" or tag), to stand at the top of the high slide, to play catch—be sure to include different types of games from around the world. At this age, cooperation in physical activities is far more important than competition.

Building becomes much more intricate during these years. Preschoolers plan and carry out elaborate ideas with blocks. They need lots of unit blocks in many different shapes. Large hollow blocks are wonderful if your budget will allow them. Smaller building blocks—such as interlocking plastic blocks, wooden logs, and stick-together pieces—add yet another dimension for building with small muscles.

Hardwood unit blocks are a superb investment. They last for generations. Best of all, they have **unlimited potential for learning** in nearly every area of children's development: physical, social, emotional, math, science, social studies, art, and language arts, for example. Pat Hutchins' book, *Changes, Changes*, if read to preschoolers, can change their imaginative play with blocks.

Fine motor coordination improves greatly during the preschool years. Every few months, 4-year-olds can work puzzles with more and more pieces. Wooden or rubber ones are the sturdiest for hard use in programs, but children also enjoy ones you make. Cut up cereal boxes or paste pictures on cardboard and cut them up. Older preschoolers can even make their own puzzles like this.

Woodworking, weaving, sewing, and other fine motor skills begin to appeal to children during these early years. The equipment and materials should always be selected to assure that children can do these projects successfully and safely: Real carpentry tools, large

Potential contributions of blocks for early childhood curriculum.

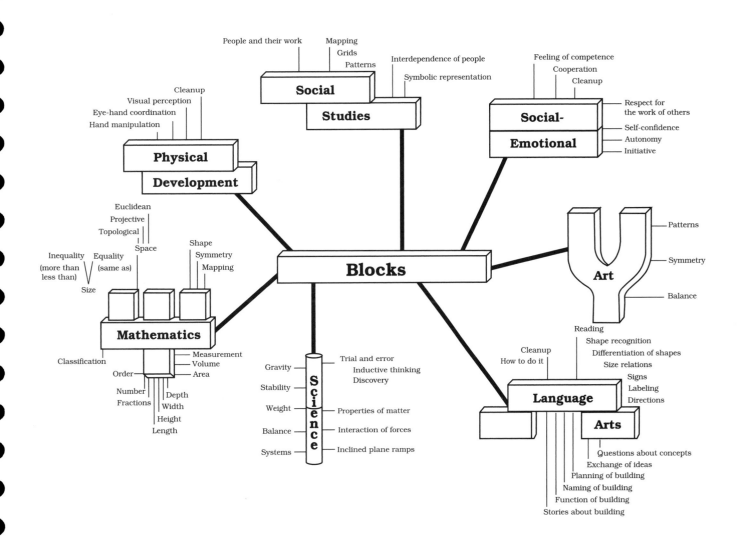

*Adapted from Charlotte and Milton Brody. The Block Book (revised) (1996) edited by Elisabeth S. Hirsch. National Associated for the Education of Young Children, 1509 16th St., NW., Washington DC 20036.

yarn needles, soft woods such as pine for easy hammering and sawing, thick yarn or open-weave fabrics such as burlap or nylon net for sewing—and guidance in how to use all these things properly.

The process of doing these types of activities is far more important than the product—never make children feel they have to make something. Sawing a small board or pasting some yarn on fabric may be all the child is interested in doing. Respect that choice.

Pretend play consumes a great deal of the day for many preschoolers. Props should represent diverse jobs and cultures, so children can try out many different roles. They can use their bodies, hands, and fingers as they play: Buttons can be smaller, children may be ready to tie bows on shoes or aprons, bandages need to be wrapped carefully around those who pretend to be injured. How much they can do by themselves!

Preschoolers also are increasingly interested in identifying and making letters or numbers (*with finer markers, crayons, pencils or pens*). They may want to make signs or write their names on their artwork. Drawings and clay sculptures, for example, start to look more realistic, but most preschoolers are still more interested in what they are doing than what the final product looks like.

Preschoolers love to cut and paste and glue all kinds of things together—discards such as fabric scraps, leaves, packing chips, bits of yarn, pictures children cut out of old magazines or catalogs are some of the best art materials available.

Although preschoolers can do a lot with their muscles, there are some activities that are really *not* developmentally appropriate, meaning they are not achievable by most of the children within a given age range:

- Preschoolers should not be expected to form letters and numbers **perfectly** when they write them. Just encourage children to write the best they can and commend them for their efforts. Their writing, like all other aspects of their development and learning, will improve with practice.

- Coloring books, tracing, and drawing with stencils are not as valuable as children's own drawing and writing attempts. Children are often more capable of coloring in lines that they have drawn. Give them the materials and see how much more interesting the results are when children use their imaginations.

- Don't make a sample of art for children to copy, or expect them to paste or assemble shapes that an adult has cut out for them. You can spend hours cutting things out, and the children will finish pasting all those pieces in three minutes. Why not let the children do their own cutting? You already know how to cut and children need the practice. And while children can try (*if they want*) to cut on the lines they draw, don't expect perfection every time.

- Jumping rope and riding two-wheel bicycles call for an incredible amount of balance and coordination of arm and leg muscles, so most preschoolers find it too difficult. Team sports with lots of rules, such as baseball, football, or soccer, are beyond preschoolers' physical and social skills. Bring out the balls and let children make up their own games or just plain exercise!

List several developmentally appropriate large muscle and fine motor development activities and materials that should be offered every day for preschoolers:

_____

_____

_____

_____

_____

Your CDA Field Advisor will want to see your list.

Develop children's senses

The whole world awaits children through their senses—hearing, smell, taste, sight, and touch. Right from birth, we can support the development of—but be careful not to overstimulate—children's senses. If you know or work with children who have limitations such as vision or hearing difficulties, you truly can appreciate just what an important learning tool our senses are.

Hearing

Children's ears open the door to spoken language and to music. Cultivate children's listening skills. Infants are responsive to sound before they are born. They recognize their mother's voice immediately. You will want to talk and sing with infants, using their home language as much as possible. Even if you are slightly off key, they will love the sound of your voice.

Play pleasing music from several cultures to acquaint them with a variety of sounds and beats. Within the first few months, infants begin to hear and repeat things that are funny—they can blow "raspberries" (*make a sputtering kiss*), create strange noises, and imitate squeak toys.

Continue to introduce more wonderful things to hear throughout the early years. Choose real musical instruments that sound pleasing and that children can play with the skills they have. If they're making music together in a band, give each child a chance to play every instrument, as they seem interested.

One game young children enjoy is to guess what made a familiar sound—a door closing, the Jack-in-the -Box popping up, or a friend's voice. Keep the game brief and the children involved in making the sounds.

Language is a joy for all ages. Talk gently to babies during diapering. Use many different ways to express ideas—elaborate on your own language. Speak and sing in the preferred languages of the child's family, including signing or cueing for those who are hearing impaired. Use short poems about topics that intrigue children, including some that don't rhyme. Tell stories with a flannel board or puppets, making sure the characters are diverse.

Remember to use language a little more advanced than the children's. Children benefit from hearing language varieties and complexities well before they can use them themselves.

Children rarely listen with only their ears—their whole bodies seem to want to respond to music and words. Action songs and moving or dancing to music are marvelous for young children. Make sure the words are appropriate, just as you choose children's books that do not stereotype others.

Listening to the teacher's voice is not the only important listening children do. **Children need to talk with each other as they play.** An appropriate classroom is one that buzzes with busy children's voices.

Children learn from each other and from expressing themselves with words. Adults should never dominate children's conversations during play.

List some appropriate activities that you offer every day for children to choose to hear.

Talk with your CDA Field Advisor about your choices.

Smell

Whether the reaction is "Yuck!" or "Now I'm hungry," children learn with their noses. Rather than making up artificial experiences in which children guess what the smell is, try to keep your nose out for everyday smells in real life. Alert the children to the wonders of smell.

"Ummm. How wonderful the freshly cut grass smells! Who can smell the grass?"

"It's almost time for lunch. You know how I know?"

A preschooler points to her nose and nods her head.

"What do you think we are having?"

"Black beans with rice!"

"Oh, my, we forgot to clean Cocoa Butter's cage yesterday. Who can figure out how I can tell we need to clean it now?"

How much there is to discover about our bodies and the world with our noses!

What was the last smell you talked about with the children in your group? How did they react?

Taste

Since babies will try to put everything into their mouths, your biggest worry will be to make sure everything they can get to is safe for small mouths.

Children are sure to have a more nutritious diet if they can choose from a wide variety of foods. And the more things they taste, the more likely they will appreciate many foods.

Without being overbearing about it, encourage children to enjoy tasting many different foods.

Every day in a full-day program, you serve at least two snacks and one meal. One snack is always served in a part-day program. Use mealtimes for conversation. Talk about how things taste, what foods taste similar to others, and other topics as you prepare and eat the food. Don't turn the snack or meal into a lesson about the color of the broccoli or the shape of the orange. Just comment on how crunchy, or salty, or sticky something tastes—or wait for children to create a natural learning opportunity.

A 26-month-old, a 3-year-old, and a 5-year-old are eating their morning snack at their family childcare provider's home.

The youngest child has never eaten apples with peanut butter. The two older children urge her on.

"Come on, Ashley. Look, you like peanut butter, right? You eat it on crackers all the time. Isn't that yummy? Well, on an apple, it's wetter. Your teeth don't stick together so much."

The 3-year-old gives the recipe. "Take the knife. Take the peanut butter. Smear it on the apple? See?"

Ashley agrees to try just a taste on a very thin slice. She shakes her head. "I want a cracker now," she requests.

Your attitude is the most important factor here. Tastes are just waiting for each of us to discover them. But everyone likes different things.

Throughout early childhood, children learn through their senses.

What new tastes do you want to introduce to the children in your group? How will you do that? What happened when you did? Write your ideas here.

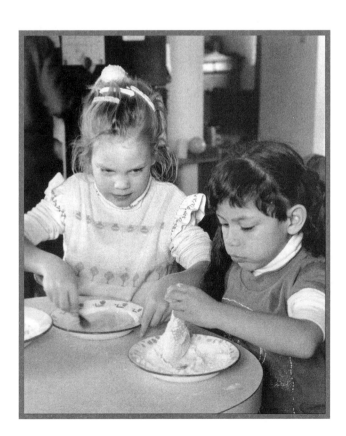

Sight

Most mothers knew better, but some experts used to claim that babies couldn't see much when they were born. Can you imagine?!

You don't want to bombard young babies or overwhelm them, but you do want them to have some interesting things to look at because they can't move around yet. Hang a mobile above the crib and another over the changing table. Be sure to choose or make mobiles that have an interesting view from the baby's viewpoint!

Hang some colorful or high-contrast pictures next to the changing table or play yard or at floor level. Put a mirror in the play yard or along the floor so babies can see themselves. Move babies about frequently so they can watch you and the other children.

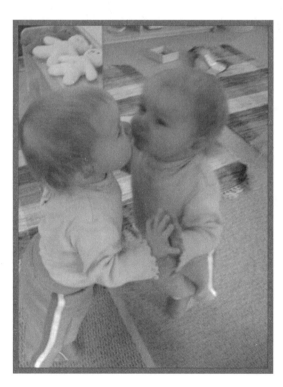

Put a mirror in the play yard or along the floor so babies can see themselves.

Choose cardboard books with bold, bright drawings and prop them within view.

Toddlers and preschoolers love colors. But be careful in decorating that you don't use such bright colors that children are over-stimulated. Maybe a colorful parachute can be hung above a crawling space. Children's cubbies could be color-coded. Keep the tempera paints at the easel fresh (so children can mix them if they want). Offer many colors of construction paper. Make sure crayons and markers have a variety of colors.

Children will learn the names of colors as they use them in their art projects, as they get dressed, and as they notice color used in many ways in real life. There are so many opportunities to use color that it is usually unnecessary to teach colors in lessons. Here are just a few of the ways color can be a part of your daily conversations with children.

"Who wants to wear the yellow apron?"

"We have three different cups for our juice. Verde, azul, rojo. Which color would you like?"

"You look so grown up in your new lavender dress, Laura."

"Today there is a special art activity for anyone who is interested. We have some gorgeous green paper, some sticky paste, and some red and white tissue paper. Who would like to start at the art table? We have space for four children at a time."

Simple children's games often rely on color recognition. Children will catch on fast to the names of colors if they want to play a board game such as "Color Lotto" with their friends.

There are many more things to see than just color, too. Every day, children can be helped to be more aware of the world around them.

Yesterday, you took a group of four toddlers down the street to visit a construction site. Later, you ask the children to choose an activity a lot like something they saw on their visit.

One child begins to work with blocks.

Another drives trucks while wearing a hard hat.

A third digs in the sand table.

A fourth asks for help to write a story. "We saw people making a new place. It was noisy." She dictates the words and you write them down. Then she draws a picture with lots of blue (*most of the noisy machines were blue*).

Children can learn so much through their eyes. Field trips provide new things to see. They should be planned often, well organized, and appropriate for the children's ages and interests (*short and not too far away, for example*).

You can provide many related but **real** experiences, before and after the trip, to help children make sense of what they see. You may need to read a book, or show pictures, or talk about what they might see (*or hear or touch or smell*). A thank you note from the children (*either one they dictate or write themselves or their drawings of what they saw, for example*) is always appreciated.

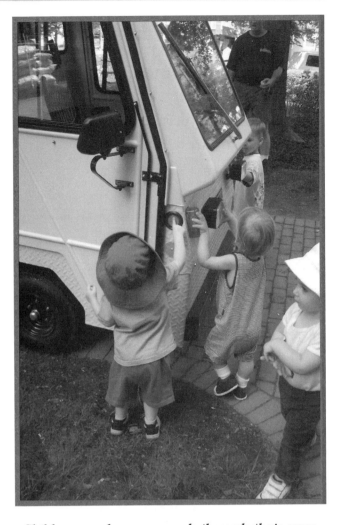

Children can learn so much through their eyes. Field trips provide new things to see.

What are some of the most interesting things happening in your program's neighborhood?

_____

_____

_____

_____

_____

Sometime within the next week, take the children on a walking trip to see one of these things. What are some preparations and follow-up activities that will help make the experience more meaningful to the children?

_____

_____

_____

_____

Talk with your Advisor about what happened.

Touch

Scratchy whiskers, soft baby skin, warm toast, smooth velvet, juicy peaches—real things are waiting for children to touch them! In addition to pictures of these objects, make sure the materials in your room have a variety of hard/soft, cool/warm, rough/smooth textures. Children will naturally experience these in their play.

Then, when a child announces, "Mrs. Duvall, these crackers have little bumps on them," you will be prepared. What would you say?

Goals for children's learning through woodworking

Cognitive

1. To develop relationship thinking: cause and effect; relatedness of things, feelings, activities; classification.

2. To understand number concepts through concrete use of counting, one-to-one correspondence, awareness of simple shapes, comparison of size, experience with metric measure in three dimensions.

3. To know and use wood and tools with purpose and satisfaction.

4. To experience joy in discovery, in active learning, in striving to find out information children need for their own purposes.

5. To increase communication skills through talking about woodworking and tools, reading directions or labels.

6. To solve problems through divergent thinking and planning creatively with three-dimensional wood constructs.

Goals for children's learning through woodworking, *continued*

Physical

1. To develop and coordinate large and small muscles, delight in movement and rhythm, feel competent in motor control and skill achievement.
2. To master physical woodworking skills: measuring, hammering, sawing, planing, filing, finishing.
3. To expand sense through smells, textures, and sounds of woodworking.

Emotional

1. To build strong, positive feelings about self.
2. To foster ability to meet new situations well.
3. To learn to sustain interest and overcome frustration successfully.
4. To become open and sensitive to feelings in self and others.
5. To expand intuitive learning through self-directed creativity such as feeling and testing hunches about performance of wood, tools, co-workers.
6. To [enjoy] satisfying firsthand experience with wood and tools.

Social

1. To cooperate with others.
2. To learn to grasp and follow rules for the safety of others as well as for oneself.
3. To accept differences among children with understanding and compassion.
4. To achieve satisfying friendships.
5. To sense responsibility to the group and status gained from this.
6. To experience joy in ... group accomplishment.
7. To achieve a deeply felt awareness that authority and group structure can promote individual fulfillment.

Note: Adapted from *Woodworking for Young Children* (p. 2–3) by P. Skeen, A. P. Garner, and S. Cartwright, 1984, Washington, DC: National Association for the Education of Young Children. Copyright © 1984 by National Association for the Education of Young Children. Reprinted by permission.

Now, on page 301, choose another activity area and try to identify three learning goals for children in each area of development. Discuss your ideas with your Field Advisor.

What new textures can you add to your teaching environment?

_____

_____

_____

_____

Through their bodies, children learn a great deal. In all the examples and ideas just discussed, did you recognize the beginnings of school subjects such as science, social studies, reading, and mathematics? Children are learning about these ideas through active, sensory experiences in **meaningful, integrated** ways that the teacher plans and guides.

All through this section, we have found how children's physical development overlaps with their intellectual and socioemotional development. We have talked about how to involve children in active learning with real objects at their own level. We have seen how you can help them build on their experiences to learn even more by relying on and expanding their curiosity.

This is how you teach and how children begin their long journey toward making the most of their lives now and in the future.

Before we move on, **really think** about these principles and how any activity, no matter what it is, can contribute to all areas of children's development. See the chart about woodworking. Then using another activity area, think about your goals for children in each area of development, using the chart on page 301.

The next long-term goal is to enable children to communicate. Let's see what learning experiences and materials lead children to improve their skills in this area.

You help children learn to speak and listen, and increase their vocabulary

The very youngest babies communicate by crying. As they grow older, they smile and look at you in the eye. They coo and then babble. Next they use gestures, and one-word utterances and before you know it, they are talking. Soon they will be reading and writing.

Language development is one of the most important tasks of the first five years of life. Children who are capable communicators are much more likely to succeed in all areas of later schooling, especially in learning to read and write. And we have already seen how crucial language is to social development. Children need command of words to be able to make friends and solve social problems.

Because children seem to learn language naturally like they learn to walk, we often assume that language just happens as children get older. But children actually learn to talk from much direct interaction with more competent speakers such as adults and older children. In fact, there is a wide range of variation in the language development of young children by the time they enter preschool. Some children are way behind in their language development and they need considerable language enrichment to be prepared for kindergarten. Building children's language capacity is one of your most important tasks as a teacher of young children.

Choose another activity area or learning center and try to identify three learning goals for children in each area of development. Discuss your ideas with your Field Advisor.

Goals for children's learning through_____

Cognitive

1._____

2._____

3._____

Physical

1._____

2._____

3._____

Emotional

1._____

2._____

3._____

Social

1._____

2._____

3._____

Strengthen children's use of spoken language

Before we look at specifics about how to promote children's language, look back at the developmental expectations chart in Unit 2. Refresh your memory about what communicative and expressive behaviors are typical for children at different ages.

Also remember that children develop at their own pace and in their own style, but that their development is heavily influenced by their experiences. Look at your daily diary for the children in your care—or at your summarized notes in Unit 3 for each child. You can probably pick out which children seem especially verbal, which ones are intent listeners, and who uses lots of nonverbal communication.

You use all of this information to figure out what to expect for each child and to decide on the best ways to strengthen each child's language learning. The strategies we suggest here for helping children learn language should all be used everyday. Language is too important to be left to chance.

Language is a joy for all ages. Talk gently to babies during diapering, feeding, and other routines. Describe what you are doing as you play with and care for them. This is sometimes called providing "play by play" because it is similar to what the television sports announcer does during a game. He or she tells you in words what you are seeing. Babies need to be surrounded by language long before they can actually produce words themselves.

As toddlers begin to use language, you scaffold their learning, providing just the right amount of assistance for them to continue to progress. You don't correct their speech, but instead you elaborate on it or extend it. So, when 2-year-old Lauren says, "Juice!", you might reply, "Oh, you'd like some orange juice." Remember to use language a little more advanced than the children's. Children benefit from hearing language varieties and complexities well before they can use them.

With all ages, use many different ways to express ideas—elaborate on your own language. Speak and sing in the preferred languages of the child's family, including signing or cueing for those who are hearing impaired.

Use books to build vocabulary

Read books to small groups of children, just two or three toddlers or three to six preschoolers. The vocabulary in books is more sophisticated than everyday speech and children can learn many new vocabulary words from well-written children's literature or information books.

When you read to children in small groups, give them opportunities to talk about the book before, during, and after the reading. Research shows that it is the conversation that surrounds the reading that is most helpful in building language. Use open-ended questions that start with "Why" such as "Why do you think Peter Rabbit went into Mr. McGregor's garden?" And ask distancing questions that require children to think beyond what actually happened in the story and relate it to their own life. "Have you ever done something naughty like Peter Rabbit? What happened?"

Use lots of expression when you read and make sure children can see the pictures. Let children act out or retell the story into a tape recorder and then listen to themselves.

Read from books with characters who reflect the identity of the children or that are written in languages other than English, or ask parents to translate some favorites for you. Your local librarian is a tremendous resource for you to check for finding all sorts of books and materials. *(See page 319-320 for ideas about using the library.)*

Now identify a good book to use to help build children's vocabulary. Prepare a series of questions to use with the children.

Discuss your ideas with your Seminar Instructor.

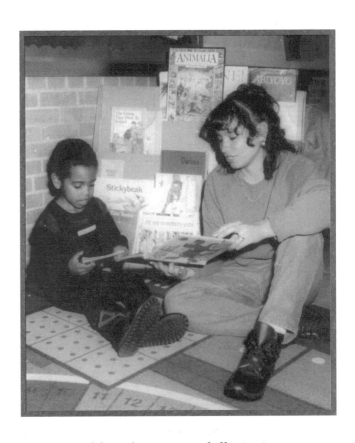

Building language skills in two languages at once requires specific strategies. Your goal is to strengthen children's ability to continue to be bilingual.

Spark conversations.

One of the most valuable things you can do to promote language development is to engage in one-to-one, extended conversations with individual children about their experiences at home, in their community, or events in the program. With preschoolers, don't limit your conversation to talking about the here and now. Talk with children about things that happened in the past, will happen in the future, or are in their imagination. This kind of talk requires more explanations and descriptions, and challenges children's developing language skill. When talking with children, try to have a conversation that extends to five turn-takings.

Don't just talk to the children who readily talk back. They don't need your support as much as those who are less verbal. All children learn to talk and appreciate the function and beauty of language when they take part in everyday conversations.

> "Good morning, DaRoyce. It's so good to see you this morning. When you have your things put away, please find something you would like to play with."
>
> "I already know," the 3-year-old smiles. "I want to play in the water."
>
> "You always enjoy that, don't you?" says Mr. Castillo. "Garrett and Melinda are already at the water table."
>
> We need more bottles," DaRoyce points out as he joins the group.
>
> "Who would like to help me get some more plastic bottles for the water table?" asks their teacher. All three children volunteer to help carry them.

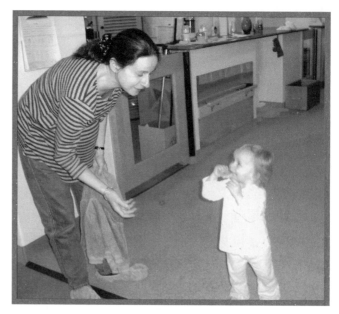

Talk with children not at them.

> As they walk to the closet, Melinda comments, "Let's get that blue one with the funny lid."
>
> "Yeah, and the one with the top cut off. To pour," adds Garrett."

> "Let's paste," Nicole says to her friend 5-year-old Shailee. They eagerly go to the art area.
>
> Shailee searches through the labeled boxes on the shelf. "Here it is. Let's paste with these bea-u-ti-ful ribbons."
>
> "OK. And here are some sequins we could add, too," suggests Nicole.
>
> "Y hojas secas," adds Shailee.
>
> "We can make a wonderful picture. What color of paper do you want to paste on, Shailee?" asks Nicole as she reaches on the shelf for a blue sheet for herself.

> "Thara, it's time for a clean diaper. Let's go change you. Christopher just got a fresh diaper, and now it's your turn. Here we go!" Patricia, the community volunteer, picks up 9-month-old Thara.

Would you like to talk on this little telephone while we change you? That's it, wrap your fingers around it tightly so it doesn't drop. Here's your clean diaper, and here are your wipes."

Thara holds the toy phone near the top of her head—she's getting the idea! Patricia picks up on her motions. "Ringgg. Ringgg. Hello, Thara. It's Patricia calling."

"Aaammm," replies Thara.

"Now we are taking off your soiled diaper. Into the trash it goes. What have you been doing this morning?"

Thara responds with, "Dadada. Bbbbaa."

"Oh, you've been looking in the mirror and making funny faces. You and Preston were trying on some hats."

"MMMM," smiles Thara.

"And then you played the drums. BOOM, BOOM, BOOM—here comes the marching band."

Gabriel, almost 3, arrives with four pussy willow sticks in his hand. The children crowd around him, eager to feel the softness. Quietly, their teacher begins one of her favorite poems:

> I know a little pussy
> Her coat is silver gray
> She lives down in the meadow
> Not very far away.
>
> She'll always be a pussy,
> She'll never be a cat,
> For she's a pussy willow.
> Now what do you think of that?

The children immediately calm down. Later, several ask for cotton balls so they can make their own pussy willows. They talk about the soft cotton and the hard sticks, and about cats, and about their favorite songs, while they work. Some of the children ask their teacher to write the poem on their artwork.

Be Spontaneous.

That's what most language with young children should be. Fun conversation as they play together, as you go about your daily routines with them such as diapering or eating together, and as you pick up on their interests. **Talk with, not *at* children. And listen.** With all children, use the kind of language you want them to use. And make sure they talk with each other.

Model good listening. Many times, adults ask children questions and then answer for them, not even waiting for a reply. With reluctant speakers, practice "wait time"—wait about 5 seconds for a child to respond to a question or comment. You'll be surprised how much more they talk. Promote listening skill with a listening center stocked with stories and songs on audiotape. Play listening games like sounds from a mystery box, Simon Says, or a treasure hunt that require listening to and following multiple directions.

Children need lots of time to talk with each other, to tell you what they need, to ask questions, to talk about feelings, to do finger plays, to say nursery rhymes, to play games with words, **and some time to listen** attentively to adults.

Children's pretend play is one of the best contexts to promote language development. When children have props, materials, and a theme for their play such as restaurant, post office, doctor's office, or supermarket, they use the words that are needed in those contexts. You might need to enter the play to get it going or extend the language interaction.

During dramatic play, children naturally try to imitate adults and their speech becomes more sophisticated and complex as a result. Block play is another classroom area where vocabulary and spoken language thrive if supported by the teacher.

While they talk and play, alone or with each other, you move about the room or playground. Sometimes you sit on the floor or grass. You are always available as a language resource. *Sometimes, as you walk through the areas where children are playing, you don't say anything* because you don't want to interfere and are not needed. You observe what is happening and make written or mental notes on children's development or ideas for future activities. You see many children talking together.

Often, you comment on what is happening— being sure not to interrupt the activity. You might say, "That's really hard to get those shapes in the right holes. You keep trying and trying, and then one fits!" And then you watch the child work or listen as the child talks.

You often expand on something a child said or did, adding new or different words to express the same idea. "Baby. Yes, that's baby Rachel. She is Jonathan's sister." Or you could repeat a child's statement, but in a second language. "Nuestra planta necesita más agua. Yes, our plant needs more water."

Sometimes you might give the child a chance to hear an idea expressed more appropriately.

You hear a child say, "He don't pick it up."

You reply, "You've noticed, he *didn't* pick up the car. He left it on the floor where we could step on it. What should we say to him about the car?"

If you change a child's use of words by directly saying, "Don't say *don't*. That's not right. You should say *didn't*," you make the child feel incompetent. Instead, just gently repeat whatever you think is a better word usage.

Children will begin to see how language styles change depending on the situation. For example, the language of the African-American community or a dialect of Spanish may be expected at home and in the neighborhood, but Standard English usages may be expected in elementary school. Children can learn both styles without being made to feel that one is correct and the other incorrect.

Sometimes you ask questions to help children take their ideas a step further. If children seem to be playing rather aimlessly in the housekeeping area, you might comment, "You are so busy in the kitchen. What are you cooking?" to help lend some direction to their play.

Sometimes you help children solve problems. "What other ways have you tried?" or "How can we find out?" or "Why do you think it's not working?" If children ask, "What letter does Dad begin with?" you respond with a brief introduction to the relationships between sounds and letters, "D—D—Dad. Dad begins with a D."

In many instances, **YOU LISTEN.** You encourage children to use their own language to figure things out for themselves or to express themselves in creative and clear ways.

Your questions lead children to think up their own ideas.

And of course, *you always speak in ways that give children an appropriate model.* You never use baby talk. Your goal is to help children want to express themselves freely in language—one or more. It takes a long time to learn all the rules. They'll learn the accepted usage in their community when they hear it often.

Build vocabularies with real experiences.

If we want children to learn to talk, we need to give them something to talk about. Conversation requires content. That's why every good early childhood program needs an intellectually challenging, interesting curriculum that opens up the world for children. Your curriculum really is what happens because you and your schedule are flexible and can make the best of every situation. Many things you plan, others happen on the spur of the moment. But you don't want to miss any opportunities for learning.

Word games—making up silly or rhyming words, for example—can be lots of fun for preschoolers. Older infants are always asking *"Dat?"* (*"What's that?"*).

Toddlers want to know *why?* Preschoolers try to figure out *how?* Perhaps a child has learned a new game or song that is part of a grandparent's heritage. It may be in another language. Ask the child to help you teach it to the other children, or invite a relative to assist both of you.

Pick up on children's cues and use what you know about language development to broaden children's vocabularies and language experiences. Take advantage of every *teachable moment*—they happen all day long every day when you know what to look for:

> The children find a fuzzy worm on the playground. You ask, "How can we find out what kind of worm it is and whether it will become a butterfly?"
>
> Or a child starts to hum an unfamiliar tune. When you mention it, the child says his aunt is visiting from Japan and she taught him a song.
>
> Or, when you ask, "What is the best way to fix the greens that Lanette's mother brought?" several children offer suggestions.

Recall at least one *teachable moment* that happened within the last week when you helped children learn new words. What did you do to help the children get the most from the experience?

_____

_____

_____

_____

_____

Share your experience with your CDA Field Advisor.

Teach more than one language.

Many of the principles of good practice discussed in early childhood education and throughout *Essentials* apply to children who speak only one language—the same language of the society in general. But you are well aware that growing numbers of children and families speak languages other than English at home and within their neighborhoods and communities. When more than one language is an issue in your program, it is important to understand how to use those principles as well as some additional ones.

There are a number of different views about which strategies are best, and with experience, you will select among them the ones that are most appropriate for you and your particular group of families. In general, however, you should start by understanding that in order to adapt your teaching strategies to match children's experiences, you must learn to distinguish between children who are **monolingual** and children who are **bilingual**.

Monolingual children speak only one language, but you want them to learn a second. Young children are quite capable of learning a second language, and they do it much the same way they learned their first one. They spend time listening—a few weeks or even four to six months—sometimes called a "silent period". Sometimes teachers or parents get concerned during this time thinking that children are regressing. But much language is being learned during this time as children listen and start to make sense of the new language. So "silent" isn't really the right word for this time. Gradually, children begin to use one- and two-word sentences and then more complicated speech, just as they did in learning their first language.

Be sure you make children feel comfortable in the program and convey an acceptance of a child's attempts at speaking the new language. Concentrate on what they are trying to say, rather than the way they say it. Speak naturally. Use one language at a time and use it in the context of first hand experiences.

Some children may suddenly stop speaking their home language. Concerned parents may be astonished that their child refuses to speak to them except in English. "English! Read to me in English ... I don't hear Spanish!" This may cause family stress, so be open to discussing this issue with parents. Lasting negative consequence will occur if children are allowed to "give up" their home language. Assure them that you provide plenty of reinforcements for the use of both languages at school.

Bilingual children have the ability to speak or at least understand two languages, and you want to build their skills in both. The level of development in the second language will vary from child to child and your observations will be important in deciding what to emphasize with each individual child. Remember, children often understand more complex language than they use—challenge growth by speaking to the child at a more advanced, but appropriate, level of difficulty. Talk, sing songs, and provide learning materials in both languages. Routinely incorporate both languages

continues on page 313

Working with English-Language Learners

By Pam Schiller and Andrea B. Bermudez

... While most English-speaking children continue to use the same language and learning styles when they enter child care or school, children whose home language is not English (English language learners) often experience an abrupt change. Therefore, it is important that teachers ... assist English language learners in making this transition.

These four items are a base for work with English language learners.

- Oral and written language proficiency in English as a second language cannot be attained unless the child's first language is strengthened.
- Involving parents and other family members in the learning experience of English language learners is necessary to establish continuity between home and school.
- Self-concept in children is the key to success in learning. However, what makes up a positive self-concept for children may vary from culture to culture.
- Learning, motivational, and problem-solving styles are different among cultures and different within cultures.

Oral and written language proficiency

Preschool children have great imagination, and they explore ideas by reaching out physically as well as verbally. As a result, language development goes hand in hand with creativity and intellectual ability.

At the same time they are expanding their home language, English language learners are faced with learning a new language. This challenge can be overwhelming unless children are allowed to experience activities in the language that is comfortable. A good way for children to use both languages is to introduce English gradually and not assume that an all-English classroom will happen overnight.

Besides contributing to creativity and intellectual ability, the comfortable language can promote a child's social development during the preschool years. Teachers recognize that 2-year-olds who bite or hit or behave in other unacceptable ways are probably frustrated because they cannot use language to express their thoughts and emotions. This frustration also occurs in older preschool children who are acquiring a new language and may lead to unacceptable behavior from them, too.

The teacher's role is to change obstacles into opportunities. Assume, for example, that two children are building a ranch house in the block center, and a third child who is learning English comes over and starts playing with blocks on the floor. The two children get angry and demand that he stop. Unable to ask why the children are angry, he kicks the blocks and starts to leave. An observant teacher will take the third child by the hand and explain that the blocks on the shelf are available for playing, and suggest that he build a corral for horses.

Involving parents

Any successful preschool program will have a high level of cooperation and communication between center and family. This is particularly true for families whose home language is not English.

Despite the best intentions, the majority of school programs ... have difficulty incorporating parent expectations for their children's schooling. It takes a sensitive teacher to recognize, for example, that a certain Latino child never asks questions or speaks up because his parents value respect for authority and view questions as rude interruptions. Or that a Vietnamese child is reluctant to use her native language because her parents believe their children should speak only English in school.

Balancing individual needs and capabilities with the goals of parent involvement is a delicate task. Parents of children whose home language is not English usually cannot communicate in the language of the center and, in many cases, do not understand their rights and responsibilities in the education of their children. Where possible, for example, the center might ask a volunteer translator to interpret for non-English-speaking parents at parent meetings and children's programs.

In many families, the parents are working full time. After-work opportunities for conferences and other activities are essential if working parents are to get involved.

Self-concept variations

Self-expression is a critical aspect of self-esteem. This makes language a focal point in the development of self-concept in all groups.

Children's abilities to express themselves are strongly related to ... cooperation, sharing, respect for others, and similar behaviors. Their prosocial behavior, in turn, is strongly related to positive self-esteem.

In order for English language learners to gain confidence socially, they must be able to interact with others in a language with which they feel comfortable and in command. A sensitive teacher will allow English language learners to communicate in their own way during social interaction with other children . . .

Independent play and outdoor play offer excellent opportunities for children to interact with each other in the comfortable language. A teacher must give verbal as well as non-verbal support to English language learners in both languages ....

Learning, motivational, and problem-solving styles

Cognitive behavior involves the ability to use prior knowledge to solve new problems. It is a child's attempt to make sense of the world.

Cognitive development for English language learners is basically the same as for children who only speak one language. Because language and cognitive development are closely linked, children who are learning a second language must have an opportunity to express their thoughts in the language that is comfortable for them. For example, when describing the events in a story a teacher has just finished, English language learners need opportunities to discuss the events in both languages. Children do not organize thoughts in the same way across cultures, so what English language learners may select as important may not agree with the teacher's ....

Challenging children is essential to motivation. Children who feel that teacher's expectations are low or too simple will often fail to strive. On the other hand, if expectations are too high, children stop trying.

Children feel successful if they use their first language in their cognitive achievements and social interactions. As children begin to use the English language, teachers should focus on ideas expressed rather than on language choice. For example, if Carmen says, "I have hungry," teachers should reward the effort rather than correct her use of grammar or pronunciation.

In addition, to promote prosocial development, teachers should encourage children to communicate in the best way they can. Discouraging the use of the comfortable language can limit a child's prosocial development and hinder self-confidence . . . .

Note: Condensed from *Texas Child Care Quarterly,* Winter 1988, 12(3), 3–8. ©Copyright 1988 by Texas Department of Human Services. Reprinted with permission.

Support home language and help children acquire English

You can support children's home language throughout the day in all kinds of ways, while also helping them become fluent in English. Linda Espinosa and M. Susan Burns (2003) offer the following suggestions for both kinds of support. Because there is such a close connection between language and literacy, these strategies support learning early literacy skills as well (which are discussed in more detail in the next section of this unit).

Primary (or home) language support

Even when teachers do not speak the child's home language, there are many strategies that support primary language development:

- Provide bilingual instructional support using teaching assistants, family volunteers, or older and more competent children.

- Incorporate child's home languages into the daily classroom activities through song, poetry, dances, rhymes, and counting. Create materials in the children's home languages to represent familiar stories, songs, or poems that will improve early home language literacy.

- Have simple print material in the child's home language in learning centers. Labeled objects and writing utensils will further support early literacy abilities for English language learners.

- Encourage parents and other family members to continue to use the home language during family activities while also supporting early literacy development in that language.

- Loan parents age-appropriate books and stories in the child's home language if available. Encourage parents to engage in playful, interactive reading times to motivate children to read.

- Make efforts to learn the children's home languages. Even a few words or phrases will communicate respect and value for the families' language and culture.

English language fluency

Many classroom and teaching approaches are effective for second language learners, such as:

- Create a consistent and predictable routine that helps English language learners know what to expect and provide regular opportunities for them to speak informally with English speakers.

- Make small peer groups to give children opportunities to learn English in non-threatening, secure environments and promote friendships among children who speak different languages. Systematically include a mix of first- and second-language children in organized small group activities.

- Read books in small groups using predictable text or concept books, and read the same book repeatedly.

- Teach English-speaking children in the classroom to act as language resources for second-language learners.

- Modify the second language so it is **comprehensible** for young second-language learners.

Adapted from "Early literacy for young children and English-language learners" by Linda M. Espinosa and M. Susan Burns. In *Teaching 4- to 8-year-olds: Literacy, math, multiculturalism, and classroom community.* Edited by Carolee Howes (2003). National Center for Early Learning and Development. Baltimore: Paul H. Brookes.

Communicating with English language learners in **comprehensible** ways, so they understand what is being said and can learn the language, is one of the most important things you can do. An excellent resource to help you learn such strategies is *One Child, Two Languages* by Patton Tabors (1997). Some of the strategies she recommends include:

- Speak at a standard speed with pauses between phrases. Do not speak loudly.

- Use simple, clear, short sentences and use gestures, movements, and facial expressions to help convey meaning.

- Simplify language when needed as you would for a slightly younger child.

- Use running commentary (what we have referred to as "play by play") to describe routines and experiences.

- Link English vocabulary to first-hand experiences with concrete objects and real-life events, focusing on the here and now until children acquire enough English to extend their language to past or future events. Children get a lot of understanding from the context.

- Use repetition.

- Provide many opportunities for children to play because their natural interest in play will motivate them to communicate with other children, speeding second-language learning.

into daily routines. Encourage children to use either language to express themselves. Provide resources to families to help them understand the cognitive advantages that bilingual children have over their monolingual counterparts. Your goal is to strengthen their ability to continue to be bilingual!

You help children learn early literacy skills

At two months of age, baby Liam already has favorites from among the lovely board books his Mom shows him. Sometimes when she reads to him, he stares intently at the book. With another book, he ignores the book and looks at her face, appearing to enjoy the sound of her voice. And with yet other books, he ignores both the book and her voice. Liam will undoubtedly grow up to be a book critic!

Learning to read and write does not happen overnight, nor does it begin with formal reading instruction in first grade. We now know that the process of learning to read actually begins at birth. Successful readers are usually children who have good communication skills, as we described earlier, and have learned early literacy skills such as book appreciation, print awareness, early writing, phonological awareness, and alphabet knowledge. These early literacy skills come before and lead up to conventional reading and writing, that is, the ability to gain meaning from unfamiliar text—the way older children and adults read.

In literate societies, children encounter written words in addition to spoken words from a very early age. The first printed word of real interest is usually their own name—

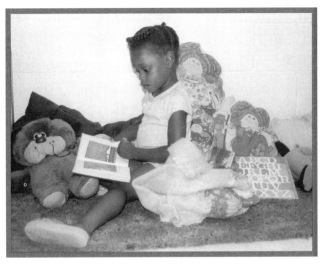

Children who have lots of experience with books during their preschool years are more successful when they learn how to read and write in elementary school.

labels on clothes, lunches, or backpacks. Toddlers begin to recognize the first letter and then later all the letters, especially if more than one child's name begins with the same letter. Preschoolers learn each other's names after a few weeks of seeing them on their artwork and cubbies.

Children also see signs in the classroom that help them know what a play area is for and how many children can fit in it comfortably: "Discovery Area: Space for 3 children." Children will soon want to know: What are the words? How many are *three*?

Soon they want to make a label for their castle. Or write a list of things to take on a field trip. As you measure windows for new curtains, they ask you what the numbers on the yardstick mean.

Written words and numbers should serve real purposes in the environment. You need to draw children's attention to print in the environment and help them make connections between written and spoken words.

Help children learn to appreciate and use books.

There is no question that children who have lots of experience with books during their preschool years are more successful when they learn how to read and write in elementary school.

When you plan your learning environment, the book area should invite children to enter. Provide a carpet to sit on, some pillows, a child-sized rocker, and maybe some pictures of children reading books.

Low, open shelves are always the best way to display any items—children can easily see what their choices are and can return the book when they are finished. Book covers should always face the children. For babies, you might stand books on the floor. One teacher found a discarded greeting card display stand to hold books. Of course, commercial bookracks are also available. Be sure to include a variety of types of books so each child can find something appealing. In order to build up their own collections, some teachers suggest that parents donate a book in the child's name instead of sending trinkets for birthday parties at the center or family childcare home.

Choose storybooks and information (non-fiction) books that meet the criteria we discussed in Unit 3. Books should always portray positive, authentic images of all people. Illustrations should be pleasing to look at so children learn to appreciate art as well as literature. Choose simple, bright, uncluttered picture books with themes that convey the messages and ideas we want children to learn: how to be friends, the world is a diverse and interesting place to live, constructive ways to deal with difficulties, information about how things work.

Go to the book area often during the day. Sit on the floor to chat or read. Children are always attracted to places where interesting things are happening.

But don't limit books to the library corner of your room. Use books in various areas of the classroom where they support the curriculum or children's interests—books about construction in the block area, or science books to support a topic of study, or reading material that might be found in a home in the housekeeping area.

Young children who have not had experience with books may need to be shown how to carefully handle them, turn the pages, and protect the spine. We want children to become independent readers eventually so they need to be able to handle books on their own. Because books are expensive and precious, teachers sometimes control access to them. Books need to be in children's hands, not on top of the piano or in the teachers' closet. Teach children proper book handling skills and when books get damaged, have children help repair them.

Selecting Books for Children

Books for infants

Infant's books should have fat cardboard pages with rounded edges or be made of plastic or fabric because infants will chew on them. Prop books up so nonmobile children can see the bright pictures.

Once children can sit by themselves, they can safely hold books and begin to try to turn the pages—these are early physical development and reading skills!

How to read stories to babies

- Get the baby's attention. (*"Oh, look!"*)
- Ask the baby a labeling question. (*"What's that?"*)
- Wait for the baby to answer, or if necessary, provide or elaborate upon the answer. (*"Yes, that's a monkey, isn't it?"*)
- Provide feedback. (*"Well, it is brown like a dog, but that's a monkey. Monkeys have long tails."*)

Note: From *More Than the ABCs: The Early Stages of Reading and Writing* (p. 34) by J. Schickedanz, 1986, Washington, DC: National Association for the Education of Young Children. Copyright © 1986 by National Association for the Education of Young Children. Reprinted by permission.

Books for toddlers

Toddlers especially enjoy simple stories about things that happen to them (*toilet learning, going to the doctor*) and about animals. They are curious about *why* things happen. Pictures hold their attention as well as the words. They love predictable books that repeat the same words or rhyme. They are beginning to understand that events happen in order. And they can begin to take care of books in responsible ways: turn pages gently, keep the pages clean, return books to the shelf when finished.

Read to groups of two or three children and don't be embarrassed to use different voices for each character! Really enjoy reading and make it a fun time for the children.

Books for preschoolers

By this age, if children have been read to often, they have learned a great deal about books. They are ready for stories with plots—real and pretend. They can find adventure, surprise, silly words, and scary situations (*with reassuring endings*) between a book's covers.

If you pause during a familiar story, they can fill in a word or a sentence. Or stop a new book just as the action gets exciting and ask the children: "Now what do you think will happen?" Or pause before you turn a page to heighten the suspense.

Preschoolers may become interested in "Where does it say that?" Show children the words they are interested in with your finger, reading each word as you go.

And remember, although preschoolers can sit longer for a lively or enchanting story, it's still a good idea to keep the group small so children have a chance to talk.

What can you do to make your book area cozy and inviting?

couch, pillows, magazines, a variety of books.

Books are best when they are read to small, cozy groups. Children can sit on the floor or in your lap. For a larger group, you sit on a chair so children can see all the pictures and hear your voice. Use all the strategies for reading aloud described by David Dickinson *(see pages 317-318)*. Have times during the day when children select their own books to look at alone or with a friend.

Children should always be active participants, not just passive listeners when you read together. Make each book come alive! Roar with the lions! Laugh heartily! Whisper to build suspense. Encourage children to play out what happens.

Ask questions that make children think about the story—not just to recall specific facts. Ask questions that begin with *why*, or *how*. Or have children think up different ways the story could have ended. Talk about how the book made children feel and why. Maybe a child will want to retell the story using the flannel board or translate it to their home language. Enjoy the adventure of every book with young children through spontaneous conversations.

Building a good collection of books for your program might take a little time. Books are expensive, and while paperbacks are more affordable, they won't withstand the wear of lots of young hands turning their pages. You might want to buy some of the best children's literature and supplement the selection from the library. Talk with children about their favorite books and authors, and encourage them to write or e-mail authors.

Libraries, too, very often have outreach programs *(see pages 319-320)*. These vary and can usually be tailored to the needs of your center or family child care home. Librarians might make a site visit and do a story program to your class; they might speak to the families about appropriate reading and what might be used with a given age of children; they might offer to teach storytelling to the teachers or parents/grandparents and give some insight on some techniques for using puppets and flannel boards to accompany storytelling.

Use your daily diary notes to decide what book topics might be of interest to your children. List them here and check out some books on those topics from the library on your next trip.

Reading in Preschool Classrooms
David Dickinson (2001)

Suggestions for Teachers

Schedule Sufficient Time for Book Reading

- In full-day programs, read aloud at least three times per day for a minimum of 45 minutes total. In partial-day programs, read once or twice per day for a minimum of 10 minutes per session.
- Divide the children into groups of no more than 8-10 (preferably fewer than six) for one or two group book-reading times. Use these smaller groups to allow time for children to ask questions and for the group to engage in thoughtful discussions about books.
- Provide individual and small-group reading experiences every day. Keep track of which children are involved, and ensure that each child is read to in such a setting at least twice per week.
- Do not withhold book reading as a punishment, and do not drop book reading from the day's activities.
- Schedule time for children to look at books alone or with a friend.

Read and Reread Various Types of Books

- Share your enjoyment of books you love.
- Read books that are related to your curriculum. Be sure to seek out some that convey important information and contain varied vocabulary.
- Stretch children's attention to books by trying out longer books and books with more text than you typically read.

- Read favorite books several times. With rereading, be alert for opportunities to extend children's understanding by asking questions about features of the plot or characters that have not been discussed before.

Be Thoughtful About Book Discussions

- Think about the book you will read before you start. Identify important words and concepts that you want the children to grasp.
- Encourage children to think by talking about aspects of the story that might confuse them. Use the pictures and children's own experiences to help them understand the story. Tell children word meanings and clarify confusion when needed.
- Respond to children's questions, especially when they deal with matters directly relevant to understanding the story. Discourage extended conversations while the book is being read and conversations on topics with limited relevance to the book.

Enjoy Reading, and Minimize Time Spent on Organizational Matters

- Establish clear routines for book reading— when it happens, who sits where, and how turn taking will be handled.
- Hold children's attention by reading with drama, asking questions when children are lost, and showing and discussing the pictures.
- Be clear about expectations related to turn taking, but beware of stifling involvement and enthusiasm with overly strict rules governing participation.

Make Books and Book Reading Part of the Full Day

- Link books to your curriculum or current topic and strive to get children interested in rereading books on their own that you present in a group setting.
- Set up a listening center with tapes of books that you have read to allow children repeated opportunities to listen to favorite stories while looking at the books.
- Display books in multiple places around the room.
- Constantly introduce new books related to your curriculum.

Encourage Parents and Other Family Members to Read to Children at Home

- Tell parents about the importance of regular reading. Encourage them to read with their child and to find others who can read to their child (such as big sisters, uncles, or grandparents). Read in home language.
- Strive to develop a classroom library with books that can be sent home.
- Encourage parents to use the library, get library cards for children, buy books, and subscribe to children's magazines.

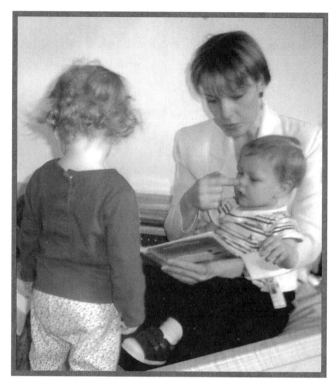

Encourage parents and other family members to read to children at home.

Dickenson, D. (2001). Book Reading in Preschool Classrooms. In D. Dickinson and P. Tabors, eds., *Beginning Literacy with Language: Young Children Learning at Home and School.* Baltimore: Paul H. Brookes. Reprinted with permission.

What the Library Can Do to Help You

Throughout *Essentials,* we suggest that public libraries can provide valuable resources and services for early childhood teachers and programs. But what specific ways can libraries support your work? Many early childhood programs enter into agreements with their local libraries, sometimes signing formal memorandums of understanding, which describe the partnership and the responsibilities of each party. Most important, you should establish a personal relationship with the children's librarian in your area. That person can then become an invaluable ally in your work. Librarians provide important services in at least three ways: in the library, at your program or in the community, and for families.

In the library, the librarian:

- Reads and compares many of the hundreds of newly published children's books each year and uses selection criteria to evaluate them.

- Provides bibliographies, critiques, and book lists of titles that can address the specific needs and interests of an individual child; reflect the cultural, linguistic, ethnic and racial backgrounds of your children; or the topics of study in your program.

- Reviews and identifies non-print and electronic media including computer software, videos, music audiotapes and computer disks, and Internet resources.

- Provides story hours for groups of children, using books, storytelling, puppets, fingerplays, music, and other developmentally appropriate strategies followed by children's choosing books to bring back to the classroom or take home.

- Help you identify books that you check out of the library regularly to maintain a rotating collection in the classroom.

At your program or family child care home and in the community, the librarian:

- May visit with the bookmobile, literally bringing the library to you, if your program is in a rural or remote location.

- Help you set up your library area in the classroom or home, and maintain a rotating collection of books.

- Demonstrate effective strategies for reading aloud and storytelling with children.

- Teach you how to work with families to enhance literacy experiences at home.

- Order books, toys, puppets, music and other materials for your program to obtain the same discount as the library.

For families, the librarian:

- Can provide story hours for parents and children to demonstrate effective reading aloud strategies and motivate parents, grandparents or other family members to read regularly with their children.

- Provide workshops for families (at the library or at the early childhood program) to help them use storytelling, puppets, fingerplays, and books with their children.

- Ensure that each family member, including each child, has a library card.

- Assists family members in accessing needed resources in the community through the Internet or direct referral.

- Sponsor classes and workshops that enhance parents' life skills such as English language learning, computer instruction, parenting, and family literacy.

To help you establish a meaningful partnership with your local library, two excellent resources are available from the Head Start Information and Publications Center (www.headstartinfo.org): *The Library-Museum Head Start Partnership: A Resource Notebook* by Virginia H. Mathews and Susan Roman, 2002 (includes sample memorandums of agreement), and *The Library Head Start Partnership* (a multi-media kit that includes a videotape for parent workshops) by Virginia Mathews, Susan Roman and Marcia Trotta, 1993.

What changes can you make in your program to ensure that *each day* children get to know books in ways that spark their interest in people, places, things, and most of all learning to read themselves?

_____

_____

_____

_____

Discuss your ideas with your CDA Field Advisor.

Promote print awareness.

Eighteen-month old Addy has discovered print! Every time she sees a printed word, she points to it and says, "Adda", assuming that it is her favorite printed word—her name.

What do children, like Addy, learn when they have lots of experiences with books and print? They learn:

- that print is permanent and should make sense;
- that print and speech are related in a specific way;
- how books work;
- that book language differs from speech;
- that print carries the message;
- that print is composed of clusters of letters called   words;
- that print in English is read left to right, top to bottom; and
- that books are enjoyable.

These skills are important for later reading and they do not just naturally develop. Teachers need to draw children's attention to the properties of print. One of the best ways is to use Big Books, oversize versions of books with limited print on the page. These often come with smaller versions for children to hold in their hands. When reading from a Big Book, you can point to the words as you read them, helping children understand the concept of *word*. Tracking the print with your finger this way also helps reinforce for children that print is read left to right and top to bottom.

To promote print awareness, be sure to have print in the environment that serves a real purpose—menus, signs, helper charts, experience charts, and more. Regularly draw children's attention to this print and its purpose. Also, play games where children find print in the environment when they take walks or go on field trips. Print is everywhere—advertising, traffic signs, names of businesses, street signs, and much more. Children become aware of print when adults draw their attention to it and help them learn its meaning.

Another excellent way to help children develop print awareness is to engage them in their own writing.

Promote early writing.

As children become familiar with words written by others, they are eager to learn to write themselves. Encouraging children to write is one of the best ways to help them learn to read. Their earliest writing attempts will look like scribbles—but those scribbles are important to the children's overall development. Sometimes children will call their marks "writing," sometimes they call them "drawings." At this early age, there may not be much difference between the two. *What's important is that they are learning to make connections about verbal and nonverbal ways to communicate.* Value these early attempts to use symbols—children have done it themselves.

Researchers have studied the development of children's writing and find that it follows a predictable pattern. First, random scribbles, then more controlled scribbles with clearer differences between circles and lines. After much practice writing and drawing and exposure to print, children will form letter-like symbols, and then actual letters, usually those in their own names. When children first begin to write, it is usually easier for them to form capital letters because upper-case letters are made-up of mostly circles and straight lines. When children begin to see the relationship between spoken language and print, they are eager to write shopping lists, train tickets, traffic signs, names on artwork, and on and on!

Many older toddlers or preschoolers ask to make their own books or to write their own stories. They may want to draw the pictures—you may need to write down the story they dictate. This is called an experience story, because it is based on the child's experience, even if it is an imaginary one. Some 4's and many 5-year-olds will want to try to write their own experience stories, or use a computer. When children write or dictate experience stories, they choose words that are powerful for them—capture each one!

While you will want to include writing materials in several areas of the class, in the pretend play and block areas (to write lists or make signs or write prescriptions, for example) and in the art area, you will want to set up a special writing area as well.

What items do you need for a writing area?

- Pencils.

- Watercolor markers with thin tips.

- Plain paper.

- Envelopes (ask parents to save their junk mail).

You can even pack everything in a box or suitcase for children to take home with them overnight. Other writing supplies such as chalk, colored paper, scissors, or paste are easy to get from the art area and can be added to the writing area if children use them frequently.

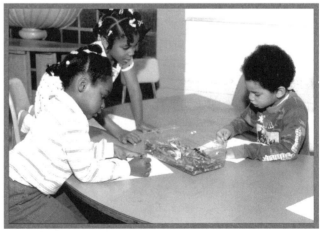

Include writing materials in several areas of the classrooms or home

Set up a small table and a chair or two in the writing area, and add some posters to make the space look appealing. Visit the area often yourself and be sure to be available whenever children have questions or need help with their writing.

Display the alphabet in the writing area at children's eye level so that they can see how to make each letter. You might even help a child make a personal dictionary, perhaps on index cards, of words that the child uses often, or of words in both of the languages being learned. Every area in your program should be open to children by choice. When you make writing an integral aspect of your program, children will be interested in figuring out how print works and will get involved.

Provide children with good models of print. Print neatly yourself. Use capital letters for the first letters of names, and lower-case letters when they are appropriate. As you write, and if the child seems interested, talk about the sounds some of the letters make. Make your own writing accurate—check your spellings if you are unsure.

Encourage children to use their own *invented or phonetic spelling*—children write down the letters they hear in the word. Spelling attempts help children learn about the relationship between letters and the sounds they stand for. Learning to spell correctly will be a goal when they are older. Just enjoy what the children write. As their muscles and minds mature, they will be able to write in ways that are more legible. For now, you want to keep children's interest and self-confidence at a peak.

Fill children's lives with print.

When children are surrounded by language and print, they see how it is used and it begins to become familiar. You don't expect young children to learn to read, although some will. But you do expect them to feel comfortable with words—ideas and feelings—both spoken and written, in one or more languages.

One important factor in nurturing eager readers is for them to see others reading. They should see you reading, and you can encourage parents to read to their children and to read for pleasure. Let children see them reading books, magazines, cereal boxes, recipes, instruction manuals, grocery lists, and coupons.

Look for real uses of print. Labels on boxes and cans ... directions for how to put something together ... a chart or simple schedule ... maybe you play the piano or autoharp with music in front of you ... you use the telephone book or the parent list to look up a number ... you make a list of children who want to use an activity area that is temporarily full ... you write a grocery or other list of supplies you need ... you write children's names on their artwork. Help children see how print is used in everything they do.

Remember to expose children to print in various languages. Empty food containers with labels in different languages are one way. Books, magazines, and newspapers are another. When you label things—artwork, areas of the room, or materials—use two languages with a different color for each. The children will begin to see how words are written in different languages.

Take a look at the kinds of print that children encounter every day in your program. Make a list of the opportunities you see.

_____

_____

_____

_____

Can you think of new materials or activities to add? List some ideas here.

_____

_____

Promote phonological awareness

Phonological awareness is the understanding that the spoken language stream is composed of discrete sounds that can be manipulated, taken apart (segmented) and put together (blended). *Phonological awareness* refers to the full range of awareness of the sounds of spoken language from rhyme (word endings sound the same) to alliteration (beginning sounds in words are the same), to syllables, and finally to the smallest sounds of human speech that are called *phonemes*. Phonemic awareness is a part of the broader concept, phonological awareness.

In English, there are approximately 44 phonemes that are represented by 26 letters either alone or in combination. For example, the word cat is made up of three phonemes: /k/, /a/, and /t/. If one phoneme is changed, /b/ for /k/, the meaning of the word changes. Different languages, and even dialects of the same language, have different phonemes.

Research shows that children's phonemic awareness ability is one of the most powerful predictors of later success in learning to read. When children lack phonemic awareness, first grade instruction in phonics and decoding does not make sense. They cannot detect the sounds of letters, words, or parts of words in speech.

Phonological awareness develops from simple to more complex abilities. In preschool, they learn rhyming words that end with the same sound), alliteration (words that begin with the same sound), sentence segmenting (hearing each separate word in a sentence), and syllable segmenting (being aware of chunks in words). The later skills of blending phonemes to make words and segmenting words into phonemes are appropriate expectations for kindergarten and first grade. But as children play with language, they may do some blending and segmenting. Just don't make it artificial or formal.

Like other early literacy skills, children do not automatically acquire phonological awareness. Teachers need to intentionally support children's phonological awareness, especially in preschool. But formal instruction is rarely needed. Most children acquire phonological awareness from fun, playful experiences that are motivating and interesting.

Everyday you should purposefully promote phonological awareness. How?

- Play rhyming games, sing songs and chant nursery rhymes, learn finger plays;

- Read and memorize poems;

- Play with language, make up nonsense words;

- Let children fill in a rhyme when reading, reciting poetry, or chanting;

- Play games such as clapping out syllables of children's names and words to songs;

- Read books that play with language like *Dr. Seuss* or include consistent sound patterns like rhyme and alliteration;

- Play games where children find objects or pictures that start with the same sound (alliteration— ball, bat, baby) and that rhyme (cat, bat).

These kinds of informal, fun experiences will successfully promote phonological awareness for most children. But you need to pay attention to whether children are able to rhyme, hear words that start with the same sound (not letter)—alliteration—and hear separate words and parts of words. For some children, you may to need to work individually with them or encourage their parents to promote phonological awareness with the same kinds of fun experiences listed above. Like other early literacy skills, phonological awareness is too important to be left to chance.

If you have not already done so, start now to collect your favorite songs, finger plays, and word games to promote phonological awareness with children. List four of your favorites here and include them in your Professional Resource File:

_____

_____

_____

You might want to keep these on file cards, in a notebook, or in an accordion file. Try to add at least one new word game or finger play to your collection each week. Don't limit yourself just to English. Use these ways of promoting phonological awareness frequently and intentionally with your children.

Children whose home language is other than English should be encouraged to develop phonological awareness in their home language, preferably with teachers who speak that language. If you do not speak a child's home language, you can encourage the child's family to engage in the same kind of experiences at home that draw children's attention to the discrete sounds of spoken language that you use in the program. Then, children's phonological awareness in their home language will transfer to English as they acquire a second language. If it is not possible to teach phonological awareness in the home language, be sure to teach it using English language words that children have already learned.

Teach the Alphabet

The ability to read and write depends on mastering the alphabetic principle—the understanding that there is a systematic relationship between letters and sounds, and that all spoken sounds and words can be represented by a limited set of special symbols called letters. In preschool, children will not fully grasp the alphabetic principle, but they should be well on their way to knowing letter names and recognizing most letters.

Like phonemic awareness, knowing the alphabet is an important predictor of later success in learning to read and write. That means that children who enter kindergarten with knowledge of letters are more likely to become successful readers. Early childhood educators haven't always believed that it was necessary to teach the alphabet. For a long time, it was believed that letters and sounds were too abstract for young children.

We now know that children can learn the alphabet the same way they learn many other early literacy skills—by being read to and having adults draw their attention to letters, by doing their own writing, by engaging in lots of fun activities that expose them to letters, and at times having adults explicitly teach letters. In fact, young children are actually learning abstract symbols from their earliest experiences—they come to recognize the stop sign, the red light, M for McDonalds! And because letters are abstract, children need lots of experiences with them over time to come to learn them well. We don't want to wait until kindergarten.

Perhaps the best way for children to learn the alphabet is to start with the letters in their own names. Those are "their" letters and they are motivated to learn how to write them and to recognize them—especially if you use names to designate helpers or for other real purposes. If children frequently see their name in print, at some point between 18 months and age 3, they will identify the first letter as their own. Even as toddlers but certainly by 3, children love to sing the alphabet song, play with alphabet blocks, and look at alphabet books. In preschool, you want to introduce the alphabet in many meaningful contexts. You don't need to teach one letter a week—that can get boring for children who already know letters. Children learn letters at different rates and are motivated to learn those letters that are most meaningful—those in their names, their friends' names, or in important words, like *Mommy* or *baby*.

Be sure to keep track of children's letter knowledge because informal experiences may not be enough for some children who need more individualized teaching and support. At times, you will want to focus children's attention on specific letters, especially for those children who don't seem to be learning letters in context.

Everyday, provide some experience that promotes letter knowledge. What are developmentally appropriate ways to teach the alphabet?

- Create sign-in sheets for children, grouping names in alphabetical order. At first, children may just make a scribble or one letter, but over time their name will become recognizable.

- Use letter knowledge for transitions. "Everyone whose name starts with a B, get your coat."

- Play games like Lotto or Concentration that require children to identify and name letters.

- Display the alphabet in places where children can see it, touch it, and use it.

- Use well-written alphabet books that clearly illustrate the sounds of letters with pictures of objects.

- Sing the alphabet song and other songs that play with letters, B-I-N-G-O.

- Provide all kinds of letter materials: alphabet blocks, alphabet puzzles, rubber stamp letters, magnetic letters, sandpaper letters, and charts of letters.

Most of all, you want to make alphabet learning interesting and meaningful. Most children get excited about learning the alphabet because they sense early on that their parents value it. Don't try to drill children on letters without any connection to words and sounds that children know. It leads to frustration and mere memorization that does not predict reading success.

Parents may ask you about teaching their child to read, or may even pressure you to begin teaching formal phonics. Be prepared to respond with a professional answer about how you do teach early literacy skills that are necessary for successful reading. Also, be aware that with this good instruction supported at home, some preschool children will progress to conventional reading. Although that is not your goal for every child, you are committed to meeting children's needs and supporting their strengths. So you will want to help those few children continue in their reading and writing development.

Parents can best help their children learn to read by talking with them to build vocabulary and providing real life experiences. Singing, reciting rhymes, and reading aloud are also important ways families can help provide a firm foundation for learning to read and write.

Let's now see how children's music, movement, and art can be used to build even further upon their ability to communicate.

You help children express themselves through music, movement, and art.

Spontaneous.

Talking with children is best when it is spontaneous and a natural part of the day. And so is music. Don't wait until 10:15 on Wednesday to sing "The Eentsy Weentsy Spider." If it's raining, sing! If a child brings in some new maracas sent by a relative in Mexico, don't put off playing them until music time. Or if a child brings in a tape or CD—put it on and dance!

What is the best part about music with young children? They love it. And they could care less whether you can carry a tune, or play an instrument, or read music, or even keep on time with the beat. Just enjoy yourselves.

Sing and sing and sing.

Sing a lullaby to babies as they fall asleep. … When something great happens—a child has just become a new sister or brother—break out in a joyous version of "If You're Happy … " When you have spaghetti for lunch, start or finish with "On Top of Spaghetti."

Don't be shy! Stand up, move around, and sing!

A soothing voice can calm a restless baby. A lively version of a favorite song can prolong a playful mood. Songs with motions are fun even when the children can't yet duplicate them all. Most babies like the Bzzzzz and the surprise ending of "I'm Bringing Home a Baby Bumble Bee."

I'm bringing home a baby bumblebee.
(hands cupped and move back and forth)

Won't my Mama be so proud of me?
(big smile)

'Cause I'm bringing home a baby bumblebee.
(hands cupped)

Bzzzzzz!
(finger wiggles through air)

Oooh! It stung me!
(then playfully pokes child)

If you want to teach children a new song, use a recording if you are embarrassed to sing it yourself. Sometimes you can use pictures to help children remember the order of the words.

Lots of times parents are eager to come in to sing with the children and teach some folk songs or songs that reflect their language or heritage. Invite them often to sing in their first language.

Choose songs with lots of action so the children are involved—that's how they learn. "The Wheels on the Bus" is an all-time favorite, and children can add or translate their own verses easily.

Make up songs, too. Children's names with five letters fit nicely in "B-I-N-G-O." Create your own tune and/or words to respond to events with children:

"Here we go on the Alphabet train, the alphabet train, the alphabet train P, P, what word stark with P?"

When children first begin to sing, they will probably be off key. Encourage them to try to match the sounds, but do not expect them to really carry a tune until the age of 3 or so. Keep the number of notes to a minimum and if possible stick to fairly low tones (*the notes from middle C to the A above it are best*). Children's voices are not as high as we sometimes think they are.

Build up your own memorized collection of songs by going to workshops or checking out books and records from the children's section of your library.

A word of caution ...
The words to some well-known songs, such as "Ten Little Indians" or "There Was An Old Lady" are demeaning to people. Always check out the words of songs to make sure they meet the same criteria as the books and other learning materials you select. Look for songs that celebrate our diverse heritages!

When you join your CDA Seminar you can exchange favorite songs with the other participants. Teach yourself a new song during the next week. Write the title and words here.

_____

_____

_____

_____

As soon as you know it well, sing it with your children.

If you can play the piano, or want to learn the guitar or autoharp, these are all excellent instruments to use to accompany children's singing. A drum provides a nice rhythm background for songs. But don't worry if all you have is your voice and the children's.

Whenever possible, have children stand while they sing. Sitting on the floor or in chairs is fine sometimes. Just remember, children need to move while they sing—did you ever see a professional singer sit to perform?

What is the best part about music with young children? They love it.

Children communicate through dance and movement.

Young children love to respond to music. Play recordings of a variety of types of music—show tunes, classical, 50s, ethnic, folk, country, contemporary—and watch children's reactions.

Most of the time, children will want to move to the music they hear. They can dance (although some parents may not want their children to participate for religious reasons) or move in other creative ways.

Always offer children a choice of another activity when others do creative movement activities. Children should not feel forced or even gently prodded into doing something that makes them uncomfortable.

Be sure you know how to expect children to be able to move based on their development and any disabilities. Babies might just wave their arms or kick their legs. Toddlers may rock back and forth, twist their whole bodies, or stamp their feet. The "Hokey-Pokey" for toddlers usually goes, "Put your whole body in" so they can follow the directions.

Preschoolers may enjoy more intricate body movements and may want to try dancing with scarves or capes. But young children never lose their interest in songs with lots of motion. Such songs keep children involved during transitions between activities or if a short wait is unavoidable.

Allow children to think up their own responses to music. See how many different ways children can express themselves to the sound of music. Sometimes children will be entranced enough by music to sit quietly to listen to a recording, but don't expect this very often or for very long. Great classics such as "Peter and the Wolf" or portions of "The Nutcracker" are lovely and usually hold their attention. Ask them to listen for something specific or to imagine what is happening.

Live performances can appeal to very young children if the music and setting is right—the performer chooses short pieces, is expressive, and is receptive to children's questions and even requests to try out the instrument. Check with families—there are probably several who play an instrument, and perhaps some of those instruments are played primarily in their cultures.

Even if you or the visiting performers only took piano lessons as a child, you will seem accomplished to young children. Make sure any guests know to expect young children to get up and move around while they perform.

Making their own music is also a good experience for children learning to communicate. We have already talked about how to select good, **real** musical instruments that are age appropriate. Slowly build up an orchestra of good instruments that children can play: drums, bells, triangles, wood blocks, tambourines, maracas, rhythm sticks, sandpaper blocks, stick bells, cymbals.

Children learn through art

Physical/perceptual development	Cognitive Development	Social and emotional development
Sensitivity to touch	Clarify and elaborate meaning	Trust
Sight discrimination	Relate information and ideas	Identity/individuality
Spatial awareness		Autonomy/independence
Body awareness	Put events in sequence	Express and deal positively
Eye-hand coordination	Understand cause and effect	with emotions
Laterality and directionality		Extend flexibility
Shape, size, color discrimination	Solve problems	Appreciate beauty
	Make	Appreciate and value others'
Figure-ground orientation	Make decisions	ideas and work
Part-whole discrimination	Generalize	Share
Fine motor control	Communicate ideas	Cooperate
Technical skills	nonverbally	Take turns (delay gratification)
		Adapt to group needs/interests
		Resolve interpersonal conflicts
		Acquire interests for leisure time

Note: Adapted from *Art: Basic for Young Children* (p. 108) by L. Lasky and R. Mukerji, 1980, Washington, DC: National Association for the Education of Young Children. Copyright © 1980 National Association for the Education of Young Children. Reprinted by permission.

List two new musical experiences for listening and movement that you can introduce to your children—try out different types of music, or, using different versions of old favorites, try out different ways to move.

· I tried a move to sound song (certain sounds mean walk, gallop, etc.)

· I tried a kid's michael Jackson free dance session.

Tell your CDA Advisor what happened when you tried out your ideas.

Children learn through art

Creating through art is one of the learning experiences through the early years that fosters development in all areas at once. We have seen how children use their arm, hand, and finger muscles in increasingly controlled ways to paint, roll and shape clay, draw, cut, paste, weave, sew ... the list seems endless. And we have discussed how to encourage and accept individual forms of creative expression to promote social and emotional development.

But in addition to these, children's involvement in creative expression through art—in all its various forms—fosters their intellectual development. As they manipulate materials according to their own ideas, **they actually make and change the world.** This is an incredibly powerful form of human intellectual capability. Since you have learned to observe children carefully, you are already aware that children can get intensely involved in the creative process of art—they finger paint with intensity (*and get paint all over their arms and faces*), they carefully select just the right materials to paste on their collage, they mix colors with delight! But children will only be this involved in expressing themselves creatively—and get the most from their experience—if you remember these four important points:

· **What children are doing**, not what they are making, **is the most important thing.** In art, as with other early childhood activities, the **process** is more important than the end product.

· Children need lots of time to see what happens when they do different things with the materials, to test out their own ideas, and to mess with the paste or paint or clay.

· Children need to get messy—they're washable! Preschoolers become more interested in making a product and can even make decisions about which of their works they judge to be their best.

· Keep your expectations appropriate for children's motor skills and cognitive abilities. Not until the end of the preschool years will children's creations resemble what adults think things look like.

It is inappropriate to give children teacher-made models of art to copy. For example, a teacher who didn't know better might give preschoolers a toilet paper roll to cover with brown paper, three packing chips to paint green and paste on the roll to look like three frogs on a log, and expect them to duplicate it. With a lot of prodding from the teacher they might be able to make one like the teacher's, but so what?

Instead of providing models that end up with all the children's work looking alike, teachers can support children's art by exposing them to photos or pictures of objects. Or if children are drawing flowers for instance, bring in real flowers for children to see and feel as they draw or paint. Children usually have good ideas of what to do with art materials.

Individuality is much more interesting than uniformity.

So put out the toilet paper rolls, the brown paper, the packing chips, the green paint, and some paste and see what exciting ideas children come up with on their own.

- Similarly, **children's art should be their own creation.** If they can't do it themselves, it is not an appropriate activity. You don't need to practice cutting and pasting—so don't do it for the children. Let each child use the materials in her or his own unique way. Don't waste your time making a clay bowl for them to copy. **Give children the raw materials** and let them experiment but be available as a resource so children don't become frustrated.

If you have always given children models to copy, the next time you are tempted to do so, just put out the materials and see what things children can do on their own. If they protest because they are used to being told what to do, just say, "This time, I want you to use your imagination. See what each of you can make with your own ideas." Children will need some time to get used to your new approach to teaching!

- Art isn't something that happens at 3 p.m. on Thursdays, or any other "art time." **Every time is art time, indoors or outdoors.**

Children's art should be their own creation. Give children the materials and let them experiment.

Provide materials.

When children arrive in the morning, and throughout the day, they should be able to choose from a wide array of tempting and appropriate creative art materials:

- 18- x 24-inch sheets of plain paper manila paper, white drawing paper, newsprint

- construction paper in many colors and colored tissue paper

- watercolor markers with broad and narrow tips, fat crayons (*for older infants and toddlers*), regular crayons (*for preschoolers*)

- blunt-end scissors and paste and/or white glue

- easel, tempera paint (*add a few soap flakes so any drips will wash up easily*), one-inch brushes, smocks, newspaper or shower curtain

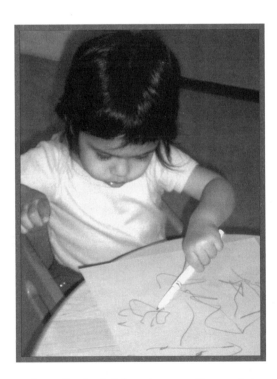

Remember that children's creative art is very personal to them. Respect children's unique creations and you respect children as well!

to put under the easel; or make a table easel with a cut-off cardboard box

- modeling dough (*make your own to save money*)

- collage materials—anything safe: fabric, yarn, packing chips, leaves, buttons, yogurt lids, meat trays, egg cartons, magazines to cut up, paper towel rolls, boxes, paper plates, paper bags

- woodworking—real tools, soft wood (*requires close supervision*), nails, glue

Each day you will probably also want to offer one or more special art activities for those who are interested. Additional materials will be needed for these occasions:

- finger-paints and smooth paper

- sponges for printing

- oil crayons (*Craypas*)

- chalk

- for older children only: water colors, charcoal, dyes, colored pencils, papier-mâché or sawdust, weaving and sewing supplies

- real potter's clay

Many teachers also use food as art materials for projects, such as stringing large macaroni, printing with potatoes, or finger painting with pudding. Other teachers object, since many children in this country and in the world do not have enough to eat. They do not feel comfortable destroying food when it could be used instead to nourish people! This is one of the many ethical decisions you will face as an early childhood educator.

How do you feel about using food as an art material?

_____

_____

_____

_____

Just wait—you're in for a lively discussion in your CDA Seminar.

While children are working in areas around the room, you are walking about, talking with them in ways that support their development. Remember, children's creative art is very personal to them. Treat it with respect. Instead of asking, "What is it?" comment on something about one or more elements of their art: color, line, shape, space, and design.

"You have used so many different colors!"

"Look how those lines go back and forth."

"Los pedacitos de papel son difíciles de agarrar. Teeny bits of paper are hard to hold."

"You really worked a long time to create your special project, didn't you?"

"What would you like to tell me about your art?"

Given openings such as these, children will not feel threatened or criticized about their art. They may tell you, "This is the fire truck that came to our apartment last night," and describe in vivid detail just what happened. Or they may say "red," or "That's fire," or just give you a big smile for being interested in what they did.

Usually, children's art is beautiful in their own eyes. Rather than make a value judgment about the art, concentrate on the child's effort instead. Children will feel good because your response supports their work, their vocabularies will expand, and they will learn more about their own creative abilities. Respect their unique creations—and you respect children as well!

Introduce new techniques.

Often children can figure out what to do with materials by themselves. Children watch you and each other and get lots of new ideas. Sometimes, you will need to demonstrate a technique for children—for safety's sake, or because the materials are completely unfamiliar to them. Here's an example of how to give some simple directions on how to get started, without limiting the creative use of materials.

You have set up a low, sturdy woodworking bench where the noise will not disturb others. First, you want these young preschool children to learn how to use a hammer. You have three light claw hammers, some roofing nails, and three 12-inch squares of 2-inch thick white pine (*some old tree stumps are even better if you can get them*).

"Today we will start a new activity," you announce enthusiastically when you gather the group on the carpet to plan for the day.

"The hammers and nails!" one child calls out excitedly.

"Yes, we have a woodworking bench, three hammers, nails, and wood. Each of you can learn how to use the hammers. We will add more tools when you show you can use the hammers safely and well. While some children are hammering, the rest can play in other places. There are some new puzzles on one table, and we have added some hard hats and nail aprons in the pretend play area. Please go to the area of your choice now."

Six children want to hammer. "We only have space for three children. Who would like to volunteer to hammer in a few minutes when the first three children are finished?" You write down the names of the three volunteers and ask them to find something else to work on while they wait.

You pick up a hammer and hold it toward the back of the handle. "This is where you hold the hammer. Here is a hammer for each of you. Show me how you hold the hammer."

"Please move your hand toward the back of the handle a little more. That way your nails will go in straighter," you point out to one child.

"Excellent! You will all soon be fine carpenters. Now we need some nails and wood and we are all set .... Spread out so each of you has room to work safely .... Choose the nail you would like to hammer. Who knows which end of the nail you hit with the hammer?"

"This flat end," shows one child.

"So which end goes into the wood?" you ask playfully.

"The pokey end, silly" giggles another.

The children hold their nails and begin pounding gently to get them started. You make sure each child holds the hammer properly. You stay with the children to help them figure out how to hammer. Each child who finishes is asked to tell the next child on the list that she or he can have a turn.

Each new material may need a little explanation so that children can see how to use it to best advantage. Be patient. It takes a long time for children to master scissors, for example, because their muscles are still growing.

You can probably see now why it is not appropriate to just put out scissors and paper with lines drawn on it so children can practice cutting, for example. Instead, put out scissors, paste, old magazines, construction paper, and let children figure out what they want to do. Maybe they will cut, maybe they will tear the paper. When materials like these are offered every day, most children will eventually get the practice they need while they pursue activities that appeal to them. For those children who don't choose art on their own, you may need to invite them to work with you.

New techniques can also be introduced by real artists. Invite artists—potters, painters, printmakers, and weavers—to visit you, or ask if you and the children can come watch them at work. Sometimes local museums or art groups sponsor special events just for children. Ask artists to share their ideas with children, or to talk about the culture in which the technique was first developed.

Use all of these real art experiences as a way to heighten children's appreciation for beauty and the elements of design. And open up new ways for them to express their own ideas and to experiment with different ways of doing things.

The creative arts, music, and movement foster growth in every area of children's development! Every really good activity for young children touches on their social, emotional, physical, and cognitive development. Let's turn now to look at how children think and try to make sense out of the world as they go about their daily activities.

You enable children to learn early mathematics concepts

Setting the table for snack, counting the crackers, finding just the right size block to span the bridge, stringing beads in a pattern, dividing the play dough so each child gets the same amount, measuring how tall we are. Yes, it's true that mathematics is everywhere in the early childhood classroom. But it is also true that too often teachers and children miss these opportunities to learn math concepts.

Just like language and early literacy, we now know that the foundation for later success in learning mathematics is laid during the preschool years. We also know that during the informal play and routines of the classroom are countless opportunities to help children learn mathematics concepts. What is needed is for you to draw children's attention to math in everyday experiences, provide the language of mathematics to describe what children are learning, and plan experiences as part of your curriculum that specifically teach fundamental math concepts.

We used to think that young children's ability to comprehend mathematics concepts was very limited, so we had very low expectations for their learning, such as counting up to 10. But new research over the last few decades demonstrates that children are capable of a great deal more if we provide them with the right kinds of environmental support and adult guidance. NAEYC and the National Council of Teachers of Mathematics (2002) developed a position statement describing what and how preschoolers should be taught. The Head Start Child Outcomes Framework (2002) also lists goals of mathematics learning. These include:

Number and operations—Preschool children:

- Demonstrate increasing interest and awareness of numbers and counting as a means for solving problems and determining quantity.

- Begin to associate number concepts, vocabulary, quantities and written numerals in meaningful ways.

- Develop increasing ability to count in sequence to 10 and beyond.

- Begin to make use of one-to-one correspondence in counting objects and matching groups of objects.

- Begin to use language to compare numbers of objects with terms such as more, less, greater than, fewer, equal to.

- Develop increased abilities to combine, separate and name "how many" concrete objects.

Geometry and spatial sense—Preschool children:

- Begin to recognize, describe, compare and name common shapes, their parts and attributes.

- Progress in ability to put together and take apart shapes.

- Begin to be able to determine whether or not two shapes are the same size and shape.

- Show growth in matching, sorting, putting in a series and regrouping objects according to one or two attributes such as color, shape or size.

- Build an increasing understanding of directionality, order and positions of objects, and words such as up, down, over, under, top, bottom, inside, outside, in front and behind.

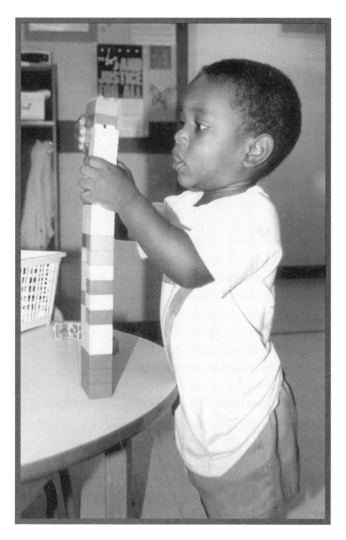

Children need lots of concrete experiences to make sense of mathematics concepts.

Patterns and Measurement—Preschool children:

- Enhance ability to recognize, duplicate, and extend simple patterns using a variety of materials (such as stringing beads, blocks, or pegs).

- Show increasing ability to match, sort, put in a series, and regroup objects according to one or two attributes such as shape or size.

- Begin to make comparisons between several objects based on a single attribute.

- Show progress in using standard and non-standard measures for length and area of objects.

The NAEYC/NCTM position statement gives excellent examples of each of these math content areas, the type of knowledge and skills children are acquiring, and the kinds of teaching strategies that promote mathematics learning. (See pages 338-339 for an excerpt. The complete position statement is online at www.naeyc.org.)

As with every other area of learning in early childhood, children need lots of concrete experiences to make sense of mathematics concepts. For young children, numbers are adjectives—they can understand "four cats" but not necessarily the abstract concept of "4" They need lots of experiences with counting and sets of objects for "4" to have a consistent meaning for them.

To promote children's mathematical thinking and learning, one of the most important things you can do is talk with children about problems and introduce math vocabulary.

continued on page 341

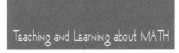
Learning Paths and Teaching Strategies in Early Mathematics

(From: Early Childhood Mathematics: Promoting Good Beginnings. A joint position statement of National Association for the Education of Young Children and the National Council of Teachers of Mathematics.)

Examples of typical achievements of 3- to 6-year-olds and teaching strategies to promote them

The research base for sketching a picture of children's mathematical development varies considerably from one area of mathematics to another. Outlining a learning path, moreover, does not mean we can predict with confidence where a child of a given age will be in that sequence. Developmental variation is the norm, not the exception. However, children do tend to follow similar *sequences*, or *learning paths*, as they develop. This chart illustrates in each area some things that *many* children know and do—early and late in the 3–6 age range. These are, then, simply two points along the learning path that may have many steps in between. For each content area, the Sample Teaching Strategies column shows a few of the many teacher actions that promote learning when used within a classroom context that reflects the recommendations set forth in this position statement. In general, they are helpful strategies, with minor adaptations, across the age range.

Content Area	Examples of Typical Knowledge and Skills From Age 3 ⟶ Age 6		Sample Teaching Strategies
Number and operations	Counts a collection of 1 to 4 items and begins to understand that the last counting word tells "how many."	Counts and produces (counts out) collections up to 100 using groups of 10.	Models counting of small collections and guides children's counting in everyday situations, emphasizing that we use one counting word for each object: ♡　♡　♡ "One . . . two . . . three . . ." Models counting by 10s while making groups of 10s (e.g., 10, 20, 30 . . . or 14, 24, 34 . . .).
	Quickly "sees" and labels collections of 1 to 3 with a number.	Quickly "sees" and labels with the correct number patterned collections (e.g., dominoes) and unpatterned collections of up to about 6 items.	Gives children a brief glimpse (a couple of seconds) of a small collection of items and asks how many there are.
	Adds and subtracts nonverbally when numbers are very low. For example, when one ball and then another are put into the box, expects the box to contain two balls.	Adds or subtracts using counting-based strategies such as counting on (e.g., adding 3 to 5, says "Five . . . , six, seven, eight"), when numbers and totals do not go beyond 10.	Tells real-life stories involving numbers and a problem. Asks "how many" questions (e.g., How many are left? How many are there now? How many did they start with? How many were added?). Shows children the use of objects, fingers, counting on, guessing, and checking to solve problems.

Content Area	Examples of Typical Knowledge and Skills From Age 3 ——————————→ Age 6		Sample Teaching Strategies
Geometry and spatial sense	Begins to match and name 2-D and 3-D shapes, first only with same size and orientation, then shapes that differ in size and orientation (e.g., a large triangle sitting on its point versus a small one sitting on its side).	Recognizes and names a variety of 2-D and 3-D shapes (e.g., quadrilaterals, trapezoids, rhombi, hexagons, spheres, cubes) in any orientation. Describes basic features of shapes (e.g., number of sides or angles).	Introduces and labels a wide variety of shapes (e.g., skinny triangles, fat rectangles, prisms) that are in a variety of positions (e.g., a square or a triangle standing on a corner, a cylinder "standing up" or horizontal). Involves children in constructing shapes and talking about their features.
	Uses shapes, separately, to create a picture. Describes object locations with spatial words such as *under* and *behind* and builds simple but meaningful "maps" with toys such as houses, cars, and trees.	Makes a picture by combining shapes. Builds, draws, or follows simple maps of familiar places, such as the classroom or playground.	Encourages children to make pictures or models of familiar objects using shape blocks, paper shapes, or other materials. Encourages children to make and talk about models with blocks and toys. Challenges children to mark a path from a table to the wastebasket with masking tape, then draw a map of the path, adding pictures of objects appearing along the path, such as a table or easel.
Measurement	Recognizes and labels measurable attributes of objects (e.g., I need a long string; Is this heavy?). Begins to compare and sort according to these attributes (e.g., more/less, heavy/light; This block is too short to be the bridge).	Tries out various processes and units for measurement and begins to notice different results of one method or another (e.g., what happens when we *don't* use a standard unit). Makes use in nonstandard measuring tools or uses conventional tools such as a cup or ruler as nonstandard ways (e.g., It's three rulers long).	Uses comparing words to model and discuss measuring (e.g. This book feels heavier than that block. I wonder if this block tower is taller than the desk). Uses and creates situations that draw children's attention to the problem of measuring something with two different units (e.g., making garden rows "four shoes" apart, first using a teacher's shoe and then a child's shoe).

Content Area	Examples of Typical Knowledge and Skills From Age 3 ⟶ Age 6		Sample Teaching Strategies
Pattern/ algebraic thinking	Notices and copies simple repeating patterns, such as a wall of blocks with long, short, long, short, long, short, long. . . .	Notices and discusses patterns in arithmetic (e.g., adding 1 to any number results in the next "counting number").	Encourages, models, and discusses patterns (e.g., What's missing? Why do you think that is a pattern? I need a blue next). Engages children in finding color and shape patterns in the environment, number patterns on calendars and charts (e.g., with the numerals 1–100), patterns in arithmetic (e.g., recognizing that when zero is added to a number, the sum is always that number).
Displaying and analyzing data	Sorts objects and counts and compares the groups formed. Helps to make simple graphs (e.g., a pictograph formed as each child places her own photo in the row indicating her preferred treat—pretzels or crackers).	Organizes and displays data through simple numerical representations such as bar graphs and counts the number in each group.	Invites children to sort and organize collected materials by color, size, shape, etc. Asks them to compare groups to find which group has the most. Uses "not" language to help children analyze their data (e.g., All of these things are red and these things are NOT red). Works with children to make simple numerical summaries such as tables and bar graphs, comparing parts of the data.

When children are building with blocks, for instance, ask them to compare the size of different blocks, or count the number needed to make both sides of a structure equal. Also explore ways of representing math ideas through words, pictures, diagrams, and graphs. For instance, make a graph of children's heights and weights.

The kind of problem-solving and investigation that is needed for mathematics is a major part of all your work as we try to help children achieve the larger goal of making sense of the world. In the next section, we describe your role in supporting children's problem solving.

You enable children to use their curiosity to make sense out of the world

Young children are constantly trying to solve problems and figure things out. But children don't see or understand things the same way older children or adults do. After all, we have years of experience with things and people. Children are still discovering ways to figure it all out.

Three 4-year-olds want to play color bingo. They make three piles of markers with the same number in each pile. Lynn takes the pile that is all spread out "because it has the most."

Your toddlers are stacking cardboard bricks. The first one in the stack is on its side. The pile topples over. The children start to rebuild again without changing the bottom block.

You and a baby are playing with a favorite rattle. You hide the rattle under a diaper. The child immediately turns to pick up another toy. Why didn't the baby just lift up the diaper?

You probably have many examples of how children see the world differently than adults or older children do. Sometimes their ideas give us a good chuckle.

Of course, now that you are becoming a professional early childhood educator, you are more than just amused by happenings like these. In fact, you will use the information you gather about how children's thinking changes as they mature to decide how to teach—to enable children to learn through experiences that provide just the right level of challenge.

Thanks to the careful observation and research of scientists like Jean Piaget and Lev Vygotsky, we know the ways children think and reason at different ages and ways to teach them. Their logic and ability to organize information are greater than was previously thought but are still not like that of adults' or even elementary school children.

You will learn more about these changes in your CDA Seminar. But for now, return to the chart of developmental accomplishments/expectations in Unit 2 and review the material in the sections, "children become aware of the world" and "children solve problems and use tools."

These characteristics will help you choose materials and plan appropriate activities to build on what you know about children's thinking. Three of the long-term goals for children's cognitive development overlap so much that we are going to consider them all at one time:

... **make sense of the world** ... **recognize real problems and figure out solutions to them** ... **think critically and logically, ask questions that lead to more questions**

Of course, we don't expect children to go off to kindergarten or first grade having mastered all of these goals! Most of **us** are still trying to make sense of the world! But a good early childhood program can give children the **confidence and the experience to begin to develop sound thinking skills.**

How, then, do you help children make sense of the world, figure out solutions to problems, and ask good questions? You put everything together that we have discussed so far.

Encourage discovery

Children are naturally curious. They are active learners. Most children are self-motivated. They have their own personal ways of learning—but all children use their language, their senses, their bodies, and their minds. They are eager to dig in and their learning is messy and noisy!

So give them a wealth of **real materials**, an abundance of **appropriate learning experiences**, lots of **choice and opportunities** to move around, some **friends**, and **your observant eye and ear**. And very important, give them **yourself as a knowledge resource** and **instructor** to stimulate and extend their thinking.

Children learn when they touch, smell, work, watch others, pretend, imitate, try out, and experiment with real things. Those real things don't need to be fancy "educational toys." Children also learn a lot from everyday items and even things that seem useless.

Geraldine has an apple tree in the back yard. Some of the apples are filled with worms. When she encourages the preschool children to pick up the apples, they are fascinated! They spend a long time just handling the apples and watching the worms crawl in and out.

Then she provides each child with a blunt knife and suggests that they carve a face or some other design in the apple. Some children want to do more than one.

"What do you think will happen if we let these apples sit on the shelf for a few days?" she asks as they finish.

Children offer several ideas—"Bugs will eat them." "They will get all yucky and brown." "We can take them home." "Nothing." "They'll get to be applesauce and we can eat it."

Geraldine writes each child's name on a paper towel, the children put their apples on the towel, and each day they check what is happening to their apples.

Events like this and the time and space for them to happen are an important part of the early childhood classroom. Of course, they can happen anytime or anywhere, provided you are open to them. But you might also want to set aside a special learning area that invites this type of exploration: The Discovery Area.

When children bring in seaweed, or some coffee beans, or an old clock, feature them in the Discovery Area. You add other things that children are curious about or that fit in with your curriculum for a week or two: a hearing aid, coins from several different countries, gardening tools, a Navajo blanket, or a children's book/tape set in another language, or some corncobs, or shells.

If the topic of study is seeds, you might want to include some snow peas, peanuts or walnuts, and a nutcracker.

If you are talking about chickens, you will want feathers, eggs, and bones. Some of the permanent items in the Discovery Area will help children explore their world: magnifying glass, tape measure, scale, small containers, paper bags. These are the tools that scientists, engineers, mathematicians, and researchers of all ages use.

In the Discovery Area and all over the playroom, children will sort ... compare ... match ... measure ... weigh ... use trial and error ... count ... solve problems ... figure out how things work ... touch ... see what happens when they drop or roll something ... try to fit things together ... squeeze ... shake ... learn from their mistakes ... smell ... dig ... saw ... pour ... estimate ... put things in order .... Children will never run out of things to do!

Discovery and exploration involve a lot of activities that seem like **math and science**—and they are! But most things in a good early childhood program are math—and science—and language—and physical skills all wrapped into one! Children see how useful numbers are, for example, when they need to measure the flour to bake bread. They see how things change as they watch the yeast

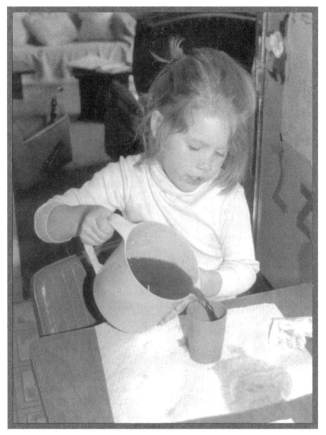

Most lunch and snack menus contain at least one item that children can help fix.

make the bread rise. They see the value of reading when they try to follow the recipe! And they know how strong their muscles are when they knead the dough! The world begins to make sense!

Most lunch and snack menus for young children contain at least one item that even toddlers could help fix. Children can help write lists, shop, scrub fruits or vegetables, stir soups, break up chunks of lettuce for tacos, pour juices, put their own sauce and toppings on their pizza—think about all the steps involved and see whether one or two children at least might participate. Tailor the tasks to the age and skills of the children.

When possible, take your group to the store

to shop. There is so much to learn—how to choose the best produce, reading labels in one or two languages, checking out, paying for the food. A grocery store in the dramatic play area will surely be a big hit. Children can bring in empty food boxes from home and set up a cash register with play money.

When you prepare foods with young children, be sure to really let the children do it. If you jump in and interfere, they will soon lose interest and won't have the opportunity to learn or practice a skill either. If you are responsible for very many children, you will probably want to break up into smaller groups. It is impossible for everyone to take part if there are more than four or five preschoolers working on one project. Two or three toddlers are more than enough.

If you are a family childcare provider, you have the advantage with cooking—you have everything you need at your fingertips! If you work in a center, you may need to bring in an electric skillet or small oven, pans, or utensils, for example. Local regulations about what appliances you may use in the classroom vary so be sure you check them first.

Be sure safety rules are established with the children and all of you have washed your hands thoroughly before you begin. Use plastic knives or table knives for children to cut with.

Real skills learned with **real** food are far more valuable than asking children to cut out food pictures and paste them on a paper plate! Always think **real** when you plan activities for children.

With everything children do in a good program, they **think**. So you set up a schedule that gives children lots of time to think—to play alone and together—to choose what they want to do and how they want to do it. You modify the materials or furnishings so those children with disabilities can be as involved as possible, too. And you are flexible, so that if something comes up during the day (*and it always does*) you can take advantage of the teachable moment.

Catch teachable moments

All day, as you move from experience to experience, you look for teachable moments that you can use to further children's thinking. Let's see how you can capitalize on some everyday occurrences.

Fourteen-month-old Daren is struggling with the stacking toy. The largest ring just won't fit because the smallest one is already on top.

"You have tried and tried to get that red ring on, but it won't go. What seems to be the problem?" asks his family childcare provider, Ms. Patel.

Daren looks underneath the green ring, his hair touching the floor. Then he dumps the ring from the spindle and smiles. "Bat," he announces.

"Now your spindle has no rings. Which one will you put on next?"

Daren was learning elementary physics—that two things won't fit in the same space at the same time.

But his teacher did not dump the ring off and show him how to make the red ring go on. She put his problem into words because he was just beginning to use language. She pointed out how persistent he had been and used words to talk about what he was doing.

Lots of trying to make sense of things, ordering, looking, trial and error, fitting together, and problem solving going on here! Science, math, language, physical development—all in one short minute!

Two toddlers are playing in the sand. "Let's do a birthday party!"

Their Head Start teacher, Mr. Rinaldi, hears the suggestion and walks closer.

"We need cupcakes," announces Michelle as she looks in his direction.

"Cupcakes usually have milk in them. Do you need a gallon of milk?" Mr. Rinaldi asks.

"Cupcakes are good with milk," Shanada replies.

"Who would like to help carry a bucket of milk for cupcakes?" their teacher asks. Both children volunteer, and they go to the storage shed to get the bucket. The three fill the bucket, and the two girls carry it back to the sandbox.

These toddlers had an idea, decided what they needed to carry it out, and knew whom to ask for help.

Their teacher was aware that their play was just beginning and knew that water adds so much to children's play with sand. He enabled them to expand their play and gave them a chance to cooperate by carrying the heavy gallon bucket of water.

The children were indeed making sense of their world, weighing, digging, pouring, recognizing a problem, and thinking about what they wanted to do!

A 4-year-old has found a long flashlight in the Discovery Area. He turns it on and watches it dance on the ceiling. Then he takes the batteries out. When he puts them back in, the flashlight doesn't work. He dumps the batteries on the floor, puts them back in, and still it doesn't work. In fact, now they jiggle around inside.

Mrs. Arias has been watching Colin's progress. She catches his eye. It looks questioning, so she walks over to the Discovery Area.

"What's the problem, Colin?" she says in a friendly voice.

"The flashlight doesn't work," he responds simply.

"Show me how it doesn't work," Mrs. Arias suggests.

"Well, see, I took this end off. Then I dumped out the batteries. I put them back in, and then it didn't work. So I dumped them here on the floor—oops! There's a battery under the shelf! No wonder it didn't work!"

Colin puts his batteries back, pushes the button— no light. "Oh no, it still doesn't work," he says with disappointment.

Mrs. Arias asks, "What do you think could be wrong?"

"Well, it is broken."

"Probably not, and if it worked today the bulb probably isn't the problem, either. Sometimes they wear out, too. What do you think it could be?"

Colin is silent. He dumps out the batteries one more time and studies each one carefully.

"Which end did you put in first, Colin?" his teacher asks.

"Does it matter?"

"Let's find out."

Those were long examples! But then, children need a long time to figure things out and Colin is still working on his problem! Mrs. Arias found out what he knew, saw that he needed a clue before he got discouraged, and offered it—he probably will have a working flashlight in a flash. And how well he will know that batteries have two ends and that it matters how they are stacked. No picture, no words, could ever substitute for this simple experience.

These are the kinds of everyday, simple, real experiences that mean the most for children's learning. These are teachable moments. And your support can make the difference in just how much children learn. What do you do?

- You **observe** what is happening. Sometimes you don't need to do anything—you already did your part by putting out the item. Children can take it from there.

- You **describe** or explain what is happening. Sometimes a simple statement will help children notice what their problem is so they can go on to the next step in solving it.

- You **ask thought-provoking questions in the child's home language**—questions that have lots of possible answers are called open-ended questions. How ... ? Why ... ? What ... ? What if ... ? When ... ? Where ... ? Ask questions so children can think up a possible solution. Help them wonder. Give them a chance to talk about their ideas.

  Avoid closed-ended questions—those that have only one right answer or that can be answered with a simple yes or no. And don't answer children's questions for them until they have given the problem their best shot at a solution!

- You **encourage children to ask questions** about what they are doing. As they ask questions, they will think through their own answers. Lots of times two or more children will discuss what they are doing, and figure out what they need on their own. Children in the block corner frequently help each other out when a block is too long or a ramp is too steep.

  Sometimes, of course, children just need an answer to their questions. "Where is the ... ?"; "How do you spell ... ?"; "Is this good wood for sawing?"; "What do rabbits eat?"

  And if you don't know the answer, say so. "What an excellent question that is. I wonder what foods are good for rabbits. Where could we find an answer to that question?" Opportunities such as these are great for helping children learn about libraries, telephones, the Internet, and how to do research.

- You **let children come up with solutions and try the ideas themselves.** Yes, even when you know something won't work. Especially when you know something won't work—children learn from trial and error. They learn from their mistakes. If it is safe, let them proceed uninterrupted.

Brandon and Rahsaan are helping prepare the toddler snack. They have cut up banana chunks and put them and the crackers on three small trays. Now they need to carry them to the tables.

Rahsaan takes one tray and places it on the closest table.

Brandon takes another tray and puts his on the same table.

The other toddlers begin to arrive for snack just as Rahsaan gets the last tray.

"Hey, this table doesn't have any food," points out Kimeon.

Rahsaan takes his tray to that table. One table still has no tray.

"Where is our snack?" asks Essence, who is always ready to eat. She looks around. "No fair, that table has two, and we don't have any."

Brandon takes one of the trays to the last table.

Children can learn so much from each other and by experiencing the consequences of their own actions! Brandon and Rahsaan are actually working on learning an important mathematical principle called *one-to-one correspondence*—one tray for each table or one serving for each child.

- Sometimes you **join in their play**. "You need an ambulance driver and they are all out? Well, sure, I can drive the ambulance. Where is the person who is hurt? How long will it take to get to the hospital?" When you play with children, you can extend their vocabulary and even draw their attention to math concepts in an informal way. You don't dominate or control the play, but rather take your cues from the children. And gracefully exit from the play as soon as you make your ambulance run.

These techniques sound a little bit like the listening you learned earlier. They are very similar—once you know how children learn and what you want them to learn, the same teaching techniques and learning experiences

---

Make the most of teachable moments

Children learn best in everyday, simple, real activities. Use one or more of these techniques to extend their learning:

- Observe what is happening.
- Describe what is happening.
- Ask thought-provoking questions in children's home language.
- Encourage children to ask questions.
- Let children come up with solutions and try the ideas themselves.
- Join in the play.

---

come up over and over again in different ways. All of children's learning is so interrelated.

Catch a teachable moment tomorrow. Practice using open-ended questions in place of closed-ended ones. Write what happened here.

Discuss what happened with your Advisor.

What materials would make a good addition to your supply?

What new techniques could you introduce to the children in your group?

Plan nine learning experiences (*across the age span served by your CDA Credential setting*) to include in your Professional Resource File. Each learning experience should promote physical, cognitive, (including language, literacy math and science) and/or creative development. Include in the description: goals, materials, and teaching strategies used.

Let's move on now to our next long-term goal for children. Like all the others, it draws on ideas and techniques we have already talked about.

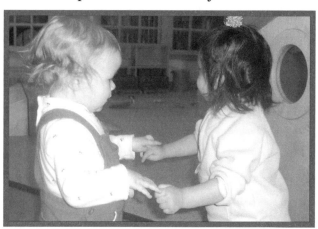
Children treat their friends with respect.

You enable children to lead well-balanced, productive lives

Life is meant to be lived to its fullest. Children are in your group for many waking hours every day. Everything you have learned through your experience and in this CDA material can be applied as you create an atmosphere and environment to support young children's growth toward happy and fulfilled lives as adults.

Children are learning how their bodies work, how to communicate, how to think, and how to act responsibly. You already know the importance of children's self-esteem and why they must feel good about themselves. You know that children need to learn self-help skills and to increase their ability to function independently. Part of feeling grown up is accepting responsibility—age-appropriate responsibility, of course.

We have talked about how children pick up bias and stereotypes from the people who are important to them—and in contrast, how they learn ways to treat other people with respect.

Likewise, children pick up a sense of responsible connectedness to a larger world outside their own families and absorb values about other more global issues such as pollution, hunger, waste/conservation, change, and war/peace.

Children need to learn respect for our natural resources. They should learn to respect the human universe and to participate in keeping it safe, healthy, and fair for all living things. They learn this respect everyday—for things and each other—primarily from what you and their parents do and say, the kinds of experiences you offer, how you make decisions, and the responsibilities children begin to assume.

- **Children respect people.** You expect children to take good care of themselves. Children treat their friends and families with respect. Children use words to work out problems. Diversity is a natural part of their everyday experience, so they are not threatened or uncomfortable with different ideas, skin colors, languages, or clothes. Children learn to speak up when they see that something is unfair or hurts feelings. These are small beginnings toward a more peaceful world.

- **Children respect nature and its resources.** Your example and attitude can make all the difference. Food is to be eaten, not wasted. You work to preserve animal life. Even if you are afraid of snakes or bugs, you are always curious and in control of yourself. You turn off the water or the lights when they are not in use. Children will soon follow your example, and as a result more resources will be available for all of us and future generations to enjoy.

- **Children accept responsibility.** Right from baby-hood, children can make choices and take responsibility for things that affect them. Babies can decide what kind of cereal to eat, which toys to play with, and whether to climb to the top of the mountain of cushions or not. They can use a sponge to wipe off the tray of their high chair or a napkin to dab at their face. They learn to be kind to other children, and to pet the cat or dog gently. Toddlers put their toys back when they are finished. They wipe up spills with a sponge. They can help make small repairs—sanding a rough block, taping a torn page, tightening a nut on the tricycle. They can turn off the water after they wash their hands.

    Preschoolers can handle even more responsibility. Sharing toys and playing cooperatively.

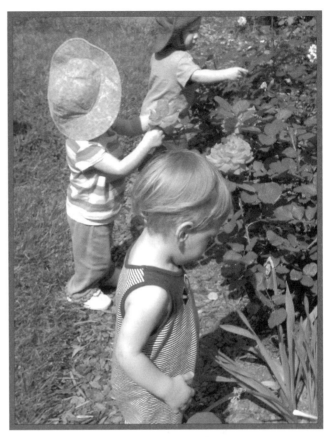

Children appreciate beauty

Coordinating their efforts to cook a holiday feast. They can keep the playground free of trash. And remind each other in the car to buckle up when it's time to go home.

What else can you think of to help children grow up to be more responsible citizens?

What global issues in society do you care most about? Think about these and be ready to discuss your ideas with the other CDA Candidates in your Seminar.

- **Children appreciate beauty.** Beauty is everywhere, not just in art or music. Beauty is the smell of hot vegetable soup on a cold winter day. Beauty is the hand of a close friend or a warm smile. Beauty is the sun glittering on water or a tall building. Beauty is the shade of a tree on a hot summer day. Beauty is a peaceful feeling of quiet after working hard on the playground. Beauty is the feel of silk, or bark, or the bricks of the sidewalk. Beauty is all around if we just take the time to appreciate it.

You make your environment appealing and reflective of children's cultural diversity.

You create a restful background on which to tastefully exhibit children's artwork, artifacts from around the world, items from nature, and a few fine art pieces.

You arrange shelves neatly with labels and/or pictures so children know where everything goes. Store extra toys and supplies in a closet or cupboard. Place plants, cut flowers, or dried arrangements where children can touch and smell them.

Let the air be filled with children's laughter and many languages. You play music that is in good taste at a comfortable sound level. Some quiet music at naptime can create a restful feeling even for adults.

You clean pet cages or aquariums often. Open the windows and shades every day to let fresh breezes and natural light stream in.

Select books, posters, and pictures that are pleasing to the eye. You avoid clutter, large quantities of dark or glaring colors, "cute" cartoon drawings. So many items intended for children are ugly and harsh. Strive for moderation.

Outdoors, you listen for birds or the leaves rustling in the wind. You use a variety of materials—sand, wood chips, grass, trees for playground design. You paint equipment to blend in with the environment rather than stand out like a sore thumb. You plant a garden that the children can watch. You keep the area free of litter.

Beauty is everywhere. It is not expensive. Experience it everyday with your group of children.

List some ways that you can help children appreciate beauty in your environment.

_____

_____

_____

_____

_____

Start to make your improvements immediately.

To be an effective teacher of young children, you need imagination and creativity . . . joy . . . curiosity . . . a sense of humor . . . boundless energy . . . a listening ear . . . a warm heart . . . enthusiasm—and the desire to learn along with the children.

You won't find these in any catalog and none of them costs a penny. But they are priceless qualities that you bring with you every day when you walk in the door, or when the children walk in your door. Use them wisely.

What is appropriate curriculum?

We have said, curriculum is what happens . . . but planning and intentional teaching on your part are key to learning. Curriculum is a written plan that describes the goals for children's development and learning, and the experiences, materials, and teaching strategies that will be used to help children achieve the goals. Every good early childhood program should have a curriculum plan so that teach-

ers are constantly aware of their goals for children and are prepared in advance. All curricula, whether commercially produced or developed within a program, must be adapted for individual interests, needs, and strengths of children.

When you plan what will happen each day, you always want to add some variety to make each day something to look forward to. Many teachers, however, like to provide variety by highlighting one or more special activities. Children are still given lots of choice about what to do, but the choices vary from one day to the next.

The curriculum will give your daily activities direction. It is easy to let your pre-planned curriculum dominate, though, so you need to be careful to balance it with the ideas and interests that emerge from children's experiences.

For instance, if children are especially excited about dinosaurs, you might want to hang up a few dinosaur pictures, put out a few dinosaurs to play with in the sand, and display some dinosaur books.

Or perhaps you could find some fossils, or some dinosaur rubber stamps, or cookie cutters to use with clay, or a couple of dinosaur puzzles. And maybe you could find a computer game with dinosaurs, or word cards in the writing area, or a card game of dinosaurs.

But you don't want all of these. It can be dreadfully boring for you and monotonous for the children as well if they have no relief from dinosaurs for every activity for a whole week. Enough is enough.

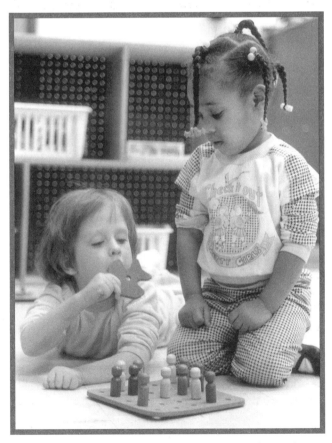

Children's development in all areas is enhanced through play.

Keeping in mind, then, the need to balance the special focus on the curriculum with routine activities, here are some curriculum topics and ideas for teaching that can be predicted to be appropriate and interesting for young children. Each of these topic areas also lends itself to children's engagement in specific projects or the use of the "project approach," described fully by Lilian Katz and Sylvia Chard in *Engaging Children's Minds: The Project Approach* (2000). They define a project as "an in-depth study that one or more children undertake," that usually extends over several days or even weeks. This approach emphasizes the importance of the teacher's role in helping children actively participate and engage with people and the environment in ways that are personally meaningfully.

We have left space with each one so you can add your own appropriate ideas. Add other curriculum topics you can think of, too. See the Resource section for more ideas.

You use appropriate infant curriculum

We are growing. Show baby pictures to help children see how much they have changed, look at hair and other body parts in mirrors, play with dolls, talk about how much children can do.

can infants do this

? — ~~Create a height chart to measure~~ Sequencing pic's (baby to adult)

What we eat. Try new foods with a sense of adventure, visit a grocery store, walk through a garden, smell foods as they cook, wash fruits and vegetables.

create a food project
Dramatic play (kitchen, food store)

People we love. Exhibit pictures of families—not just parents but aunts, uncles, cousins, grandparents; talk about how friends treat each other; sing songs in many languages; invite relatives to visit and cuddle with the children; read stories about all kinds of families.

Family Tree
classroom picnic
family play day in classroom

Animals. Watch fish swim, pet furry animals, sniff a wet dog, play guessing games about which animal makes the noise, imitate animal sounds.

• animal sounds on cd
• animal puppet show
• ~~touch tank~~ ? with infants

What happens. Roll different kinds of balls (*fabric, rubber, textured, smooth*), pour water, slide down the slide, pick flowers, play instruments, send a small vehicle down a ramp.

- magnets
- pour/dump w/ sand/water
- mix substances (mud)
-

We move our bodies. Move and sing to music from many cultures, climb a mountain of cushions, crawl through an obstacle course, ride vehicles, roll in the grass.

Head, shoulders (song)
hop like bunnies
roll around

You use appropriate toddler curriculum

How big we are. Compare what infants can do with what toddlers can do (*baby pictures/ real children*), weigh and/or measure each child once a month and chart their growth.

height chart
draw persons to show how big
we are in comparison

Food comes from plants. Plant a garden or at least a tomato in a sunny window, pick pumpkins or apples, make spaghetti squash and tomato sauce, sprout seeds, taste different colors and shapes of foods from several cultures.

ok • Field trip to pumpkin patch/farm
ok • grow bean plant in class
• class food project — what?

Food comes from animals. Watch a cow being milked, make ice milk, have a picnic, visit a poultry farm, make books of pictures on how many ways you can eat eggs.

• ~~Shared writing what animal~~
~~foods do you eat at home~~?
• ~~match game~~ (animal to food)
• Field trip to farm — ok
• pictures of animals matched
w/ food.

remember almost more preschool

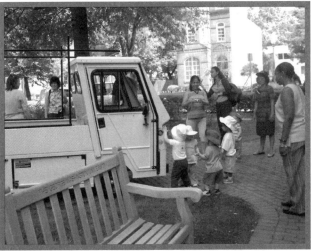

Curriculum topics like trucks and buses are likely to be appropriate and interesting for toddlers.

Where we live. Visit children's homes or have them bring in pictures, talk about similarities and differences, walk through the neighborhood to look at where people live, watch a building being erected (*visit every week, not just once*), introduce carpentry skills.

for toddlers!

- Community helpers visit (police, fireman)
- Traffic signs (shapes, print)
- Building structures (blocks)

Where animals live. Tour a farm, read books or see movies about animal's natural habitats, watch an ant hill, walk through the woods and look for tracks and sounds, use animal puppets, set up a barn with animals.

more used from Toddler

- Butterfly habitat in room
- Animal hunt (clues in room)
- picture books (pop-up
- Fish tank

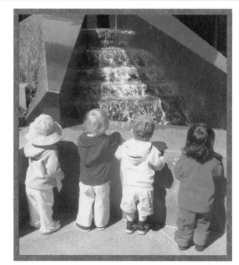
Sometimes the curriculum is finding out what happens.

At the beach. Play in sand and water with beach toys, collect shells or other debris, play with rubber sea animals, let water sit out and evaporate—what is left?, pretend to spend a day at the beach in the middle of the winter.

- sand/water table (seashells, mud, etc.)
- touch tank
- aquarium visit

What we can smell. Ask children to bring in something they like to smell, play guessing games with smells, look at each other's noses, cook lots of ethnic dishes.

- 5 senses kit (sauces, candles, etc.)
- food projects
- nature walk
- Dif types of odor

How things feel. Collect fabric scraps for children to paste or make into books, give each child a small bag to fill with treasures on a walk, touch a Braille book.

- Materials in sand table (rough, smooth)
- Mystery box.
- Display board of textures
- Cardboard books about texture

Harvest time. Shell corn, feed birds, collect and paste colored leaves, plan and cook a harvest feast, talk about things children are thankful for, how families celebrate harvests.

- Field Trip to pumpkin farm
- Collect Leaves
- bring harvest foods

Weather. Put a thermometer on the playground and watch how it changes, watch the clouds, fly kites in the wind, provide dress-up clothes for each season.

- track weather (patterns?) toddlers ?
- Dark/white clouds (rain)
- Feel wind (fans) ok
-

Trucks, trains, and buses. Ride a bus or train, read *Freight Train*, watch and listen to a train go by, find different kinds of trucks—what is in them, visit the fire station, listen for engine sounds.

- match sound to correct vehicle
- Dramatic Play clothes (trucker, conductor)
- play w/ different toy motor vehicles
- watch for vehicles on outside walk

remember this is toddlers

needs more

You use appropriate preschool curriculum

All the topics for toddlers are appropriate, but with more ideas and activities to expand children's thinking even further.

People have different jobs. Provide props for pretend play from a variety of types of jobs, talk about what parents do, and visit many different job sites.

- Job dress-up day
- Career Day (parent's visit)
- Community Helpers (fireman, police will visit)
- Dramatic play / block people

People are the same and different. Make charts of hair color or eye color, feel different hair and skin textures, watch authentic movies about food and shelter and dress in other cultures, eat with utensils from other cultures, let children try out a wheelchair or glasses.

is this DAP

- Bring in Artist to draw charactures
- Attempt to draw a person (add texture pieces for clothes)
- Chart (height, color, hair, etc.) differences/similarities
- use dolls (if have realistic ones)

Where clothes come from. Watch a sheep being sheared or a weaver at work, grow cotton, paste cotton balls, feel the smoothness of silk, compare leather with vinyl, sew with yarn and burlap, visit a seamstress or tailor, add some new dress-up clothes.

- mystery box (materials)
- fashion show
- visit a store
- picture books showing where clothes are made.

Milk and dairy products. Visit a dairy farm, prepare milk shakes and write down children's original recipes, compare tastes and textures of cheeses, make a barn with a cardboard box.

- make smoothies (fruit)
- visit a farm
- food (cream cheese cubes & cheddar cheese cubes)

How plants grow. Plant a garden, collect different seeds from food you eat, care for plants.

- grow sunflowers
- visit botanical gardens
- books about plants, dirt, etc.
- grow grass

Money. Compare coins from many countries, set up a lemonade stand or tricycle wash, obtain a popular advertised item and decide whether it really performs like the commercial says it does, write "checks," set up a post office or grocery store with a cash register.

- Foreign money vs. Domestic (compare)
- numerical value ($5 = 5 singles)
- weight of money

Time. Talk about birthdays and ages, find different kinds of clocks, compare to see whether older always means taller, bake bread.

- 60 min. real clock (timer)
- egg timer
- Tomorrow, yesterday

Water. Freeze it, let it evaporate, make steam, pour and measure it, add food coloring, swim, raise fish.

- ice cubes (colors)
- freeze water bottle (watch melt)
- freeze a large cube of ice to put in water table, put food coloring in it.

There are hundreds of other curriculum topics that interest children and that are intellectually engaging enough to advance physical, intellectual, social, and emotional development—listen every day and pick up on their ideas and questions.

WELL . . . now that you have seen all the videos and completed the exercises in these first five units, you have most of the basic tools you need to implement curriculum with the children in your classroom or home.

But you are not finished—for in order to pull EVERYTHING together to plan for your children you must establish positive working relations with their parents. We'll cover this in the next unit.

Meanwhile, to practice what you have learned so far, complete the following exercise of working out a weekly plan and be prepared to discuss it in detail with your Field Advisor and put a copy in your Professional Resource File.

Weekly plan

Curriculum topic ____5 senses_____

Special events ____Veggie Pizza_____

	MON.	TUES.	WED.	THURS.	FRI.
Child-initiated experiences	Language Master (sounds)	~~Listening Station~~ (CD sounds) "I spy" board	Ooblik (water table)	~~Play Dough~~ Veggie Pizza	scratch n' sniff
Teacher-guided experiences	Mystery Box - 5 senses	~~Food project~~ ~~(Veggie pizza)~~	Art (5 senses book)	~~textures~~ smell ingredients	smells + ~~sounds~~ of community
Special materials needed	Lang. master cards various materials for box	~~various veggies~~ ~~pita, sauce~~ cardboard 5 sense materials	glue, markers, texture materials, construction paper	~~seashells, rocks~~ ~~etc~~ ~~playdough~~ bread, veggie sauce	books w/ smell various sounds made w/ objects
Arrangements to make	Be sure there are enough cards	Buy materials + create board	buy materials	reserve kitchen staff	reserve time to walk
Special focus for individual children	speech; saying simple sentences	I spy simplified (colors, shapes)	identify one sense to create in art	display veggies to be easily accessible	bring camera to take pic's

(*Include modifications for children with special needs*)

not finished

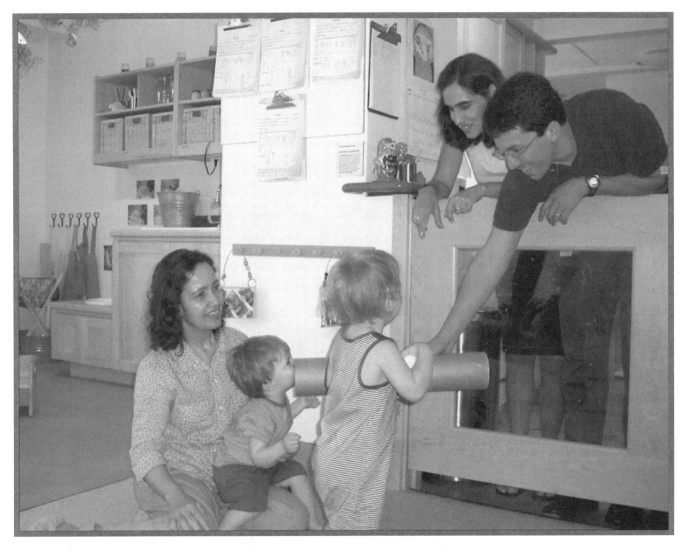

Make parents feel welcome to visit anytime.

At last! You have put everything you know together to come up with an honest-to-goodness plan for teaching. It has taken a long time to get to this point, and you have worked hard on your CDA.

Turn to your CDA progress record and make a BIG check for having finished the self-study portion of Unit 5. Pause to take a deep breath, and then come back to finish Unit 6.

Resources for more information

A creative adventure (4 videos). (2000). Washington, DC: Educational Services, Inc. Available from Head Start Information and Publications Center (HSIPC).

Althouse, R., Johnson, M.H. & Mitchell, S.T. (2002). *The colors of learning: Integrating the visual arts into the early childhood curriculum.* New York: Teachers College Press. Available from NAEYC.

Bergen, D., Reid, R. & Torelli, L. (2000). *Educating and caring for very young children: The infant/toddler curriculum.* New York: Teachers College Press. Also available from NAEYC.

Bowman, B. (Ed.) (2002). *Love to read: Essays in developing early literacy skills of African American children.* Washington, DC: National Black Child Development Institute. Also available from NAEYC.

Bowman, B.T., Donovan, M. S. & Burns, M.S. (Eds.) (2000). *Eager to learn: Educating our preschoolers.* Committee on Early Childhood Pedagogy, National Research Council. Washington, DC: National Academy Press.

Bredekamp S. & Copple, C. (Eds.) (1997). *Developmentally appropriate practice in early childhood programs (Rev. ed.)* Washington, DC: National Association for the Education of Young Children.

Bredekamp, S. & Rosegrant, T. (Eds.) (1995). *Reaching potentials: Transforming early childhood curriculum and assessment, vol. 2.* Washington, DC: National Association for the Education of Young Children.

Burns, M.S., Griffin, P. & Snow, C.E. (Eds.) (1999). *Starting out right: A guide to promoting children's reading success.* Washington, DC: National Academy Press. Available for purchase from www.redleafpressorg. Available free at www.nap.edu. Also available in Spanish: El aprendizaje de la lectura ej l escritura: Practicas apropiadas para el desarrollo infantile.

Campbell, R. (2001). *Read-alouds with young children.* Newark, DE: International Reading Association.

Chalufour, I. & Worth, K. (2003). *Discovering nature with young children* (book and video). St. Paul, MN: Redleaf Press. Also available from NAEYC.

Children at the center: Reflective teachers at work (video). Seattle, WA: Harvest Resources. Available from Redleaf Press, www.redleafpress.org.

Copley, J.V. (2000). *The young child and mathematics.* Washington, DC: National Association for the Education of Young Children and the National Council of Teachers of Mathematics.

Curtis, D. & Carter, M. (1996). *Reflecting children's lives: A handbook for planning child-centered curriculum.* Seattle, WA: Harvest Resources. Available from Redleaf Press, St. Paul, MN.

Dickinson, D. (2001). Book reading in preschool classrooms. In D. Dickinson & P. Tabors (Eds.), *Beginning literacy with language young children learning at home and school.* Baltimore: Paul H. Brookes.

Head Start Bureau, U.S. Department of Health & Human Services. (2003). *The Head Start path to positive child outcomes: A guide for education leaders.* Washington, DC: Author.

Helm, J.H. & Katz, L. (2001). *Young investigators: the project approach in the early years.* New York: Teachers College Press. Available from NAEYC.

Hemmeter, M.L., Joseph, G., Smith, B., & Sandall, S. (2002). *Recommended practices program assessment: Improving practices for young children with special needs and their families.* Longmont, CO: Sopris West.

Hohmann, M. (2002). *Fee, fie, phonemic awareness: 130 prereading activities for preschoolers.* Ypsilanti, MI: High/Scope Press.

Howes, C. (Ed.) (2003). *Teaching 4- to 8-Year-olds: Literacy, math, multiculturalism, and classroom community. National Center for Early Learning and Development.* Baltimore: Paul H. Brookes Publishing Co.

Katz, L.G. & Chard, S.C. (2000). *Engaging children's minds: The project approach.* Rev. ed. Ablex. Available from Redleaf Press.

Koralek, D.G. (Ed.) (2003). *Spotlight on young children and language. Collection of articles from Young Children.* Washington, DC: National Association for the Education of Young Children.

Koralek, D.G. (Ed.) (2003). *Spotlight on young children and math. Collection of articles from Young Children.* Washington, DC: National Association for the Education of Young Children.

Koralek, D.G. (Ed.) (2004). *Spotlight on young children and play. Collection of articles from Young Children.* Washington, DC: National Association for the Education of Young Children.

Koralek, D.G.& Colker, L.J. (Eds.) (2003). *Spotlight on young children and science. Collection of articles from Young Children.* Washington, DC: National Association for the Education of Young Children.

Lasky, L. & Mukerji-Bergeson, R. (1980). *Art: Basic for young children.* Washington, DC: National Association for the Education of Young Children.

Mathews, V. H. & Roman S. (2002) *The Library-Museum Head Start Partnership: A Resource Notebook.* Washington, DC: National Association for the Education of Young Children.

Mathews, S. H., Roman, S. & Trotta, M. (1993) *The Library Head Start Partnership.* Washington, DC: National Association for the Education of Young Children.

McDonald, D.T. (1979). *Music in our lives: The early years.* Washington, DC: National Association for the Education of Young Children.

National Association for the Education of Young Children and the National Council of Teachers of Mathematics. (2002). *Early childhood mathematics: Promoting good beginnings. A joint position statement of NAEYC and NCTM.* Washington, DC: Author.

Neuman, S.B., Copple, C. & Bredekamp, S. (1999). *Learning to read and write: Developmentally appropriate practices for young children.* Washington, DC: National Association for the Education of Young Children.
Ready to Learn, A PBS Initiative.
www.pbs.org/readytolearn

Sandall, S., Schwartz, I.,& Joseph, G. (2001). A building blocks model for effective instruction in inclusive early childhood settings. *Young Exceptional Children*, 4(3).

Sandall, S., Schwartz, I., Joseph, G., Chou, H-Y. Horn, E., Lieber, J., Odom, S.L., & Wolery, R. (2002). *Building blocks for teaching preschoolers with special needs.* Baltimore, MD: Brookes Publishing Co.

Sanders, S. (2002). *Active for life: Developmentally appropriate movement programs for young children.* Washington, DC: National Association for the Education of Young Children.

Schickedanz, J.A. (1998). *Much more than the ABCs: The early stages of reading and writing.* Washington, DC: National Association for the Education of Young Children.

Schiller, P. & Bermudez, A.B. Working with non-English-speaking children. *Texas Child Care Quarterly, 12*(3), 3-8.

Seefeldt, C. & Galper, A. (1999). *Active experiences for active children: Social studies.* Merrill, an imprint of Prentice-Hall. Also available from NAEYC.

Setting sail: An emergent curriculum project (video). Seattle, WA: Harvest Resources. Available from Redleaf Press, www.redleafpress.org.

Shonkoff, J.P & Phillips, D. A. (Eds.) (2000). *From neurons to neighborhoods: The science of early childhood development.* Committee on Integrating the Science of Early Childhood Development, Board on Children, Youth and Families. Washington, DC: National Academy Press.

Tabors, P. (1997). *One child, two languages: A guide for preschool educators of children learning English as a second language.* Baltimore, MD: Paul H. Brookes Publishing Co.

Torbert, M. & Schneider, L. (1993). *Follow me too: A handbook of movement activities for three-to five-year-olds.* Addison-Wesley. Available from NAEYC.

Weitzman, E. & Greenberg, J. *Learning language and loving it: A guide to promoting children's social and language development in early childhood settings (2ⁿᵈ Ed.)* From Hanen Centre. Available from NAEYC.

Wolery, R.A. & Wilburs, J. (Eds.) (1994). *Including children with special needs in preschool progams: Research and implications for practice.* Washington, DC: National Association for the Education of Young Children.

Worth, K. & Grollman, S. (2003). *Worms, shadows, and whirlpools: Science in the early childhood classroom.* Washington, DC: NAEYC copublished with Heinemann.

Keys to establish productive relationships with families

IN EARLY CHILDHOOD EDUCATION you always work in partnership with families to foster children's development. Together, you will assess children's strengths, needs, and interests; plan their experiences; and make decisions that influence how your program unfolds from day to day, month to month, and year to year. Your ability to develop effective relationships with parents is so important that parents' opinions of your work will be weighed in the final decision about your competence as a CDA!

As an early childhood educator, you play a very special role in the lives of families. Most of you see the children's parents daily, sometimes twice a day. You will celebrate happy occasions with families and cry with them at difficult times. Programs for young children enable parents to continue their education or to earn a living. You not only teach children—parents look to you, an experienced and knowledgeable professional, for ideas about how to be a good parent. You support parents in the challenging task of childrearing.

In this unit you will build upon your own experiences and learn new strategies to establish positive, productive relationships with families.

Programs usually have policies describing what the program must do for parents, and what is expected of parents. To begin this unit, review your own program's policies that affect your work with families: enrollment, arrival and departure procedures, conferences, screening, visits, and resource referral guidelines, for example.

These policies sometimes are written in lengthy form, such as the Head Start Program Performance Standards. There may be a brief program brochure, handbook, or even a simple typed sheet. Put a copy of all the policies for your program regarding parents and families in your Professional Resource File.

> We will use the terms parents and families to mean those people who are primarily responsible for the children in your care, whoever they are—parents, stepparents, grandparents, cousins, guardians, foster families, or other household members.

PART 1

How do you get off to a good start?

You make good first impressions

Although your involvement in the enrollment of children will vary depending on whether you are in a large group program or providing family child care, you need to be aware of the process to start off on the right foot to build and maintain a professional relationship with parents.

If you are a family child care provider, every time you pick up the phone you could be welcoming a prospective parent. In a center, you may first meet a potential family when they visit your classroom. Regardless of when or how you meet, both of you need some time to get to know each other before a decision about the child's enrollment can be made.

During these first conversations, family members are asking themselves, "Is this the kind of person we want to care for and teach our child?" You are asking, "Is my program a good match for this child and family?"

Don't dismiss the importance of these first impressions and early reactions to you and your program. You are establishing the foundation for a long, close, professional relationship. Both you and the families want to make the right decision for the children.

Start off in a professional manner by being friendly and explaining the highlights of your program on the phone or in person. Then either you (*if you are a family child care provider*) or your program administrator will mail, or give the parents a copy of your program's written policies.

Timelines

This is the final unit to be completed during the self-study phase of your CDA Professional Preparation Program. You will need about two weeks to finish these tasks:

1 Prepare for conference with your Field Advisor to discuss three topics (*get off to a good start with new families, collaboration each day, and effective ways to exchange information*).

2 Complete three assignments (*observe a parent conference, plan a parent meeting, and complete two home visits*) and two entries for the Professional Resource File.

3 Complete three assignments for Seminar (*explore ways to involve parents, refine skills in conducting parent conferences, and resolve typical dilemmas that arise between parents and teachers*).

4 Distribute and collect the CDA Parent Questionnaires.

These policies cover basics about such things as enrollment qualifications, fees, holidays/vacations, illness, emergency procedures, discipline, and educational philosophy. When these policies are in writing, you greatly reduce the chances for conflicts about these issues later—and you probably already know from experience that disagreements do arise. So much is at stake.

Encourage parents to visit your program at least once before they decide to enroll their child. Welcome the family warmly and with respect. Show them where their child would spend the day, including the playground, and the sleeping areas. Tell parents your expectations about working with them. Ask them about theirs.

Invite them to watch what happens and how the children are treated. Encourage the family to ask questions and share their concerns about what is important to them.

During the visit, your guest parents will want to talk with you (*and perhaps your program director*) about what happens in a good program for young children. You or your director will explain how your program is sensitive to families from a variety of cultures or who speak a second language. All of you want to be comfortable that your program is a good match for the child and family.

You observe business and legal responsibilities

Business is the order of the day when a new child enrolls. Make sure contracts and emergency procedures are signed, deposits and fees paid, health forms complete, and all other paperwork is complete **before** the child's first day.

Your program provides families with a clear written statement about your responsibilities—and theirs—so that all of you know exactly what your roles are. Why? Because accidents do happen and misunderstandings arise.

For example, rather than wait until it is too late, clarify at the beginning who is responsible for children, especially during the critical times of arrival and departure. Put your policy in writing for every parent. Then, if a parent forgets the child's lunch in the car and rushes back to get it, there will be no question about who is responsible—you or the parent—in the event of an accident.

On page 366 is a list of some program and parent responsibilities in early childhood settings. Add other responsibilities to these lists that fit your program. **Check to see that these responsibilities are covered in writing for your program. If they are not, talk with your CDA Field Advisor about ways you can work together to have them added.**

If you are a family childcare provider, you can begin immediately to make changes.

You work with parents on the child's first day

Advance planning is needed to get ready for a family's first day. One good idea is to send the child a postcard or note of welcome in advance. Children love to receive mail and will sometimes arrive clutching this precious object in their hand. You put the child's name on a cubby and cot or crib. Add the child's name to the sign-in list. Put

The Program's Responsibilities

- To meet all federal, state, local, and program regulations for health, safety, nutrition, staffing patterns, program, emergencies, illness, and other matters.

- To release child only to those people designated in writing by the custodial parent or guardian.

- To administer medicine only when authorized in writing by the parent or guardian.

- To plan an appropriate program for each child, taking into account language, culture, age, differing abilities, and all other pertinent factors.

- To communicate with parents in the language most comfortable for them.

- To keep records of budgets, income, expenses, licenses, permits, insurance, and other business information.

- To obtain parent permission whenever the child leaves the program premises during contract hours with staff (such as on field trips).

- To maintain confidential records of children's development and progress, and to make these records available to parents upon request and only to others (another program or school, for example) if authorized in writing by the parents.

- To report any suspected indicators of child abuse.

- To establish other policies where needed and apply them uniformly among staff, children, and parents. For example, policies about exclusion due to illness and about who is responsible for the child when the parent is present.

- To request parent permission and involvement when possible for developmental screening, photographs, and other similar activities.

- To include parents in establishing the program's goals and objectives for children's development and learning and negotiate openly any areas of discomfort or parental concern.

The Parents' Responsibilities

- To be involved with the staff in setting the program's direction and daily experiences by volunteering or serving on policy boards, for example.

- To agree in advance and in writing to follow all program policies.

- To provide any information about a child or the family that may affect decisions about the child's development.

- To discuss any areas of concern with the appropriate staff member(s).

the family's name on the parent bulletin board.

Make a cheery welcome sign using the family's preferred language. If the children in the group are old enough, ask those who are interested to help you. Plan a familiar snack. Little touches can mean a lot toward helping a child and family feel really welcome.

Discuss in advance with parents what you expect on the first day. For example, make sure parents know to bring diapers, an extra change of clothes, bedding, a bag lunch, or other items.

Agree upon how long the parent will stay with the child and how the parent can help ease the separation for herself or himself as well as the child, knowing that the time may need to be extended or shortened depending on how it goes.

When the child and parent(s) arrive, warmly greet them. We already talked in Unit 4 about how to help children handle separation, so let's think now about how to help **parents** deal with their child's first day.

Parents may react in many different ways to leaving their child. Every family is different. Some adults may find it very difficult to leave. Others will know just when to say "Goodbye" or "¡Hasta luego!" to their child. Still others would prefer to rush out the door and not deal with their own, or their child's, feelings about this major change in their lives.

All parents will benefit from your support and understanding during what may be for them a difficult time—even if they treat it casually. You set the tone by being calm and friendly, welcoming parent and child alike. You

will briefly want to suggest what the parent is expected to do, "You may hang your coat here and get a cup of coffee if you like. Here's a grown-up chair if you would like to sit where you can see what the children are doing. Then Nichole will know just where to find you."

Then turn your attention toward helping the child be comfortable. As we said in Unit 4: call the child by name, walk to the child's cubby together, show her or him where the bathroom is and explain any procedures for using it. Perhaps arrange for another child or adult who is fluent in the new child's language to act as a guide, and serve a snack or lunch with foods common to the child's culture or personal preferences.

During those first few hours especially (*depending upon the child's age, personality, and previous group experience*), the child may have more or less difficulty getting used to the new people and surroundings. Watch carefully and take any steps necessary to make the child, and the parent, increasingly feel a part of your program. You may want to talk informally with the parent about signs you see that the child is beginning to feel a part of the group. Or you may suggest that the parent feel free to read a story to the children who are gathering with her in the book corner.

Parents of very young children, or of those who are enrolled in a group for the first time, may want to stay one full day, and then gradually decrease the number of hours over the next week or two.

Some parents do not have the luxury of that much time and some children do not need to return to their "home base" as often as others. Talk with the family about the best arrangements for everyone involved. Saying goodbye is not easy, but it is not in the best interest of child or family to prolong it unnecessarily, either.

If a parent must leave a clinging child in tears, be sure to take a minute later in the day to call the parent and offer reassurance that the child is indeed feeling more comfortable in the group. (*And let the parent know that it is OK for her or him to call.*) Then at the end of the day, again describe how well the child settled into the day.

How can you improve your ability to help parents and children say goodbye to each other?

_____

_____

_____

_____

Ask the parents in your program how they felt about their first days and whether they have some suggestions for making enrollment work better.

_____

_____

_____

_____

PART 2

How do you work together each day?

Every day is a golden opportunity for you to learn more about the children and their families.

- Your enthusiastic greeting in the child's home language . . . makes everyone feel welcome.

- Your insistence that children and parents say goodbye when they separate . . . builds trust within the family.

- Your sharing about events in the child's day . . . provides continuity between home and program.

- The program's respect for parents' concerns and ideas . . . enables them to feel valued as people and reaffirms their child care choice.

- Your willingness to have families visit at any time . . . reassures them that their children are being well cared for.

- The staff's encouragement for parents to be involved in your program . . . builds support for your partnership on behalf of children.

- Your model of how to treat children . . . provides an example that most families will begin to follow.

And most of all—

- The spirit of working together when planning all that happens in your program . . . creates an atmosphere of joint responsibility for the child.

All these close contacts happen for the most part in just the few short minutes each day that you have with families. So let's look at how to use that valuable time to build solid, productive relationships with families.

Be partners with parents each day

- Greet families enthusiastically

- Share events in the child's day

- Respect parents' concerns and ideas

- Welcome parents as visitors

- Encourage parent involvement

- Exchange appropriate child rearing techniques

- Clarify legal responsibilities

You and parents share important information

Each day, you and the parents will need to exchange information about important events that occurred since you saw each other last. Take just a few seconds when the child arrives and again when the parent returns to fill each other in on what is happening with the child. Most providers prefer to do this in casual conversation with parents.

"Good morning, Marie. How are things with Elyse today?" Gwen asks.

"Elyse didn't sleep very well last night. She seemed especially hungry this morning. Maybe she is in a growth spurt."

"That could be. She's growing up so fast. We'll see how she does with food and naps today and let you know when you pick her up."

Daily Infant Record

Child_____ Day_____

Bottles at_____ am _____ pm_____

Solid food_____

Naps at_____ am _____ pm_____

Bowel movements_____

Supplies needed_____

Interesting things that happened_____

_____

_____

Parents of infants need to know how much and when their child ate, how many bowel movements she or he had that day, and when the child took naps. You might want to use a chart like the one on page 369 to keep track of this information and then tuck it in the child's bag when it is almost time to go home. Translate the chart into all the languages spoken by families in your program.

Most information about toddlers and pre-school children can be shared as you talk with parents. It usually takes just a few well-spent seconds of your day.

A mother arrives one morning brimming with pride. "Oh, Diane, Ayuko is so proud of the finger painting she did yesterday. We hung it up near the stairway at home so all of us can enjoy it."

"She had the best time making it, too," confirms Diane. "She just couldn't wait for it to dry so she could put it in her cubby to take home. She must be thrilled to see it hanging in a place where you all can see it."

If you work in a large program with many staff members, written notes between each other may be essential. If staff change between arrival and pick-up time, work out a system that is easy to use and yet allows everyone to feel well informed about the children. The system should work for both parents and staff.

If parents don't have the time to spend in even a few moments of casual conversation, you might want to arrange a time when you can call them to talk a bit or e-mail them about how their child's day has been. Or if parents are nearly always in a hurry, jot down a quick note about the day's events and pin it to the child's backpack. You can find a way to share information, even if it is only briefly.

Sometimes, in addition to individual information about health, projects, and learning experiences, you want to share general information with all parents. Perhaps you are planning a field trip, or a child has just gotten chicken pox, or a parent cooked a family recipe with a group in the program and it made a big hit.

Written forms are best for this kind of information, just to be sure everyone has been given all the details. You can use brief memos, letters, or even newsletters, depending upon the resources and staff available to help get them ready. **Always, always**, use the primary language of the parents for all written communications.

Be sure to keep a copy of all your notices to parents—many of them can be used when the situation arises again.

What ways do you use to communicate with parents?

_____

_____

_____

_____

_____

How can you increase everyday communication?

_____

_____

_____

_____

Ask your Field Advisor for other suggestions.

Find out where to obtain resources, materials and translation services for families whose home language is not English. Provide the agency's name and contact information in your Professional Resource File.

You discuss major issues openly and negotiate differences

Each family is different from every other. Some are outgoing and talkative while others are quiet and reserved. Some like lots of space while others thrive on intimacy. Some are compulsively neat while others are more casual about maintaining order. Some value cooperation while others build a strong sense of individual responsibility. Some extend their roots to friends and relatives while others may be just one parent and child.

Culture, income level, aspirations, and religious beliefs all play a part in determining how parents raise their children. Because families are so different you will want to make sure—right from the beginning—that your program is a good match for the parents and children. And for as long as the child is enrolled, you want to continue to keep the dialogue open, so that the good match can be maintained.

New issues arise as children grow and changes will probably need to continue as you work with parents to reach agreeable solutions on issues, such as:

- how and when to respond to a baby's cries,
- how to introduce new foods/utensils,
- ways to support the child's growing independence,
- the best method for toilet learning,
- appropriate discipline and guidance,
- dealing with separation anxiety,
- why children need to spend a lot of time playing,
- how to prepare a child for kindergarten, and
- the role of child's first language in her or his development.

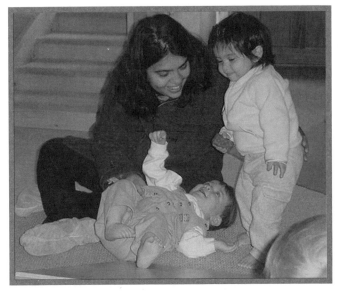

Each family is different from every other. Culture, income level, aspirations, and religious beliefs all play a part in determining how parents raise their children.

Parents' values and feelings should always be discussed openly and treated with respect, even when you disagree. Your listening skills are very helpful in working out a solution. You may need to set aside a special conference time if an issue seems to hold the potential for disagreement.

Many times you can adapt what you do to include parents' preferences in your program so that families feel more comfortable.

I can see how a long afternoon nap for Rachel means she doesn't want to go to bed at night. But she also seems too cranky at the center when she doesn't get her nap. If she stays up late, that takes away from the little time you and your husband have together each evening. Instead of letting her sleep for two hours, perhaps we could awaken her after an hour so she will be more ready to sleep at bedtime. Would you like to try this for a week or so and see whether she gets enough sleep that way?"

When parents learn more about how children develop and learn, they may be willing to be more flexible in their ideas, too. For instance, sometimes parents do not know that children will learn English better if they are firmly rooted in their first language. You may have to help them understand that children who speak their first language *and* English will have a real sense of competence. And by reinforcing their language and culture, their child builds pride and positive self-concept.

You can provide reading material designed for parents (*you already have collected some in your PRF*). Brochures and pamphlets are available from NAEYC, NBCDI, NAFCC, and other groups, as well as from libraries and pediatrician offices. The Public Health Service too has brochures on many child development topics. Start to collect some whenever you see them. They'll come in handy as you encounter issues with different families. One especially good and timely brochure based on a topic we've talked about so much in *Essentials* is "Teaching Young Children to Resist Bias: What Parents Can Do" (*NAEYC*). You should find it helpful in convincing parents about more effective ways to prepare their children for successful living.

Your approach should be to negotiate with parents when areas of disagreement arise. **Listen** to their views and share your own. Try to reach an agreement that you both can live with.

Sometimes you will have to make a hard professional decision, however, about what is in the child's best interests. Sometimes parents will ask you to do something that makes you uncomfortable:

"Why do you spend so much money on juice? Jeremy just loves Kool-Aid at home."

They may even ask the impossible:
"I have to work until 10:00 tonight. Could you take Kristi home with you?"

Or the unethical:
"Just spank him if he doesn't listen. Then when he gets home we'll get out the belt to make sure he has learned his lesson."

When situations like these happen, you must always make your decision based on what is best for the child. How would you respond to these dilemmas?

Junk food

_____

_____

_____

A parent's last-minute overtime

_____

_____

_____

Spanking

_____

_____

_____

Most likely, you phrased your position in ways that didn't put down the parents. Here are some responses to think about:

"The children do love sugary drinks, don't they? But we prefer to buy the most nutrition for the money. Juice is so much healthier for the children."

"I'm really sorry but I have my own family to take care of in the evening. Here is a list of emergency caregivers who might be able to help you out. Please give us a call so we will know who is picking her up."

"I'm afraid we could never do that. Licensing standards prohibit spanking. If you remember in our program policies, our philosophy is never to hit children and never to let them hit anyone else. Instead, we use words to figure out how to solve problems. We have found that children learn to control their own behavior much better with this type of discipline. Would you like to meet to discuss discipline ideas?"

When you are respectful, understanding, honest, fair, and ethical, you can work **together** with parents to resolve problems and disagreements in a manner that benefits everyone.

At times, it will be necessary to negotiate differences over goals for children's development or childrearing practices. For example, a parent's cultural value may be for children to learn to use the toilet by 12 months of age while you believe that children should begin toilet learning when they are older and able to be more responsible themselves. This difference of opinion could cause real friction with the family.

In such cases, negotiation is required. There are four steps to a successful negotiation process. First, clarify your own preferences; know where your belief comes from. Is it based on how you were parented or can it be defended on the basis of research? Then communicate openly and clearly with the parent what your preferences are and why you feel the way you do. Listen carefully to the parent's concerns. The third step is to negotiate, to find some common ground about which you can agree. In this case, you agree on the ultimate goal: you both want the child to eventually learn to use the toilet. But explain that you are responsible for a large group and cannot take this one child to the toilet as often as a parent could. Hear the parent's concern: she wants her child dry. The final step in a successful negotiation is that both parties need to be willing to learn and change. As a result of this respectful communication, you no longer judge the parent as having inappropriate expectations or being ignorant. The parent understands your thinking and ceases to press you about potty training at school.

We will talk more about the ethics of providing high quality care and negotiating differences in the Seminar.

Negotiation Process:

STEP 1: Clarify preferences

STEP 2: Communicate

STEP 3: Negotiate

STEP 4: Learn and change

What issues have come up where you and parents disagree? What techniques have you used to resolve them in a harmonious way?

_____

_____

_____

_____

_____

_____

Talk with your CDA Advisor about what you have done. She will help you prepare for the discussion in your CDA Seminar.

You encourage impromptu visits

Parents should always be welcome in your program. There should be no exceptions. If you provide appropriate learning experiences, you have nothing to hide. Don't leave yourself open to criticism or accusations—keep your door open to parents. If parents don't seem eager to visit, encourage them to do so, even if they can only stay a few extra minutes at one end of the day or the other. Or videotape what happens in the program and share the video with parents.

You find meaningful ways to involve families

What do we mean by parent involvement? Parents already lead busy lives. Involving them in meaningful ways takes careful thought. Keep your expectations reasonable and gently urge parents gradually to become more involved as they feel comfortable and see how much it means to them and to their children to be an **active partner** in their child's education.

Programs such as Head Start and co-ops started a trend long ago of parent involvement. In these programs, parents are decision mak-

Involve parents in your program

Time in the program

- Read books with a small group
- Cook a family recipe together
- Accompany the group and /or drive on a field trip (perhaps to the parent's work or neighborhood)
- Sing with the children
- Teach children a dance or art technique
- Write down children's experience stories
- Eat lunch with the children
- Breast-feed their infant during lunch break
- Talk with children
- Assist with screening children for possible disabilities
- Help out with filing, typing, or other business duties
- Answer telephones
- Contribute to curriculum planning meetings

Time at home or after work

- Mix new supplies of clay dough
- Make minor repairs to equipment
- Build toy shelves
- Write down a favorite recipe or words to a song
- Locate music, clothing, everyday objects, or a work of art from their own culture
- Save "beautiful junk" such as toilet paper and paper towel rolls, plastic bags, (for dirty clothes), meat trays, egg cartons, packing chips
- Read books children bring home with them
- Hang up children's artwork
- Talk with children about their day
- Help prepare for a special event (harvest feast, school picnic)
- Write/edit a program newsletter
- Assist with fund-raising activities
- Serve on parent policy/advisory board

ers, staff, and volunteers. These parents—who first get involved in education through early childhood programs—stay involved with their child's school throughout their children's elementary and later years as well. Your efforts to involve parents will pay off far beyond today and tomorrow!

In order to encourage parents to become involved, you must make them feel a real part of what happens with their child. Each parent can make a different contribution. Some may have time to spend with the children during the day. Others can help out by doing things in the evening or on weekends. Some will be eager to serve on policy boards or the board of directors for the program, making policy, financial, and other major decisions about the program. Parents can be involved at the center, in your home, or at their own homes!

Some families will feel honored to be asked to participate, while others will feel intimidated at first. Some are willing to contribute time and skills, some have materials to donate, and some can give financial gifts to benefit the program.

Whatever parents do, their efforts will add to the continuity between home and program. Only then will children feel as if they truly belong in both their homes and your care.

Your role is to match each parent with a comfortable type and level of involvement in your early childhood program. On page 375 are some ideas about things parents can do. Other early childhood educators have used these techniques to encourage families to share their cultural experiences and talents with all of the children. **Add your own ideas to this list.**

Parents often have great ideas about how to improve the program, but they may prefer to be asked first. You need to make sure that parents always feel free to make suggestions, attend staff planning meetings, or raise questions about what you do with children all day.

Perhaps a parent notices frequent traffic jams on the playground and has in mind a few simple changes to eliminate it. Other parents may have suggestions for menus that are more nutritious or offer greater variety.

Parents can help shape the curriculum in many ways. Children often ask parents questions—and some of those questions could lead to new curriculum areas to explore. Encourage parents to share with you interests their children have expressed.

Perhaps a parent has a special skill (*such as speaking a foreign language, carpentry, sewing, art*) or knows a lot about a subject of interest to young children (*insects, gardening, how shoes or other familiar products are made*). With these parents, plan several activities and experiences for children to introduce and build upon the parent's involvement.

Parents often see new angles on how to arrange play areas, know about interesting places to visit on field trips, or see minor problems that you may have overlooked because you've grown so familiar with the program. When parents participate in board meetings or in staff meetings on a regular basis, they will feel more comfortable in offering ideas and solutions. Stay alert to hearing about ways to improve your program for children and parents.

You and the parents of the children in your care are truly partners in your efforts to raise happy, healthy, well-adjusted children. When you work together to share ideas and work through problems, you, the parents, and the children will all benefit.

How do you enlist parent participation in your program?

_____

_____

_____

_____

Looking at the list of things parents and other family members can do in the program, what could you do to involve them more fully?

_____

_____

_____

_____

You will exchange ideas about parent involvement with others in your CDA seminar.

You strengthen parenting skills

Teachers and parents change with experience. We all start out as rookies. At first, most of us are baffled and a little overwhelmed by the responsibility and time and work involved.

Once we begin to see how successful our efforts have been—the child seems healthy and happy—our confidence is bolstered. As a professional, you have the advantage of your experience and CDA Professional Preparation Program. But new parents usually don't have any training, and especially in the beginning, mothers and fathers alike are looking for ideas about how to parent.

You play a key, but often very subtle, role in shaping parenting skills. You set an example for parents to pick up. How you treat children every day can slowly but surely begin to make a difference in how parents treat their children.

You listen and observe how parents act with their children. Some parents apply all the principles professionals know. Others may not be aware of the long-term consequences of their actions. So, when the parent seems

You and the parents of the children in your care are truly partners in your efforts to raise happy, healthy, well-adjusted children.

to be open to a different way, you can offer a new or different idea in a non-threatening, uncritical way. For example, if a parent is having a difficult time with discipline, you might purposefully demonstrate a positive technique with another child while that parent is present.

You support their positive efforts to be good parents in both indirect and direct ways:

"One of these days soon we would love to have you stay with us for a few minutes to watch Amy. Ever since she started to wear play clothes she has been trying so many new things—she paints with a smock, builds with the blocks, and seems to have such a marvelous time on the playground. She is learning to control her muscles so well now that she is more comfortable."

"Lauren, don't forget to say '¡Adios!' to Dad. He will be busy at work all day, and I bet a good hug will make his day a lot better."

"What a thoughtful idea to put those notes in Kirk's lunch box. He looks forward to lunch every day. He usually talks about his wonderful family while he eats."

A resource shelf can contain parenting books, brochures, and videos on topics of great interest. Encourage parents to take materials home. You are always happy to discuss any questions and listen to parents' concerns. Put those listening skills into practice every day— you never know what might be troubling parents or children.

You can also help parents improve their own skills by building ties with other parents. Connecting families can be fostered if you provide a space for parents to chat together when they arrive or leave. A parent lounge area, if possible, is a nice idea. If space is limited, you might set up a message board so parents can share ideas and build networks with other families. This is the place to post a thought-provoking newspaper or magazine article. Tack up a brochure or notice about a community service or event and see what happens.

Encourage parents to put up business cards or service notices so they can share their skills with each other. Promote self-sufficiency and bolster confidence!

Your example of positive, appropriate ways to treat children may be the most long-lasting effect of your work as a CDA. Make every minute count.

Go to your local library and look through the parent books and videos that are available or search the Internet. List several titles that would be of special interest to parents in your group.

_____

_____

_____

_____

Set up a parent message board if you do not already have one. Where is the most visible place? What are some good ideas to get it started? How will you encourage parents to contribute?

_____

_____

_____

_____

How can you encourage parents to make use of the resources in your program and community?

_____

_____

_____

_____

Discuss everything you are doing to make sure parents play a more active role in your program with your CDA Field Advisor.

Exchange information with parents during:

- conferences
- meetings
- home visits
- telephone calls, e-mails
- screening
- arrival and departure times

PART 3

How do you effectively exchange information?

In addition to daily contact, you also need to set aside some time when you and the parents can talk a little more about their children and parenting in general—or any other topic of special interest to the parent such as job interviews, nutrition, moving, or home budgets.

Parent conferences, parent meetings, home visits, e-mails, and even telephone calls give you and the parents an opportunity to focus on the children or family needs.

Good early childhood programs can also offer another important service to families by helping to identify any possible disabilities. In most cases, the sooner any problems are found and something is done about them, the more likely they are to be resolved. When disabilities are discovered early, children can lead more productive lives. Parents should always be involved in any developmental screening.

In all of these more formal contacts, as well as those that are informal, you keep any information you learn about the family in strict confidence (*except suspected child abuse*). You are a professional and must not allow yourself to make private information a public matter.

You hold parent conferences

Most parent conferences provide regular checkpoints for you (*and any other staff involved*) and the parents to share information and plan for their children. Conferences should be held whenever they seem like a good idea—at least twice a year—and preferably more often for infants and toddlers because they change so quickly. Occasionally, you will need to schedule a special conference to discuss a problem. But don't let your first communication with families be about a problem. Establish a relationship of mutual trust through daily communication about everyday, small things. Then when problems arise, as they inevitably do, they will be more easily resolved because you and the parents already have a relationship to build on.

Make arrangements

You demonstrate respect for parents when you schedule conferences at their convenience. Many parents cannot take off work except in an emergency. Evenings and weekends may be the best times. If transportation or childcare are problems, make your plans accordingly.

Be sure your time will not be interrupted and the setting will be comfortable. Create a warm, informal setting where you can be alone without distractions.

If you use a classroom for conferences and have to sit on child-sized chairs, make sure ALL of you sit on child-sized chairs so you don't tower above the parents. Better yet, sit around a table. Sitting behind a desk or in an office will not create a friendly atmosphere of working together.

Include parents with custody as well as the non-custodial parent whenever possible (*two conferences may be necessary*). Perhaps an interpreter will be needed if you do not speak a common language. Careful planning is essential for an effective conference!

Set up a mutually agreeable time and place for all participants, then follow up with a note to remind the parents. You might also suggest some things they could be thinking about that they might want to discuss with you.

Prepare a written agenda for yourself in advance. Use your daily diary to pull out your major points and questions for discussion. Look for lots of examples of the child's social, emotional, cognitive, and physical development.

Prepare in advance to start the conference off with a positive statement about the child's accomplishments. Parents often feel that they are being judged by their child's behavior and will be anxious. Be prepared to set them at ease from the start. You could provide a pot of coffee so parents can serve themselves. Perhaps the children could fix a snack for their parents.

Generate discussions

Just as with all other interactions with parents and children, you will listen **at least** as much as you will talk. All of you want to get to know each other better so you can continue to keep the child's best interests in mind. A cheerful, positive atmosphere will help parents feel more comfortable, too.

You will probably start with a few friendly comments to make the family feel welcome.

Be sure to indicate that the parents should feel free to ask questions at any time. Then move into a brief, upbeat discussion of some positive examples of the child's experiences.

A conference is a time to look both back and forward. Together with the parents you see just how much progress the child has made. Save artwork and writing samples—it's an excellent way to demonstrate the child's progress. Point out changes that show the parents just how much their child is growing. Ask parents which changes they have noticed at home. Share your insights about the child.

If the child has any type of problem, indicate what behaviors have led to your concern. Again, ask whether parents have observed similar difficulties at home and how they handle them there. Together, work out a plan to help the child, or discuss setting up a screening or counseling session, depending on the nature of the difficulty.

Avoid using labels (aggressive, destructive, learning disabled, slow, or hyperactive, for example) but instead concentrate on concrete examples of the child's behavior.

If things are going well for the child, talk about ideas each of you have for the future: activities, trips, enrollment in elementary school. Making these plans together will reaffirm your joint efforts with the family.

Always close on a positive, friendly note. Say how pleased you are to work with the family to provide good experiences for the child. Thank the parents for coming and bid them goodbye.

Developing skills in conducting parent conferences takes lots of experience. Start by observing during one. Ask permission to do so. Your CDA Advisor will help arrange it if you need assistance. When you observe, listen and watch. Fill in this information:

What did the teacher do to help the parent relax?

_____

_____

_____

_____

What positive examples of the child's behavior were reported?

_____

_____

_____

_____

What questions did the teacher ask the parent?

_____

_____

_____

_____

What information did the parent share?

_____

_____

_____

_____

What examples of children's work were shared?

_____

_____

_____

_____

What plans were agreed upon for the future?

_____

_____

_____

_____

You will discuss this experience during your CDA Seminar.

You hold parent meetings

Many larger programs have regular or special parent meetings. These can serve a variety of purposes: to share information, to build parenting skills, to do specific activities together.

A number of parents have had unpleasant experiences with schools and may be reluctant to join in these groups. Some have com-plications with time, language, travel arrangements, or childcare.

Use your own judgment about whether meetings will be successful with the parents of children in your group. If you think they will be well accepted, ask parents to suggest topics or speakers. These are some ideas that have worked well in other programs. Add to this list any topics you might like to consider for parent meetings:

- discipline
- bedtime
- allergies
- meal planning/nutrition
- gift ideas for children
- children's books
- early literacy skills
- sick child care
- getting ready for kindergarten
- TV and movies
- holidays
- budgeting
- family recreation activities
- baby sitters
- home play activities

_____

_____

_____

_____

Plan your group meetings in much the same way you do the individual conferences to increase your chances for good participation. You may need to locate a community room in a library or church to accommodate the size of your group. Your classroom or living room may simply not be big enough! Adult furniture is almost a must if you expect to sit longer than 15 minutes or so.

Arrange for healthy refreshments, get any keys needed to get in or lock up, and make sure you know where to turn on the lights and how to close the building for the evening. You may need to make child care arrangements for a wide age range of children, including your own. Be sure you determine in advance how this person will be paid. Arrange for someone to answer the phone so you won't be interrupted.

Parents who speak English as a second language or who do not speak English need interpretation. Participating in a large group setting is difficult for many adults; it becomes doubly difficult if you don't fully understand what's going on. If need be, arrange for an interpreter, either to sit next to one or two parents, or to interpret collectively for a group of parents. Headphones are used in some meetings to not lose time stopping for the translations. Parents may have other strategies.

Give lots of enthusiastic publicity at least a week ahead of time and talk with parents about the event as well. Make sure parents have a clear set of directions to the meeting site and know what time the meeting will start.

During the meeting, make parents feel welcome and keep them involved in the action. Any speakers or videos should take just a few minutes, leaving lots of time for discussion and questions. People of all ages learn best when they are part of the action. A lively meeting will lead to more lively meetings!

Someone is sure to suggest that a parent meeting include some entertainment by the children. Rather than a live performance, which is difficult at best, a more useful and manageable strategy is to display documentation of children's learning and projects they have completed. Show a videotape or slides of children at work and play. Eat snacks the children have prepared.

If you feel a group meeting with parents would be of interest to the families in your program, work with your CDA Field Advisor, director, assistant, other staff, or parents to plan what you will do. If at all possible, ask to conduct a meeting yourself. Jot down your ideas here.

Topic/speaker _____

_____

_____

_____

Time and place _____

_____

_____

_____

_____

Meeting plan

What could be improved another time?

After you have conducted the meeting, write what happened here. What was successful?

Discuss your experience with your CDA Field Advisor and/or program director.

You make home visits

Since the very beginning of early childhood education, home visits have been a part of many programs—either where the teacher spends an hour or so just visiting a child and

Think about your conference with parents as time to discuss with not talk to or talk at.

Home Visits

Select two families in your group who might be receptive to home visits. Ask if you could arrange a visit soon. Write your plans here and carry them out. Then write a brief summary of what happened and discuss it with your Field Advisor.

Family _____

Plan _____

What happened _____

Family _____

Plan _____

What happened _____

family at home, or where the teacher conducts a formal parent conference at the child's home.

Today some parents and teachers are reluctant to have home visits. These visits may seem like an invasion of privacy or an intrusion on the family. Others still welcome them as a way to further cement the continuity between program and school. Think very carefully about whether a home visit would be

appropriate for the parents in your program. If not, you could meet parents on "neutral ground" like in a coffee shop.

Often, the children benefit the most from such a visit. They are nearly always delighted to show their teacher where they sleep, to introduce their grandmother, or to share some other favorite part of their home.

If you decide to make home visits, arrange them well in advance and make it clear what your agenda is: You want to spend a few minutes getting to know the parent and child in their own comfortable surroundings, away from the busy program. Reassure parents that no special arrangements are needed except for them and the child to be there.

Think of all the ways in which you can help parents feel comfortable with this visit: your professional but casual manner, how you dress, where you sit, how long you stay, how you will handle any language or custom differences. Try to adapt to the family's individual style so that all of you will feel comfortable.

You use the telephone and e-mail

The telephone and/or e-mail are marvelous ways to deal quickly with questions or minor concerns. Use them often. On the other hand, respect parents' time at work—if receiving phone calls or e-mail is a problem, leave a message and ask the parent to return the call during a break.

---

5 Cs of parent relations

COMMON SENSE

CONSISTENCY

COMMUNICATION

CARING

CONFIDENTIALITY

Note: From Opening you door to children: How to start a family day care program (p.15) by K. Modigliani, M. Reiff, and S. Jones, 1987, Washington, DC: National Association for the Education of Young Children. Copyright ©1987 authors. Reprinted by permission.

Similarly, encourage parents to call you if they would like to discuss something that will take a few minutes. Let them know when good times are for calls (*naptime, for example*).

If you are a family childcare provider or work in a small program, an answering machine can be a real asset. Whenever you need time to devote to the children, just turn on the machine. Of course, you will want to check for messages often and return calls promptly so parents don't feel they have lost touch with you and their children.

What do you do when you encounter difficulties?

Whenever people work together as closely as you and parents do, and whenever the issue involved is someone as dear as a child, there are bound to be times when there is conflict. Rather than wait for an argument to erupt, or an issue to get blown out of proportion, prepare yourself now so you will be ready to use a positive approach to deal with the problem.

We have seen how putting program policies in writing can help head off disagreements about fees, illness, and even teaching methods. You also know the steps involved for reporting suspected child abuse, whether it is physical or emotional. And you are prepared to communicate with parents in their preferred language, either by learning it yourself or using an interpreter.

Of course, sometimes family difficulties go beyond the issue of childcare. In Unit 4, we discussed helping families deal with life's stressful events. Your support of families is especially critical during difficult times, so you want to constantly polish your skills so you can put them into practice at a moment's notice.

Each family has its own style of living and strategies for coping with difficulties it must face. Some families have tremendous resources and seem to be able to solve any problem that comes their way. Other families have few resources and from time to time may need or rely on you or your program administrators for help.

Try to understand each family's circumstances. Financial problems can cause a great deal of stress. Perhaps the parents had a difficult childhood. Racism may affect their lives. Is the family's home language one that is rarely spoken in your community? Are the parents under pressure at work? Do other children in the family require most of the family's emotional or physical resources? Most often, many different factors have led to the family's current state.

When the difficulties are minor, you can use your listening skills and resources to help the parents make progress. However, a great deal of specialized training is needed to help families directly deal with major difficulties. In those cases, consult with your director or other trusted professional about recommending a specialist—a family therapist, financial planner, or other community resource. Then the family can begin to solve the problem with your support as the childcare provider.

You can help families move in directions that will enable them to have more productive lives. Think about any families that you believe might benefit from professional assistance. Consult with your Advisor about how to find two or three appropriate referrals. Ask your Advisor for guidance on how you can present your recommendations to the families in tactful, respectful ways.

You recognize parents' mixed emotions about child care

Professional childcare is a relatively new idea in our country. The American ideal used to be (*and is still for some*) that the mother stayed home to raise the children. For most families, this is no longer an option, and for many it never was.

Even so, most parents are never sure they have made the right decision. Some "experts" have the opinion that childcare, especially for infants, is harmful to children.

Grandparents may also be critical about "baby sitters" raising the next generation. Parents may worry about giving their children "quality" time. They may feel guilty that they are doing all they can for their children.

You need to be aware of these mixed feelings. Some parents will have them more than others. Generally, if the parents are happy in their work, school or training program, and are confident they have chosen high quality childcare for their children, they are content with their decisions.

Families who are less happy with their work or who don't really like their child care arrangements usually worry the most about whether they have done the right thing for their children.

First of all, you need to be aware that high quality programs for young children are not harmful and indeed, as you might expect, do promote children's healthy development. So when you do a professional job, you—and children's parents—can rest assured that children will thrive in your care.

Children can and should have emotional attachments to both their family members and their teachers/caregivers. In fact, when they do, they are more likely to be successful learners and become healthy, productive adults.

With your understanding and patience, parents will eventually begin to see just how much high quality child care supports their entire family. You supplement, not replace, the family's childrearing responsibilities. Together, you want the best for young children.

How do you help families accept that they have made a good decision about the care of their child?

_____

_____

_____

_____

_____

_____

You acknowledge competitive feelings about the child

Sometimes parents worry that their child will love the caregiver best. They may feel threatened when their children don't want to go home at night or when the teacher hugs and kisses their child each morning. It may be a shock when a child calls Mother by the teacher's name, or vice versa.

Infants usually become attached to their parents, and especially their mother or the other most important person in their lives, very early in their lives. They know that Mom and Dad are special.

Occasionally, this early attachment does not happen, even if the mother is the primary caregiver. In these rare instances, someone skilled in working with infant/parent relationships is needed to help the family develop more emotional closeness.

Ties between children and parents in most families are very strong, however. As a professional, your role is to build upon these ties with both your actions and your attitudes. Ideas about how to do this have been woven throughout this entire book.

For example, you build a warm personal relationship with each child, support children's development within their own cultural context and encourage bilingual children to express themselves in the language of their choice. You encourage parent involvement and readily share children's successes.

You may have other ways to help parents feel you are a partner, not a competitor. List what you do to help parents know that your role as a teacher is different, but complementary to, their role as parents.

_____

_____

_____

_____

_____

PART 5

What are parents' opinions about your work?

By the time you have all these kinds of contact with parents, they should know you well and you should know them well. Their opinions about your work with their children are valuable in helping you know how effective you are.

During your final evaluation for the CDA Credential, you will survey parents using the Council's CDA Parent Questionnaire. This questionnaire provides parents an opportunity to express their views of your competence. The information that parents provide is used by the Council to determine whether you have acquired the skills necessary to become a CDA.

We recommend that you use the Parent Questionnaire at this point in your studies to get a picture of what parents think about your work. You can use the information to help identify your strengths and weaknesses and to help you improve your practice with children and families.

Your CDA Field Advisor will assist you with distributing and collecting the questionnaires, and will discuss the results with you during a conference.

Look at the items on the sample questionnaire that follows. What do you think parents will say about your contact with them and their children? Do you think every parent can answer "YES" to every question? What areas will you need to improve before your final evaluation as a CDA?

_____

_____

_____

_____

_____

CDA Parent Questionnaire

Cuestionario CDA de Opinion de Padres

CDA Candidate's Name _____

Nombre del Candidato/a CDA _____

<table>
<tr>
<td>

For each statement, circle the answer
you think is best.

YES = CDA Candidate does this

NO = CDA Candidate does not do this

N/A = Do not know or does not apply

</td>
<td>

Haga un círculo alrededor de cada respuesta que
usted considere como la más correcta.

SI = **La Candidata CDA lo hace**

NO = **La Candidata no hace esto**

N/A = **Ud. no sabe o no es pertinente**

</td>
</tr>
</table>

The CDA Candidate
El Candidato CDA:

YES NO N/A 1. Reports accidents or any first aid given to my child.
SI NO N/A 1. Reporta accidentes o primeros auxilios dados a mi niño.

YES NO N/A 2. Requires my written permission to give any medication to my child.
SI NO N/A 2. Requiere mi autorización por escrito para poder dar cualquier medicina a mi niño.

YES NO N/A 3. Tells me about my child's eating, sleeping, and toileting/diapering.
SI NO N/A 3. Me dice como mi niño come, si duerme, sobre sus hábitos en el uso del baño, o cambio de pañales.

YES NO N/A 4. Follows feeding instructions for my infant or for my child with allergies.
SI NO N/A 4. Sigue instrucciones para la alimentación de mi bebé o la de mi niño que sufre de alergias.

YES NO N/A 5. Allows my child to be picked up only by people I have named.
SI NO N/A 5. Permite que a mi niño lo recojan sólo aquellas personas a quienes yo he autorizado.

YES NO N/A 6. Reports to me about my child's development and learning.
SI NO N/A 6. Me mantiene informado/a sobre el desarrollo y el aprendizaje de mi niño.

YES   NO   N/A   7.   Organizes toys and play materials so my child can reach them easily.

SI   NO   N/A   7.   Organiza los juguetes y materiales de juego de manera que mi niño pueda alcanzarlos facilmente.

YES   NO   N/A   8.   Provides a place for my child to store his or her own things and makes sure I can find the things I need to bring home.

SI   NO   N/A   8.   Provee un lugar para que mi niño pueda guardar sus pertenencias y se asegura de que yo pueda encontrar todas las cosas que necesito llevar a casa.

YES   NO   N/A   9.   Has enough toys and materials so children do not fight over popular toys.

SI   NO   N/A   9.   Tiene juguetes y materiales en número suficiente para evitar que los niños peleen por los juguetes más populares.

YES   NO   N/A   10.   Takes my child outdoors to play every day, except in bad weather.

SI   NO   N/A   10.   Lleva a mi niño a jugar afuera todos los días excepto cuando el tiempo esta muy malo.

YES   NO   N/A   11.   Talks with my child frequently.

SI   NO   N/A   11.   Habla frecuentemente con mi niño.

YES   NO   N/A   12.   Listens with interest when my child talks and encourages my child to talk.

SI   NO   N/A   12.   Escucha con interés cuando mi niño habla y lo anima a hablar.

YES   NO   N/A   13.   Helps my child learn to control his or her own behavior without spanking or other harsh punishment.

SI   NO   N/A   13.   Ayuda a mi niño a controlar su propio comportamiento, sin pegarle o sin usar castigos duros.

YES   NO   N/A   14.   Reads to my child often.

SI   NO   N/A   14.   Le lee a mi niño, con mucha frecuencia.

YES   NO   N/A   15.   Provides many music, art, block and pretend activities that my child can do in his or her own way.

SI   NO   N/A   15.   Provee muchas actividades de música, arte, bloques, actividades de pretender, que mi niño puede hacer a su manera.

YES   NO   N/A   16.   Helps my child feel proud of what he or she can do.
SI   *NO*   *N/A*   16.   *Ayuda a mi niño a sentirse orgulloso de lo que él puede hacer.*

YES   NO   N/A   17.   Encourages children to enjoy getting along with each other.
SI   *NO*   *N/A*   17.   *Anima a los niños el disfrute de llevarse bien entre ellos.*

YES   NO   N/A   18.   Gives me the feeling that she is truly interested in my child and me.
SI   *NO*   *N/A*   18.   *Me hace sentir que ella/él está verdaderamente interesada/o en mi niño y en mí.*

YES   NO   N/A   19.   Is pleasant and friendly with me.
SI   *NO*   *N/A*   19.   *Es agradable y amistosa/o conmigo.*

YES   NO   N/A   20.   Is available to discuss my concerns.
SI   *NO*   *N/A*   20.   *Esta disponible para hablar conmigo sobre mis preocupaciones.*

YES   NO   N/A   21.   Asks me for ideas to use with my child, including activity ideas.
SI   *NO*   *N/A*   21.   *Me pide ideas para usarlas con mi niño, incluyendo ideas sobre actividades.*

YES   NO   N/A   22.   Asks me what I think is important in raising my child.
SI   *NO*   *N/A*   22.   *Me pregunta sobre lo que yo pienso que es importante en la crianza de mi niño.*

YES   NO   N/A   23.   Talks with me about any fears or problems my child has.
SI   *NO*   *N/A*   23.   *Me habla sobre cualquier temor o problema que tenga mi niño.*

YES   NO   N/A   24.   Maintains confidentiality; does not freely discuss my child or family in the presence of others.
SI   *NO*   *N/A*   24.   *Es reservada/o, mantiene información confidencial; no habla sobre mi niño o mi familia en la presencia de otras personas.*

YES   NO   N/A   25.   Encourages me to visit at any time.
SI   *NO*   *N/A*   25.   *Me anima a visitar en cualquier momento.*

YES   NO   N/A   26.   Lets me know of parent meetings and other ways I can become involved in the program.

SI   *NO*   *N/A*   26.   *Me hace saber cuando hay reuniones de Padres y me informa sobre otras maneras de participar en el programa.*

YES   NO   N/A   27.   Schedules conferences at times that are convenient to me.

SI   *NO*   *N/A*   27.   *Señala fechas para reunirnos, en días y horas que me son convenientes.*

Indicate language(s) you use at home_____.

Language(s) Candidate uses with your child_____.

Indique el idioma/s que usted habla en su casa_____.

Idioma/s que el Candidato habla a su niño_____.

· ·

Please write your opinion about this Candidate's work with your child:

Por favor escriba lo que usted opina sobre el trabajo de este Candidato con usted y con su niño:

DATE you completed this questionnaire_____

FECHA en que usted completó este cuestionario_____

Remember that parents are a vital part of your program. Some of them will want to become more involved in their children's learning. And you will be able to provide opportunities for them to do so.

You can ask parents to assist you in looking in the community for learning opportunities for their children. These may include:

- Parents identifying local collections children would like, such as art, history, plants, and animals.

- Parents identifying outdoor sculptures and monuments to tell the story of where children live

- Parents organizing a field trip without children to preview and evaluate learning opportunities for children

- Parents scouting the community for postcards to link community resources to the classroom.

- Inviting parents to bring music, food, and objects from home to showcase family traditions and interests.

What happens next?

You are now ready to share and build upon your experiences with other CDA Candidates in a group Seminar. This second phase of your CDA credentialing process is sure to be an exciting one!

These group sessions will build upon your knowledge and skills in early childhood education and prepare you to complete the Early Childhood Studies Review. After the Seminar ends, you and your Field Advisor will work together to complete the last two units in Essentials. If you have any questions, review the information in the introduction to this guide (pages I–IV) or call the Council on the Candidate Connection Hotline—**800-424-4310**.

Check that you have completed Unit 6 on your CDA progress record and then get ready for thought-provoking group experiences yourself!

Resources for more information

Baker, A.C. & Manfredi-Petitt, L. A. (1998). *Circle of love: Relationships between parents, providers, and children in family child care.* St. Paul, MN: Redleaf Press.

Beginnings Workshops, *Child Care Information Exchange*, Redmond, WA. Includes many resources for working with families. Available at www.childcareexchange.com

Building bridges between teachers and families. (Video). Seattle, WA: Harvest Resources. Available at www.ecetrainers.com.

Child Health Talk: A Publication for Parents. Washington, DC: National Black Child Development Institute. www.nbcdi.org.

Diffily, D. & Morrison, K. (Eds.) (1996). *Family-friendly communication for early childhood programs.* Washington, DC: National Association for the Education of Young Children.

Dodge, D.T. & Phinney, J. (2002). *A parent's guide to preschool. Rev. ed.* Washington, DC: Teaching Strategies. Also available from Redleaf Press. Also available in Spanish: *Una guia para padres a la educacion preescolar.*

Dodge, D.T. & Heroman, C. (1999). *Building your baby's brain: A parent's guide to the first five years.* Washington, DC: Teaching Strategies. Also available from Redleaf Press. Also available in Spanish: *Como estimular el cerebro infantile: Una guia para padres de familia.*

Early Childhood Parenting Collaborative website: http://ecap.crc.uiuc.edu

Pruett, K.D. (2000). *Fatherneed: Why father care is as essential as mother care for your child.* The Free Press. Available from www.zerotothree.org.

Helping children cope with crisis: A guide for African American parents (brochure). (2002). Washington, DC: National Institute of Child Health and Human Development, U.S. Department of Health and Human Services and National Black Child Development Institute. To order: 1-800-320-2943 or www.nichd.nih.gov.

Lerner, C. & Dombro, A.L. (2000). *Learning and growing together: Understanding and supporting your child's development.* Washington, DC: Zero to Three.

Manolson, A. with B. Ward & N. Dodington. (1995). *You make the difference in helping your child learn.* The Hanen Centre. Available from Zero to Three. Also available in Spanish *Usted Hace la Diferencia.*

Mathews, V.H. & Roman, S. (2002). The Library-Museum Head Start partnership—A resource notebook. Washington, DC: The Center for the Book. Available from www.headstartinfo.org.

National Black Child Development Institute, Parent Empowerment Project (PEP) www.nbcdi.org.

National Center for Family Literacy, 325 West Main Street, Suite 300, Louisville, KY 40202-4237. www.famlit.org.

Parenting Exchange, an electronically published parenting column that focuses on the daily life of families. Available from Child Care Information Exchange, www.childcareexchange.com.

Parents as Teachers National Center, Inc. 2228 Ball Drive, St. Louis, MO 63146. www.patnc.org. *Parent Page* available in English and Spanish in newsletter and on website.

Pawl, J. & Dombro, A. (2001). *Learning and growing together with families: Partnering with parents to support young children's development.* Video package also available. Washington, DC: Zero to Three.

Stonehouse, A. (1995). *How does it feel? Child care from a parent's perspective.* Redmond, WA: Exchange Press. www.childcareexchange.com.

Putting it all together as an early childhood professional working with preschoolers or infants and toddlers, or providing family childcare

WHAT A LONG WAY you have come since you first started your CDA Professional Preparation Program! You have worked hard on your own. You have met many other CDA Candidates in your Seminar group. You have had exciting moments of discovery along the way when you saw how things fit together. You undoubtedly disagreed with a few ideas. You probably spent your weekends and evenings completing assignments and putting together your Professional Resource File. But now your CDA Credential will soon become reality.

You are almost at the end of one phase, and at the beginning of an even more challenging one in your work life. You are about to be recognized as an early childhood professional. You will be faced with problems to solve every day in this field. You will have to make decisions that affect the lives of children, parents, or your colleagues. You may be faced with the need to take action on behalf of children, families, or early childhood educators you don't even know.

And you are probably aware of just how much more there is to learn about how young children develop and learn. Our field, like young children themselves, is constantly changing and growing. After you have earned your CDA, you will enter the early childhood profession and will be qualified for employment in a number of responsible, professional positions. In order to make progress on your career path, you must keep on building your skills through continuing education and through collaboration with your early childhood co-workers.

Will you accept the challenge? Where do you go from here?

This unit and the next are to be completed during the final phase of your CDA professional preparation program. You will need about two weeks to complete Unit 7 and will continue to apply what you have learned as you:

1 Prepare for conference with your Field Advisor to discuss three topics (*using resources to efficiently manage, making good professional decisions, acting on behalf of children*).

2 Complete two assignments (*complete the final floor plan and interview your Field Advisor*) and add one entry to your Professional Resource File.

3 Prepare any remaining questions or concerns for discussion during your CDA Seminar.

PART 1

Putting together all that you have learned

To be able to put everything together to create a high-quality program means using all the teaching strategies you know to foster development and learning in children. Doing this will take yet another skill area: working as a member of an early childhood team.

Lots of **adults** are involved in programs for very young children: families, licensing personnel, teaching assistants, staff (*cooks, bus drivers*), volunteers, community service people, consultants, medical personnel, substitutes, provider networks, supervisors, other teachers, neighbors. All of you must work as a team to provide the best possible care for children in your community. How can you do that?

Establish cooperative relationships

We have already talked about how to work with families: you both share information and plan together, you treat each other with respect, and you listen more than you talk. You use informal conversations, notes or letters, conferences, meetings, telephone calls, e-mails, newsletters, and a variety of other ways to keep in touch with families. You are always pleasant, courteous, and tactful. You try to understand their point of view and keep their needs in mind. You are open to suggestions and are always trying to improve yourself.

When you work with families of infants and toddlers, you probably sense that you are in a unique position. New parents are eager to learn more about their unfamiliar roles. At the same time, they may feel uncomfortable about leaving very young children in the care of another person, and they may feel quite guilty. Some parents might even see you as competition for their child's love. These feelings of guilt and competition often take the form of criticism. A parent who feels, "no one can take care of this child as well as I do," may have a new complaint or concern everyday. It is important for caregivers to understand why a parent like this complains so, and should help her get in touch with her real issue. It is very easy to become defensive when a parent is overly critical, and seemingly unappreciative of all your hard work. Your warmth, sensitivity, and understanding will be challenged as you work to help parents see how all of you can work together as partners to provide care for their youngest family members.

As a professional early childhood educator, you will use these same skills when you collaborate with all the other people involved in your program. Whether you work in a large Head Start program, a medium-sized center in a nationwide chain, in a small local childcare center or as a family childcare provider, your work puts you in touch with many other people. You are part of a team of professionals. And you are expected to conduct yourself in a professional way.

Whenever these other people are together with you and the children, you are showing children how adults get along with each other. When people respect each other, the day goes much more smoothly, too.

A new substitute is working with you today. She was called at the last minute and arrives after some of the children. You welcome her to the program, give her a statement of your program's philosophy and a quick summary of the activities for the children, and briefly outline what you expect her to do during the morning. "We're so glad you are here today. I will introduce you to each of the children. They can wear their nametags today if you would like.

Please help me walk around the room as the children play. We'll show interest in what they are doing, talk informally, ask questions to make them think, and offer assistance if we see the need. Around 9:30, I'll show you how to fix snack."

OR in an infant/toddler setting you may say, "Please sit with me on the floor as the children play. We'll talk informally with them, sing songs, read books, and offer assistance if we see the need. We'll change diapers when they're needed. Our rocking chairs are for reading, snuggling, and bottle-feeding. Around 9:30, I'll show you how to fix snack for the toddlers. Feel free to ask questions."

Helping volunteers, substitutes, and visitors feel welcome and comfortable requires some advance organization on the part of the staff person supervising the classroom. These are just a few of the things you must remember to prepare in advance so that the day can go as smoothly as possible:

• Have a copy of your program's expectations for children—the program rules and the daily schedule—written out for the newcomer to read. Or for infants/toddlers, have the basics of how you work with infants and toddlers written out for the newcomer to read. These guidelines will help ensure that methods are consistent and promote positive behaviors. This system eliminates surprises for children and adults, too. Make sure any questions the visitor might have are answered as soon as possible throughout the day.

- **Write out your plans for the day, and explain how you expect the volunteer or substitute to assist you with each activity.** If the person is new to working with young children, you may need to explain some basic principles about this kind of teaching. For example:

Finger painting at about 10 a.m.

Supplies: Place these supplies on the art table (*supplies are in the cupboard above the sink*): Orange, yellow and black finger-paints; enough large sheets of finger-paint paper for each child in the group.

Supervision: Three or four children may finger paint at a time. Ask them to help each other snap on their smocks and roll up their sleeves. Children may use their hands and arms to paint. They may choose any or all of the three colors, and can work as long as needed to finish. After washing and hanging up their smock, they can ask someone else in the group to take their place in the art area. Encourage conversation and experimentation.

Things to talk about: Talk with children about what they are doing. Ask them to think about how the paint feels on their hands. You might suggest words such as cool, slippery, slimy, wet, gushy, mushy—make up a word or two. Point out how different techniques make different marks on the paper as the children use them: One finger makes a thin line, the side of the hand can

erase everything. If children make a design and then cover it up, do not express disappointment or criticize, but rather focus on what the child is doing. If the paper gets too wet and tears, offer another sheet if the child wants to continue.

A similar plan for infants and toddlers might be: Dough clay for toddlers at about 10 a.m.:

Supplies: Place these supplies on the low table (*supplies are in the cupboard above the sink*): large jar of dough clay, box of accessories for clay.

Supervision: Three or four children may play at a time. Clay stays on the table. It may be rolled, pounded, squashed, and otherwise worked with their hands and fingers. Encourage conversation and experimentation. Please do not make a model for the children to copy. It is important for the children to be original. Remember, the fun children have is more important than whatever the results are.

Things to talk about: Talk about what the children are doing. Children learn by doing. Ask children to think about how the clay feels on their hands. Suggest words such as cool, soft, mushy—make up a word or two.

Clean up: Return dough clay to container. Seal, so it stays moist. Rinse rollers and hammers in sink.

- **Introduce the children and visitor by name.** Some children may want to introduce themselves. Explain to each child who the person is and why she or he is there. If a teacher is ill, tell the children. If the visitor will be doing some testing, briefly explain the process. If you are being observed, say what the observer is looking for. Use name tags if your visitor prefers.
- **Observe the person as she or he works with the children.** Throughout the day, comment on how things are going. "You've been such a help to notice just where to

be when the babies needed a hug or to be engaged with a finger play. I'm so glad you're here today." Jot down any topics that need to be discussed later.

Many early childhood programs have support staff such as nutritionists, social workers, bus drivers, office staff, and janitors. To make sure they feel like a real part of your program's team, exchange information with them on a regular basis . . . about individual children's preferences or moods . . . about program plans . . . when you'll need something special, for example. Encourage children to draw pictures or write letters for the staff who are responsible for special efforts.

With the nutritionist/cook: "In two weeks, on Wednesday, the 23rd, we have a field trip planned to the vegetable farm. We'll be needing bag lunches for the children that day. Think about what foods might travel well, and then we'll talk about how to organize our lunch plans at the end of this week."

With the cleaning staff: "I know that this has been a busy week for you. We brought in all those colorful leaves and then pasted them. Making

applesauce really created quite a sticky mess, didn't it? We do try to have the children clean up after themselves, but are so glad you can handle the really big jobs for us. We really appreciate having a clean space to play every morning."

With the driver: "Sharee has really been working hard to sit quietly in her seat lately. We've been talking about safety on the school bus. How has she been doing?"

Throughout the year, you may also work with other adults from outside the program. Sometimes they will support your efforts, sometimes they will be critical of what you do, and sometimes you will work together on behalf of a child or family who has requested information about a topic. Or sometimes a staff member within your program, such as your supervisor may offer a negative opinion of your work.

Teachers are put on the spot a lot, and it is hard sometimes to accept criticism. Ask for a private conference time when you both are unhurried and can calmly discuss areas of concern in a productive way.

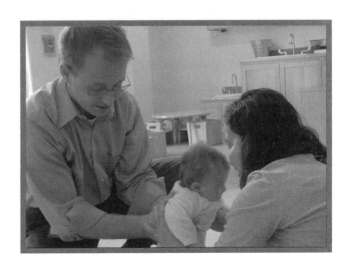

Helping volunteers, substitutes, and visitors feel welcome and comfortable requires some advance organization.

Your director has finished her evaluation. You are nervous about the results, even though you have tried hard to do your best. Sure enough, you are rated low in one area: children need to be offered more opportunities for small group interaction throughout the day.

You are disappointed at the criticism but eager to find out just what you can work on to do better. "We are trying hard to do that. Can you give us some examples of what you mean to improve our program?" Your director begins tactfully, "I can see you have a good start. But instead of always reading the story to the whole group requiring a lot of time spent managing behavior, you might try reading to small groups of 4 to 6 children. In the smaller groups, children can see the book better, listen more attentively, and engage in conversation and answer questions about the story." You reply, "Oh, I agree that it would be better to read to small groups. But I don't know what to do about the rest of the children in the group. I'm afraid I'll lose control."

"Naturally, that's a concern. The children may take a while to adjust to thinking more for themselves, but you have a lot of great materials. Let the others pursue their own interests from the choices you have prepared. Try giving them a little more freedom to choose their own learning experiences. Make small group reading interaction with you one of the choices. The children will gravitate to you."

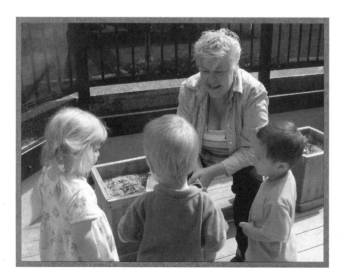

"It's really helpful to see what you mean. I'll try the small group reading and see if it engages the children more."

What techniques have you developed to respond to criticisms or challenges in productive ways?

_____

_____

_____

_____

You probably also have encountered the need to build support for what you do within your neighborhood or community.

Your childcare program or family childcare home is located in a residential neighborhood. One person who is home all day has been stirring up the people on your street by complaining about all the noise from the playground area.

A parent hears about the stew from a friend, and tells you what is happening. "Thank you for cluing us in to the problem. We'll need to think of some ways to become better friends with our neighbors."

You come up with several ideas to try: Send a newsletter to everyone in the area, or have a noon picnic and invite neighbors, or issue invitations for people to visit the program, or ask the local paper to do a story on what a good program you have.

Some of these ideas may not work, but the process has been started. You meet with two parents to try to figure out what to do.

Children should benefit from your
professionalism.

In a situation like this, it's very important for you to remain calm and "professional." This is true even if the accusations are false, or make you angry. The parents will pick up on your tone and attitude.

What ideas do you have to maintain good community relations with your program's neighbors?

_____

_____

_____

_____

As a professional, you may also be called upon to lend your expertise to discussions of issues beyond your own program.

A condominium homeowner's association in your city has just ruled that their policy against home businesses will be enforced. This means no family childcare in a nearby neighborhood. And already there is a shortage of good care in your community. Parents are dismayed.

You ask for a few minutes at the next AEYC meeting to raise the issue with your colleagues. You form a committee that includes several parents and a city administrator. Your goal is to plan strategies to increase the availability of childcare.

A teacher brings in an "English Only" leaflet that is being circulated in your neighborhood. It calls for a petition to do away with all bilingual services in the community.

You call a meeting with staff and parents to discuss a strategy. A parent suggests an "English Plus" leaflet supporting diversity. Staff and parents take various responsibilities to work on it.

Are you ready to handle these kinds of responsibilities? As a CDA, others will look up to you. You will be expected to work with lots of people. The future of children is in your hands.

Use community resources

All through your _Essentials_ curriculum, you have tracked down resources:

- the legal requirements and your program's policy for reporting suspected incidents of child abuse or neglect
- your county Extension Service for nutrition information
- field trip possibilities
- services to screen children for possible disabilities and to take appropriate action
- resources for parents
- translation/interpretation services for the languages spoken at your center

Now is the time to become familiar with all the other resources in your community that can help you be more effective in your work with children. Following are just a few of the typical resource agencies that serve families. You can probably list more. Use the Internet, get together with your program director, members of your provider network, or perhaps talk with your licensing representative, if you need help to find out what your community offers.

Begin a card file of resources such as these, that you can share with your colleagues and with parents. Then call each group and find out what services or materials they have to help you.

- Parenting programs
- Red Cross
- Easter Seal Society
- Safety groups
- Mental health clinics
- Medical clinics
- Food stamps
- WIC programs
- Financial planning
- Gymnastics classes
- Childcare resource and referral
- Cultural resource groups
- Resale shops
- Educational supply stores
- Performing artists' groups
- Food cooperatives
- Public library
- Community-based organizations
- Children's book stores
- Early and periodic screening programs for very young children.
- Any service organization that might contribute people or funds to your program.

All of these resources can broaden your ability to support the needs of the families in your program—and your program itself. Most have Websites, brochures, information, even curriculum materials appropriate for parents and/or young children. Take advantage of what is available in your community through government agencies, volunteer groups, and citizen action coalitions. Unless you use these wonderful supplements, you, the children, and their families will miss out on a lot of marvelous opportunities. Expand your horizons today.

BOOKS GIVE US WINGS

And, do not forget your local library. It contains a vast amount of resource material!

Manage efficiently

You are well aware that not all of your time is spent with children. Regardless of the type of program you work in, you have other responsibilities as well. You manage space, materials, activities, records, and other adults every day.

Organize space and materials

We have already seen how important it is to arrange your teaching space to make the most of it. But remember, maintaining a safe, healthy learning environment means rearranging it occasionally. Because children grow and change, and new children enter your care, you will want to periodically look carefully at your room arrangement and make changes to keep it fresh and interesting. Rotate equipment and materials as children's skills improve. Rejuvenate the outdoor play area with a fresh supply of sand or a new set of containers for water play.

Each time new material is added or a new topic is introduced, you have to examine these materials for bias. It is easy to slip back into a routine of what was done before.

Storage areas need to be neatly arranged and cleaned occasionally so you know what you have and where to find it. Who knows what buried treasure is lurking in the back of your closets.

Thoughtful planning of the environment also means you keep track of supplies so they can be ordered before you run out. One busy day and you can suddenly be out of glue! And you certainly don't want the guinea pig to go hungry! Periodically check the first-aid kit to make sure it is well supplied.

You plan ahead, too, to decide which special materials you will need—pipe cleaners, tissue paper, or foods for a cooking project. Perhaps you need parents to bring in paper bags or scraps of fabric or empty coffee cans for stacking. Give them a little advance notice so they can save things.

Take a look at the floor plan you developed in Unit 3 of *Essentials* (*page 165*). Now that you have many new ideas, complete the final design using the chart on page 166, or review the design you completed during Seminar.

Discuss your design with your Field Advisor.

Plan ahead for daily curriculum experiences

Long before you start a new curriculum topic, gather all the materials needed so you won't have to scramble for something at the last minute. Check with your library to make sure the book titles or videos you want are available, and reserve them if possible. Contact community resource groups about materials or visitors and arrange dates well in advance. The curriculum in your program will set the framework for what daily experiences the children will have. But being prepared for each day will require you to think ahead.

For instance, most field trips must be scheduled far in advance because there are so many details to arrange. You will need to visit the place yourself and talk with the people there about how they can best accommodate young children. Travel, emergency medical permissions, and other forms must be signed. Remember not all field trips are appropriate for toddlers, and few are appropriate for ba-

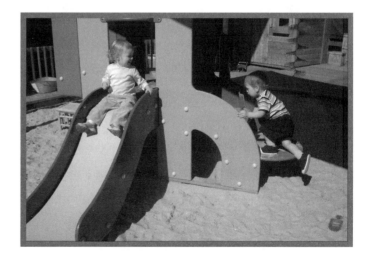

Allow children the freedom to choose some of their own learning experiences.

bies. Bus or car arrangements have to be made. Appropriate car seats need to be available for every young child. Special preparations may be needed for children with disabling conditions. Volunteers to go with you must be contacted. Be sure to include some type of exercise or activity that helps prepare children for the trip. Money may need to be collected.

Arrange for special visitors by giving them enough notice. Be sure to talk with them, in person or by phone before their visit, about the children's interests and attention spans and clarify what you expect the visitor to do.

Plan ahead to stay late on days when an activity will require a lengthy cleanup. Arrive early when preparations for the day require extra time.

You may also need to make arrangements for parent meetings—make sure refreshments are ready and supplies (*napkins, coffee, and so forth*) are provided, and arrange for interpreters and translators as needed.

Allow time in your day to keep notes for future planning. Sit down at the end of each day and look at your plan for tomorrow—do you have everything you need?

Keep records

By now, you should have quite a large collection of observations of the children recorded in your daily diary. By building a record of how each child develops and learns, you can use the information to plan curriculum, to tell parents how much progress their children are making, and to help identify any potential disabilities or special needs. Don't stop just because you have finished your CDA!

Date records and have a folder for each child. Records of children can also help families when the child leaves your program. For bilingual programs, for example, records on the first language of the child and his or her usage and understanding of the second language will be critical to planning. Families may want you to share some of what you have learned about the child with their child's next teacher. Always ask the parents first—summaries of your observations should only be released to others **if the parents approve**. Obtain permission from parents in writing. Remember, this is confidential information. They will usually be quite agreeable if you explain that this is one way you can work together to build a bridge between the two programs for their child.

In every program, some written records are needed just to ensure children's welfare while they are present. Proper procedures to report illness or accidents should be established. Attendance records must be accurate, especially in the event of an emergency evacuation. All programs must keep up-to-date health records, emergency forms, and written policies.

Depending on the type of program you work in, you may or may not be responsible for keeping other types of records. Family childcare providers, for example, must maintain records for licensing/registration and for taxes. Your program director or finance officer must prepare a budget, maintain a checking account, and obtain liability insurance coverage. Zoning records may be needed. You may participate in the Childcare Food Program or serve children whose education is subsidized or paid for by an agency, and all of these require some paperwork. If you have any assistants, you will need health and wage records for them as well. And you may need to advertise your program. Early childhood programs are indeed businesses!

All written records must be legible so others can read them, and should be organized and kept in a place where they can be located easily. If your program is bilingual, records may need to be kept in more than one language.

Communicate

Your ability to listen and respond appropriately—to children, parents, and others—keeps coming up in your professional studies. That's because listening is such a valuable tool in your everyday work. Sometimes people are subtle and sometimes they are pretty direct.

But you **will** find out what people think about your work, what they need, and how you could improve what you do. Keep your eyes and ears open to clues that something needs to be changed or that you are really doing a good job. It's a mark of a professional to be able to make positive changes in response to constructive criticism.

Here are some typical examples of the subtle types of feedback you may get. What would you do in each of these situations?

1. A child gets wet and you discover there are no extra clothes in her cubby. As you look around, you see other cubbies with few or no extra clothes as well.

What are these families telling you?

_____

_____

_____

_____

What should you do about it?

_____

_____

_____

_____

_____

2. You sent field trip permission slips for a neighborhood walk out two weeks ago, and you have only three of the seven permissions you need.

Why have so few been returned?

_____

_____

_____

_____

What should you do?

_____

_____

_____

_____

3. Group time is about 10 to 15 minutes for your oldest children. About half of them sit quietly, but the other half listen only a minute or two, and then they begin to wander around.

Why are the children so restless?

_____

_____

_____

_____

What should you do?

_____

_____

_____

_____

4. A parent of a just-enrolled 8-week-old seems very anxious when she leaves her child each morning. At pickup each day, she has complained about something in the program.

What is worrying her?

_____

_____

_____

_____

What should you do?

_____

_____

_____

_____

5. One parent constantly compares her child's development to another child in the program. She is usually critical of her child and sees her child as "slow."

What is she concerned about?

_____

_____

_____

_____

What should you do?

_____

_____

_____

_____

6. In your newsletter, you ask parents to provide healthy snacks for birthday treats. The first three birthdays after your notice are all celebrated with cupcakes and Kool-Aid.

Why did parents ignore your request?

_____

_____

_____

_____

_____

_____

_____

How can you get parents to plan more nutritious birthday snacks?

_____

_____

_____

_____

7. Three monolingual Spanish-speaking parents in a row have asked to move their children from your group to the group of a monolingual English-speaking teacher.

What do their actions tell you?

_____

_____

_____

_____

_____

What information about language development of bilingual children would you share?

_____

_____

_____

_____

_____

_____

How could you present it?

_____

_____

_____

_____

8. Your director gets a phone call from the local TV station about qualifications of childcare providers. They would like to interview her. She agrees, and suggests they use your room as the setting.

What does the director's choice mean?

_____

_____

_____

_____

What can you do to prepare your room?

_____

_____

_____

_____

Managing efficiently means being sensitive to these indicators of feedback and making adjustments accordingly.

Every day you will make hundreds of decisions—about how to interact with children, about what to say to a parent, about how to

work more effectively with colleagues. The more resources you have at your fingertips, the more likely you are to make good decisions. The field-work and Seminar parts of your _Essentials_ curriculum have covered the basic information you need to make sound judgments. How you use that information professionally requires discussion of one more topic—professionalism.

PART 2

You try to make good decisions

Throughout your _Essentials_ curriculum you have picked up information to build on your teaching experience. You have seen ways to make good decisions about how you teach, how you work with other adults, and how you plan and organize your work. You will look back again and again at some parts of this material as you continue to extend your ability to work with the youngest of children in a professional way. There is so much to absorb—people have learned a lot from research on children's learning and development over many years.

Making good decisions means always being ethical. Members of NAEYC have developed a Code of Ethics, which you will find in Unit 1 of _Essentials_. As a CDA, you are expected to agree to abide by it.

With this code to help, each of us in the profession must work out our own thoughts on what kind of teaching behavior is truly professional. We'll offer some guidelines here to help you make ethical decisions. While there are no right answers, here are some ways to help you consider as many factors as possible before you decide what to do in a specific situation. **Presented on the following pages are several situations. Think about each of these situations and discuss them with your Field Advisor.**

Have a healthy attitude about your power

Young children, especially infants and toddlers, are so helpless and dependent upon adults. They are with you for so many of their waking hours. Their parents depend on you to give children the best experiences possible during those impressionable early years. In addition, parents need reliable childcare so they can earn a living or prepare to earn one.

It is easy to abuse this power, either with children or adults. Some teachers are tempted to use physical force because they are stron-

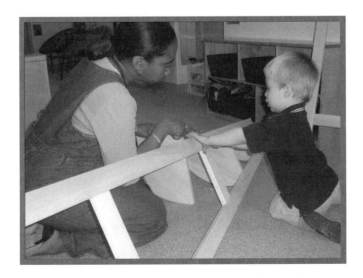

Giving children the help they need in a positive way enables them to be strong and competent.

ger than children. Some teachers are tempted to take advantage of children psychologically because they believe children learn to be obedient out of fear. Some teachers fail to prepare children to become good world citizens. And some teachers think they can get away with almost anything because the parents are so desperate for affordable, convenient childcare.

Think for a minute about how much power you have and use every day. You have the power to enable children to grow strong and competent—or to be weak and inept. You have the power to help children become kind and generous—or mean and stingy. You have the power to validate children's home language and culture or make them feel inferior to other people. You have the power to help children get along with each other—or to hate and fear people who are different from them. You have the power to provide high-quality education and care—or minimal custodial care. What is the ethical approach?

As a professional, you make a commitment never to take advantage of children or their parents—physically, emotionally, intellectually, or financially. You respect them as people and treat them accordingly. You use your power to build strengths and to help overcome weaknesses.

How would you use your power in situations such as these? Jot down notes and discuss your responses with your Field Advisor.

1. A 4-year-old boy has been crying for 10 minutes. You have tried listening, hugging, and offering a favorite stuffed animal, all to no avail. *Do you scream at the*

boy and tell him to shut up, that big boys don't cry? Do you spank him and isolate him in the director's office?

What is the professional thing to do?

_____

_____

_____

_____

2. A 4-month-old has been crying for half an hour. You have tried a clean diaper, a bottle, rocking, a warmer blanket, and soothing music, all to no avail. *Do you scream at the baby and tell him to shut up, that big boys don't cry? Do you spank him and isolate him in his crib?*

_____

_____

_____

_____

What is the professional thing to do?

_____

_____

_____

_____

Children will often look to you for reassurance and comfort. You have the power to do both.

3. Two toddlers are fighting in the sandbox. Before you can get there, one has thrown sand into the other's eyes. *Do you grab the child who threw the sand and drag her indoors to sit in the office? Do you tell both children to get out of the sandbox and that they may not play there for a week?*

What is the professional thing to do?

_____

_____

_____

_____

4. A new family has moved into your community. Their 5-year-old is hearing impaired. *Do you discourage the family when they inquire about enrollment? Do you accept the child but dread having him because more effort is needed on your part?*

What is the professional thing to do?

_____

_____

_____

_____

5. An English-speaking child announces she won't play with Marisol because she is stupid and can't talk. *Do you frown and tell the child she is wrong and you never want to hear her say anything like that again? Do you ignore the comment and act like you didn't hear it?*

What is the professional thing to do?

_____

_____

_____

_____

_____

Keep confidences

During the course of your work, you will learn a great deal about families' personal lives. A parent may confide in you some upsetting de-tails about a spouse. A child may blurt out, "Momma told me not to play with you because you are dumb." Parents may fill out financial forms so your program can qualify for financial reimbursement. Bruises on a Monday morning may lead you to suspect child abuse.

Whatever you hear or see as a CDA is privileged information. You are a professional, so you must take the appropriate steps to remedy the situation if there is a problem. Often you refer people to the appropriate community resources. You provide an accepting environment in which children feel good about themselves and others. You keep written records confidential. And you immediately report any possible abuse or neglect to the appropriate authorities. Professionals do not announce what they have learned about a family to all the other teachers in the program, or to any other parents, or to their friends.

What do you do to stop yourself when you feel tempted to break a confidence about a family or a particular child in your program?

_____

_____

_____

_____

Families trust you to keep information about them confidential. Families have a right to privacy. Of course, you must balance that with the need to protect the child.

Protect children

You are legally and ethically responsible for the protection of all children in your care. Not just their safety, but also their emotional well being, their physical and intellectual development, and their social skills. You do not allow children to hurt themselves or each other. You do not allow any other adult to hurt children either. You show value for the way each child speaks and include their home language in the program. You are constantly alert for signs of any type of abuse. You base your decisions about what to do on the children's best interest.

Professional early childhood educators are constantly alert to conditions within the program to assure that children are protected in all these ways. For example, you scan the outdoor play area for new hazards every time you enter it. You arrange for enough adult assistance on field trips so children are kept in small groups for easy supervision. You evaluate each new order of materials (*or each donation*) for safety and appropriateness. You always listen to and watch the children so you can promote cooperation and friendly behaviors. You are eager to learn more about what types of learning experiences are most beneficial for early childhood development, and you implement what you know. You keep up with the latest information about preventing injury and illness in children in group settings.

Your role as a professional demands that you report suspected child abuse. Here are some examples of other situations that may arise, in which you will need to act as a protector for children.

Write down how you would handle each of these dilemmas, and then talk with your Field Advisor about your responses.

1. One child frequently hits and shoots pretend guns at the other children.

_____

_____

_____

_____

2. Often one of your 4-year-olds is listless all morning, then devours lunch and seems livelier in the afternoon.

_____

_____

_____

_____

3. The parents of a 2-year-old have purchased a kit with flashcards to teach their child to read. They are pressuring you to use it with all the children in the toddler group.

_____

_____

_____

_____

4. Grandmother and mother are pushing an 18-month-old boy to get toilet trained. Whenever he arrives in training pants and wets himself, he sobs so much that you have reason to believe he is being punished at home for his inability to stay dry.

_____

_____

_____

_____

Provide good quality care

There are many different types of programs for young children. You can adopt one of the models, or set up your own approach. Either way, as a professional you always provide developmentally appropriate materials and learning experiences for all the children. You know children learn best through play and other teacher-guided learning experiences. You want children to enjoy themselves and to learn ideas and behaviors that they will keep throughout their lives. You provide good, safe care for children. To do less would be unethical.

One of the most difficult aspects of working with young children is to avoid the temptation to lapse back into your old ways of teaching and disciplining. Catch yourself before that happens.

Maybe it's so easy for you to use baby talk. Or perhaps you want toddlers to sit quietly for 20 minutes to listen to your favorite music. A parent might expect an 18-month-old to be toilet trained. Now you know why these are not appropriate methods or expectations.

There are still many commercial (*and homemade*) materials available that are not appropriate for young children. Some methods or materials are better used with older children. Parents may request worksheets for 4-year-olds, for example, and you now realize that there are more effective ways to teach children concepts and early literacy skills.

You will need to put everything you know to work every day in making the right decisions about how to best foster the learning and development of young children.

Transitions from one activity to another also often prove to be difficult with a group of wiggly young children. The time between one activity and another may simply involve sitting and waiting . . . and waiting . . . and waiting. But now you know that's not an appropriate expectation. You know it's best to minimize the number of transitions required and to involve children in the transition to keep it smooth, and make it a learning experience that is not wasteful of anyone's time. Children can carry out the baskets of sand toys, for example. If you are waiting for another child to wash hands before lunch, do some finger plays or sing songs with movements until everyone is ready. Keep children involved rather than waste their time.

Move about in small groups rather than herding children like cattle from place to place, or expect them to walk in a straight line with hands clasped behind their backs. If your schedule still isn't working to make transitions easier, revise it again with the long-term goals for children in mind. Remember, children are learning from everything they do!

You will be faced again and again with the need to make on-the-spot decisions about the best quality of care. It helps to think ahead about how you would handle problems that are sure to arise.

What would you do if . . .

. . .a toddler in your program consistently kisses other children on the cheek, and then bites them?

_____

_____

_____

_____

. . . a young preschooler drew a beautiful picture with lots of colors, and then scribbled black all over the top of it?

_____

_____

_____

_____

. . . a child began spanking a doll in the housekeeping area?

_____

_____

_____

_____

. . . a 4½-year-old boy always forces his way into a play situation, demanding to be involved or destroying children's projects?

_____

_____

_____

_____

Discuss your responses with your Field Advisor, who can help you think about how to apply what you have learned about young children in dealing with these and similar incidents.

As a CDA, you will always strive to keep knowledgeable about the standards of the profession. You will need to know about other national voluntary self-evaluation systems designed to improve and recognize the quality of programs. Group programs can benefit greatly by going through these review processes, much as you are going through the CDA credentialing system.

If you feel your center is an excellent one, you may want to find out about getting it accredited through NAEYC's accreditation system. For information, go to NAEYC's website online at www.naeyc.org. Then talk with your program director about whether your program should take advantage of this excellent opportunity to be nationally recognized.

If you are a family childcare provider, contact the National Association for Family Childcare (*refer to the National Organizations list on page 26*) about the Family Childcare Home Accreditation System.

What else do you and other program staff do to constantly monitor whether you are providing good care for children?

_____

_____

_____

_____

What steps can you take to improve how your program's quality of care is assessed?

_____

_____

_____

_____

Respect parents' authority

Parents do have the ultimate authority to make decisions about their children—within legal limits, of course. Every cultural group stresses some values more than others, and then there are individual differences among families.

Parents may have standards of behavior for children at home that are not necessarily the same as those you have set in the program. Some families may live by a different code of morality than you accept. Parents may place a higher value on some things—wardrobe or financial status, for example—than you prefer.

We all know how important it is to respect differences, but sometimes it is difficult when you disagree with how parents are raising their children. Often, parents who have radically different ideas than you will probably not choose your program. At other times, however, they may have no choice but to enroll their children in your program. When that happens, you need to get to know each other well and work out a way to be as cooperative as possible. You must make a concerted effort to learn all you can about the family and their way of life or beliefs. You may eventually agree to disagree. You will respect each other's differences—and agree that children will be expected to act differently at home and at school. That way, at least in your program, you can keep what you believe to be the child's best interests in mind.

Children also need to know that some differences between home and your program are acceptable and natural. A simple explanation that "Yes, you say grace before each meal at home. That is so important for your family. But here we wait until everyone is seated and then we begin to serve ourselves."

Without a doubt, as a CDA you will encounter some thorny value issues. Just remember there is more than one way to make things work for the benefit of the children. Be willing to listen and try new ideas.

As a professional, how would you deal with situations such as these?

1. Parents insist on dressing their 4-year-old boy in a white shirt almost every day, and they want to keep him clean.

_____

_____

_____

_____

2. A child clearly has not been bathed in many days—she has offensive body odor, her hair is tangled, and her fingernails are imbedded with dirt. The child is developing a rash.

_____

_____

_____

_____

3. One 2-year-old boy has been biting other children. You know you should speak to the parents about it—but you also know that if you do they will probably beat the child.

_____

_____

_____

_____

4. Each morning, one parent stops at your sidewalk in front of the center, honks the horn, and then sends her child alone up to your door.

_____

_____

_____

_____

5. A 10-month-old who is fairly new to your program usually cries when the parent leaves. The parent has asked that you get the child busy with something so the parent can sneak out without saying goodbye and the child won't cry.

_____

_____

_____

_____

Support diversity

As you have seen, all people are biased—we all think we are right and the best. And we all need to admit that we have those biases if we are to become good teachers. Your CDA Seminar experiences helped you see how these biases can affect your work.

Hard as it is, there is no room for favorites when you teach young children. Instead, you must do everything possible to help children feel good about themselves, their family, their heritage, their beliefs, their abilities, and their language—and to appreciate and respect those same characteristics in others.

We are helping to make it possible for children to become productive citizens of the world of today and tomorrow. The world is filled with many ethnic groups and people with varying capabilities who must get along with each other. Ultimately, our survival depends on peacefully resolving our differences and learning to live together. We all must accept and appreciate our wonderful diversity as human beings.

These are some ethical issues in this area that you may face. How would you deal with them?

1. You have just admitted a new infant and you are in a program that requires records on ethnic/racial background—one parent is white, one black. A staff member using a strained voice says, "What is this kid anyway?"

2. Another teacher in your program always asks the older children to sit "Indian style."

3. You accept a child with HIV infection into your group. The other parents threaten to withdraw their children.

4. A child brings in a copy of *Little Black Sambo* or *The Five Chinese Brothers*.

5. A group of 2-year-olds have a new classmate who is dark-complected with lots of dark, black hair. The other children have fair skin. One child points and says to you, "He dirty." What do you do? OR Two White children say they are afraid that a Spanish-speaking child's "dirty color" will rub off on them if they hold hands.

Help protect consumers

Every state has different laws regarding programs for young children and qualifications for staff. You have already seen how important it is for good programs to be licensed or registered and for staff and providers to obtain professional education. Sometimes, we forget that the purpose of the licensing and registration laws is for consumer protection. In fact, most regulations provide only a **minimum** form of protection—far less than in many other areas that we take for granted, such as driver's licenses or pet food standards, for example. Adhering to those laws is a must.

Regulations generally are designed to establish at least a floor for child-staff ratios, safety, staff qualifications, space, materials, and a variety of other important areas in programs for young children.

An ethical early childhood educator:

- never abuses power with children or families

- keeps information confidential

- protects children's best interests

- provides good quality care and education

- respects parents and co-workers

- supports diversity

- favors consumer protection of programs

- improves personal habits

- keeps on learning

- advocates for children, families, and the profession

Your role as a professional is to protect children and families and advocate for what is in keeping with good practice. Above all, you should assure children's safety, health, and general well being. All these while maintaining the ethical standards already discussed.

Here are some sticky consumer protection situations. What would you do?

1. The landlord has instructed that the heat must be set no higher than 62 degrees in the winter. The children and staff are too cold. Do you report your own program to the health department?

2. Your director doesn't count part-time children when reporting enrollment levels because "there are always some children out sick anyway."

3. In your state, family childcare registration is voluntary. If you register, you will have to report your income on your taxes. This means you may lose your rent subsidy.

Working with young children is demanding—of your energy, of your time, and of your conscience. Are you ready to become a professional? Are you prepared to take the most ethical action in difficult situations?

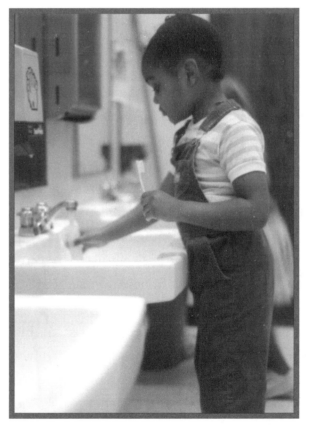

Your role as a professional is to protect children and families, and advocate for what is in keeping with good practice. Above all you should assure children's safety, health, and general well being.

PART 3

You keep learning

By now you probably have realized how much there is to learn about young children. Even if you have been working with young children for years, or are the parent of several, you have surely discovered that it is much more difficult to be a professional early childhood educator.

You are always learning from your experiences. The profession is constantly changing, as we learn more from research about how children develop and learn. This information affects how we teach. How can you keep up with the challenges to get better at what you love to do?

Improve yourself personally

All of us have things we would like to do better. These may include bad habits we want to break, or attitudes that have been questioned.

What are some of the areas you need to work on?

These are the areas you will want to begin to improve so you can be a better teacher. Perhaps you need to read more, improve your vocabulary, eat more healthy foods or you are always late.

Choose just one of the things you listed and write what steps you need to take to change your behavior.

_____

_____

_____

_____

You don't have to do it alone. Rely on the same community support groups to which you refer parents. Or talk with your supervisor, spouse, friend, or a respected colleague about how they can support your efforts. After you have made some progress in one area, select another and begin to work on it. As you make the most of your life, you can better help others make the most of theirs!

Learn more about your profession

How lucky you are to become a professional today. Just a few years ago there weren't many places you could turn to for information. Now nearly every community has an organized group of early childhood educators. Some of these groups are affiliates of NAEYC, NBCDI, NHSA, NAFCC, SECA, or other large organizations. Some are state groups, and others are composed of active local people.

These professional networks are important. Most of you work alone or with just a few other professionals—and you never come in contact with the hundreds of thousands of other people who share the same commitment you do.

The next task in building your network is to find the names of all the professional early childhood support groups in your area (a few national organizations are listed in Unit 1).

If you have not already done so, contact several groups to learn more about their activities. Then select one or two organizations that seem to be good matches for you. Attend their meetings (go with a co-worker or your CDA Field Advisor, if possible). **Join at least one.** If there is no local chapter, consider starting one in your area. Be an active member! Volunteer!

Most of these groups have Websites, publish newsletters, journals, books, videos, posters or other professional development materials. Obtain a sample copy of any regular periodicals that sound interesting. Which publications seem to be most useful to you? You might want to subscribe regularly to a journal or magazine. A few are listed in the Resources for More Information section at the end of this unit.

Find out what resources are available in your program or local library. If not, how can you include some of these items in your program budget? Use the Internet to order others as your personal budget permits.

Read! Read! Read! Or you will soon be left behind in your own profession. Become famil-

In Unit 1, you began networking by interviewing an early childhood professional in a job different from yours. You should continue to build this network by interviewing your CDA Field Advisor—you know each other well by now. Make a list of questions you would like to ask about what the distinctive issues are for a career working with preschoolers, infants and toddlers, or in family childcare:

_____

_____

_____

_____

_____

_____

_____

_____

_____

Now set up a time when the two of you can talk in general about the early childhood profession for at least half an hour. Jot down what you learned here:

_____

_____

_____

_____

_____

_____

_____

_____

_____

iar with the "Resources for more information" found at the end of each unit of *Essentials*.

Workshops, conferences, and classes are excellent ways to meet other people and learn more about how to care for and educate groups of young children. Once you have completed your CDA, keep up with the profession by regularly enrolling in a course or taking a workshop. Better yet, keep climbing that career ladder and continue to work on your college degree!

What topics would you like to learn more about?

_____

_____

_____

_____

Write up a plan to accomplish at least one of these goals. Find out where to go or what to read and continue to become even more professional. Then do it.

Becoming a professional also means contributing to the professional development of others. How do you share your new found knowledge with others?

_____

_____

_____

_____

These are just a few of the issues you will encounter as you continue to work with young children. Your thinking about ethics will be constantly challenged. Are you prepared to meet those challenges and to act on behalf of young children?

PART 4

You act on behalf of young children

A teacher's work is never done. You already know that. And now we are going to suggest that you do even more. Just working with young children day-to-day is not enough. Thousands of children in our country and around the world are hungry, homeless, unhealthy, or have been harshly treated. Children are unable to defend themselves, so we must take it upon ourselves to act in their behalf.

Stand up for good programs and services for children and families

You are now a committed early childhood professional. You have a responsibility to act in your local area, your state, nationally, and even on behalf of children in other countries you have never met. Here are some ways you can reach out, directly or indirectly, to improve

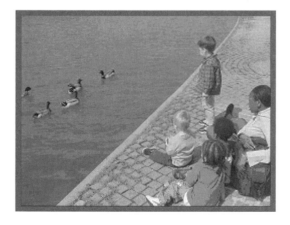

Children need opportunities to develop their language skills.

the lives of children everywhere. **Add others to this list that you can think of or that you are already involved in.**

Don't wait another minute. If you are not taking an active role on behalf of all children and families, choose at least one activity from this list and **get involved now!**

Advocate for your own profession

One of the most difficult issues facing us as early childhood educators is how to balance the need for affordable childcare with our need to support ourselves. Salaries are low. Benefits are inadequate. Many people still view our work as babysitting. But public recognition of the positive long-term consequences of high quality early education is increasing everyday. Research on early brain development raises awareness about the importance of experiences during the first three years of life. And calls for universal preschool are becoming more prevalent across the political spectrum. We now need to turn this public awareness of the value of early childhood education into recognition of the value of early childhood educators, and improve their compensation accordingly!

Good programs for young children are especially expensive because so many staff are needed, so many materials are used, and so much space is required. We don't want to shortchange children. Nor do we want to settle for less than we deserve for the professional knowledge and skill required for this important work.

Remain committed to the entire profession.

Act on the Behalf of Children. . .

- Write letters to support stronger childcare legislation, programs to strengthen families' self-sufficiency.

- Become active in child advocacy groups.

- Remember early childhood begins at birth. Do something to stay in touch with issues affecting the welfare of babies and toddlers.

- Help parents become child advocates.

- Stay informed about public policy through the e-mail updates from NAEYC and their website.

- Vote in every election.

- Speak up on behalf of developmentally appropriate practice: tell others, buy only appropriate materials, challenge others to learn more about how young children develop and learn.

- Build an appreciation for diversity in the groups you are involved in: civic, church or synagogue, volunteer organizations, community service.

- Volunteer for Week of the Young Child activities.

- Support groups participating in strategies to improve compensation of early childhood professionals.

- Set up a network of supportive colleagues to phone for help.

- Work with your school board or kindergarten teacher's association to ease the transition for children entering public school.

- Advocate for appropriate services for children with disabilities.

Don't isolate yourself only among workers who are like you. Keep learning about others — Head Start, infant/toddler centers, private programs, parent educators/home visitors, church sponsored programs, family childcare.

Don't fall into the old trap of "divide and conquer." Don't allow yourself or your program to be pitted against other programs serving children. That's where "listening" comes in. Support the efforts of early childhood professionals working in other communities as well. Get involved in coordinated compensation strategies that benefit all early childhood professionals.

What can you do to improve the quality of life for staff as well as families in programs for young children?

_____

_____

_____

_____

_____

You will end this portion of your CDA Professional Preparation Program process by going back to where you began—by reaffirming your commitment to professional work with children. This statement first appeared in Unit 1. Now that you are nearly finished with your CDA—at last—this statement will probably have new meaning for you.

The National Association for the Education of Young Children Statement of Commitment

As an individual who works with young children, I commit myself to furthering the values of early childhood education as they are reflected in the NAEYC Code of Ethical Conduct.

To the best of my ability I will:

- Ensure that programs for young children are based on current knowledge of child development and early childhood education.

- Respect and support families in their task of nurturing children.

- Respect colleagues in early childhood education and support them in maintaining the NAEYC Code of Ethical Conduct.

- Serve as an advocate for children, their families, and their teachers in community and society.

- Maintain high standards of professional conduct.

- Recognize how personal values, opinions, and biases can affect professional judgment.

- Be open to new ideas and be willing to learn from the suggestions of others.

- Continue to learn, grow, and contribute as a professional.

- Honor the ideals and principles of the _NAEYC Code of Ethical Conduct._

Congratulations for taking on a very difficult task—enrolling in the CDA Professional Preparation Program. You can check the box on your CDA Progress Record. Your Professional Resource File is now, or soon will be, complete and you will take part in a final assessment. Our best wishes are with you during these final stages of meeting the requirements for your CDA Credential.

We welcome you as a professional early childhood educator. May your work be more rewarding than you ever dreamed possible and may you grow in your professional competencies each day. The world's children are counting on you.

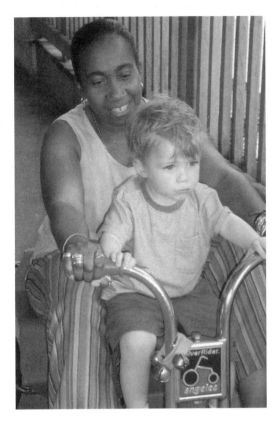

Children look for and often need your guidance to help them do the things they like to do.

Resources for more information

Accreditation standards for early childhood programs. Contact www.naeyc.org for center-based standards. Contact www.nafcc.org for standards for family child care homes.

Feeney, S. & Freeman, N.K. (1999). *Ethics and the early childhood educator: Using the NAEYC Code.* Washington, DC: National Association for the Education of Young Children.

Gonzalez-Mena, J. (1991). *Tips and tidbits: A book for family child care providers.* Washington, DC: National Association for the Education of Young Children.

Lombardi, J. (2003). *Time to care: Redesigning child care to promote education, support families, and build communities.* Philadelphia: Temple University Press. Available from www.naeyc.org

Modigliani, K., Reiff, M., & Jones, S. (1987). *Opening your door to children: How to start a family day care program.* Washington, DC: National Association for the Education of Young Children.

National Child Care Information Center, funded by the Child Care Bureau, U.S. Department of Health and Human Services. www.nccic.org.

Raphael, D. & Weisman, D. *How to start a family day care* (video and book). St. Paul, MN: Redleaf Press.

Robinson, A & Stark, D.R. (2002). *Advocates in action: Making a difference for young children.* Washington, DC: National Association for the Education of Young Children.

Professional Publications

Child Care Information Exchange
www.childcareexchange.com

Child Health Talk
National Black Child Development Institute
www.nbcdi.org

Children and Families Magazine
National Head Start Association
www.nhsa.org

Childhood Education
Association for Childhood Education International
www.udel.edu/bateman/acei

Dimensions
Southern Early Childhood Association
www.southernearlychildhood.org

Head Start Information and Publication Center (HSIPC)
www.headstartinfo.org

MenTeach—a Website with resources for men teaching young children
www.MenTeach.org

NABE News
National Association for Bilingual Education
www.nabe.org

The National Perspective (newsletter)
National Association for Family Child Care
www.nafcc.org

Young Children
National Association for the Education of Young Children
www.naeyc.org

Young Exceptional Children
Division for Early Childhood of the Council for Exceptional Children
www.dec-sped.org

Zero to Three, professional journal of
Zero the Three: National Center for Infants, Toddlers and Families
www.zerotothree.org

Resources for bilingual programs

Compiled by Chimere Jones and Sarah Kinderknecht, with Barbra Lancelot, Director Early Detection and Intervention Project, Center for International Development, 2003
www.cirnetwork.org

- **Babies On the Web**
  Bebes en la Web
  http://www.bebesenlaweb.com.ar/intervenciontemprana.html\

Bebes en la Web is provided by the Institute for Pedagogical Psychology. This site contains an article titled "Intervention Temprana para lactantes y deambuladores", which addresses early detection of disabilities in children. This article, written in Spanish, focuses on what parents can do to detect birth defects and illnesses within their child at an early age.

This article focuses primarily on:
- o Incorporating parents in the developmental work of their child.
- o To accentuate the possibility of success in the development of the child.
- o To strengthen the bond between a child and his parent.
- o To re-evaluate the image that the parent has of their child.
- o Educating parents on the disability of their child under three years old.

Contact: Lic. Silvia Zaffirio
Barrio Norte (Ciudad de Buenos Aires) – Escobar Argentina
Teléfono 011-15-4-022-3099
Email: primeroscuidados@bebesenlaweb.zzn.com

- **The California Childcare Health Program**

  http://www.ucsfchildcarehealth.org/webpages/links.htm#childdevelopment
  With in this site The California Childcare Health Program provides links to other helpful sites, pertaining to the following subjects:
  - o Child Abuse Prevention, Child Care,
  - o Child Development,
  - o Child Passenger Safety
  - o Children with Special Needs,
  - o Diversity,
  - o Health and Safety
  - o Health Insurance and Child Welfare Services
  - o Parenting
  - o Public Policy
  - o California Government Sites

  Contact: The California Childcare Health Program
  1322 Webster Street, Suite 402
  Oakland, CA 94612
  Phones: (510) 839-1195
  Fax: (510)839-0339
  Email: cchp@ucsfchildcarehealth.org

- **CLAS: The Early Childhood Research Services on Culturally & Linguistic Services**
  CLAS

  http://clas.uiuc.edu

  This is a bilingual website in both Spanish and English for the Early Childhood Research Institute on Culturally and Linguistically Appropriate Services (CLAS). The CLAS Institute identifies, evaluates, and promotes effective and appropriate early intervention practices and preschool practices that are sensitive and respectful to children and families from culturally and linguistically diverse backgrounds. The site includes links to additional resources and includes a bilingual search option to find catered materials throughout the site including publications available in Spanish. These publications can be used by early childhood/special education practitioners to help them select culturally and linguistically appropriate materials for early intervention practices. The link to the publications site is as follows:

  http://clas.uiuc.edu/publications.html

  Contact: CLAS Early Childhood Research Institute
  ATTN: Acquisitions Coordinator
  61 Children's Research Center
  51 Gerty Drive
  Champaign, IL 61820-7498

- **Early Start Online Library**
  http://www.edgateway.net/cs/es/view/lwe/472
  http://www.edgateway.net/cs/es/view/lwe/473
  http://www.edgateway.net/cs/es/view/lwe/3438

  These links are a part of the Early Start Online Library. The links are titled in Spanish as Companeros en el Idioma: Guia para Los Padres (A Guide for Parents). http://www.edgateway.net/cs/es/view/lwe/472 is a bilingual pictorial guide pertaining to early speech and language progression. This site also addresses ways that families can stimulate their infants' growth. http://www.edgateway.net/cs/es/view/lwe/473 is a bilingual pictorial guide that addresses language and speech progression for toddlers. http://www.edgateway.net/cs/es/view/lwe/3438 is a Spanish Language site that discusses what scientist feel that parents should to help their baby's brain grow during their first five years.

  Contact: California Department of Developmental Services
  P. O. Box 944202
  Sacramento, CA 94244-2020
  Telephone: (916) 654-1690

- **The Magic of Everyday Moments**
  La Magia de la Vida Contindiana
  http://www.zerotothree.org/magic/Spanish

  This is a Spanish language site that provides health care information to parents regarding developmental learning techniques and procedures. This links is provided by Zero to Three and the Johnson & Johnson Pediatric Institute.

The links provide information pertaining to the building self-confidence, curiosity, social skills, self-control, and communication skills. This site provides information to parents of children ages:

- o 0-4 months
- o 4-6 months
- o 6-9 months
- o 9-12 months
- o 12-15 months

Contact: ZERO to THREE
National Center for Infants, Toddlers and Families
2000 M Street, NW, Suite 200
Washington, DC 20036
Phone: 202- 638-1144

- **Migrant Head Start- Disabilities Services Quality Improvement Center**

    El Centro para el Mejoramiento de la Calidad de los Servicios para Niños con Discapacidades de Head Start para Familias Migrantes (MHS DSQIC)

    http://www.mhsdsqic.org/newsletter/newsletter1sp.pdf

    This is a link to a Spanish newsletter from El Centro para el Mejoramiento de la Calidad de los Servicios para Niños con Discapacidades de Head Start para Familias Migrantes (MHS DSQIC).

    Contact: Migrant Head Start- Disabilities Services Quality Improvement Center
    1825 Connecticut Avenue, NW
    Washington, DC 20009
    Phone: 877-371- 2088, Fax: 202-884-8113
    Fax: 512-476-2286

- **The National Early Childhood Technical Assistance Center**
    NECTAC- El Centro Nacional de Asistencia Técnica para la Niñez Temprana en español

    http://www.nectac.org/about/bienvenidos.asp

    http://www.nectac.org/about/elcentro.asp

    http://www.nectac.org/default.asp

    Their technical support is targeted to aid administrators from all states and other U.S. jurisdictions responsible for planning and implementing services under IDEA and also additional state agency personnel, service providers, families, community and higher education representatives, TA providers, and individuals from multiple levels of the service system. Their website provides information and links for the IDEA, the ERIC Clearinghouse and also for relevant projects and publications. The organization's mission is to strengthen systems at all levels to ensure that children (birth through five) with disabilities and their families receive and benefit from high quality, culturally appropriate and family centered supports and services.

    Contact: Chapel Hill, NC 27599-8040
    Phone: (919) 962-2001
    TDD: (919) 843-3269
    Fax: (919) 966-7463
    E-mail: nectac@unc.edu

- **Parents Helping Parents INC**.

    Padres Ayudando a Padres

    http://www.php.com/dopage/espanol

    This is the Spanish language information site of Parents Helping Parents Inc., the Family Resource Center Inc., http://www.php.com. Their mission is to help children with special needs receive the resources, love, hope, respect, healthcare, education and other services they need to achieve their full potential by providing them with strong families and dedicated professionals to serve them. Their website provides references to programs, support groups, events and outside resources.

    Contact: 3041 Olcott Street, Santa Clara, CA 95054
    Voice: (408) 727-5775 Fax: (408) 727-0182

- **UNICEF**

    UNICEF Manual
    Manual de UNICEF
    http://www.unicef.org/spanish/ffl/pdf/factsforlife-sp-part4.pdf

This website contains an article titled information about the importance of infant development and early intervention in detecting illnesses within the first eight years of a child's life. This article is completely in Spanish and it is dedicated to the fundamental value of early education in child care development. This article emphasizes the importance of the quality of attention and care that the child receives during the first eight years of their life. The article also highlights the important of early intervention and child care during the first three years of the child's life. There is an emphasis placed on the first eight years of the child's life because these are the child's most formative years.

Para la Vida- La Lactancia Materna
http://www.unicef.org/spanish/ffl/04/index.html

This website provided by UNICEF and is in the Spanish language. This website is dedicated to educating mother on the health issues that are associated with breast feeding. This website informs mother on the nutritional and developmental values of breast feeding along with other health care issues including HIV/AID's, immunization, and malnutrition.

Contact:

UNICEF House
3 United Nations Plaza
New York, New York 10017
Telephone: 326.7000

Fax: 887.7465 or Fax: 887.7454

Email: information@unicef.org

You are almost there. . .

As you prepare to demonstrate your competency as a teacher of young children, you will complete these tasks in Unit 8:

1. Collaborate with your Field Advisor to distribute the Parent Opinion Questionnaire to all the parents of children in your group.

2. Complete your CDA Professional Resource File.

3. Be observed by your Field Advisor as you demonstrate your skills with children in the appropriate setting depending on your endorsement—a preschool or infant/toddler classroom setting, or with children in a home setting.

4. Submit your application to complete the final assessment—take the written exam and oral interview, and submit your Professional Resource File and other materials about you to the Council for Professional Recognition.

Preparing for final assessment as a Child Development Associate

Now, you should be prepared to complete your final assessment. The process will determine your ability to integrate the knowledge and skills outlined in the *Essentials* curriculum and to demonstrate your competence as a CDA working with young children and their families.

Once you submit your application and fees, a specially trained Council Representative will be assigned by the Council for Professional Recognition to conduct an on-site visit to collect evidence of your competence working with young children and their families. The Council Rep will interview you, administer the written Early Childhood Studies Review, review the results of the Formal Observation and Parent Opinion Questionnaires, and examine your Professional Resource File. A summary of the results of this evidence will be forwarded to the Council office in Washington, D.C. Or, if you are eligible, you may submit materials to the national office and complete the interview and written Early Childhood Studies Review online.

If you successfully complete the final assessment, the Child Development Associate Credential will be awarded with an endorsement for center-based programs serving either preschoolers or infants and toddlers, or for family child care (depending on the credential setting for which you applied).

Candidates working in bilingual settings and completing special additional requirements will be awarded the Bilingual Specialization.

Definition of a CDA

The Child Development Associate (CDA) is a person who is able to meet the specific needs of children and who, with parents and other adults, works to nurture children's physical, social, emotional, and intellectual growth in a child development framework. The CDA Credential is awarded to child care providers and home visitors who have demonstrated their skill in working with young children and their families by successfully completing the CDA assessment process.

PART 1

CDA Competency Standards

As a Candidate for the CDA Credential, you will be assessed based upon the CDA Competency Standards. These criteria are the national standards used to evaluate a teacher's performance with children and families. The Competency Standards are divided into six *Competency Goals*, which are statements of a general purpose or goal for teacher behavior. The six goals are defined in more detail in 13 *Functional Areas*, which describe the major tasks or functions that a teacher must complete in order to carry out the Competency Goal. The national Competency Goals and Functional Area definitions are common to all early childhood settings, whether in centers or family child care homes.

All of the evidence you collect to demonstrate your competence as a CDA will be judged by these standards.

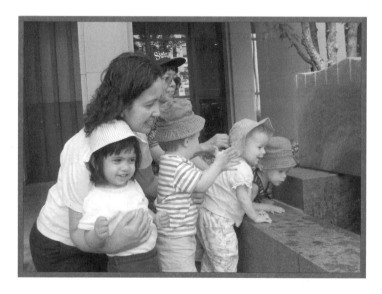

As you become more professional in your role as an early childhood educator, your ability to work with children will be enhanced.

"Through the years of providing child care, I finally took a step forward to see what I can gain and accomplish with my work. The obstacles were sometimes hard to climb over, yet it was all challenging and well worth it. It is amazing, and yet, it is an honor to be listed among the CDA's nationwide."

Windy Sherman, first Family Child Care CDA on Hopi Reservation, 2003.

CDA Competency Goals	Functional Areas	Definitions
I To establish and maintain a safe, healthy learning environment	1. Safe	Candidate provides a safe environment to prevent and reduce injuries.
	2. Healthy	Candidate promotes good health and nutrition and provides an environment that contributes to the prevention of illness.
	3. Learning Environment	Candidate uses space, relationships, materials, and routines as resources for constructing an interesting, secure, and enjoyable environment that encourages play, exploration, and learning.
II To advance physical and intellectual competence	4. Physical	Candidate provides a variety of equipment, activities, and opportunities to promote the physical development of children.
	5. Cognitive	Candidate provides activities and opportunities that encourage curiosity, exploration, and problem solving appropriate to the developmental levels and learning styles of children.
	6. Communication	Candidate actively communicates with children and provides opportunities and support for children to understand, acquire, and use verbal and nonverbal means of communicating thoughts and feelings.
	7. Creative	Candidate provides opportunities that stimulate children to play with sound, rhythm, language, materials, space, and ideas in individual ways and to express their creative abilities.
III To support social and emotional development and provide positive guidance	8. Self	Candidate provides physical and emotional security for each child and helps each child to know, accept, and take pride in himself or herself and to develop a sense of independence.
	9. Social	Candidate helps each child feel accepted in the group, helps children learn to communicate and get along with others, and encourages feelings of empathy and mutual respect among children and adults.
	10. Guidance	Candidate provides a supportive environment in which children can begin to learn and practice appropriate and acceptable behaviors as individuals and as a group.
IV To establish positive and productive relationships with families	11. Families	Candidate maintains an open, friendly, and cooperative relationship with each child's family, encourages their involvement in the program, and supports the child's relationship with his or her family.
V To ensure a well-run, purposeful program responsive to participant needs	12. Program Management	Candidate is a manager who uses all available resources to ensure an effective operation. The Candidate is a competent organizer, planner, record keeper, communicator, and a cooperative co-worker.
VI To maintain a commitment to professionalism	13. Professionalism	Candidate makes decisions based on knowledge of early childhood theories and practices, promotes quality in child care services, and takes advantage of opportunities to improve competence, both for personal and professional growth and for the benefit of children and families.

PART 2

Documentation of Competence

Your final assessment as a CDA will involve a documentation of your competence. Five components make up the documentation:

> 1. *Early Childhood Studies Review*
> 2. *Professional Resource File*
> 3. *Formal Observation*
> 4. *Parent Opinion Questionnaires*
> 5. *Oral Interview*

First, you will prepare to present evidence of your competence from the following three sources:

> 1. *Professional Resource File*
> 2. *Formal Observation by the Field Advisor*
> 3. *Parent Opinion Questionnaires*

Then, you will complete your Oral Interview and Early Childhood Studies Review either during the Council Rep's Verification Visit or online.

Professional Resource File

The Professional Resource File is a collection of materials that you will use as an early childhood professional in future work with young children and families. It is compiled for two purposes:

> 1. *It provides a picture of what information Candidates find valuable in their work as a basis for assessing competence as a CDA; and*
> 2. *It provides Candidates an important experience in locating resources, using them in their work, and evaluating their effectiveness in early childhood programs.*

The Professional Resource File is a working resource—one that should be USEFUL to you as a CDA during your career in early childhood education. In your Professional Resource File, you should include resources that you are familiar with and that you use in your daily work with children, families, programs, and the community. The process of preparing the File provides you with plenty of opportunity to create, gather, select, use, and evaluate the most appropriate resources available. Therefore, the collection included in the Resource File ultimately must reflect your own situation, and your own work and activities.

You have already collected most, if not all, of the materials you need for your Professional Resource File and have drafted Statements of Competence for five of the six Competency areas. Now it is time to revise and complete all three sections and arrange them in their final form.

Arrangement of the Resource File

The material in the Professional Resource File can be arranged in any one of many creative ways (*e.g., bound in a notebook or contained inside file folders in a box*). It should be professional looking and manageable in size. The File should be organized and easy to add to or delete from. *There are no requirements about <u>how</u> it should look.* Whatever its physical form, the Professional Resource File should be portable—designed to be carried to and from a work site, on a home visit, or to a meeting—wherever early childhood professionals work.

Contents

The Professional Resource File has three major sections: (1) *Autobiography*; (2) *Statements of Competence*; and (3) *Resource Collection.*

1. **Autobiography:** Write a statement about yourself of about 300 words. In the first part tell who you are, and in the second part, tell what things about your life influenced your decision to work with young children. *If you wish, you may attach a formal résumé of your education and work experiences.*

2. **Statements of Competence:** In your own words, describe what you do with children and families that demonstrates your ability to meet the specific needs and support the learning and development of children in each of the following six Competency Goal areas. The description in each area should be 200-500 words in length and should state your goals for children and give specific examples of what you do to achieve those goals. *For Bilingual Candidates, statements must be specific to the goals of bilingual programs and the statements in three Competency Goal areas must be written in Spanish.*

Begin each section by writing out the Competency Goal Statement:

1. To establish and maintain a safe, healthy learning environment

2. To advance physical and intellectual competence

3. To support social and emotional development and to provide positive guidance

4. To establish positive and productive relationships with families

5. To ensure a well-run, purposeful program responsive to participant needs

6. To maintain a commitment to professionalism

Remember, your statement for each Competency Goal should contain no more than 500 words. Of course, you cannot describe everything you do in such a limited space. Choose the most important goals you have for children and the best examples of practices that you feel represent your competence.

Write about your *current practice*, using examples of your work now (within the past six months). As you review the draft statements you wrote when you first started reading *Essentials*, you may need to revise them based on changes in your beliefs and practices as you progressed through your study.

3. Resource Collection: The third part of your Professional Resource File consists of 17 specific items called the Resource Collection. Even though you have collected them as you worked through *Essentials* chapter by chapter, you should check them again for completeness. They should now be organized by Competency Goal areas and numbered so that each item can be located easily during the Council Representative verification visit. *Do not mix them with your statements of competence. For Candidates applying for the Bilingual Specialization, the resources used directly with children and families must be in two languages (English and another language). These are items 4, 5, 6, 7, 8, 10, 11, 12, 15, and 16. For Monolingual (other than English) Candidates. Items 4, 5, 6, 7, 8, 10, 11, 12, 15, and 16 must be in the other language.*

Note: Some Resource File items vary slightly depending on the setting for which endorsement will be granted.

●●●●●●●●●●●●●●●●●●●●●●●●●●●●●●●

COMPETENCY GOAL I

To establish and maintain a safe, healthy learning environment

1. Provide a summary of the legal requirements in your state regarding child abuse and neglect (including contact information for the appropriate agency), and also your program's policy regarding your responsibility to report child abuse and neglect.

2. Include the current certificate of completion of a certified pediatric first-aid training course (that includes treatment for blocked airway and providing rescue breathing for infants and young children). Certification must have been within the past three years.

3. Use the Internet, public library, or your program's professional library to obtain the name and contact information for an agency that supplies information on nutrition for children and/or nutrition education for families (e.g., *Cooperative Extension Service* or *Child Care Food Program*).

4. Provide a sample of your weekly plan that includes goals for children's learning and development, brief description of planned learning experiences, and also accommodations for children with special needs (whether for children you currently serve or may serve in the future).

●●●●●●●●●●●●●●●●●●●●●●●●●●●●●●●

COMPETENCY GOAL II

To advance physical and intellectual competence

5. Select four songs, fingerplays, word games, or poems that you can use to promote phonological awareness. Describe strategies to promote phonological awareness among children whose home language is other than English.

6. **For preschool endorsement**: Describe nine learning experiences for three, four, and five year old children (three for three-year-olds, three for four-year-olds, and three for five-year-olds). Each learning experience should promote physical, cognitive, and creative development. Describe the goals, materials, and teaching strategies used.

For infant/toddler endorsement: Describe nine learning experiences that promote physical, cognitive, and creative development—three for young infants, three for mobile infants, and three for toddlers. Describe the goals, materials, and teaching strategies used.

For family child care endorsement: Describe nine learning experiences that promote physical, cognitive, and creative development—three for infants, three for toddlers and three for preschoolers. Describe the goals, materials, and teaching strategies used.

• •

COMPETENCY GOAL III

To support social and emotional development and *to provide positive guidance*

7. Provide the titles, authors, publishers, copyright dates, and short summary of ten age-appropriate children's books **that you use** to support development of children's self-concept and self-esteem, and to help children deal with life's challenges. These books may support development of cultural and linguistic group identity; gender identity; children with disabilities or special needs; separation, divorce, remarriage, or blended families; everyday activities and routines; and/or the cycle of life from human reproduction to death.

8. Use the Internet, public library, or your program's professional library to obtain at least two resources designed to assist teachers in constructively dealing with children with challenging behaviors (such as aggressive behavior like hitting or biting, or shyness).

9. Provide the name and telephone number of an agency in the community where you work for making referrals to family counseling.

• •

COMPETENCY GOAL IV

To establish positive and productive relationships with *families*

10. Find out where to obtain resources, materials, and translation services for families whose home language is other than English. Provide the agency name and contact information.

11. Document your program's policies that specify parents' responsibilities and what the program does for parents.

• •

COMPETENCY GOAL V

To ensure a well-run, purposeful program responsive to participant needs

12. Provide three samples of record-keeping forms used in early childhood programs. Include an accident report, emergency form, and a third form of your choice.

• •

COMPETENCY GOAL VI

To maintain a commitment to professionalism

13. Use the Internet, public library, or your program's professional library to obtain the name, address, and phone number of your state's agency that regulates child care centers and homes. These regulations are available electronically at the website of the National Resource Center for Health and Safety in Child Care

(http://nrc.uchsc.edu/STATES/states.htm). Make a copy of the section(s) that describe qualification requirements for personnel (teachers, directors, and assistants). For family child care: If your state does not regulate family child care homes, review the accreditation standards of the National Association for Family Child Care. Describe two important requirements related to your job responsibilities.

14. Review the websites of two or three national early childhood associations (one with a local affiliate) to obtain information about membership, their resources, and how to order (if necessary, use the public library for Internet access). Download and include at least two resources from the Internet that will enhance your work.

15. Obtain four pamphlet(s) or articles (may be downloaded from the Internet) designed to help parents understand how young children develop and learn.

For preschool endorsement: Articles must help parents understand development and learning of 3 to 5 year olds. At least one article must relate to guidance.

For infant/toddler endorsement: Articles must help parents understand how babies and toddlers (birth to age 3) develop and learn. At least one article must relate to brain development.

For family child care endorsement: Articles must help parents understand development and learning of children birth to 5. At least one article must relate to guidance.

16. Locate an observation tool to use in recording information about children's behavior. One copy should be blank; the other one should be filled out as a sample of your observation of an individual child. (*The child's name should not be included.*)

17. Obtain contact information for at least two agencies in the community that provide resources and services for children with disabilities (in most communities, the local school district provides these services).

Formal Observation

A vital source of evidence of your skill is your actual hands-on work as primary caregiver with children and families. Documentation of these practices is collected through a formal observation.

You will be observed by your Field Advisor while you are working with young children in your field placement setting. This observation will be carried out exactly like the first formal observation conducted during Unit 6 of *Essentials* using the *CDA Assessment Observation Instrument*.

Your Field Advisor will arrange a time to conduct the observation. S/he may complete the formal observation in one visit or it may take several. Once the observation form is completed, it will be presented to the Council Representative during the Verification Visit. The instructions for your Field Advisor are included with the *CDA Observation Assessment Instrument*.

If you are seeking an infant/toddler endorsement, your Field Advisor must document your skills with young infants (*birth-8 months*), mobile infants (*9-17 months*), and toddlers (*18-36 months*). Therefore, it may be necessary for her/him to complete the observation/interaction requirement by *conducting a separate observation in a classroom or group other than where you work on a daily basis.* Following the instructions on the Observation/Interaction Form, your Field Advisor will accompany you to a setting where you can spend a few hours interacting with children.

Keep in mind that the purpose of the observation is to rate your skill in the following specific performance areas. The items the Field Advisor will look for are listed on the next two pages.

In a bilingual setting, the Field Advisor will look for examples of your performance that show your skill in achieving bilingual development in children.

Good early childhood practices include encouraging children to work together and to respect each other's differences.

Candidate Performance Items to be Rated by Field Advisor

Functional Area 1: Safe

1.1 All toys and materials provided for use by children are safe.

1.2 Supervision is appropriate for developmental level of children.

1.3 Emergency procedures are well planned in advance and are well organized.

Functional Area 2: Healthy

2.1 General hygiene practices are implemented consistently to prevent the spread of infectious disease.

2.2 Health maintenance habits in children and adults are encouraged.

2.3 Diapering/toileting procedures are organized to maintain health.

2.4 Meals/snacks meet the developmental needs of children.

2.5 Pleasant and appropriate environment conducive to rest is provided daily.

Functional Area 3: Learning Environment

3.1 Well-arranged space, that meets the developmental needs of children during routines, play, and other learning experiences is provided.

3.2 A variety of developmentally-appropriate materials are made available.

3.3 Materials for play and learning are well organized.

3.4 Schedule provided meets children's needs for routine and play.

Functional Area 4: Physical

4.1 A variety of learning experiences are offered that enable children to develop their large muscles.

4.2 A variety of learning experiences are offered that enable children to develop their fine motor skills.

4.3 Program experiences and environment are adapted to meet individual needs and special needs of children with disabilities.

4.4 Opportunities are offered to help children develop their senses.

Functional Area 5: Cognitive

5.1 A variety of age-appropriate materials and learning experiences that encourage curiosity, exploration, and problem solving are accessible to children throughout the day.

5.2 Interactions provide support for play, exploration, and learning.

5.3 Individual learning styles are recognized.

5.4 Developmentally appropriate learning experiences are provided to promote learning of early literacy and number skills.

Functional Area 6: Communication

6.1 Communication with each individual child is frequent.

6.2 Talk with children is frequent, individualized, and developmentally appropriate.

6.3 Children are encouraged to talk.

6.4 Children's attempts to communicate are responded to positively.

6.5 A developmentally appropriate, print-rich environment, in which children learn about books, literature, letters, sounds, and writing, is provided.

Functional Area 7: Creative

7.1 Individual expression and creativity are appreciated.

7.2 Many appropriate music experiences are available to children.

7.3 Art experiences are age-appropriate and varied.

7.4 Dramatic play experiences, with a variety of age-appropriate props, are available.

7.5 Variety of age-appropriate block play opportunities are available.

Functional Area 8: Self

8.1 Children are given the message that each is important, respected, and valued.

8.2 Individual children are helped to develop a sense of security.

8.3 Diapering/toileting procedures are developmentally appropriate and are organized to encourage self-help skills.

Functional Area 9: Social

9.1 Each child is helped to feel accepted in the group.

9.2 Feelings of empathy and respect for others are encouraged.

9.3 Non-biased curriculum is used.

9.4 Children are encouraged to respect the environment.

Functional Area 10: Guidance

10.1 Methods for avoiding problems are implemented.

10.2 Positive guidance techniques are used.

10.3 Guidance practices are related to knowledge of each child's personality and developmental level.

Functional Area 11: Families

11.1 Various opportunities to appreciate children's families are part of the regular program.

11.2 Information about families' culture, religion, and childrearing practices is used in classroom experiences.

11.3 Various opportunities are offered to help parents understand the development of their child and understand their child's point of view.

11.4 Resources are provided to help families meet their child's needs.

In addition, the Field Advisor will rate your performance in the two additional CDA Functional Areas where it may not be possible to actually observe your behavior during the formal observation. The Field Advisor may need to ask you some questions in order to complete her/his evidence of your skill in the following areas:

Functional Area 12: Program Management

Candidate manages by using all available resources to ensure an effective operation. Candidate is a competent organizer, planner, record keeper, communicator, and a cooperative co-worker.

Functional Area 13: Professionalism

Candidate makes decisions based on knowledge of early childhood research and practices, promotes quality child care services, and takes advantage of opportunities to improve competence, both for personal and professional growth and for the benefit of children and families. Candidate keeps abreast of regulatory, legislative, and workforce issues and how they affect the welfare of young children.

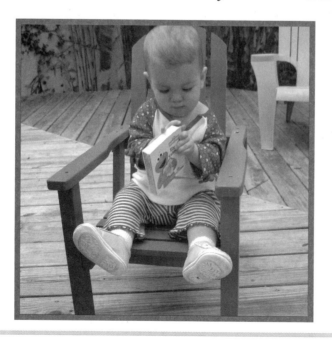

PART 3

How much do parents know about me?

Parent Opinion Questionnaire

Parent perceptions about your skills and knowledge are extremely important in assessing whether you conduct yourself in a professional manner. Your Field Advisor will assist you in this process of gathering parent opinions. Each family with a child in your care will be given an opportunity to complete a questionnaire. At least 75% of the questionnaires distributed must be completed. Your Field Advisor may have to make follow-up telephone calls in order to get the questionnaires returned.

The questionnaires are confidential and you will not be able to read the parents' responses. The Field Advisor will collect the questionnaires and place them in a sealed envelope for you to present to the Council Representative. Instructions for distributing and collecting the responses to this questionnaire are included in the *Field Advisor's Guide*, along with the following cover letter and questionnaire.

Paying close attention to children reassures parents that you have their child's best interests at heart.

CDA PARENT OPINION QUESTIONNAIRE COVER LETTER

Dear Parents:

I am applying to be assessed for the Child Development Associate (CDA) Credential. Located in Washington, D.C., the Council for Professional Recognition (*Council*) awards the CDA Credential. The Credential is awarded to competent caregivers and home visitors who have demonstrated their ability to teach effectively and meet the needs of children and parents on a daily basis.

The Council believes that parents have the right to know that the individuals caring for their children are competent. Therefore, parents have a very important role in the assessment of a person who wants to become a Child Development Associate. You can make an important contribution to a national effort to assure quality child care for young children by evaluating my work with your child and family.

As part of my assessment, I am required to collect the opinion of all parents who have children in my group. Therefore, I am asking you to fill out the questionnaire included with this letter. Your answers will be confidential. Please do not sign your name. Think about each question and answer it openly and honestly. Your specific comments at the end of the questionnaire will be very much appreciated.

I would be grateful if you would return your completed questionnaire to me in the enclosed envelope (**sealed**) by

_____.

If you have any questions, please contact me at
_____, or you may contact the Council hotline at 1-800-424-4310.

Thanks for your help.

Sincerely yours,

_____
CDA Candidate

Queridos Padres:

Estoy solicitando ser evaluada/o para obtener mi Credencial de Asociada/o en el Desarrollo del Niño (CDA). Esta Credencial es otorgada por el Concillo ("*Council*") para el Reconocimiento Profesional de la Educación Infantil/Pre-escolar/Temprana, localizado en Washington, D.C. La credencial es otorgada a personas que demuestran ser capaces de satisfacer las necesidades específicas de los niños, y quienes trabajan con los padres para fomentar el progreso del niño.

El Concilio ("Council") cree firmemente que los padres/madres tienen el derecho de saber que los individuos a cargo del cuidado de sus niños son profesionales competentes, es por eso que los padres juegan un papel muy importante en la evaluación de una persona que desea convertirse en un Asociado en el Desarrollo del Niño (CDA). Usted podría contribuír grandemente a este esfuerzo nacional, de asegurar la calidad en el cuidado infantil/pre-escolar, evaluando mi trabajo con su niño/s y su familia.

Como parte de mi evaluación, tengo la responsabilidad de recolectar la opinióm de todos los padres de los niños en mi grupo. Por esta razón, le pido que llene el cuestinario adjunto a esta carta. Sus respuestas se mantendrán confidenciales. Por favor no escriba su nombre. Piense y responda a cada pregunta en forma libre y honesta. Sus comentarios específicos al final del cuestionario serán apreciados.

Le agradezco anticipadamente se sirva devolverme este cuestionario completo en un sobre **sellado**, antes del

_____.

Si Ud. tiene alguna pregunta, por favor comuníquese conmigo al_____, o Ud. puede llamar a la línea de ayuda del Concilio (*Council hotline*) al 1-800-424-4310.

Gracias por su apoyo.

Sinceramente,

_____
Candidata/o CDA

CDA PARENT OPINION QUESTIONNAIRE
CUESTIONARIO CDA DE OPINION DE PADRES

CDA Candidate's Name _____

Nombre del Candidato/a CDA _____

For each statement, circle the answer you think is best.

Haga un círculo alrededor de cada respuesta que usted considere como la más correcta

YES = CDA Candidate does this
NO = CDA Candidate does not do this
N/A = Do not know or does not apply

SI = La Candidata CDA lo hace
NO = La Candidata no hace esto
N/A = Ud.no sabe o no es pertinente

The CDA Candidate/ El Candidato/a CDA:

YES NO N/A 1. Reports accidents or any first aid given to my child.
SI NO N/A 1. Reporta accidentes o primeros auxilios dados a mi niño.

YES NO N/A 2. Requires my written permission to give any medication to my child.
SI NO N/A 2. Requiere mi autorización por escrito para poder dar cualquier medicina a mi niño.

YES NO N/A 3. Tells me about my child's eating, sleeping, and toileting/diapering.
SI NO N/A 3. Me dice como mi niño come, si duerme, sobre sus hábitos en el uso del baño, o cambio de pañales.

YES NO N/A 4. Follows feeding instructions for my infant or for my child with allergies.
SI NO N/A 4. Sigue instrucciones para la alimentación de mi bebé o la de mi niño que sufre de alergias.

YES NO N/A 5. Allows my child to be picked up only by people I have named.
SI NO N/A 5. Permite que a mi niño lo recojan sólo aquellas personas a quienes yo he autorizado.

YES NO N/A 6. Reports to me about my child's play and learning.
SI NO N/A 6. Me mantiene informado/a sobre el desarrollo y el aprendizaje de mi niño.

YES NO N/A 7. Organizes toys and play materials so my child can reach them easily.
SI NO N/A 7. Organiza los juguetes y materiales de juego de manera que mi niño pueda alcanzarlos facilmente.

YES NO N/A 8. Provides a place for my child to store his or her own things and makes sure I can find the things I need to bring home.
SI NO N/A 8. Provee un lugar para que mi niño pueda guardar sus pertenencias y se asegura de que yo pueda encontrar todas las cosas que necesito llevar a casa.

YES	NO	N/A	9.	Has enough toys and materials so children do not fight over popular toys.
SI	NO	N/A	9.	*Tiene juguetes y materiales en número suficiente para evitar que los niños peleen por los juguetes más populares.*

YES	NO	N/A	10.	Takes my child outdoors to play every day, except in bad weather.
SI	NO	N/A	10.	*Lleva a mi niño a jugar afuera todos los días excepto cuando el tiempo esta muy malo.*

YES	NO	N/A	11.	Talks with my child frequently.
SI	NO	N/A	11.	*Habla frecuentemente con mi niño.*

YES	NO	N/A	12.	Listens with interest when my child talks and encourages my child to talk.
SI	NO	N/A	12.	*Escucha con interés cuando mi niño habla y lo anima a hablar.*

YES	NO	N/A	13.	Helps my child learn to control his or her own behavior without spanking or other harsh punishment.
SI	NO	N/A	13.	*Ayuda a mi niño a controlar su propio comportamiento, sin pegarle o sin usar castigos duros.*

YES	NO	N/A	14.	Reads to my child often.
SI	NO	N/A	14.	*Le lee a mi niño, con mucha frecuencia.*

YES	NO	N/A	15.	Provides many music, art, block and pretend activities that my child can do in his or her own way.
SI	NO	N/A	15.	*Provee muchas actividades de música, arte, bloques, actividades de pre tender, que mi niño puede hacer a su manera.*

YES	NO	N/A	16.	Helps my child feel proud of what he or she can do.
SI	NO	N/A	16.	*Ayuda a mi niño a sentirse orgulloso de lo que él puede hacer.*

YES	NO	N/A	17.	Encourages children to enjoy getting along with each other.
SI	NO	N/A	17.	*Anima a los niños el disfrute de llevarse bien entre ellos.*

YES	NO	N/A	18.	Gives me the feeling that she is truly interested in my child and me.
SI	NO	N/A	18.	*Me hace sentir que ella/él está verdaderamente interesada/o en mi niño y en mí.*

YES	NO	N/A	19.	Is pleasant and friendly with me.
SI	NO	N/A	19.	*Es agradable y amistosa/o conmigo.*

YES	NO	N/A	20.	Is available to discuss my concerns.
SI	NO	N/A	20.	*Esta disponible para hablar conmigo sobre mis preocupaciones.*

YES	NO	N/A	21.	Asks me for ideas to use with my child, including activity ideas.
SI	NO	N/A	21.	*Me pide ideas para usarlas con mi niño, incluyendo ideas sobre actividades.*

YES	NO	N/A	22.	Asks me what I think is important in raising my child.
SI	NO	N/A	22.	*Me pregunta sobre lo que yo pienso que es importante en la crianza de mi niño.*

YES	NO	N/A	23.	Talks with me about any fears my child has.
SI	*NO*	*N/A*	*23.*	*Me habla sobre cualquier temor o problema que tenga mi niño.*

YES	NO	N/A	24.	Maintains confidentiality; does not freely discuss my child or family in the presence of others.
SI	*NO*	*N/A*	*24.*	*Es reservada/o, mantiene información confidencial; no habla sobre mi niño o mi familia en la presencia de otras personas.*

YES	NO	N/A	25.	Encourages me to visit at any time.
SI	*NO*	*N/A*	*25.*	*Me anima a visitar en cualquier momento.*

YES	NO	N/A	26.	Lets me know of parent meetings and other ways I can become involved in the program.
SI	*NO*	*N/A*	*26.*	*Me hace saber cuando hay reuniones de Padres y me informa sobre otras maneras de participar en el programa.*

YES	NO	N/A	27.	Schedules conferences at times that are convenient to me.
SI	*NO*	*N/A*	*27.*	*Señala fechas para reunirnos, en días y horas que me son convenientes.*

Indicate language(s) you use at home_____.
Language(s) Candidate uses with your child_____.

Indique el idioma/s que usted habla en su casa_____.
Idioma/s que la Candidata hable a su niño_____.

• •

Please write your opinion about this Candidate's work with your child:
Por favor escriba lo que usted opina sobre el trabajo de esta Candidata/o con usted y con su niño:

DATE you completed this questionnaire _____

FECHA en que usted completó este cuestionario _____

PART 4

Final assessment: Verification visit or online

Once you have completed your Professional Resource File, Formal Observation, and Parent Opinion Questionnaires, you are ready to submit your application for final assessment either by a Verification Visit by the Council Representative or online. An online assessment is conducted electronically and you will receive detailed instructions by mail or e-mail.

If you opt for a verification visit, the Council Rep will telephone you to schedule a date. You will need to provide a private place for the Council Rep to review your documents, administer the Early Childhood Studies Review, and conduct the interview. It is preferable to use space at the Center where you work. Be sure to get permission from the Program Director, and if you need help arranging a place, ask your Field Advisor to assist you.

For family childcare providers, it is preferable to locate space outside the family childcare home, such as at a library, community center or church. However, if no other space is available, the provider's home may be used, as long as the rooms are completely private and free from traffic, telephone calls and other interruptions, AND another adult is on the premises providing substitute care for the children. If you need help arranging a place, ask your Field Advisor to assist you.

Before the Council Rep arrives, prepare your documentation in the following way:

1. Put your Professional Resource File in final form. The Council Rep will check to see that all entries are complete and then return the File to you. *Make a photocopy of your "Autobiography" and "Statements of Competence"*—the Council Rep will mail these to the Council office in Washington, D.C.

2. Get the completed CDA Assessment Observation Instrument from your Field Advisor. It should be in a sealed envelope for the Council Rep to mail to the Council.

3. Get the completed Parent Opinion Questionnaires from your Field Advisor. They should also be in a sealed envelope. The Council Rep will mail these to the Council.

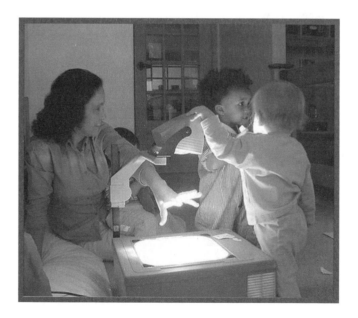

As a professional early childhood educator, you play an important role in stimulating children's learning through creative play.

During the Verification Visit, the Council Rep will:

1. Check the "Autobiography" in the Professional Resource File and send one copy to the Council.

2. Check the "Statements of Competence" in the Professional Resource File and send the copies to the Council.

3. Check the Resource Collection in the Professional Resource File and return it to you.

4. Check the Parent Opinion Questionnaires and send them to the Council.

5. Check the CDA Assessment Observation Instrument and send it to the Council.

6. Conduct the Oral Interview.

7. Administer the Early Childhood Studies Review.

Oral Interview

The Oral Interview provides an opportunity for you to show how the information you have learned would be applied in a variety of early childhood settings.

The interview consists of 10 structured situations and takes about one to two hours to administer. The situations will be specific to your endorsement as a preschool teacher, infant/toddler caregiver, or family childcare provider, and if you have chosen the Bilingual specialization, specific to bilingual programs.

Bilingual Candidates will be interviewed in the language of their choice.

For each situation, the Council Rep will show you a picture with a written description of the activity pictured. The Council Rep will read the description as you read along. Then s/he will pose a question and ask you to respond. As you respond, the Council Rep will listen, make notes and identify various aspects of your response. S/he may ask additional questions to help you give a clean and complete response.

Sample interview questions follow:

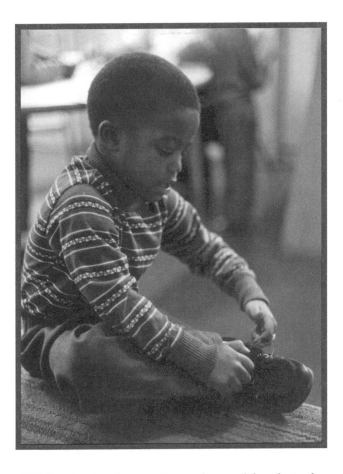

Children's development is enhanced by their desire to perform some tasks independently.

SAMPLE
INTERVIEW
QUESTION

The adult in charge of ten children ages birth to 14 months believes that all of them should be put to sleep every four hours. She thinks children learn discipline from a very young age. Their sleeping time provides her and her assistant with time to plan, clean the classroom and take breaks. All children are supposed to sleep for 45 minutes at a time. The adult says that she and her assistant have tried very hard to implement this routine, but when they get the children ready for bed, some become fussy, cry and do not want to listen.

What do you think of this situation?

"Taking the courses and receiving the training necessary for the CDA was a challenge as a working mom, but "the key was not giving up. I am challenged every day. The variety of cultures and traditions present in our center makes each day interesting, and the opportunities to learn and grow are great for providers as well as the children,"

Jeannie Flowers, Center-Based CDA, 2003.

Three teachers from three different groups take their children outside every day for outdoor activities (each teacher has one assistant). The teachers believe this is a great time to share information among themselves, so they gather together on the entrance steps drinking hot coffee, and allow the assistants to take a break and go inside the building. The children are allowed to play in the different areas of the playground. They play on the swings, in the sandbox and with the outdoor toys and equipment. Although the teachers are not near, they know the children are safe because the playground is fenced in. Also, they have told the children to come tell them if anyone gets hurt or gets in trouble.

What do you think about this?

When the interview is finished, the Council Rep will score your responses and send the results to the Council.

After the Council receives the documentation of your competence, a committee will conduct a review and make a decision. If Credential award is recommended, the official Credential is sent to you, the new Child Development Associate. If the committee recommends more professional education, the Council will notify you and inform you of appeal procedures.

A CDA Credential is valid for three years from award, after which it must be renewed.

Renewal Procedures

A CDA Credential is valid for three years from the date of award, after which it must be renewed for five-year periods. At the request of the CDA, a renewal packet may be purchased from the Council, or downloaded for free from the Council's website: www.cdacouncil.org. CDAs may renew their Credential only for the original setting, age-level endorsement, and specialization. **A Credential for a different setting, endorsement, or added specialization may be earned by applying for a** *Second Setting CDA.*

Under the renewal procedures, all CDAs must complete the following and submit materials to the Council with payment of a renewal fee:

- Document proof of a current **pediatric First Aid Certificate.**

- Document proof of at least **4.5 Continuing Education Units (CEUs), or a three credit-hour course in early childhood education/child development.** These hours must be in addition to the original 120 clock hours or three formal or informal educational experiences required when the Candidate obtained the CDA Credential. Bilingual CDAs must meet this requirement with coursework incorporating bilingual issues.

- **Document proof of recent (within current year) work experiences with young children (a minimum of 80 hours).**

- Select an Early Childhood Education Professional to complete a Letter of Recommendation Form regarding the CDA's competence with young children.

- Document proof (within current year) of **membership in a national or local early childhood professional organization.** A list of suggested national organizations will be included in the renewal application packet.

CONGRATULATIONS!

You have completed all the requirements for the CDA Professional Preparation Program and will soon be assessed as a CDA. In just a few weeks after that, you will receive notification from the Council of the decision about your Credential award.

There are more than 200,000 CDAs across the country, the Commonwealth of Puerto Rico, and the U.S. territories of Guam and the Virgin Islands, and on U.S. military bases worldwide. You will join their ranks, as well as the ranks of the early childhood education profession.

The choice to work with young children and their families is one of the most important career decisions that one can make in our society. Best wishes for a rewarding and successful career ahead!

CDA Progress Record

Keep track of your progress toward your CDA by using this form. Each time you complete a milestone in your CDA Early Childhood Studies, check it off.

You are to be congratulated for each check—it shows that you are learning about how to be a better teacher of young children.

Phase of your CDA Early Childhood Studies

Section of curriculum		Self-Study	Video	Seminar
Unit 1.	Introduction to the early childhood profession	❑	❑	❑
Unit 2.	How children develop and learn	❑	❑	❑
Unit 3.	Safe, healthy environment to promote learning	❑	❑	❑
Unit 4.	Children's social and emotional development	❑	❑	❑
Unit 5.	Children's physical and intellectual competence	❑	❑	❑
Unit 6.	Productive relationships with families	❑	❑	❑
Unit 7.	Putting it all together as an early childhood professional	❑	❑	❑
Unit 8.	Preparing for final assessment as a CDA	❑	❑	❑

Progress on other CDA activities

Date first-aid course completed_____

Parent Questionnaire discussed with Field Advisor on_____

Initial site visit and program observation by Field Advisor completed on _____

Glossary of CDA terms

Bilingual Specialization—Open to Candidates who work in a bilingual program and speak, read, and write both English and a second language. Contact the CDA Candidate Connection at 800-424-4310 for more information.

Candidate—Individual enrolled in the Child Development Associate credentialing process through the Council for Professional Recognition.

Candidate Connection—A toll-free telephone number to find the answers to your questions about the CDA credentialing process. Call weekdays from 9:00 A.M. to 5:00 P.M., Eastern Time: 1-800-424-4310.

Child Development Associate (CDA)—A person who is able to meet the specific needs of children and who, with parents and other adults, works to nurture children's physical, social, emotional, and intellectual growth in a child development framework. The CDA Credential is awarded to child care providers and home visitors who have demonstrated their skill in working with young children and their families by successfully completing the CDA assessment process.

Council Representative—Person designated by the Council for Professional Recognition to verify successful completion of final phase of CDA Professional Preparation Program. The Council Representative records Candidates' successful completion of the CDA Early Childhood Studies Review. This Representative also interviews the Candidate and determines that the Candidate is applying the basic knowledge of professional practice.

Early Childhood Studies Review—Written assessment of knowledge about children from birth through age 5 gained from field experience, completion of *Essentials*, and participation in the CDA Seminar.

Field Advisor—Person who assists CDA Candidate in completing the self-study and final evaluation phases of the credentialing process. The Field Advisor is in touch with the Candidate at least once a week to discuss ideas and answer questions. The Field Advisor determines that the Candidate's responses to exercises are accurate and developmentally appropriate and verifies completion of designated exercises by the Candidate.

Professional Resource File—Materials and topics collected to use in teaching and for final assessment as a CDA. Includes regulations, policies, observations, telephone numbers, teaching resources, and ideas.

Seminar—A group of CDA Candidates that meets with a Seminar Leader to deal with issues, sensitive topics, and in-depth concerns related to teaching young children. At the completion of the Seminar, Candidates will complete their written Early Childhood Studies Review.

Seminar Instructor—Individual who conducts Seminars for groups of Candidates. The group will discuss controversial, sensitive, and timely topics. Assignments will be made. The Seminar Instructor will advise Candidates of the date to take their CDA Early Childhood Studies Review.

Index

eating breakfast, 136

nutrition principles, 138

"Especially good foods," 138-139

"Favorite lunches," 142

meal and snack planning, 141

new guidelines, 139

"Yummy snacks," 141

settings for mealtimes, 143

sources for food, 143

field trips, 143

formal observation, 442-446

friendship and cooperation children's, 188

fostering friendships, 188

being friendly, 188-189

environment, 190, 196-197, 200, 202

reinforce cooperation, 227

toys, 227-228, 237

listening to children, 226, 229

G

goals for children, 191-192, 195

competence, 193, 195-196, 238

curiosity, 153, 238

independence, 195

individualism, 194

love of others, 194

parents' unrealistic expectations, 191-192

security, 194, 201, 207

self-esteem, 192, 196, 209,

and use of home language, 192

self-regulation, 187-188, 193, 195-196, 201

trust, 191-192, 195, 201

H

hand washing, 8, 101, 119, 128-129

I

illness and hospitalization, 253, 260

dramatic play, 256, 258

terminally ill children, 261-262

using children's books, 252

visits to doctors and hospitals, 261

Immunizations, 120-121

implementation of developmental principles, 175-176

evaluating books, 176-180

popular/unpopular activities, 175

Inclusion. See disabilities, children with.

intellectual development. See cognitive development.

L

language, 11, 14-15, 37-38, 43, 47, 50, 58-59, 63-66, 70, 73-75, 78, 86, 89, 115-116, 134, 148-149, 152, 169-173, 179, 191, 193-194, 203, 205, 213-215, 218-220, 227, 230, 240, 244, 246, 261

appropriate model for, 305-306

bilingual children, 308-313

building vocabularies, 305-306

everyday conversations, 302-303

monolingual children, 308

teaching more than one language, 308-313

"Working with second language learners," 308-313

learning materials appropriate . See also developmental accomplishments, 174

dramatic play, 66, 71, 73-74, 173-174, 227, 256, 258

toys, 64, 67, 72, 170-174, 227-228, 253, 255

legal requirements, 20, 22

libraries, 79, 219, 221

literacy, 173-174

experience story, 321-323

invented spelling, 323

print materials use of, 323-324

using books, 314

children's participation in, 313-314

criteria for selecting, 315

M

mathematics, 143

membership organizations, 23, 26

music children and, 327-329

creative movement choices of, 327, 329

live performances, 316